Esteemable Acts

10 ACTIONS
FOR BUILDING REAL SELF-ESTEEM

Francine Ward

Broadway Books

New York

10/21/03

Julie—
Self-esteem comes from doing esteemable acts.

Francine

ESTEEMABLE ACTS. Copyright © 2003 by Francine Ward. All rights reserved. No
part of this book may be reproduced or transmitted in any form or by any
means, electronic or mechanical, including photocopying, recording, or by
any information storage and retrieval system, without written permission
from the publisher. For information, address Broadway Books, a division of
Random House, Inc., 1745 Broadway, New York, NY 10019.

Broadway Books titles may be purchased for business or promotional use or
for special sales. For information, please write to: Special Markets Department,
Random House, Inc., 1745 Broadway, New York, NY 10019.

PRINTED IN THE UNITED STATES OF AMERICA

BROADWAY BOOKS and its logo, a letter B bisected on the diagonal, are
trademarks of Broadway Books, a division of Random House, Inc.

Visit our website at www.broadwaybooks.com

First edition published 2003

Book design by Elizabeth Rendfleisch

Cataloging-in-Publication Data is on file with the Library of Congress.

ISBN 0-7679-1218-7

3   5   7   9   10   8   6   4   2

$\mathcal{A}$CKNOWLEDGMENTS

In 1993, *Esteemable Acts* was just an idea, and in 2003, it became a reality thanks to the love, guidance, inspiration, and encouragement of many people. While it's impossible to individually thank every single person who contributed to the realization of my dream, my desire is to make the effort. I give thanks to the following:

Louise Robertson, the principal inspiration behind this book, was the first person to teach me that self-esteem comes from doing esteemable acts. She believed I could be a woman of substance long before I believed I could.

Dr. Paul Ohliger, the first person who told me I could write a book because I had something to say.

My husband, Richard, one of the most wonderful and courageous people I know.

My mother, because she loved me in spite of myself and didn't ask for much in return.

Hal Marley, an example of the father I never had.

Carole Bidnick, my fabulous agent, who believed in me and *Esteemable Acts* from the first time we met and has consistently proved her support through action.

Janet Hill, my Broadway editor, who worked tirelessly with

me throughout the process and who was my advocate from day one. To her assistant, Toisan Craigg, and everyone else on my incredible Broadway team: Heather McGuire, Catherine Pollack, Steve Rubin, Gerald Howard, Jean Traina, and Chava Boylan.

Stuart Horwitz, my book doctor, without whom I would not have been able to get through the rough times of writer's block. Thank you for knowing just the right questions to ask to get just the right answers.

Patti Breitman, for being my friend, for introducing me to my agent, and for having the vision to see the possibilities in *Esteemable Acts*.

Gita Vrat and Dee Roby, at the San Francisco Admirals Club, for helping to create a special place for me to write, while waiting for many a plane to take off. You are two of the sweetest people I know.

Terri Hohener, a very special Weight Watchers instructor, who was a light on those days I had writer's block, due to stress and overeating.

My Mastermind Group: Carolyn Kellams, Diane Parente, Gloria Dunne, and Jim Prost, for just always beng there and keeping me accountable.

Reverend Dr. Michael Beckwith, for helping me realize that I could survive without being a lawyer.

Reverend Mary Manin Morrissey, for being a phenomenal example of a successful woman, a loving wife, and a spiritual teacher.

Peggy Byrne, for having me write a weekly gratitude and fear list, even when I didn't want to.

My publicist, Jill Siegel, whom I liked the moment we met, and who helped make this book possible.

Lorraine Friedman, my best friend from law school, who showed me that a lawyer could leave the practice of law and become a successful author.

Michael Larsen and Susan Page, for always being willing to answer my questions and for writing two of the best books on how to write a book proposal.

All the women and men who have ever asked me for guidance and all those who used it, you are the reason I give and you are the reason I keep on giving.

All the people who believed I'd never amount to anything or that my dreams were too big, all I can say is "thank you." You motivated me to try harder. There were days when I showed up in spite of myself, simply to prove you wrong. While at the time it wasn't the healthiest motivation, in the moment, it got me into action.

Finally, to everyone who has ever loved, inspired, motivated, supported, encouraged, or believed in me. Your love and strength carried me long before I was able to carry myself. Thank you.

$\mathscr{C}$ONTENTS

Esteemable Acts

$\mathcal{A}$N INVITATION FOR YOU

- At fourteen, I was a drug-addicted alcoholic; now I'm clean and sober for twenty-three years.
- At eighteen, I was a high school dropout; now I'm a graduate of Georgetown University Law Center.
- At twenty-one, I was a call girl, paying lawyers lots of money to keep me out of jail; now I am a lawyer, a successful businesswoman, and a loving wife.
- At twenty-six, I was hit by a car and told I'd never walk again; in my forties I ran two marathons within three months of each other.
- At twenty-eight, all I could think about was what's in it for me; now, at fifty, I'm an active participant in my community.

Today I live a life beyond my wildest imaginings, and you can, too. How was such a miraculous transformation possible for me? How is it possible for you? By doing those things that genuinely make you feel good about yourself, things that almost always give you an opportunity to walk through something you're afraid of. Having the courage to live your dreams, staying focused on what you say is important to you, taking care of your health, making better choices are all examples of things you can do to make you feel good about yourself. Self-esteem comes from doing esteemable acts, and it's an esteemable act to walk through your fear.

In this book you'll be encouraged to move past your limitations—whether imposed by yourself or others—to a new and more appealing picture of your life. This will require work. Work that at times will appear to be more than you can handle. Just do the best you can. What do you have to lose? Give yourself six months to see a change. You may think, "Six months, that's too long. What about six days?" All I can say is that lasting change does not happen overnight.

This book is divided into ten "Actions" that will help you change your life, ten esteemable actions. As you read the book, you'll encounter exercises that invite you to think about, reflect upon, or identify a problem or issue. Each exercise is designed to move you closer to real and lasting self-esteem by helping you walk through your fear. Do as many exercises as you can. Confront the issues in your life. Work at your own pace, but do the work.

To get started on this incredible journey of self-discovery you will need a notebook, which will become your Esteemable Acts Journal, and a pen. Make sure these items are close at hand at all times. Your journal will be a living document to which you can and will refer over and over again. Any size notebook will do, as long as it has lots of pages. Make it your own special book, reflective of you. Color it, paste on pictures, write in it, make it personal. This will be your treasure book, filled with lessons learned, questions asked and answered, pictures and ideas reflected upon, and the exercises you'll be encouraged to do throughout your journey.

If you do all the exercises, if you challenge yourself to walk through your fear and take actions that will make you feel better about yourself—if you take esteemable actions—you will come out the other side different from when you started. You will develop healthy self-esteem.

I invite you to take the challenge.

PART ONE

Living your dreams is an esteemable act

If you can dream it, you can have it

It's an esteemable act to have the courage to dream.

 ntil I had the courage to dream of a better life, I wasn't able to have one. And as far back as I can remember, I was afraid to dream. I saw what happened to people like me who thought they had a right to dream, who thought they were special. They ended up hurt, disappointed, and disliked, and I didn't want to go there. You see, I was a poor black kid from Atlanta, Georgia, and later New York's South Bronx, and, as I saw it, for people like me, there were no such things as hope, dreams, or endless possibilities. And to think otherwise was a set-up for failure and despair. I got the message early in my life that dreams were for people who were rich, people who were smart—people who were white. The message that I'd never amount to anything and that I'd never leave the ghetto was presented to me at home, at church, in school, at the movies, in the newspaper, and on television. The message was subtle, yet at other times, not so subtle—disadvantaged black girls like me couldn't become anything other than drug addicts, alcoholics, or prostitutes.

Many self-esteem experts believe that as children we go through a phase in which we stumble and fall as we try to find our way. We experience adolescence and the teen years often hating ourselves and feeling disconnected from life and limited by what we feel is a lack of choice; a time in our lives when we feel stuck and unable to change our circumstances. Then, according to those experts, when we get to our late teens, we grow out of it and begin to think in terms of possibilities, infinite possibilities. We feel empowered and hopeful. We start to realize, as young people, that life is full of opportunities.

The point those experts miss is that the kids who get to that next level are often encouraged to do so. Frequently they have mentors who motivate and inspire them to live their dreams. Their passion is encouraged and their imagination is fired up. And when they come across an obstacle that frightens them, they're taught to walk through their fear and go for what they want. Sadly, this was not my experience. The people in my neighborhood reminded me that the life I was leading was as good as it gets and not to expect much more. And for a long time I didn't. So I, like many others, became a casualty of limited thinking. I was paralyzed by fear. My fear became as much a part of me as my skin color and my DNA—it was the essence of who I was, and I didn't even know it. After years and years of fear taking hold of me, it would take years of hard work for me to find release from its demoralizing grip.

Dreams are what life is made of. They give you a reason to get out of bed in the morning and a reason to go to bed early at night, so you can wake up and start all over again. Living your dreams is the first, but not the final, step in building real and lasting self-esteem. When you follow your heart, when you live with intention and passion, everyone benefits, because you're happier and you feel more vital. And when you do what you love, not only do you feel good about yourself, it's easier to feel good about others. On the other hand, when you allow external or internal forces to prevent you from doing or having what you want, everyone suffers, because when you're unhappy you make everyone around you unhappy.

But like anything worth having, dreaming takes work, which often requires that you walk through something you're afraid of. Unlocking the courage to dream is the essence of Action #1. This Action invites you to see past your fears and your limitations to a new and more appealing picture of your life. It also encourages you to step out of your comfort zone and go for what you really want. Self-esteem comes from doing esteemable acts—things that make you feel good about yourself. It's an esteemable act to live your dreams.

Bring to mind one of your childhood dreams. Maybe you wanted to be a teacher or a doctor, or to own your own business. Maybe you wanted to be a scientist. Maybe you wanted to be president of the United States. Are you living your dream? If not, what got in your way? What excuses did you buy into? Write out your answers in your Esteemable Acts Journal.

Walking Through the Fear

In 1981, at the age of twenty-eight, tired of feeling stupid and determined to prove that I wasn't, I went back to school. It was one of the hardest decisions I ever made because it brought up all my insecurities. Fears I never knew I had surfaced, such as fear the of being too old, the fear of failure, the fear of not being smart enough, the fear of not being able to grasp the concepts, the fear of not fitting in, the fear of going back to school, the fear of the coursework being too hard—the list continued. But one day at a time, after talking to advisers, researching the necessary steps, and auditing classes, I decided to face my fears and embark on a journey, one that proved to be an entry into a life far beyond my wildest imaginings.

What do you dream about when you're by yourself and left just with your own thoughts? What do you wish you could do "if life were different"? What would you be doing if you could snap your fingers and make it all happen? What experiences would you participate in if the canvas called your life was blank? You can make your dreams come true and this book will help you. In the beginning, what's being asked of you might seem hard. It might appear that more is being asked of you than is reasonable or fair. The journey to positive self-esteem is your experience; you may do as you please. All I ask is that you do the best you can. You'll be invited to stretch beyond your comfort zone, then stretch just a little bit more, because often change doesn't happen without a push.

So let's get started. In your Esteemable Acts Journal, write out your answers to the questions at the beginning of the previous paragraph. Don't rush through them. Give yourself plenty of time to really think them through. This is the first step in building real and lasting self-esteem.

Obstacles That Get in Your Way

You'll encounter many obstacles along the road to living your dreams. Some obstacles may be real, some imagined, some may be tangible, and some may be intangible. Some of those obstacles will be created by others, and some will be self-imposed. However they manifest, you will always be given the choice as to whether you give them power.

Before we move on to specific actions you can take to eliminate obstacles or lessen their potency, let's examine three of the most common stumbling blocks that can stand between you and living your dreams.

CORE BELIEFS AS OBSTACLES

We are what we believe. We create our reality based on what we think. For example, what do you do in your life that stems from a childhood belief? As a kid, were you taught that vegetables are good for you? Were you taught to brush your teeth after eating because it protects your teeth and gums? Some of you will say, "Well, yes, I was taught certain things, but now I do the opposite of what I was taught." Sometimes we rebel against what we know to be right simply because an authority figure told us to do it, and that's a therapy session all by itself. But it's likely that even if we don't like what we were taught, if it was pounded into our heads over and over again, those beliefs have become an integral part of who we are unless we have made a concerted effort to change them.

In your Esteemable Acts Journal, take a moment and identify some beliefs you were raised with. For example, as a kid, what were your thoughts about television, football, piano lessons, dating, cats, poor people, and rich people? What were your thoughts about success, failure, education? To get past the obstacles that bind us we must first know what they are.

Like it or not, your beliefs determine the assumptions you make about yourself and other people, and the assumptions you make determine your attitude and your behavior—and how you behave is what defines you. When I believed I wasn't smart enough to go back to school, my actions supported my beliefs; I never even tried. Once I started believing I could do something to change the course of my life, I took actions that supported those beliefs: I enrolled in school. Getting to the place where I believed I could do what I set out to do has been a long, slow, arduous process that has required constant vigilance. I realized that if I was ever going to live the life I wanted, I'd have to confront what was holding me back, face my fears, and walk through them.

Despite the negative feelings I often had about myself, I became willing to behave contrary to those feelings. For example, when I thought I wasn't smart enough to read my schoolbooks, I forced myself to read them anyway. I acted as if I knew what I was doing, even though I didn't. Every time I did something I didn't think I could do and got to the other side, I felt great. One small step toward the building of my self-esteem.

We are what we believe.

It's not easy to know what you really believe, so one thing you can do to better understand your beliefs is to listen to what you say. The words that come out of your mouth often reflect what you really believe, as do the thoughts you keep in your mind.

FEAR AS AN OBSTACLE

Underlying our beliefs is fear—fear that we won't get something we want or that something we have will be taken away from us. Sometimes fear is a motivator, compelling us to take affirmative action. For example, after escaping the South Bronx at eighteen, I knew I never wanted to live there or be poor again. Fear was my motivator. On the other hand, fear is sometimes an obstacle, making it difficult or impossible for us to take action. For example, suppose you loathe your job, but you're afraid to quit and look for another one. It's your fear that keeps you stuck in a job you hate. Fear is a real, human emotion. While it's okay to feel afraid, it's not okay to give in to fear, making it your master. It's not okay to give it permission to stand between you and your dreams. The key to managing fear is to acknowledge it and walk through it.

I'm quick to share how afraid I am, because people need to know that you can be afraid and still walk through your fear. Often they are surprised to find out I'm afraid, because for them, if you're afraid, you're paralyzed. Fearful people, in their minds, are unable to take action. Fear is a real and valid emotion; it's what you do with it that can cause trouble. In a recent interview with twenty-five men, each admitted that it was easier to admit they were angry than to admit they were afraid. "You just never let people think you're scared," said Jimmy D. The more that seemingly strong people have the courage to share their fears, the easier it is for others to do the same.

Fear is a clever foe. Of all the obstacles that stand in our way, fear is the most powerful, because it can so easily be denied. It comes disguised in many ways, as anger, resentment, jealousy, envy, hurt feelings, and self-pity, to name a few. But whatever the label, fear is still fear, and it has the power to capture your soul, disintegrate your spirit, and eat away at your self-esteem until you are incapable of separating the real from the unreal. You're left blaming someone else for your choices. You give up. So think about it: What are you afraid of? How has fear stopped you from living your dreams? In your Esteemable Acts Journal write out your answers. Then identify how you have faced your fear and achieved your goals. What specific actions have you taken?

PEOPLE AS OBSTACLES

Sometimes it's not just your fear that gets in the way; other people's fear can set you back, too. No doubt you've encountered people who always have a negative word to say about a project you're starting or a great idea you have. They quickly focus on the reasons you won't succeed. It could be your parent, a teacher, your spouse, or a friend. Regardless of who they are, in most cases it's someone you trust enough to share the idea with in the first place. Meet your dream busters. They bust open your dreams and stifle your spirit—when you let them.

When I decided to become a lawyer, I expected the people who initially encouraged me to go back to school to be happy I was living my dream. Every day John, Mary, Susan, and Betty would say, "Francine, you can do it." So it was especially hard to understand why they weren't supportive when I started doing what they told me I could do. After my pain subsided, I realized they couldn't be there for me, because they couldn't be there for themselves. In most cases, they weren't living their own dreams. They were stuck. It wasn't personal. They just couldn't celebrate my success because I reminded them of what they could be doing but weren't. "Why don't you try something easier? What happens if you fail?" they asked. Or, "Won't you be too old to practice law?" Then there were those who were less subtle, who said, "You're an ex-hooker with a criminal record, you'll never get through school, so why even try?"

It wasn't only my so-called friends who tried to discourage me. Some of my professors were dream busters, too. One day I excitedly told my professor at UNLV (University of Nevada, Las Vegas) I was going to become a lawyer. Knowing my past, he simply laughed and said, "What an imagination you have." He was one of the people who, without even knowing it, motivated me into trying harder than I thought I could. I stretched far beyond my comfort zone often to prove him and other dream busters wrong.

Now, I'm not suggesting you completely avoid the dream buster, because he has an important role to play. His perspective can help you understand what you're up against—the challenges that lie ahead. You can be prepared for an obstacle only if you know it's there. But the idea is to learn how to deal with him, to take what he says for what it's worth. While writing this book, I had input from many people. Sometimes I liked their feedback and sometimes I didn't. At all times, however, the feedback was useful. When they were confused or misled or repelled by something I had written, I realized some of my readers might be as well. So instead of being angry at anyone I perceived to be a dream buster, I saw their comments as an opportunity to better my writing. The best way to deal with a dream buster is to identify him, listen to what he says, and ask yourself, "Is there any truth to what he says?" Or, "What can I learn from this?" Take a moment, and in your Esteemable Acts Journal make a list of your dream busters; next to each name write a sentence illustrating something they have said to you. In some cases the message may be communicated nonverbally. Describe in your own words how they communicated their negative message or describe what you perceive to be a negative message. Recognition of the obstacles that prevent you from living your dreams is the first step in taking charge of your life.

Once you recognize your obstacles, it's time to move past them.

Moving Beyond Obstacles—It's Time to Start Living Your Dreams!

We all have dreams. Some of us make them come true, some of us talk about making them come true, and some of us wish we had made them come true. Some of you know what your dream is—it's your heart's desire, a passion that burns inside you just waiting to be nudged into action. Then there are those of you who need some assistance either because you have no dream at all or because it's been stuffed so deep inside you that only a gentle yet firm act of love and support can bring it to the surface. And for the rest of you, perhaps at one time you had a dream—and now you don't. So let's begin by identifying your dream. How do you go about doing that? For this, you will need to tap into the right side of your brain—your creative side, your playful, imaginative, and inspired side. Here are some specific steps you can take to help you unlock the dream inside you.

CREATE A COLLAGE

Let's start by creating a visual image of things you like, things you find appealing. Gather together your favorite magazines, no fewer than two and not more than five. Also select one or two magazines you wouldn't normally read. For example, if you primarily read business magazines, such as Forbes or Fortune, step outside your comfort zone and buy GQ, Redbook, O Magazine, Men's Health, VIBE, National Geographic, Self, or even Black Enterprise. Explore something new and different. Allow your mind to wander and be curious. With no particular objective in mind, other than to choose things that you like, select pictures, words, and phrases that appeal to you. Maybe it's because they're pretty, maybe it's because they interest you, or maybe it's a product you like or someone who is doing something you enjoy. Whatever the reason, cut it out. If you're not accustomed to working with the creative side of your brain, don't fret, just do the best you can. Remember, all you're doing is browsing through magazines, cutting out pictures you like—the idea is to have a little fun. This stress-free exercise may help you identify your dream and bring it to life.

After you've gathered your pictures and phrases, you're now ready to create your collage. In your Esteemable Acts Journal, designate at least four pages for your collage. Glue your cutout pictures, words, and phrases into your journal. It doesn't matter how you put them on the paper, just allow each picture to fall where it will. Again, fun is the operative word for this exercise.

After you've finished, step back and observe what you did. What does your visual say to you? What does it say about you? Is there a pattern of things you like, things you enjoy, and things you're interested in? Are you surprised certain things are there or that certain things are missing? Is there a color scheme? Is there a business theme? In your Esteemable Acts Journal, write about your observations, then spend some time reflecting upon your thoughts.

Now I'd like you to start thinking about who you are and what's important to you. With your collage in front of you, answer the following questions. Allow yourself time to answer each one as honestly as you can. You're in no rush, but you do want to keep moving.

What do you value?
A value is something you hold dear. Values are often concerned with ethics, the moral fiber of a culture. Values speak to the good, the bad, the right, and the wrong. Our values are reflected in whom and what we punish and whom and what we reward. We tend to like people who share our values and dislike people who don't. For example, let's suppose you believe in a strong work ethic. You celebrate and applaud people who work long hours in order to make sure a job is done. Consequently, if someone leaves at 5 P.M. when there is still work to be done, you won't think well of them. In your Esteemable Acts Journal, identify three or four things you value in your life. Refer to your collage for possible clues.

What is your personal mission statement?
What is your mission in life? What do you believe you are here on earth to accomplish? Why are you doing what you do? What

drives you? What inspires you? What keeps you going on those days you want to give up? Think for a moment about what's important to you and what you perceive as your calling. Write your answers in your Esteemable Acts Journal.

What is your passion in life?
What are you passionate about? What excites you? What turns you on? Is there any cause or belief you'd give your life for? What causes do you donate time and/or money to? What causes would you donate time and/or money to if you had it to give? Write your answers in your Esteemable Acts Journal.

What are your talents?
Getting clear as to what you are good at will help you. What are your top five talents? What do you do best? For example, are you good at handling money? Are you good with putting things together? Are you good at taking things apart? Are you good with words? Are you the creative type? Can you inspire people? Do you work well with people or do you work best alone? Are you good at planning and organizing? What skills/talents do you bring to the world, to your relationships, to your job, to any situation? In your Esteemable Acts Journal, acknowledge what you do well.

How would you spend your money?
This is another exercise designed to help you explore some of the things you like that could be converted into a dream. If you had ten million dollars to spend in any way you wanted, how would you spend it? Would you save it all? Would you spend it

all? Would you share some? If so, with whom? What would you do with all that money? Write your answer in your Esteemable Acts Journal and be as detailed as possible.

What Do You Dream Of?

By now your thinking has been jogged a little and there should be many ideas floating around in your head. Your next action step is to make a list of twenty-five things you'd like to do or places you'd like to go. Write your answers in your Esteemable Acts Journal. We will call this your Twenty-five Dreams List, a wish list of sorts. Use your collage or any of the previous exercises as a reference guide. Don't worry about prioritizing—just make the list. This is a living document, something you can add to whenever a new dream comes to mind. Nothing is too small or too big to put on your list. Every dream counts. Include in your Dreams List things you'd really like to do in your life if lack of money or education were not obstacles. Don't rush the process—it's too important—but don't give yourself too much leeway either. A week is plenty of time to add to and subtract from your Dreams List. Have fun. This is a very important step on your journey.

Let your Twenty-five Dreams List sit for a few days. Keep copies in your car, on your desk, in your computer, in your date book, in your purse, in your wallet—wherever you frequently are. This will remind you of your heart's desires. The old adage "Out of sight, out of mind" holds true here. Keep your dreams fresh in your mind so you won't forget them. Think about your list and take note of the feelings that surface. Record these feelings in your Esteemable Acts Journal. This is an exciting process you are embarking upon, one in which you will explore thoughts and ideas you've never explored before. By the time you complete this phase of your journey, you'll be amazed at how excited and empowered you feel, just because you were willing to take a few baby steps.

Next, reduce your Twenty-five Dreams List to the twelve things you'd most like to do. Reread your list at least three times a day, for one week, paying particular attention to what you're most affected by (either positively or negatively). I read my list as soon as I wake up, then around noon; I look at it again around 3 P.M. or when I start to feel weary, and again before I go to bed. It's not important what schedule you set; just be sure to read your list at least three times a day.

Sometimes your list will excite you, sometimes it will depress you, and sometimes it will make you feel uncomfortable. Take note of your reactions. They will give you vital information about the fear-inducing obstacles you've let stand in your way.

Now, reduce your Twelve Dreams List to six. Once again, acknowledge your feelings and thoughts along the way. Whatever they are, write them down in your Esteemable Acts Journal and move on. About now, you may feel like quitting. I encourage you to resist the temptation to quit the dream list exercise. This temptation is just fear rearing its ugly head. Instead, continue to allow yourself to dream. Why? Because with each esteemable action you take, your dreams become more powerful than your fear. By now, you should be closer to connecting with what you really want in life. If you've made it to this point in the exercise, you've overcome a few mental hurdles. Bravo! But don't stop now. Your next step is to reduce your Six Dreams List to three. Take a few minutes to think about each one individually. Why is each important to you? How would making each of those dreams a reality change your life? By when would you like to accomplish each dream? Now, prioritize your dreams on a separate page in your Esteemable Acts Journal entitled "My Top Three Dreams."

Now let's move on to making them manifest.

From Dreaming to Manifesting

It's one thing to dream, it's another to make a dream happen. So, how do you get from dreaming to manifesting? You eat, sleep, and drink your dreams. The more you resonate with your dreams, the more likely it is you'll start to live them. First, take a moment to remember successes you've had in the past. Success leaves clues. What personal accomplishments have you had? Something magical takes place when you identify the two or three things you've done in your life that make you feel proud. They could be small or big things; what's important is that they are things you've done that you feel good about.

The next step in getting from dreaming to manifesting is to choose current goals. A goal is a specific plan, a blueprint, for making your dream come true. Having specific goals gives you a sense of direction by letting you know where you're going and how you'll get there. This is how the seemingly unattainable becomes attainable. The key to accomplishing this is breaking your actions into small, manageable pieces that enable you to see and celebrate your progress—one step at a time.

When I decided to become a lawyer, first I created a plan, then

I divided the big plan into manageable tasks, and finally, I broke the tasks into even smaller pieces. Each piece became a doable part of the whole. Had I focused on tackling the big plan all at once, it's unlikely I would have succeeded, because the plan would have been too big, too overwhelming, and too seemingly unreachable. Big would have given me an excuse to avoid. So I created small, reasonable goals—mini-goals—within my big goal. It worked. Taking small steps was the answer.

Esteemable Acts

Let's begin the process of making one of your three dreams come true. Suppose your dream is to go back to school. You don't like your job and you understand that the best way for you to change jobs is to get additional training. Work with me through the next three exercises in order to create a plan that really works.

EXERCISE 1

First, begin by converting your dream into a specific, measurable goal, that is, to go back to school within eighteen months. Your goal needs to be specific, so you know exactly what you want to do, and measurable, so you know when you get there. In your Esteemable Acts Journal write out your goal and include today's date. Next, specify the proposed finish date. While you can always change your date, it's good to start with the end in mind. For the purpose of this example, the end date is eighteen months from today. Assume today is May 16; your goal might look like this: "My goal is to start school by September 10 of next year." When selecting a date, think in terms of what's reasonable. The quickest way to set yourself up for failure is to create an unreasonable goal: For example, today is May 16 and you want to go back to school in August but you're not prepared, you work a full-time job, and you have three small children at home.

EXERCISE 2

Make a list of everything you can think of that you'll need to do to get you from where you are now to where you want to be in the time you've stated. For example, going back to school within a year and a half requires getting transcripts, deciding which classes to take, finding the money to pay for school, securing child care if you are a single parent, and scheduling time for classes in light of the other things you have to do. After you've identified the overall steps in the process, define the tasks within each step; for example, in deciding which classes you will take you must ask yourself: Which courses are required? What times are they given? How will that work with your schedule? How many credits can you take a semester and still remain sane? Is there a chance you can exchange life credits for school credits? These are the kinds of questions you'll need to ask.

Now we're going to gather together the steps you've decided are necessary to reach your goal, and plug them into your Goals Matrix. In your Esteemable Acts Journal, draw a grid that looks like the one on page 21. Feel free to adjust the Matrix format to fit your needs if your goal will take longer or less than eighteen months. For example, two years can be broken into eight quarter-year segments, and a six-month goal can be divided into six thirty-day segments. For easy access and the option of modifying your Matrix at will, you might consider creating the Matrix on your computer.

The idea behind the Matrix is that by the end of each time segment—for instance, thirty days—you will have completed the task in the box—that is, created a plan. Feel free to do more if you finish early, but aim not to do less. By breaking a task into small, manageable pieces, you're guaranteed success. Below is an example of what I mean.

30 DAYS	60 DAYS	6 MONTHS	1 YEAR	18 MONTHS
Create a plan	Order school brochures	Research ways to pay for school, (i.e., loans, grants, scholarships)	On paper, realistically think through plan for child care	Start school
Determine your objectives for going back to school (i.e., get a degree, get a promotion, make more money, learn a new skill)	Determine credits needed	Send out applications	Wait for results and create plan B, just in case you have to try again	Send thank-you notes to people who helped you reach your goal
Honestly assess where you are and where you want to be, by when	Get transcript	Start talking to spouse, parents, kids, managers—anyone who will be affected by your schedule change	Gratefully receive acceptances	Start on your next goal

EXERCISE 3

Talk your plan over with a trusted friend or confidant, someone who is supportive of what you want to do. It's important to have a connection with someone who is also on the road to living his or her dreams. Whoever it is, let's call that person your Esteemable Acts Buddy. It's best to use the same person, if you can, throughout this process. This allows you to build rapport and establish the kind of trust that can only come from a long-term relationship based on honest sharing. It might even be more effective to select someone who is also going through the Esteemable Acts experience. You might also consider an Esteemable Acts Mastermind Group, a group of people with the same objective and a desire to support one another in getting there. Brainstorm ways to walk through each obstacle and listen to what your Buddy has to say. Don't be so quick to say "Yes, but," or totally dismiss the person's thoughts.

Just Do It!

If you've been doing the exercises in this chapter, you should already be feeling much better about yourself. You've got something to aim toward and you know how to recognize and avoid falling prey to paralyzing fear. Now you're ready to tackle the next esteemable act—getting rid of the stuff that distracts you along the way. Don't stop now, just do it!

Don't let stuff get in the way

It's an esteemable act to stay focused on what's most important in the moment.

Have you ever started something you really wanted to do and not finished it? Have you ever made a commitment to yourself or someone else and not kept it? Have you ever allowed stuff to just get in the way of your doing what you said was most important to you in the moment? I suspect at some point in your life you have. Choosing to do what is least important in the moment may seem like the best decision at the time, but it rarely is. It's merely the easiest. Each time you take a detour, each time you allow something to steer you away from what you say and know is most important to you, you pay a price—knowingly or unknowingly. And over time, the price gets higher.

Your reasons for not fulfilling your commitments are always valid—at least at the time. For instance, emergencies and other people's urgencies, unforeseeable conflicts of interest, not having the money to do what you're committed to do, insufficient information, lack of time, not having someone to take care of the kids, and health issues can all get in the way of fulfilling a commitment. But regardless of the validity of your excuses, the impact those excuses have on your relationships and on your self-esteem can be damaging. You don't feel good about yourself when you don't follow through.

Eventually, for us to succeed at whatever we want to do in life, we simply must get started doing those things that lead to our success, regardless of the distractions that get in our way. We must be willing to take action despite how we feel. It's the very act of doing something that relieves us of the pain of feeling like someone who can't be counted on. Taking an action, regardless of how small, is the key.

Action #2 will help you identify the stuff that gets in your way and help you create a plan for developing new habits.

Think of a time when you followed through on a commitment. Perhaps it was a promise to take your kids to the zoo or a movie. Perhaps it was a commitment to spend time or have lunch with a friend. Perhaps it was an obligation to complete a task at work by a certain date, or maybe it was simply that you agreed to give someone a ride. Whatever the promise, think about how they felt when you did what you said you'd do. Think about how the other person felt the moment they knew you could be counted on. Now think of a time when you followed through on a commitment you made to yourself. Perhaps it was a promise to clean your closet or your garage, or to send that long-overdue thank-you note. Maybe you made a commitment to yourself to start being on time or maybe you agreed to walk one mile every day. How did you feel after you did what you said you'd do?

Now think about a time when you didn't follow through on a commitment you made to someone. Take a moment to recall the details, and as best as you can, visualize your experience. How was the other person affected? Was he or she angry? Disappointed? Sad? Understanding? Tolerant? Have you broken your promise(s) more than once? How were you affected? What price did you pay for not doing what you said you'd do? Now, what about a time when you didn't follow through on a commitment you made to yourself. How did you feel? What price did you pay? Have you broken promises to yourself before? Why? Write out the answers to these questions in your Esteemable Acts Journal.

You're probably wondering how you can compare a commitment to your family to a less important commitment to clean your closet. Well, the truth is, a commitment is an agreement, and breaking an agreement with yourself is as important as breaking agreements with other people. Self-esteem comes from doing esteemable acts, and it's an esteemable act to value yourself enough to follow through.

Procrastination, the Enemy

It's so easy to get diverted from the task at hand, from the thing you say is important. Doing that once or twice might be acceptable, but continually breaking agreements with yourself and other people takes its toll on your spirit, your integrity, and your self-esteem. The more you procrastinate—put off until tomorrow what can be done today—the less likely you are to feel good about yourself. Like it or not, there is a connection between doing what you say you'll do and your self-esteem.

The power of procrastination, a debilitating and destructive force, is so subtle you hardly know it has taken hold of you. Indeed from afar, the lives of procrastinators seem fun and appealing—they just do what they like and what's easy and leave the rest. But when you just keep putting off until tomorrow what you can do today, before you know it the unimportant becomes important, and the important becomes urgent or completely overlooked. Contrary to popular belief, putting off a task doesn't make it go away, it only prolongs the inevitable, and you suffer the consequences. At the end of the day, success in life comes from doing the hard things that don't always feel good yet are necessary for the desired outcome.

Once you start making excuses for not doing what you say you'll do, it becomes easy to continue making excuses. Then one day, you find putting off a task becomes a working part of who you are. It becomes so natural to procrastinate, you just don't do what you've agreed to do. Then, of course, you open the door for procrastination's companion: guilt, that nagging, annoying voice that tells you you've done something wrong—yet again. The more you procrastinate, the guiltier you feel. The guiltier you feel, the more you procrastinate. And because procrastination and guilt are such uncomfortable feelings, you seek ways to get rid of them, often finding someone to blame. In some cases, you blame the person you were committed to, because in your mind, he or she forced you to make the commitment in the first place.

I put off sending a thank-you note to a friend for a valuable re-
ferral. While my excuse was that I was so busy I forgot, in truth,
there was no valid reason for not taking three minutes to write a
note of appreciation. Every day I thought about it and every day
passed without my taking action. Days turned into weeks, weeks
turned into months, and eventually it was almost a year before I
took action. During the year, I avoided seeing my friend because I
was ashamed and felt guilty. I felt guilty because I did something
that made me feel guilty: I didn't keep an agreement I made to myself. But I didn't feel guilty enough to send a note. On occasion I
thought about calling her and acting as though I had sent the note
and was wondering why I hadn't heard back from her. But I knew
that was a lie. The truth was I allowed stuff to get in the way of my
doing what I claimed was important to me at the time: saying
thank you to my friend for her generous gift. I procrastinated my
way into a corner and didn't come out until the pain had become
so great. Finally, one day I summoned the courage to tell her the
truth. What a relief. And because I had the courage to walk through
my fear of what she would think of me, there was a happy outcome. Of course, the outcome won't always be positive, but we do
the right thing for ourselves, not for the glory to be gotten. At the
end of the day success in life comes from doing the hard stuff that
doesn't always feel good, not from doing those things that are necessary for the desired outcome.

In your Esteemable Acts Journal, write about a time when you
felt guilty. Describe the specific event that caused the feeling. Was
there a valid reason for you to feel guilty? Was there something
you didn't do that you agreed to do? Be mindful of your answers.
If you are having a difficult time identifying where you might

have been at fault, take a step back and try to find the unfulfilled commitment. This is a useful tool for helping you identify the source of your feelings. Almost always attached to guilt is something you didn't do that you said you would do. I bet if you're honest with yourself, it won't be too hard to find.

What Causes Procrastination?

On the surface, we procrastinate because we are too busy, we have more important things to do, or because the task at hand is too challenging, boring, painful, or simply not fun. But here's a thought: Underneath procrastination lies fear of taking action. *Procrastination* is another word for *fear*. Fear of failure, fear of success, fear of the process, fear of the unknown, fear of trying something new, fear of change—these are fears that prevent us from fulfilling our commitments. Coming to terms with how powerful fear is in your life is the first step in changing old habits.

Right about now you may be growling, saying to yourself, "What does she know? It's easy for her to say that I'm afraid, but I know I'm really not. I'm just really too busy." But are you *really* too busy or is there something important you're putting off right now because you're afraid to tackle it? If your answer is a resounding "no," then skip the rest of this chapter, you're ready for Action #3. But if you're like most of us, there's something you're avoiding doing. It could be for a variety of reasons: You don't understand all that's expected of you, you are confused as to how to get started, you don't have all the resources you need. What will you find if you scrape away your excuses for procrastinating?

What are you procrastinating about today? What one thing are you putting off until tomorrow? Do you have unfinished business to attend to? Is there a task you need to complete? A dream that needs to be acted upon? Why are you procrastinating and what price are you paying? Take a moment and record your answers in your Esteemable Acts Journal. You might be tempted to rush through this important phase, but please don't. Give yourself the gift of acknowledging the underlying causes of your procrastination. Don't put off until tomorrow what can be done today, because tomorrow may never come. Get started now!

It's inescapable that this book talks so much about fear, because fear gets in the way of everything, even though you may not have identified it as fear. Until you're able to see fear as the perpetrator, you'll never get past it. So the first step is to acknowledge it, then walk through it.

When I first started on my writing journey, I said my intent was to write a book. But was it really? For years I said I wanted to be a writer and for years I found excuses not to write. "People will judge me." "They'll judge my writing." "I don't have time." "I don't have money to stay home and write." "I don't know how to get an agent." At the beginning of every year I'd put on my goals list "Write my book proposal." And at the end of every year I was sadly disappointed that I hadn't even started the process. I talked about writing, but somehow couldn't manifest putting pen to paper. With each passing year, my fear became increasingly more powerful than my dreams. And not doing what I said was most important to me at the time affected how I saw myself, because I became a person who didn't follow through.

Had I really wanted to write, I would have found a way to do it—as I've done with most everything else I wanted to do. Think about something you really wanted to do and did. How long did you let stuff get in your way, if at all? I bet your answer is no time at all. Because when you really want to do something, you just do it! You find a way because it's important. It took me nine years to write this book. No doubt there were some important things that got in the way, but nine years' worth? I think not. I had what I thought were valid reasons, but when left in the quiet of my own mind I knew the truth, and so do you.

In your Esteemable Acts Journal, next to each of your Top Three Dreams, identify what prevents you from achieving each one. Be as truthful as you can. An honest look at the obstacles that stand in your way will help in knowing what actions to take.

Keep Your Eye on the Blue Chip

Activities that take up your time with little to no payoff are white-chip items, those low-priority tasks that are generally plentiful, easy to tackle, and fun to do. Most often they have little to do with the task you claim is most important at the moment and are time wasters and distracters. Imagine a white poker chip or a white one-dollar casino chip and think about how plentiful they are compared to the single stack of higher-denomination chips. When pondering the value of a white poker chip or a one-dollar casino chip as opposed to a red or blue or one-hundred-dollar chip, we realize that white chips aren't worth as much. Likewise, the white chips in your life aren't worth as much as the reds and the blues, yet often, as an excuse for not doing what we say is really in the moment, we get sidetracked by them. Examples of white-chip items are checking your e-mail several times a day when once or twice would do, spending time socializing and talking on the telephone when you have work to do, or playing with your pets when you have something else to attend to. In your Esteemable Acts Journal identify some of the white chips in your life, those things that are preventing you from doing what's important to you today.

Important activities that contribute to the accomplishment of your goals and objectives but which could be done by someone else are red-chip items. Examples of red-chip items might be attending a meeting that your representative could attend as easily as you, having a travel agent secure your reservations instead of you spending hours on the Internet or on the telephone yourself, or hiring someone to do your tedious data input. Now, in your Esteemable Acts Journal, take a moment to name some of your red chips, those important tasks that need to be done as soon as possible so you can live more in alignment with your dreams but which can be done by someone else in your behalf.

Finally, those high-payoff activities that lead directly to fulfilling your goals and objectives are blue-chip items. Examples of blue chips are writing that résumé, making that phone call to get additional information, sending away for that college brochure, going to the gym, or writing that first page of the book you always wanted to write.

Red and blue chips are often harder to stay focused on, because they are your boring and/or challenging items. Even so, working through them renders you a greater, more rewarding, end result. They are the high-maintenance, high-stake assignments that, when done, will make you feel good about yourself simply by virtue of your having done them.

Courage to Stay on Track

It's been proven that the only effective way to deal with fear is to walk through it, through the pain that accompanies doing something you're afraid to do. It takes courage to fulfill your commitments, courage to stay on track, courage to follow your dreams, courage to reach your goals, and courage to walk through your fear. Remember, reaching goals is not so much about doing big things when the feeling hits you; it's more about doing little things every day that move you toward your dream. It's about staying steady and on course. Action #2 is about not letting stuff get in the way of your stated goal. It's about having the courage to fulfill your commitments, follow your dreams, reach your goals, and say "no" to distractions that take you off track.

Remember what you identified as your Top Three Dreams in the previous Action? Continue to allow them to sink into your mind. Hold them close to you. Own them. Defining what's most important to you is the first step in getting on track. The next step is to stay on track. So if your dream is to complete your education, deciding when, where, and what classes you will take should be a priority on your to-do list. If your dream is to buy a house, creating a financial plan and sticking to it will be on your list of things to do. If your dream is to lose weight, you should see exercise as a regular working part of your schedule. The keys to success are being clear about your purpose, staying focused on your goal, and being willing to make sacrifices. If you consistently allow outside forces—whether people, places, or things—to control your destiny, you will never reach your goals. And you will not feel very good about yourself.

My friend Denny paid a high price for not having the courage to stay on track. Now it's too late. He's sixty-five years old and has a cancer that's quickly eating away at his spine. With little time and less energy left, he reflects often about his life— what he did, what he didn't do, and what he wishes he had done. It's sad sometimes because all I can do is listen, hold his frail hand, and say I love you. Denny will die with three dreams in his heart: to heal the relationship with his estranged daughter, to see the Atlantic Ocean, and to get a college degree. It's probably too late for him to realize those dreams, but it wasn't always. Every day something else was more important than the commitments he made to himself. Every day he found a reason for not sending his daughter that letter. Every day he had an excuse for not taking that trip. Every day he was too busy to complete the two classes he needed for a degree. Each day he let fear get in the way. And now, he looks back and says, "I wish I had."

On the other hand, my friend Shauni had a dream to pay back a debt. As a single parent with very few skills and little money, she nonetheless decided she would eliminate her debt within a year. Every week she paid a little toward reducing the loan, until one day it was all paid off. How did she do it? She made a commitment, an agreement with herself to pay off the money she owed. Every day she focused on the red and blue chips that allowed her to move closer to living her dream of being debt-free. No doubt, kids, school, and personal emergencies got in her way from time to time, but even when she was temporarily taken off track, Shauni was able to succeed because she was clear about her purpose and willing to make the necessary sacrifices to accomplish her goal. She called me the day she sent off her last check to the creditor, crying because she felt so good about herself.

Bring to Mind . . .

. . . a time in your life when you didn't reach your goal or when you didn't get something that you really wanted. How did you feel? Take a moment and reflect on that experience. Write your answers in your Esteemable Acts Journal. I encourage you to do the exercise once, take a break, and then repeat the process a second time, allowing yourself to go deeper. You may find more truth will surface the more you allow yourself to open up. This process can be somewhat painful, but it's the only way to step through your fear. Now take yourself even deeper. Ask yourself: "What kept me from reaching my goal? Why didn't I make it to the finish line?" Your first response may be that someone or something was in your way. And maybe you're right. But try going past the initial blame and think about what you could have done differently. What part did you play?

Now bring to mind a time when you reached your goal. Perhaps you lost weight or you got that advanced degree. What did it take? What did you have to do? What sacrifice did you make? How did you feel when you fulfilled a commitment to yourself? How has staying focused on your goals affected your self-esteem? It's important that you remember the experience, because, again, success leaves clues. When you remember what enabled you to get to your goal the first time, it will serve as motivation for the second and third and fourth times.

So How Do You Let Go of Stuff That Gets in the Way?

Here are fourteen steps to help you on your journey to staying focused on your dreams and commitments:

STEP #1:
ADMIT STUFF GETS IN YOUR WAY

Denial is the enemy of success. Excuses prolong the misery and keep you further from the solution. As long as you continue to say, "Not me, I'm fine, there are no distractions," you'll continue the pattern. Have the courage to admit you procrastinate.

STEP #2:
TAKE RESPONSIBILITY FOR YOUR PART

The more time you use to blame your habits on others, be it your parents, your spouse, your friends, the government, or anyone else, the less time you have to do what you need to do to move forward. Blame is a lose/lose game. While you may feel good in the moment because you've shifted responsibility, ultimately it will come back to you.

STEP #3:

FEEL YOUR FEAR AND TAKE ACTION ANYWAY

Fear keeps you in bondage. Walking through fear sets you free. The very act of walking through a problem or difficult situation empowers you. Not taking action because you're afraid feeds into your belief about yourself that you can't do something. Fear is just a human emotion. It goes away when you do something contrary to it. Take an action!

STEP #4:

SHARE WITH ANOTHER PERSON

Acknowledge on paper and to another person what's really important to you in this moment. As you did with your dreams in Action #1, visualize it, see it as clear as if it were in your mirror. Take hold of it. Know it's possible. Remind yourself of it.

STEP #5:

REMIND YOURSELF OF YOUR AGREEMENT

Reflect back on the promise you made with yourself in Action #1, the agreement to live your dreams. Keep it uppermost in your mind. Repeat it over and over again, perhaps in the form of an affirmation, such as "I am not distracted from my primary purpose of living my dream. Today I deserve the life I want and the universe supports my efforts to make it happen. Today I am focused on my purpose and loving every delicious moment of it. I am grateful for the chance to do what I love. I am thankful for the opportunity to take actions that move me closer to living my dream of _____."

STEP #6:

BREAK THE HARD STUFF INTO SMALL PIECES

It's easier for the mind to accept a small piece than a big chunk that appears too hard to handle. So reduce all tasks into smaller, more manageable pieces and then do something. Take some action regardless of how small. It's better to do something than nothing at all. Once you get moving, it's amazing how the next action will follow. When infants start to walk, they don't immediately break into a sprint. They start with small steps (baby steps!) and before you know it, they are on the other side of the room! Think about something you've been putting off because it's so hard. How can you reduce it to a manageable size? What are the small steps you can take just to get started?

STEP #7:

ALTERNATE BETWEEN THE EASY AND THE HARD TASKS

For some of you the best approach will be to tackle the hard tasks first. For others, it will be more rewarding to do the easy tasks, then move on to the more difficult ones. Still others will find it more appealing to alternate between the easy and the tough tasks. Regardless of your preference, find a methodology that works and use it. The last time I studied for the bar exam I felt overwhelmed. Just the idea of studying fourteen comprehensive subjects one more time sent me emotionally spinning. So I tackled my least favorite subject first: property law. Then I chose my favorite subtopic, which was tenancies. Before I knew it I made it through all fourteen subjects—by alternating between the easy and the more difficult tasks. What tasks can you alternate between today? Identify an easy step and a more challenging step. Perhaps, do the easy one first.

STEP #8:

TAKE IT A DAY AT A TIME

There will be days when you'll feel as if you're on top of the world, in the flow, in sync with the universe. You'll be taking action and feeling good. Then there will be days where nothing goes right and you feel horrible and can't for the life of you get started. The lyrics to an old song by the Shirelles say, "Mama said there'll be days like this. . . ." Know that those days will come. Also know you have options. Consider using the time to take a needed break or to regroup, or just let it be, knowing that this too shall pass.

STEP #9:

SCHEDULE EVERYTHING

Visual reminders are powerful, and scheduling is a visual reminder. Schedule time to do the things that will take you closer to what's important to you. Some people hate calendars. It's okay if you do, but use them anyway. If you write down a task in your daily or weekly calendar it's more likely you'll do it. Committing to paper the things you need to accomplish will make it easier to accomplish them. Why? Because when tasks to be completed are out of sight, they are out of mind. Also, if something is in writing, it becomes a part of your routine and you're more likely to take it seriously. On my calendar you'll find the gym, writing time, meditation time, and birthday reminders of friends and family. While I prioritize all my tasks, my goal is to complete each one.

STEP #10:
DELEGATE TASKS WHEN YOU CAN

Delegation is a learned skill that begins with selecting the appropriate person for the job. If someone else is willing and able to perform a task for you, let them. The operative words being "willing" and "able." The person you choose must not only be *qualified* to do the task, meaning they have the requisite skill and the authority, but they must also be willing to do it. The worst possible scenario is asking someone to do a job he or she can't do or doesn't want to do. That's a setup for disappointment. It's also an excuse to put off doing what you say is most important to you, because you're busy cleaning up someone else's mess. Lastly, in choosing the appropriate person to delegate a task to, ask yourself, "Can I trust this person to do the job as I want it to be done?" If all of the above requirements aren't met, then perhaps the person you have in mind isn't the best person for the job. But don't stop there, that's not an excuse not to delegate. Just look for someone else. What tasks can you delegate today? Who can you delegate to? In your Esteemable Acts Journal, answer those two questions.

STEP #11:
SEE DISCIPLINE AS A GOOD THING

In today's "I want what I want when I want it" world, the quick fix is the order of the day. We are always looking for the faster and easier way around every situation. And sometimes our quest for all things immediate has us bypassing the real lessons to be learned, such as patience and discipline. Doing the things you need to do to be where you want to be requires consistent action over time and self-control—discipline. Your willingness to practice discipline can make all the difference in the world.

STEP #12:
AVOID BEING A PERFECTIONIST

Understand that every time you say "I'm just a perfectionist," you're giving yourself permission not to try. It's good to want to do a job well. There is a certain amount of pride that comes from putting your best into all you do. But when doing your best becomes an excuse not to try, that's not a good excuse—it's fear preventing you from keeping your agreements to yourself or someone else. Striving for excellence, not perfection, is a better goal.

STEP #13:
DON'T WAIT FOR THE RIGHT TIME

Forget about waiting to be in the right mood—it will never come. There is never a right time to do the hard things you've been avoiding. You'll just have to do them, and once you start, often you'll be amazed at how good you feel, and how easy it goes!

STEP #14:
ACT AS IF

Even if you don't believe you can complete the task—just do it anyway. Act as if you are doing it and enjoying it, and then before you know it, you will be where you want to be. Some of you might feel this is an invitation to be phony, because you are doing something you don't believe in. Do it anyway. The truth is, you're not phony by acting as if—you're just practicing. It's all in how you look at it.

Esteemable Acts

EXERCISE 1

What's most important to you today? What unfinished business needs attending to? What task needs to be begun that you've been putting off? In your Esteemable Acts Journal, if you haven't done so yet, list those things that call out for your attention, those things that you've placed on the back burner for a long time or perhaps only a day. Now is the time to move closer to building real and lasting self-esteem by doing what you say you're going to do. What is most important to you? What do you value? What task would you like to complete?

EXERCISE 2

What stuff gets in your way? What distractions keep pulling your attention away from the things you say are most important to you? Having the courage to write them on paper makes them real and takes away some of their power. List all the things you use to procrastinate. Getting that stuff out of you and onto the paper is a first step in moving closer to being where you want to be in life.

EXERCISE 3

What steps will you take today toward moving past your procrastination, past your fear? In your Esteemable Acts Journal, make a list of the possible actions you can take. What resources will you turn to?

Just Do It!

Right now, get up from wherever you are and do something. Perhaps it's writing out your goals if you haven't listed them yet, or creating a visual that will help you stay focused on what you want to do. Maybe it's that you just need to sit down to write to a loved one that letter you've been putting off. Whatever it is, just do it or tackle a small, manageable piece of it today.

Have the courage
to risk failure

*It's an esteemable act to get up, dust yourself off,
and start all over again.*

have failed at many things in my life—driver's tests,
school exams, relationships—but nothing compared
with failing the New York State Bar Exam. It was significant because this was the first time I had really worked so hard to accomplish a goal, the first time I'd put my all into something. The
first time I was willing to see if I could succeed based on my
own hard work. Everything I had went into passing, and from
this experience I learned firsthand how it felt to fail—and fail
miserably. I failed the New York Bar not once but twice, before
passing and going on to become a licensed attorney in the State
of New York. After finally being admitted to the New York Bar,

I went on to struggle through the California Bar more than six times.

Have you ever worked really hard to reach a goal, only to fail? Have you ever done your very best and it just wasn't good enough? Have you ever sacrificed everything for a dream and it did not turn out the way you wanted it to? If you answer yes to any of these, allow me to congratulate you for having the courage to try something new and risk failure.

To fail at something you must first be present for the event. Many people will never experience failure because they will never put themselves in a position where it's possible. *Defeat* is not a word in their vocabulary because they make safe choices that will keep them out of harm's way. And many people equate safe choices with the good life. In a recent conversation, a friend who prides himself on being brave insisted he wasn't afraid of anything, citing countless examples of his fearlessness.

"And," he continued, "I'd never do anything that I'd fail at."

Yet, as he continued to talk, I got the impression that something was missing. There was a hole that seemed unfilled, a need that appeared unmet as he complained about his life and what was missing. Perhaps safe wasn't so safe after all.

In truth, relying on safe choices can sometimes be the enemy of self-esteem, because you're never encouraged to stretch beyond your comfort zone. And if you don't stretch, while you may never fail, you also may never experience the joy of real, hard-earned victory. It takes great courage to fail because it takes great courage to try—having the willingness to show up in the first place is an esteemable act.

No one likes to fail, whether it's making a mistake in public, getting divorced, being fired from a job, or, as in my case, failing exams over and over and over again. But contrary to popular belief, failing is not the worst thing that could happen to you—not trying is. Action #3 is about having the courage to risk failure, and if you do fail, having the courage to get up, dust yourself off, and start all over again.

Why Do We Fail?

Failure is what happens when you're living a full and rich life. And there are times it can be avoided. There are many reasons for failure and arguably there are times when we fail for no reason at all. Not being fully prepared, not being prepared in the way you need to be, not being prepared at all, being overprepared, a belief that you'll fail, the need to be perfect, and missed opportunities are all reasons for failure. Let's explore each of these a little further.

NOT BEING FULLY PREPARED

This is a surefire way to fail at reaching a goal. Sometimes it's because we don't know what's required of us, but mostly it's because we don't take the time for advance planning. We think we can slide by without doing the necessary work. Take Jules, for example: He scheduled an appointment with a potential new client but didn't take the time to research the company thoroughly. So during his meeting, when he was asked questions he should have been able to answer, he couldn't. The client, thinking this was strange for someone who claimed to be organized, efficient, and scrupulously detailed, chose to give his business to another consultant. All Jules needed to do was spend a little time looking at the company's Website and reading a few articles about it, to get a general idea of who they were.

For many people the idea of preparation is too time-consuming. They believe it takes away from the things they think are more important. But the time you spend planning will not only pay big dividends, it will lessen your chances of not knowing what you're doing or what you're talking about, which wastes your time and other people's time! If you fail to plan, you plan to fail.

I failed the New York State Bar exam the first time because I wasn't fully prepared. While I studied and put a lot of effort into preparing for the test, I didn't work as hard as I could have. I was so happy to be out of school, having just completed eight straight years, that I wasn't as diligent as I should have been. On some level I thought the bar exam was like my law school exams. I was wrong—and I failed.

Have you ever failed at something because you weren't fully prepared? What did you learn? What would you do differently now? Recall the experience and write about it in your Esteemable Acts Journal.

NOT BEING PREPARED IN THE WAY YOU NEED TO BE

Sometimes you really have done your best and your best just isn't good enough, usually because you prepared in the wrong way. Perhaps your focus should have been on A and you mistakenly focused on B. Despite its being a careless mistake, you still fail. Take, for example, Jenny, who had a homework assignment to review math for a quiz the next day. She wasn't paying attention when the teacher said algebra would be the topic, she just heard *math*. Jenny focused on trigonometry and failed the quiz. While she was very well prepared for a trig quiz, she was not prepared for an algebra quiz.

It's irrelevant that Jenny really knew her trig. It's also irrelevant that she didn't know what was expected of her. All that mattered was that she was not prepared in the way she needed to be to successfully pass the exam. It's easy to be angry at the teacher, but wasn't it Jenny's responsibility to know what was expected of her to get a passing grade?

Have you ever failed at something because you weren't prepared in the way you needed to be? What happened? What lesson did you learn from that experience? Write about your experience in your Esteemable Acts Journal.

AN EGO THAT SAYS YOU DON'T NEED TO BE PREPARED

Sometimes we assume that because we've had past successes we don't need to be prepared this time. For example, my friend Jimmy, a motivational speaker, was standing in front of his audience giving a presentation when he froze. Not a single word came out of his mouth. It was as though he had never given a speech before. In that moment, he wasn't the charming and engaging public speaker who in the past had brought audiences to laughter and tears within a fifteen-minute time span. In that moment he wasn't bigger than life—he was just human. Very human. What happened was he hadn't prepared. He didn't know his audience and didn't do the necessary prep work required of a participant-centered professional. Instead, he thought he could wing it. In the past he got away with it. This time he didn't.

How easy it is to think that because you've done something many times you don't need to prepare—even a little bit. The ego says, "I know all there is to know." That's a setup for failure, because even if you know the material, your audience changes, and material constantly needs to be updated and made current. I've led legal training seminars for several years, and while I know my material backward and forward, my group is always different and I like to stay current and interesting. For that reason, I am always preparing.

Have you ever failed at something because your ego got in the way? Perhaps because you thought you were too smart to need to study? What lesson did you learn from that experience? Do you continue to do the same thing over and over again expecting a different result? Write your answers in your Esteemable Acts Journal.

BEING OVERPREPARED

My experience as a professional speaker has taught me a lot about being overprepared. Sometimes you can be so prepared for a program that you create unnecessary tension, setting yourself up for failure. You become more focused on the outcome than on enjoying and participating in the process. You become plastic, stiff, and totally inaccessible to your audience. You're so scripted that you leave no room for spontaneity. There is a fear that if you deviate from your script, you'll fail. Once I was so overly prepared for a program and so concerned about failing that I lost sight of why I was really doing it and failed. It was a self-fulfilling prophecy. I was too prepared.

On the contrary, being prepared, when done right, gives

you the freedom to be more spontaneous, not less so. Take for example public speakers who are well grounded in their material; they spend less time trying to remember their lines and more time building rapport with their audience.

What does it mean to you to be overly prepared? Have you ever been overly prepared for something? Describe examples in your own life of overpreparedness. What beliefs made you feel that you had to be overly prepared? What lesson did you learn from that experience? Write your answers in your Esteemable Acts Journal.

PHYSICALLY UNPREPARED

Sometimes we fail simply because our bodies and our minds are so worn out, they can't function in the way they need to carry us through. That was my problem the second time I failed the New York Bar. The day before the exam, I stayed up all night studying, trying to get every last drop of information into my head. I was so tired going into the exam, I couldn't think clearly enough to answer the questions.

Have you ever allowed yourself to get so tired or physically worn out that you couldn't do the very thing you were working hard to do? Perhaps you had a presentation and the night before you stayed up all night preparing or worrying? How did you feel the next day? How able were you to handle the work before you?

OUR NEED TO BE PERFECT CAN SET US UP FOR FAILURE

You either do something flawlessly or you fail; there is no in-between for perfectionists. You reach the goal or you fail. You either reach the goal in the stated period of time or you fail.

Somehow making the effort just isn't good enough. Learning to accept being human as a desirable character trait is a gift.

When I tell people I've run two marathons, the first question they usually ask me is "How long did it take you?" For the longest time, admitting it took me six hours each time was a devastating blow to my ego. I wanted to be perfect, and perfection meant finishing the race in under four hours. It didn't seem to matter that in both instances I ran without stopping for six hours, or that I finished a 26.2-mile race twice. All I focused on was the time it took me to run.

It took me some time, but I finally recognized that self-esteem comes from making the effort and genuinely doing the best I can. Striving for excellence, not perfection, is the key. Today, in response to the question "How long did it take you to run?" I say, "I ran and ran and ran and ran—and I finished."

What does perfection mean to you? Describe a time in your life when you thought you had to be perfect. How did it feel? How has your need to be perfect affected your life? What does excellence mean? Identify a time when you allowed yourself to do the best you could do but not be perfect. Write your answers in your Esteemable Acts Journal.

MISSED OPPORTUNITIES

Lastly, you can fail because you've allowed an opportunity to come and go. Missed opportunities occur when you're afraid to take some action or don't know how; then the choice is removed. How many opportunities have come and gone in your life because you were afraid to take an action? How many chances have you let pass by simply because it was easier to live in the fear than to walk through it? What could you have done differently? In your Esteemable Acts Journal answer the questions and describe how you felt when you missed those opportunities.

FAILURE IS PART OF LIFE

Many of us grow up believing that failing and making mistakes are the worst things that can happen to us. As children, we're discouraged from making mistakes, so we never have to learn from them. If it appears we're about to make a mistake, our parents and teachers quickly either stop the process or, if they can't, they try to take away the pain rather than allowing us to experience it in the moment, and then showing us how to get up, dust ourselves off, and start all over again. We're taught that if we fail, life is over, or that we won't succeed, or that people won't like us, or that people will look down on us, or that making a mistake is a sign of weakness. So we hold on to our unconscious fear of failure, thus giving it power to direct our thoughts and energy.

What we need to create is a new picture of ourselves, a new belief that we are successes, not failures. The worse thing in life is never to try. Further, we must imagine ourselves living the life we want, rather than consciously or unconsciously attracting the experience of failure. What do you believe about your ability to succeed? Why do you believe what you believe? In your Esteemable Acts Journal make a list of your fears regarding failure. Then, cut up as many pieces of paper as you have fears. Write one fear per piece of paper. In a ceremony, burn them, release them into the universe. The trick is to let them stay there. As you physically release your negative beliefs around failure, you must emotionally release them as well. I invite you to let go of the shackles that bind you to failure. This is a significant step in seeing yourself as a success, not as a failure. But the emotional letting go is only part of the answer; you must be willing to follow up with action and more action.

EVERYTHING HAPPENS FOR A REASON

Sometimes when you're disappointed because you didn't get an outcome you hoped for, it's hard to understand why you had to experience the pain of defeat. It feels unfair that you try so hard and yet can't achieve your goals, especially if you really did your very best. "Why me?" you ask yourself. "Why is this happening to me?"

There are no mistakes and no coincidences. Painful as it feels, nothing, absolutely nothing, happens in this world by accident. This lesson I learned the hard way. Every time I failed the California Bar Exam a piece of me died. I saw each failure as one more reason to feel worthless. Finally, standing at the door of despair yet one more time, I came to appreciate the gift I had been given: the gift of myself. Failing the California Bar Exam repeatedly was the single most painful experience of my life, but it was the one that has provided me with the greatest opportunities. I didn't like it when it was happening, but years later I came to understand that it was all part of a master plan. I needed to learn the lesson of surrender—not giving up, but letting go.

When I became willing to let go of the exam that had appeared to be my reason for living, I was awakened to a new life. Out of the darkness came the opportunity of a lifetime, and that led me to where I am today—training, consulting, speaking, and writing this book. Self-esteem comes from doing esteemable acts and it's an esteemable act to know when to let go.

How do you know when it's time to let go or when you're charged with trying again? Unfortunately, there is no one-size-fits-all answer. It's not that simple. The timing is different for each of us and many factors are to be considered: what the project is, how long you've worked on it, how consumed you are with the outcome, the financial implications, the strain on your family, and its impact on your health. Your answer will come as you trust your intuitive self. You might also wish to invite the advice and counsel of someone who can see more clearly than you, someone more objective. Perhaps this a job for your Esteemable Acts Buddy or your Esteemable Acts Mastermind Group. Invite them into your process.

How Do You Handle Failure?

So what do you do if you fail? How do you handle it and still be able to look yourself in the eye and feel okay? Here are some suggestions.

ACKNOWLEDGE THE FAILURE

The first step is to admit you failed, that you made a mistake, not that you are a failure. The hardest thing for many of us is to accept our failures, especially when we've worked long and hard for a particular outcome. We have an investment in doing things perfectly, and when we don't, we think it's a reflection on who we are. As in recovery from anything, the first step is to admit you have a problem; then and only then can you recover. Acknowledging your mistakes is a key factor in handling failure. The more you deny a mistake or blame someone else for it, the more difficult it will be to get past the experience.

TELL SOMEONE ELSE

For many of us, there is so much shame and stigma attached to making a mistake, that the idea of then sharing what happened, in detail, with another person is incomprehensible. We often think it's better to suffer alone than to expose ourselves to judgment and ridicule. So you become a prisoner of your secrets. The truth is you are as sick as your secrets, because you are always worried that someone will find out.

Revealing who you are and what you've done can, at times, be painful, but after the initial sting has subsided, it is a freeing experience that makes you more humble—more open to receiving the help you need to get to the next level.

KNOW YOU'LL GET THROUGH TO THE OTHER SIDE

When you're in the middle of the pain, it's hard to believe you'll get through it to the other side. Sometimes it feels as if you've taken one step forward and two steps backward. You're in that place where you feel stuck and don't know which way to go. Life is sometimes about being in what I call "the hallway." That place that sometimes feels stagnant where there is no movement. That place where you look for an answer for why something has happened and you just can't get it. So there you are, having to live with your feelings and still do the next right thing. Don't give up; this, too, shall pass. You will survive the experience, particularly if you are willing to take action.

LEARN FROM YOUR MISTAKES

Failures and mistakes are useless unless we learn from them. Seeing them as opportunities to understand yourself better will help you to grow. It is often said that insanity is doing the same thing over and over again expecting a different result. Think of the people who put their finger in a flame and get burned. You'd expect that they'd never put their finger in the fire again. What often happens, however, is that they put their finger in the flame again and again, expecting that, at least one time, the flame won't burn. Making mistakes is human. Not learning from them is a setup for disaster.

ASK FOR FEEDBACK ABOUT WHAT WENT WRONG

The only way you can learn from your mistakes is if you are willing to hear what you did wrong and how you could have done it differently. Knowing what works and what doesn't gives you the tools to correct the problem. Have the courage to ask for feedback. A few years ago I lost a client, and as hard as it was to ask, I requested honest feedback. She gave it to me, and while I didn't like what I heard, it provided me with enough information so I won't make the same mistake with another client.

PLAN YOUR NEW/REVISED STRATEGY ON PAPER

Something magical happens when we put our thoughts on paper. It makes an idea real. Make friends with paper and pen. Be aware that you are creating a new plan for yourself, not repeating the one that led to failure. Put pen to paper, and write out your plan in detail: how you will approach the situation, where you will begin, what steps you will take, how much time you will allot to each task, and when you will begin.

BREAK TASKS INTO SMALL PIECES

Big dreams can appear daunting unless they are broken into small, manageable pieces. Taking baby steps is the key to success, because it almost always guarantees success. It's easy to do a small task, such as call directory assistance for a telephone number or make a list of things to do. Not only does the task become doable, but there is a way to measure each assignment. Breaking tasks down into small pieces allows you to celebrate each success you've achieved. You can feel good about taking that one action, that esteemable action.

COMMIT TO DOING SOMETHING

There is a power in making agreements and a reward in keeping them. Make an agreement with yourself to do each piece of your larger task—one piece at a time. The smaller the agreement, the more likely it is you'll keep it. Action is the key to success, regardless of how you define success. Fulfilling your obligations is an esteemable action. If you successfully get through each piece, you can't fail. But if you don't successfully get through each piece, you can at least applaud yourself for having made the effort.

STAY MOTIVATED

We all need motivation from time to time, including the person who motivates others. Staying on track is hard over the long term because we all get into the doldrums. We get stuck in the hallway and find it difficult to see our way out. Sometimes all you'll need is a little push, at others times you'll need a shove.

Being willing to get the help you need is a key to dealing with disappointments. Books, tapes, pictures, supportive friends, whatever you can use to keep you going—use them!

BE PATIENT WITH YOURSELF

You've heard it a million times, but it's true. Do your part—all the work involved in getting you to where you want to be—then let go of the outcome. Sometimes going for your dream is a painful process because it feels as if failure visits you more often than success, or it feels as if it's taking you forever to get where you want to go. But if you're busy taking the necessary action, it only appears that you're not moving ahead. In truth, you are. Don't be discouraged, and if you are that's okay. Just keep showing up anyway and be patient with your progress. That's your job.

IF YOU FAIL AGAIN, GET UP, DUST YOURSELF OFF, AND START ALL OVER AGAIN

Failing is not fun, and it can even be debilitating at times. It can rob you of your spirit and your will to keep going. But the key to getting through a disappointing experience is not to give it more power than it deserves. Failure is temporary. Indeed, the slap to your ego will linger for a while, but eventually you'll forget the intensity of the pain you once held so dear. My advice: Get up, dust yourself off, and start all over again.

Esteemable Acts

EXERCISE 1

In your Esteemable Acts Journal, reflecting back over the top five to ten dreams on your Dreams List (page 16), are there any dreams that require skills and/or talents you need to develop? What action can you take to develop those skills? What would prevent you from taking that action? How far along are you in making your dream come true? If far along, what has enabled you to move forward? If not, what stands in your way?

EXERCISE 2

Think back on a recent challenging, difficult, or uncomfortable experience you've had. How did you handle the situation? Did you look for reasons not to talk about it? Did you make excuses for avoiding the situation? Did you become angry or confrontational as an excuse not to look at what really happened? Allow yourself an opportunity to really think through your responses, and then in your Esteemable Acts Journal, write out your answers.

EXERCISE 3

In going back to your Dreams List, do any of your dreams involve a previous failure, such as sending out one hundred résumés to get one job interview or working hard to get a promotion, only to have it go to another person? Explore your previous failure(s) and allow your feelings to surface. Then write out your thoughts in your Esteemable Acts Journal, if you didn't already address them in Exercise #2.

EXERCISE 4

Feeling our feelings is the hardest thing many of us will ever have to do, because the very act of feeling highlights our essential vulnerability. Further, our feelings take us to places we'd rather not go, because we just might have to do something about them. Let's move into your feeling place for a moment and explore the difficult things you may not want to admit, the past failures you've had, the embarrassing mistakes you've made, and possibly the part you played. Harboring dark feelings keeps you from success.

1. Write out those feelings in your Esteemable Acts Journal.
2. Then, in your journal, answer the following questions:
   - Do you believe life should be easy?
   - Do you believe you must work harder than most people in order for you to get anything out of life?
   - Are you sometimes angry that life is hard for you?
   - Do you wish you could have just a little break?
   - Do you sometimes regret that you've been handed everything and that life was made easy for you?

Write at least a paragraph answering each question. Then go back over your answers, paying close attention to any underlying beliefs you hold that may have influenced your response(s).

Just Do It!

Take a look at your Dreams List. What can you do right now, this moment, to move you closer to overcoming the obstacles in your path? What one action are you willing to take right now? The key to handling failure is to become willing to risk failure. Commit to one small piece of your goal before moving to the next Action.

PART TWO

Becoming your own best friend is an esteemable act

Self-examination begins with seeing yourself clearly

$\mathcal{I}$t's an esteemable act to have the courage to see yourself as you really are.

It's Not My Fault!

As far back as I can remember, everything bad that ever happened to me was always someone else's fault. "It's not my fault, I'm not to blame" was one of my favorite sayings. I was never inclined to take responsibility for anything. And why should I have? There was always someone to blame. It was my mother's fault. Had she been a better parent, I wouldn't have turned out as I did. It was my father's fault—he wasn't there. Had he been a stronger presence, I would not have sought relief in the arms of older men. It was their fault.

"If you had my life, you'd do what I did, too" was my battle cry. I didn't have the same opportunities as other kids, I was a high school dropout, I'm a woman, I'm black—the list of excuses I used to justify my life circumstances was endless. There was one reason after another for not seeing my part in the conditions that unfolded in my life. The problem, however, was that none of those reasons excused my behavior—they simply explained it. No doubt growing up poor, female, and black in America affected the way I saw the world, and no doubt this influenced my experience at times and my behavior. But like it or not, fair or unfair, in each and every case, I made the ultimate decision to choose my fate. And the choices I made moved me closer to or further away from real and lasting self-love.

Every one of us alone has the power to direct the course of our lives by choosing what actions we will or won't take. While sometimes it's easier to believe you don't have a choice, the reality is that you always have a choice to behave differently. Action #4 is about having the courage to recognize both your strengths and your challenges, own them as yours, and change your behavior when it no longer works. It's only in seeing yourself as you really are that you become able to genuinely love yourself. It's hard to love yourself when you don't know who you really are. Begin now to think about who you are and the myriad excuses you have used for your behavior. In your Esteemable Acts Journal take a moment and write a paragraph describing yourself in fifty words or less. Don't worry about doing it perfectly, just write.

Self-esteem and Self-examination

Identifying and learning how to take responsibility for your actions is the critical first step in seeing yourself more clearly. It's also a step toward building real and lasting self-esteem, because you can love yourself only when you really know who you are.

Remember, this Action is about examining your own behavior. You may be tempted to think, "Jim and Jane should read this book or they should be doing this exercise. They really need to look at their behavior." And while they may benefit from the material, this Action is specifically designed for you. In a thoughtful yet purposeful way, you'll be encouraged to continually ask yourself, "What's my part in the situations I experience?" "What can I do differently?" "How does my behavior affect the way I see myself?" "How does my behavior affect the way others see me?"

Benefits to Seeing Yourself as You Really Are

There are many benefits to seeing yourself as you really are. Here are a few:

FREEDOM FROM CHARACTER DEFECTS

Our character defects control us, whether you believe it or not. We are driven by a hundred forms of self-centered fear. And the more we deny their existence, the more control they have over us. It's like the elephant in the living room: The more you ignore it, the more you know it's there. By acknowledging the elephant, your defects, you take a first step toward being released from their grip. Bring to mind a time when you were angry and you allowed that anger to spill over into totally unrelated other areas of your life. Maybe someone at work upset you and you took it out on your family when you got home. Write about that experience in your Esteemable Acts Journal.

FREEDOM FROM SECRETS

We are as sick as our secrets. The more secrets you keep, the more imprisoned you feel. The more secrets you keep, the more you give other people power over you. The more secrets you keep, the more ill at ease you are, always afraid someone will discover who you really are. The flip side of that is the more open and honest you are with yourself and others, the more free and empowered you become. This is a step toward building greater self-love. In writing this book, there was a real concern about revealing certain aspects of my past, because up until now, only a select few knew my complete history. I knew that the story behind the story is always more interesting, and that eventually some reporter would dig up my past, so I thought it best if I brought it out into the open first. Now, I feel free and I have nothing to be afraid of. What secrets are you holding inside? What prevents you from letting them out? What's the worst thing that could happen to you if your secret was out? Is the price you pay to hide who you really are worth it?

AN ABILITY TO LOVE OTHERS

It's hard to genuinely love others unless you love yourself. Loving yourself opens you up to deeper and richer relationships with people, because you can be fully present. You're less tormented by jealousy, envy, anger, and resentment, because you are living your own best life. When you're doing what you love you can celebrate the success of others. Also, the more you know about yourself and the more you can own your humanness, the better able you are to connect with others. When you recognize your own faults, it becomes easier to see the humanness in others.

Performing the exercises throughout this Action will bring you all the benefits listed above, taking you another courageous step toward self-discovery and a revitalized life.

Getting Past Your Filters

Self-examination can be difficult, because you're looking past your filters to the truth, and it is our filters that protect us, that shield us from real and perceived dangers. But filters, by their very nature, cloud your thinking and distort your vision, preventing you from seeing things as they really are. For example, a photograph taken with a filtered lens can make the subject more appealing. There are fewer blemishes and wrinkles. Think of the old saying "seeing things through rose-colored glasses." The idea is when you wear these glasses, the world becomes rosy. Through filters, we see only the good in us. And as our filters make us more perfect and less human, they make other people more flawed.

Other filters include moods, attitudes, and other people's behavior. When you're not feeling well, it's easy to see yourself as someone who's misunderstood and who should be given a

break. While we all could be a little more tolerant of one another's feelings, when moods and attitudes are used continually
as an excuse for bad behavior, it doesn't work. Everyone has a
bad day or two, but to always be in a bad mood and expect people not to react is asking a lot.

Then sometimes we use other people's behavior as a reason
to behave poorly ourselves, thus justifying our actions. For example, "She talked about me to my boss, that's why I sent a hurtful e-mail about her to everyone on the company's e-mail list,"
said Stella. While you may think you have a valid reason for acting a certain way in response to someone's behavior, over the
long haul ask yourself, "How does it make me feel?" Does your
behavior bring you closer to or push you further away from real
and lasting self-esteem? What could you do differently?

Other Obstacles to Self-discovery

If self-examination is such a life-transforming experience, why
don't more of us do it? Why do so many of us avoid looking at
ourselves? The answer is our old friend fear.

FEAR OF WHAT YOU MIGHT FIND

If you are like most people, you have never done a personal inventory and have no desire to do so. The very idea of seeing and
admitting things about yourself is an excruciatingly painful
process; most of us are quite content living in the dark. Plus, you
have an investment in being right. It's one thing to say in jest
"I'm a bitch," it's another to acknowledge it to the world. An
honest admission involves true ownership of your behavior. And

while this book strives not to attach judgment to a particular word or character trait, make no mistake about it, you do.

FEAR YOU WILL BE EXPECTED TO DO SOMETHING

You may be afraid that once you've discovered and uncovered who you are, particularly those things that have gotten you into trouble or caused you grief in your relationships, you will have to do something about them. It's one thing to admit your faults; it's another to do anything about them. Changing old behavior is hard work, even if you know the old behavior no longer works.

FEAR PEOPLE WON'T LIKE YOU

Another fear is that once you honestly reveal yourself to others, they won't like you. Living behind a mask is easier and safer. Masks come in the form of our clothes, our makeup, our cars, our homes, the schools our kids attend, and even the way we speak. We put forth the image we want the world to see and we go to great lengths to protect it. As a result, we're always afraid that someone will peek behind the mask and see who we really are. This is not scary if you are who you claim to be. But if who you are is very different from the image you project, you're in trouble, because you fear you'll be found out.

The truth about being found out is that most people know who you are long before you admit it. People who deal with you see who you are, even if you can't or choose not to. Your admission simply validates what is already known and makes you more human and humble.

FEAR OF BEING JUDGED

Most of us are averse to anything that looks or smells like criticism. Sadly, for some of us it's because we've had so much criticism in our lives. People have hurt us under the guise of helping us by telling us something for our own good. But with or without your permission, people will judge you. You are judged every day, all the time, as you judge others. Sometimes their judgments are valid and sometimes not. If you are to gain any real advantage in this process of building real and lasting self-esteem, you must be willing to hear what they have to say. Getting past the sting of criticism and possible rejection to the truth is an esteemable act.

YOU DON'T THINK YOU NEED TO TAKE INVENTORY

Some people feel that what others think about them is none of their business. They don't care and aren't interested in your opinion. All I can say is that if you lived on an island all by yourself and you never had to come in contact with another person, then there would be no need to worry about their feelings or what impact you'd have on them. However, since you don't live on an island, learning how to interact is important.

In your Esteemable Acts Journal, identify the obstacles that prevent you from seeing yourself more clearly. If, in the past, you've made an effort at self-discovery, what stopped you from going deeper? What got in the way? If this is your first attempt at looking inward, what makes you willing to take this courageous step now? The road to real and lasting self-esteem is paved with opportunities for self-discovery. Take one step. You can do it!

Seeing Yourself More Clearly

Bravo, for having the courage to take this very important step toward building real and lasting self-esteem. At this beginning stage of your journey, start paying particular attention to your interactions with others. This will provide you with valuable information as to how you are seen in the world. For example, if you find you are in a conflict with someone, take a moment and ask yourself, "Is there something I did or could have done to make the other person react the way he or she did?" "Could my tone of voice, my body language, a look, or a word I chose to use have triggered the person in some way?" Because we don't see ourselves as others do, it might be hard to assess this, but do the best you can. It's a beginning.

To assist you on your journey, consider the following affirmations:

- I am not afraid of knowing who I am.
- I welcome the opportunity to know myself better.
- I am open to knowing and loving all of me.
- I am willing to step out of the darkness into the light.
- I am willing to see the part I play in my interactions with others.

Who do you think you are right now? How do you see yourself? Without giving it too much thought, write out your answers in your Esteemable Acts Journal. This is a start. We will develop your assessment further in the next section.

Your Honest Inventory

An honest inventory is a written assessment of who you are. It's a catalogue of your strengths, traits that make you effective—and your challenges, things that get in the way of your effectiveness. Admitting who you are triggers two powerful forces: humility and honesty. Acknowledging your specific character flaws is an act of honesty, one that takes you closer to building real and lasting self-esteem. And the admission of these character flaws is humbling.

Having the courage to see both strengths and challenges is an esteemable act. An honest inventory requires that you see both. When doing your inventory, if you see only the good, you're fooling yourself, because no one is all good. If you see only the bad, you're doing yourself a disservice, because there's not a day that goes by when you don't do something good for yourself or for someone else.

Finally, an honest inventory requires constantly being on the lookout for fear. Fear is a powerful foe and at every opportunity will step in to frustrate your best intentions. It may try to convince you that there's no need to look inward, no need for self-improvement, and that you're fine just the way you are. And while you may be a wonderful person, there is always room for personal improvement. Fear will also tell you to stop the process of self-discovery when it feels too real. Resist the temptation to do so! And keep going. Any pain you may feel is only temporary and will cease to control you as you work through the process. On the other hand, if you choose to give in, at some point in the future you'll have to face your demons once again. Avoidance serves only to increase and prolong the pain.

To get you started on your inventory, circle all the words from the list below that in your opinion describe you. As you go down the list, think about each word carefully and how it applies to you. Remember, your goal is to be honest.

controlling	easily distracted	fun to be with
self-motivator	assertive	risk taker
often late for appointments	self-absorbed	avoids confrontation
goal-oriented	argumentative	creative
organized	disciplined	competitive
focused	honest	demanding
poor listener	intimidating	impatient
follows through	critical of others	critical of self
desperate	stuffs feelings down	ethical
kindhearted	not goal-oriented	angry
consistent	values education/learning	high energy
talkative	cautious	too giving
provocative	passive	persistent
open to feedback	supportive	a bright light
frugal	ambitious	depressed
a gossip	a nongossip	responsible

Next, in your Esteemable Acts Journal, on a new page, write at the top "My Strengths." Underneath, identify five strengths, things that make you a good friend, a good employee or employer, a good spouse or companion, a good person. If they apply, you may wish to add to your list some of the words and phrases you circled above.

Now turn your attention to your challenges, areas that need

improving. In your Esteemable Acts Journal, on a new page, write at the top "My Challenges." Identify five challenges, those things that make you less effective than you want to be. Again, you may wish to use the words and phrases you circled above. One question you may want to ask yourself is "How can I be even more effective than I already am?" Here the presumption is that you are already effective, you're just looking for ways to improve.

Some Additional Words to Consider

Let's examine your more visible and destructive human characteristics in more detail. In your Esteemable Acts Journal, on a separate sheet of paper for each word, write the following seven words: angry, fearful, dishonest, critical, self-pitying, intolerant, jealous. Allow yourself two to three pages for each word. Then write one or two sentences describing what the word means to you. As you continue with the process of seeing yourself clearly, identify a time when you exhibited that character trait—for example, a time when you were angry. What made you feel angry? How did you behave? How did others react to your behavior? How do you feel when someone is angry with you? Go through this process for each word.

Now, let's shift your focus to one behavior you exhibited in the last seven days. Record your experience. How did it affect the people around you? Did you have any regrets?

When you are finished, take a moment to think about what you wrote. What conclusions can you draw about yourself based on your lists of strengths and challenges? What conclusions can you draw from the process you went through to come up with your list? Write down your thoughts in your Esteemable Acts Journal.

What About G-u-i-l-t?

An intoxicating and abominable feeling, guilt eats away at the essence of who we are. We're taught early in life to recoil from it as if from a hot flame. Yet I invite you to consider guilt in a different light. Instead of running away from it and being willing to do anything to get rid of it, I propose that you see guilt as a sensor letting you know there is a problem afoot and there's work to be done. Consider looking at the underlying behavior causing guilt instead of blaming someone else for it. Complaining once about how guilty I felt and hoping the person I complained to would say, "Oh, Francine, don't feel guilty, it's not your fault." I was told instead that if I didn't want to feel guilt, I needed to stop doing the things that made me feel guilty. Who did she think she was? I was looking for sympathy and instead I got forced accountability, and I didn't like it one bit.

For years I felt guilty about not calling my mother on a regular basis. And she encouraged my guilt. Every time she said "How come I don't hear from you?" my response was always "Stop running a guilt trip on me." My guilt never led me to change my behavior. It was not until I started calling her at least once a week that I let go of the guilt. The truth is that my mother couldn't make me feel guilty without my consent. The guilt was a result of my not doing something, for me, that I needed to be doing. Calling my mother on a regular basis is an esteemable act. What are you feeling guilty about? Is there any valid reason for your guilt? What can you do to get rid of it?

Really Going Against Your Nature

Self-examination requires that you go against your nature and do what you're unaccustomed to doing—honestly assessing yourself. Then it goes a step farther and asks you to really step outside your comfort zone and solicit feedback from others.

"Now she's gone too far with this self-examination stuff," you're probably thinking. "You want me to ask someone how they feel about me? No way!"

No doubt this is one of the most courageous things you'll be asked to do, and also one of the most rewarding. Not only do you get valuable and useful information about how to be the best you can be, the fact that you are willing to ask gives you another opportunity to walk through your fear. When was the last time you asked a friend what he or she really thought of you? Have you ever asked your supervisor or manager to give you feedback about your work and your attitude? What about your coworkers? When was the last time you asked them their thoughts about you? Or your clients—have you ever asked them to critique your work style? Your effectiveness? Do you really want to hear how you affect others or do you think it's their problem if they don't like you? While it may be their problem, you would be well served if you considered what they have to say.

Unless you hear how you affect others, you're likely to think you don't affect them at all. And if you think your behavior doesn't have an impact on others, then you'll believe there is no need for you to change. It's an esteemable act to have the courage to hear the truth and to do something about it. It's one thing to casually say "I'm controlling and that's just the way I am." It's another to have it validated by those you encounter on a day-to-day basis.

Imagine you're a thriving, successful business. To remain healthy and financially stable, you must identify your needs and resources, as well as do a continual review of your assets and liabilities. Smart businesses hire outside, nonaffiliated consultants to do this job, because they are better able to be objective. Your mission—if you choose to accept it—is to select an outside consultant to assist you in your inventory process. Pick someone you trust—a buddy you can count on to be honest and caring at the same time. Once you've chosen the person, explain that your purpose is to see yourself as others see you, so you can improve the areas that need improving. Tell them you want to be the best you can be. Give the person the following list of words, the same list you looked at earlier, and ask this person to circle all the words he or she believes describe you. For example, she may see you as someone who's fun to be with, in which case she'd circle that phrase. She may also see you as controlling. Then she'd circle that word. This will help you understand how others see you—always useful information.

controlling	easily distracted	fun to be with
self-motivator	assertive	risk taker
often late for appointments	self-absorbed	avoids confrontation
goal-oriented	argumentative	creative

organized	disciplined	competitive
focused	honest	demanding
poor listener	intimidating	impatient
follows through	critical of others	critical of self
desperate	stuffs feelings down	ethical
kindhearted	not goal-oriented	angry
consistent	values education/learning	high energy
talkative	cautious	too giving
provocative	passive	persistent
open to feedback	supportive	a bright light
frugal	ambitious	depressed
a gossip	a nongossip	responsible

By this time, you should have an honest inventory, or at least the beginnings of one. Now that you have this information, what do you do with it? Put your inventory aside for a few days. Just let it be. Don't peek at it or edit it. In two or three days, revisit your list and ask yourself the following questions:

- What attitudes, behaviors, and/or beliefs surfaced during my self-examination process?
- What assumptions did I make about myself?
- What feelings did I have as I made each selection?
- What barriers got in the way of my being honest?
- What thoughts went through my mind?
- How did I feel asking someone how they feel about me?
- Could what they say be true?
- What am I willing to do now?

Allow your feelings to surface, don't run from them. Just be with them and record them in your journal.

In reviewing your list, what do you most appreciate about you? What are your strengths? And in keeping with a sense of balance, what prevents you from being even more effective than you are? How do you know? Did you ask for feedback from a buddy? If not, why not? What did this teach you? Are you more capable of being honest with yourself? Record your answers to these questions in your Esteemable Acts Journal.

Esteemable Acts

EXERCISE 1

Imagine you have just made your transition from this life to the next and your life as you've known it is over. What legacy would you like to leave behind? How would you like to be remembered? What would be your epitaph? In your Esteemable Acts Journal, write out your answers.

EXERCISE 2

Take careful note of where you are now. Who are you? Now recall from Exercise #1 where you want to be. What would it take to get from where you are to where you want to be? What resources are available to you to help you on your journey of feeling better about yourself? What stands in the way of your accessing those resources?

Just Do It!

If you haven't begun your honest inventory yet, I invite you to select just one thing you agree to do, within the next forty-eight hours, that will move you closer to taking that inventory. Choose one thing you're willing to start—not finish. Perhaps it's sitting down with pen and paper prepared to take your own inventory. Perhaps it's asking a friend if she'd be willing to support you by giving you some honest feedback. Whatever it is—and it will be a different beginning for each of you—I invite you to get started. Just do it.

Take care of your body and it will take care of you

It's an esteemable act to treat your body like the precious vessel it is.

In our fast-paced world, we're encouraged to keep going and going, faster and faster. We're so busy producing and doing that we routinely lose sight of the need for balance and self-care, and eventually we crash.

Putting all your effort into your job might seem like a good idea at the time, but over the long haul you deplete your energy and weaken your resolve, making you less effective. Likewise, even at home, if all your time is spent doing for others, to the point that you neglect yourself, eventually your body will respond. Heart attack, exhaustion, illness, and addiction are ways our bodies tell us they've had enough—we've gone too far and need to slow down and focus on our health. Being good to your body and your mind is the greatest investment you can make. The focus of this Action is to explore ways for better self-care. What investment are you making in your health today?

Self-esteem and Self-care

When it comes to our health most of us are more concerned with how we look than how we feel. For many people, the outside takes priority over the inside. We spend hours in front of the mirror focused on the shape of our muscles rather than the condition they are in. We've been taught to believe that the better our bodies look, the greater our self-love. Not so. How often have you seen a beautiful body attached to an unhealthy mind? Or a pretty woman with a cigarette hanging out of her mouth? Or a gorgeous guy addicted to alcohol or drugs? How often have you seen a thin, well-shaped person who has bad skin?

Good health is a result of choices: smart, courageous, proactive, well-thought-out choices, which aren't always easy to make. Choices that sometimes require that you say "STOP" when everyone says "GO," or that require you to say "YES" when others say "NO." Self-esteem comes from doing esteemable acts, including making the right choices for your health. What choices regarding your health are you making today? In your Esteemable Acts Journal, take a moment and identify one smart choice you've made in the last week. Now identify one courageous choice you've made. A proactive choice. A well-thought-out choice you've made in the last month. How did you feel about yourself after you made those choices? What were the outcomes?

Good Health Is a Privilege

Good health is not a right, it's a privilege. Most of us are born with a functional body and healthy parts. As children, many of us learn how to take care of those parts: regularly brushing our teeth, washing our skin and hair, eating properly, doing exercise, getting checkups, practicing mental stimulation and emotional self-care. But even with the best early training, we often still fall prey to bad habits. Sometimes when we're young we think we can do anything to and with our bodies. But young habits, over time, become old habits, which are hard to break. Good health is not owed to us by virtue of our being on earth; we have to earn it. For many people, it's only when they lose their health that they realize just how important it was. But you don't have to wait until it's too late to wake up and practice self-care. You can start now, regardless of how old you are.

When I learned this lesson, it was almost too late. As an adolescent, I was convinced my body was indestructible, like those of the television characters I loved: Batgirl and Wonder Woman. But after years of addiction, I'm paying the price for my previous lifestyle. Sometimes the price I pay is looking at the physical scars on my body that will never go away. Sometimes the price I pay is the inability to use a part of my body with total range of motion, or chronic back pain. Or it's that I have to reread material over and over again in order to understand it, because my brain cells have been destroyed by drug and alcohol abuse. Sometimes it's the difficulty I have breathing through my nose because I smoked three packs of cigarettes a day for sixteen years.

In your Esteemable Acts Journal, take some time to explore the consequences of your previous health and lifestyle choices. Sometimes reality hurts, especially as we get older and realize we can't go back and change the past. But the good news is that no matter what our past choices, we can start anew today and live the healthiest life we can, for as long as we can.

Your Health Is Your Business

Your health is your business. And because it's your business, it's your responsibility to take care of it. Your health is not your mother's, your spouse's, or even your doctor's responsibility. For example, when you pay your doctor to advise you on health matters, how often do you then expect her to be on top of everything regarding your health? Do you just assume it's her job to monitor your behavior? Do you expect your doctor to remind you of the things you need to do for yourself? Do you relinquish responsibility and simply wait for your doctor to do for you what you're not willing to do for yourself?

The truth is, your doctor is not the gatekeeper of your good health; you are in partnership. There are things you must do and things your doctor must do, and he can do no more than you help him do. Initially that means giving your doctor all the information she needs to make a proper diagnosis. It's hard to properly diagnose a condition without all the facts. Does your doctor know the truth about your health habits; for example that you are a smoker? Does your doctor know whether you are physically active or sedentary? Does your doctor know you lead an active sexual life? Does your doctor know about your family's health history?

Being in partnership with your doctor also means asking questions if you don't understand something that's been told to you. In addition, it means inquiring as to the meaning of documents you're asked to sign. It's easy to be intimidated by authority, especially when the authority figure wears a white coat and stethoscope. But if you don't understand something, don't think ignoring it will make it magically clarify itself. Ask your doctor to explain what it means. Before I became a lawyer I was afraid to ask questions about the medical forms and releases doctors gave me to sign, so I just signed them. I recall a time when I paid the price for my fear. A few years ago when I was preparing for surgery, my doctor gave me several documents to sign. Since he was the gatekeeper of my good health (or so I thought at the time), I didn't ask him any questions, even though I was confused by what I read.

After the surgery, there was a question about the procedure. In addressing the issue, I discovered it wasn't my doctor but his assistant who had performed my operation. "I feel deceived," I cried. "I hired you to do my surgery, not your assistant."

Then he told me, "You signed a release stating it was okay for me to substitute another doctor," and he showed me the document to prove it. I had no idea I had done that. Why not? Because I never read what he gave me to sign—I just blindly signed it.

Remember, your health is your business. Have the courage

to ask your doctor questions. Read everything you're asked to sign before you sign it. Ask about what's in your medical file. While you may have a great doctor who volunteers answers to anticipated questions, it's more likely that you don't. Take responsibility for keeping yourself informed, knowing that sometimes being informed means getting a second opinion from another reputable doctor.

Also, being in partnership with your doctor means that after being informed—especially when you know what she's saying is right—you do what she suggests. You can have the greatest doctor in the world and ask all the right questions, but if you're unwilling to take her advice, you're not doing your part. Do you follow your doctor's advice or do you think you know what's best? Think of a time when you went against the advice of your doctor. What happened? How did you feel? How long did it take for you to heal from your condition?

For example, after leg surgery Quinton was told to stay off his feet for six weeks. And under no condition was he to return to work before the six weeks were up. Against doctor's orders, he prematurely went back to work and suffered another injury more severe than the first. Now he has no choice but to stay off his feet—he's bedridden for one entire year.

What choices are you making regarding your health?

You Are in a Relationship with Your Body

Relationships work best when we respect one another, and respect is an action. Listening to your body when it says it needs something and giving it what it asks for—such as rest and relaxation when it's tired, water when it's thirsty, nutritious food when it's hungry, and pampering all the time—are behaviors that demonstrate respect. It's not enough to say you love your body, then abuse it. Forcing yourself to stay awake past your body's bedtime is not a respectful act, particularly if it's done on a regular basis. Stuffing yourself with more food when your body says "I've had enough" is not a good thing either.

TAKE RESPONSIBILITY

The relationship between you and your body will improve when you take responsibility for your actions. It's easy to use your past or your environment or even your feelings as excuses for not taking care of yourself, but to have and maintain good health, you must take responsibility for what you have done and continue to do to your body. What excuses are you making? Who are you blaming for the condition your body is in? How can you start taking responsibility now? Please record your answers in your Esteemable Acts Journal.

Taking responsibility begins with gathering information. Read up on health matters in your favorite magazines. Most have a column or a regular department addressing health issues. Go to the library, look on the Internet, and ask questions of health care professionals. Gather information about your body. When was the last time you had a regular physical? Do you know what's going on with your body? Are you confused about which medical exams/screenings you should have and when? While identifying which exams you need can be overwhelming and frightening, it's worth the effort. Ask your doctor which tests are appropriate for someone of your gender, race, and age. There may even be specific tests given to people who live in certain geographical regions. Look into it. The Internet is a wonderful resource. The more you know, the more you can help yourself. This is an important step in taking care of your health. Here's a short alphabetical list of screenings you might want to consider: AIDS and other sexually transmitted diseases, blood pressure, bone density measurement, breast exam, cholesterol, fecal occult blood test, glucose, hearing, mammogram, PAP smear, problem-drinking assessment, prostate-specific antigen test, thyroid-stimulating hormone measurement, and vision. Find out which ones you need, and take them.

BE PROACTIVE

Another step in the process of self-care is being proactive—that is, taking positive action before there's a problem. The opposite of proactive is reactive, where you wait until your body, in desperation, cries out for help. And sometimes you wait until great damage is already done. Many people take the "wait and see" approach to their health. They believe if they wait long enough, whatever problems that might exist will go away or that if they wait long enough, they can convince themselves that there really wasn't a problem after all. Don't wait and see. Find out now. If there is a problem that needs to be addressed, take care of it immediately. Don't wait until it's too late.

Damon hated going to the dentist and he didn't want anyone telling him how to take care of his teeth. To him, brushing once a day was sufficient and flossing was a waste of time. Recently, he developed pain and bleeding in his gums, and reluctantly he made a dental appointment. An unhealthy buildup of plaque and tartar had caused a serious infection. Ten thousand dollars later, his teeth are in great shape, but the price he paid for not being proactive regarding the health of his teeth and gums was high.

In a recent edition of *Essence* magazine there were five illustrious examples of women who had taken control of their health. Ranging in age from forty-eight to eighty, each woman talked about the secret to her youthful appearance and healthy body. While each woman shared her story and tips on having and maintaining good health, the common denominator was that they were all proactive. They ate consciously, exercised regularly, and consistently made their health a priority. What choices are you making today regarding your health? What proactive steps are you taking? In your Esteemable Acts Journal, please record your answers.

KEEP AGREEMENTS

Keeping agreements means doing what you say you'll do, and that includes keeping the agreements you make with yourself to maintain the health of your body. Josie made an agreement with herself to do some form of exercise daily and to avoid sugar. For years, she kept her agreement. As a result, she was rewarded with a healthy, strong, and slim body. She felt and looked good. Then she moved to a new town where the weather was different from what she was accustomed to. She found excuses not to exercise. "It's too cold," "It's too rainy," she would cry. Before she knew it she was working out only once a week, then not at all. Once she got out of the habit of working out, she gave herself permission to eat whatever she wanted—she broke her agreement with herself entirely. Josie gained sixteen pounds and three dress sizes. Not only was the weight gain unhealthy, it made her feel horrible inside.

Her friends said, "Don't be so hard on yourself, it's no big thing, you're only human." No doubt they meant well by discouraging her from beating up on herself. But what Josie needed was compassionate yet firm advice. Fortunately, she was able to give the answer she needed to herself. She took responsibility for what she had allowed to happen, she became willing to do something about it, and she forgave herself for her lapse in self-care. She is now back down to a healthy weight and feels and looks great.

Keeping your health agreements to yourself is an esteemable act. What agreements did you keep this week? Today? What agreements have you made in the last week that you were unable to keep? Why weren't you able to keep them? The more honest you are, the better you'll feel about yourself. Perhaps you've been afraid to make health agreements with yourself. If so, why? What would it take for you to willingly make a health agreement with yourself? Let's make an agreement, now: "I, [your name], promise to [choose one thing to do] today in furtherance of my health and I will be forgiving of myself if I fall short of the goal." Write your answers in your Esteemable Acts Journal.

Make Amends Wherever Possible

The body has amazing restorative powers and is often quite forgiving, if only you are willing to make the effort. Here are some suggestions on how to make amends to your body.

MOVE IT!

Movement is critical to good health. Don't just think about moving your body, do it. It doesn't matter what you do: going to the gym; taking a stretch, yoga, dance, or Pilates class; walking or jogging. And remember, little things count, too, such as using the stairs instead of the elevator or escalator, lifting light weights while watching television, or just walking around the block once or twice. Every minute of exercise adds up, and the minutes don't necessarily need to be consecutive to count. So what are you waiting for? Start moving!

DRINK LOTS OF WATER

Water is a miracle tonic. It flushes out the system by getting rid of impurities that accumulate from everyday exposure to toxins in the environment, and it's great for the skin. If you don't like the taste, try alternatives such as plain seltzer water (not club soda, which is loaded with sodium); herb teas such as chamomile or peppermint; or sugar-free beverages. While you may be tempted to sweeten your beverage, I would encourage you not to unless you absolutely can't help yourself. Adding sugar is counterproductive to the cleansing properties of water.

AVOID TOXIC CHEMICALS, SUCH AS ALCOHOL, DRUGS, CAFFEINE, AND CIGARETTES

Not only can these toxins be habit-forming, but they can damage your internal organs and your skin. If you don't want to stop, ask yourself, why not? If it's hard to stop using: *get help!* Addiction to anything not only zaps you of your energy and your money, it negatively affects your self-esteem—it's hard to love you when pouring contaminants into your body on a regular basis. It's an esteemable act to let go of the shackles of addiction. Are you addicted to something? Alcohol? Drugs? Cigarettes? Coffee?

EAT LOTS OF VEGETABLES

Whether green, red, yellow, or purple, vegetables, in addition to vital vitamins, also provide your body with the fiber it needs to aid in regulation and digestion. A diet consisting primarily of fresh vegetables also aids in healthy weight loss. Raw or lightly steamed vegetables are preferred because the steaming process allows the vegetables to keep their nutrients. There are many books available on the benefits of raw foods. For flavor, add fresh salsa with cilantro to steamed veggies, such as chard, broccoli, peas, collards, and spinach. This over rice makes a great-tasting and nutritious meal. How many helpings of vegetables have you had today? Consider adding one more to your plate before you retire tonight.

KEEP TRACK OF WHAT YOU EAT

If you're overweight or you have a bad relationship with food, you may consider keeping a journal of what you put into your mouth right down to that breath mint. With tracking, you set a daily goal of how many calories you want to consume, then keep track of what you eat. It's another visual support tool for staying on track. Tracking allows you to be more conscious and aware of what you eat.

GIVE YOUR BODY A REST THROUGH FASTING

Periodically cleansing the body is an excellent way to give your body a rest, but consult your doctor, nutritionist, or medical adviser before you begin. Fasting allows you to purge your body of toxins and gives your internal organs a needed rest. If you like to eat as I do, your body needs a rest every now and then. Three times a year I go to a wonderful cleansing facility in San Diego to detoxify my body from food. I feast on such delicacies as raw veggies, sprouts, and wheat grass. Then for three days of the weekly program, I participate in a fresh juice fast. After one week, my skin is glowing and my body is working optimally again.

SET MINI-GOALS FOR YOURSELF

You can do the unimaginable if you break the task into small, manageable pieces. For example, today commit to drink one extra glass of water and lift one weight five times with each arm, perhaps while watching television. While I believe there is no such thing as an unreasonable goal, it is unreasonable that you should expect yourself to accomplish your goal overnight. Unreasonable expectations are a setup for failure, so be sure to separate your goal into small, manageable steps.

GET SUPPORT

You don't have to do anything alone, even if you are able. In reality, most of us succeed when we have encouragement along the way. I attend a regular Weight Watchers group. Our group leader is the most incredible motivator and helps me to stay on track. She's high energy, positive, and authentic, never hesitating to share with the group how she sometimes stumbles and falls, then picks herself up and starts all over again. It doesn't matter who is in your support group; the idea is to have someone or a group of people you can count on to support you in staying on track. Perhaps for you it's a nutritionist, a personal trainer, a health adviser, or even a therapist. The key to success is use them and take their advice.

GO ON RETREAT

This could mean a day without running errands or checking e-mails or voice mail. It could mean a day without the kids. It could also mean a day filled with small luxuries, such as a very long bubble bath with lots of candles around the tub, or you could curl up in bed with a good book or watch all your favorite reruns on television. If you are able, you can take your body to a spa. There are weekend retreats and weeklong adventures. And if money and/or time are issues, why not consider a day spa? The idea is to pamper your body or allow someone else to do so as often as you can. I'm hooked and have been for some time now. Monthly I get a half-day spa treatment: massage, facial, manicure, pedicure, and lunch. What a deal! When I want to get away for a week, I give myself the gift of Rancho la Puerta, a vegetarian fitness spa in Mexico. In between spa visits, I take full advantage of my gym's sauna and steam room.

IGNORE THE MYTHS

A myth is a tale that's been repeated so much over time that we've come to believe it, such as:

- You can lose weight without exercising.
- You can eat all you want and lose weight.
- You can take a pill and feel better.

- You can take a pill and lose weight.
- You can wear a vibrating belt and lose weight.
- When you get to your ideal weight you'll be perfect.

Don't buy into these myths. In truth, good health is about lifestyle change, not a quick fix. It requires small, incremental changes over time.

A Word About Depression

Emotional fitness is an important part of good health. What goes into your mind is as important as what goes into your body. Even if your physical body is healthy, if you're imbalanced emotionally, your self-esteem can be affected. Therefore, investing in the care and feeding of your mind is a critical next step to good health.

One consequence of not taking care of your mind is depression, a buildup of unaddressed, unacknowledged, and invalidated anger—anger turned inward. Feeling powerless, unheard, unappreciated, alone, as if you lack control over your life, ill-equipped to handle life on its own terms—these are conditions that often drive us to depression. And some of the symptoms are not eating, overeating, isolating, or resuming an old destructive habit, such as smoking, drinking, or gambling. At some time or another we all face problems—financial, personal, family, health, spiritual—and must deal with the realities of depression. How we handle depression and how long we remain in it are determined by our willingness to take certain actions.

While it would be easy to say all depression can be remedied with one solution, that's not true. However, the following suggestions have worked for me and countless others, and may work for you, too. However, if you are severely depressed and have had suicidal thoughts, please contact a health care professional immediately.

TAKE ACTION

For many people, action is the key to alleviating or eliminating depression. Often this means behaving contrary to the way you think and feel. Sometimes the action will be to do something that moves you in the direction of your fear, such as speaking up for yourself, going for a brisk walk or a swim, plodding through complicated or difficult material, putting together your résumé, or even quitting your job.

At other times, the action may be to give to someone in need. Giving of ourselves, what I call being of service, is one of the best antidotes for depression, because the more you give, the less time you have to dwell on your depression and the more time you'll have to feel useful and valued. When you are giving to others, it's hard to be focused on what's wrong with you in the moment.

The curative effects of positive, affirmative action are so profound that it is hard to grasp that such a simple concept can really work, but it can and it does when practiced diligently. When people take action, amazing things happen. They feel empowered and hopeful. Yet, ironically, when you're depressed, the last thing you feel like doing is taking action. Sometimes it's hard just to get out of bed, so start small. If you're depressed, commit to one action today; do one little thing that will make you feel better. Maybe it's getting off the couch. Perhaps it's turning off the television. Maybe it's not eating that second helping, even though to do so would temporarily make you feel better. Just remember, doing something is better than doing nothing, especially if the action moves you closer to your goal of better overall health.

BE PATIENT

It's normal to want instantaneous results after you've taken an action. But in truth, results rarely happen immediately, even when you're taking prescription medication for your depression. Trust the process, and know you won't die from a little pain as you're moving through your depression. It's better to have a little pain while you're taking action than a lot of pain because you refuse to.

ENLIST A FRIEND

Having someone to talk to about your feelings is important. Sometimes it's the very act of sharing that helps you get past the depression. Enlist a supportive friend who understands what you're trying to accomplish. It could be your Esteemable Acts Buddy or someone different. The idea is to find someone you can trust. Tell your friend about the actions you've taken. He or she can cheer you on when you take a positive action and can remind you of the great job you're doing, especially when the results are not happening as quickly as you'd like.

Depression is a mental health condition that can keep you stuck and feeling bad about yourself. In your Esteemable Acts

Journal write out your answers to the following: Are you depressed? If so, what do you think is the cause? What steps have you taken to get out of the depression? If you're unable to get out of your depression, what do you think stands in the way? If you have been depressed in the past but aren't now, take yourself back to that time and place. Remember how you felt. Describe your feelings in your journal. What did it take to get through the depression? Remember, success leaves clues. When you've successfully dealt with a situation in the past, it often becomes easier to deal with it in the present, because you can draw on your previous experience.

The Piece That Brings It All Together

It's impossible to ignore the power of spirituality in guiding people to lasting self-esteem. One way to recognize the spiritual realm without calling it by any specific name is to acknowledge it as "good orderly direction," that inner force that helps you to make right choices regarding your physical and mental health. Here are suggestions for connecting with your spirit:

READ DAILY MEDITATIONS

Consider beginning each day with selected readings from positive, uplifting books. It doesn't matter what you read. The key is to focus on material that shifts your thinking. Among my personal favorites are *For the Inward Journey* by Howard Thurman; *Don't Sweat the Small Stuff* by Dr. Richard Carlson; *Each Day a New Beginning*, a Hazelden publication; *Reflections in the Light* by Shakti Gawain; *As Bill*

Sees It, an AA World Service publication; Science of Mind, a Church of Religious Science publication; and anything by Louise Hay.

LISTEN TO INSPIRATIONAL TAPES

Sometimes it's easier to pop an audiocassette into your tape player than to read a book. It doesn't matter which method you select. The choice is yours. The idea is to have something close at hand that will aid you in staying centered and often uninvolved in the chaos of the moment. Louise Hay, Deepak Chopra, Marianne Williamson, Rev. Mary Manin Morrissey, and Rev. Michael Beckwith have all recorded inspiring audiotapes.

SPEND QUIET TIME ALONE IN CONTEMPLATION

There are times when you just need to be with yourself, times when the noise and stress of everyday life need to be shut out. By allowing yourself daily quiet time you create a balance between the doing and the being aspects of your life. What your daily practice is isn't important as long as you choose something. It may be meditation, prayer, or even yoga.

CONNECT WITH A SPIRITUAL COMMUNITY

Find a place where you can connect with like-minded people. Such a community may be a church, a synagogue, or a mosque; it could also be a service or social group. The idea is to find a group that can satisfy your need for community. Finding one that suits you is key to a feeling of connectedness.

In your Esteemable Acts Journal, define spiritual. Is there a difference between spiritual and religious? What does spiritual health mean to you? Does talk about spiritual matters bother you? If yes, why? If talk of spiritual matters doesn't bother you, share your thoughts with someone who wants to listen to your journey about how spirit works in your life.

Esteemable Acts

EXERCISE 1

The first step in changing poor health habits is to identify and assess your current state of health. In your Esteemable Acts Journal, answer the following questions: What condition are you in? What's your health history? What's your family's health history? Do you know what's in your medical records? How do you feel? Do you have ailments, sores, or lingering coughs that won't go away? What do you eat? Is there a health issue you're ashamed or embarrassed to talk about? Is exercise a part of your daily routine? Make the effort to be as honest as you can.

Next, find a current photograph of yourself or take one. The better you are able to see yourself as you are, the sooner you can and will move toward taking better care of yourself. Open your Esteemable Acts Journal to two blank pages facing each other. Paste your photograph on the left page with today's date. On the other side paste a picture you've cut out from a magazine of how you'd like to look or an old picture of a healthier you.

Finally, map out what it will take to transform you into the picture on the right. Remember to break it down into small, manageable pieces.

EXERCISE 2

As soon as possible, and if possible, get a complete physical, including blood work. It's worth the investment of time and money to do it now. Before we can change, we must know what needs to be changed. Be honest with your doctors, or else it's a waste of time—yours and theirs. When was the last time you had a physical? Write out the results in your Esteemable Acts Journal or tape the final copy of the paperwork given to you in your journal.

Just Do It!

What can you do right now, this moment, to move you closer to better health? What one small action are you willing to take right now? Perhaps getting a physical exam or just making the appointment with the doctor, or quitting smoking or drinking? Maybe calling your doctor to ask questions about your health? Eating a green salad, buying a quart bottle of water and drinking it all, making a spa appointment, going for a brisk walk outside or on the treadmill, or reading an agreement before signing it? The key to your good health is understanding that your health is your business. Commit to one action toward better health before moving to the next Action.

Financial freedom begins with a plan

It's an esteemable act to manage your finances.

inancial freedom means having the courage to take control of your finances and effectively manage your money. And it means honestly looking at what may be preventing you from doing so.

Why is it so important that you manage your finances? Because the way you manage your finances reflects the way you manage your life. If your finances are out of order, chances are your life is, too. And if your life is out of order, most likely your self-esteem is pretty low.

Think about it, are you having difficulty managing your personal affairs or some aspect of them? Do you feel lost and confused more often than you'd like? Unbalanced? Do you feel as if everyone but you is in control of your life, and that people are always telling you what to do? Do your feelings of lack of power and control affect your self-esteem? I bet they do. And if so, I'd suspect, with few exceptions, your money is also in a state of imbalance.

This Action Step challenges you to honestly examine the way you manage your financial life. It encourages you to take charge of your money, and by extension, increase your self-esteem. Action #6 will show you how to accomplish the seemingly impossible by taking baby steps, one step at a time. The more control you have over your finances, the better you will feel about yourself. Imagine for a moment that you have enough money to satisfy your needs and a few of your wants. Imagine you have no debt. What would your life look like? Imagine that your money is multiplying. Wouldn't that be a great feeling?

I know all too well how it feels to be dependent on someone or something for my financial support. And I have experienced the shame and degradation attached to having to ask for financial assistance, and the pain that comes from asking. Sometimes I felt worse when people loaned or gave me money than I did when they said "Sorry, I can't help you," because I was ashamed that I needed to borrow the money in the first place. I also know how it feels to grovel before people I did not even like simply because I wanted their financial backing. Likewise, I know what it's like to walk through my fear, through the door marked financial freedom. I will show you how you can walk through that door, too. You have the power to take control of your finances and build real and lasting self-esteem in the process.

What Does Financial Freedom Mean to You?

How do you define financial freedom? Is it having all your financial needs met? Is it being able to care for those you love? Does it mean having enough money to give to others in the way you'd like? Or maybe financial freedom is having enough money to buy new clothes, a new car, take a vacation to wherever you want, or enough money so that dinner out is not considered a treat but a lifestyle. Is financial freedom having enough money to buy a new home in the neighborhood you want, enough money to fund your stock portfolio, to buy a boat, or to pay for your kids' education? Or is financial freedom simply knowing you have enough money in the bank if you need it? In your Esteemable Acts Journal, write out the answers to the above questions carefully, exploring what financial freedom means to you. Money is a sticky issue for lots of people, so be as honest and forthright as you can.

To get the most out of this Action it is important for you to clarify your definition of financial freedom. It's hard to realize a dream, unless you define it. While achieving your dream is by no means easy, it is easier once you have clearly identified your intentions, once you have established what you want your worry-free financial life to look like. Establish your intention first, then create a plan. If you don't know where you're going, you can't figure out how to get there. In your Esteemable Acts Journal write out your thoughts to the questions, "What does financial freedom mean to me?" "How would my life look if I were free from financial worries?"

Wealth, Money, and Self-esteem

For some people, money is intricately connected to self-esteem. How much money they have, the car they drive, the neighborhood they live in, how big their house is, the private school their kids attend, the size of their stock portfolio, where they went to school—are all things that define who they are. In short, the more toys they have, the better they think they are and the better they feel about themselves. This thinking has many flaws. First, it erroneously makes self-esteem contingent on how much you have. Second, it implies if you have things and lose them, you also lose your self-esteem. Third, it creates a heavy burden to keep and maintain things at whatever cost, forcing people to behave in a way contrary to what's required for real and lasting self-esteem. And fourth, it suggests you disregard the significant number of rich people who hate themselves and the large number of less rich people who don't.

No doubt for some people money equals self-esteem, but I invite you to see money as the means to an end, not as the end itself. Certainly, having toys adds to our comfort level, but the key to financial freedom is not how much we have, but how well we manage what we have. Financial freedom can be attained by anyone willing to understand the universal laws that govern money and wealth, its acquisition, and its use. People who grow up in abject poverty can become wealthy by their own efforts if they come to understand these laws and the importance of a mind-set of abundance, and put behind them poverty-consciousness. Also,

know that because financial freedom may mean something totally different for you than it does for someone else, the amount
of money you have or acquire is irrelevant. It's how you manage
it that counts.

Financial freedom, like everything else worth having, is
earned. It starts with a real desire to have it, followed by disci-
plined and painstaking action. Do you want financial freedom?
Are you willing to do anything for it? Does the idea of painstaking effort scare you? If you're ready to at least make the effort,
this chapter will show you how to walk through your fear and
attain financial freedom. Let's start by exploring the obstacles
that prevent us from being financially free.

What Gets in the Way of Financial Freedom?

The road to financial freedom is littered with roadblocks called beliefs. Their influence is powerful; their reach, extensive. Over time
they so control your financial life that it becomes difficult to separate the real from the unreal with regard to your ability to attain the
financial freedom you desire. Here are a few examples of some
common myths you may have encountered at some time or another:

"Money is the root of all evil."
"Once in debt always in debt."
"You work hard and you get nowhere."
"Money can buy anything."
"Everyone has a price."

"Poor people are lazy."
"Rich people are greedy and selfish."

Your beliefs about money will determine how you relate to it, and how you relate to money will define your level of financial freedom. How do you feel when the issue of money comes up? Does it make you uncomfortable? Do you think to yourself, "Let's just change the topic"? Do you get defensive? Does the idea of financial freedom seem like a lovely, yet inaccessible concept, as opposed to an attainable ideal for you? Please take a moment and record your answers in your Esteemable Acts Journal.

Our past experiences often shape the beliefs that get in the way of our financial freedom. Without knowing it, we develop opinions about money based on our historical perspective as children. Often, these are opinions held by our parents or other influential adults, or sometimes they come from the environment we're raised in. For example, my earliest memories about money came from growing up in poverty in New York's South Bronx. The message I was taught was that there was never enough. That message came across loud and clear, as day in and day out my mother struggled to pay the bills. As a single parent, she conscientiously labored to support her two small children. While my mom did the very best she could with what she had, what she had was limited. That experience was indelibly imprinted in my brain. I knew when I grew up, I didn't want to be poor.

For some of you who grew up poor, the opposite is possibly true. The poverty mentality followed you into adulthood. Perhaps you find yourself still thinking in terms of lack and limitation even if the poverty you experienced as a child is very much a part of your past. Poverty consciousness makes you act poor even when you no longer are. Why? Because it triggers the essential obstacle to financial freedom: self-centered fear.

Self-centered fear is fear that you won't get what you need, or that what you have will be taken from you. When you're afraid of losing something, you hold on to it, unwilling to let go. For example, for years after I gained some measure of financial success, my childhood belief that "there would not be enough for me" continued to haunt me. I was afraid to buy myself even the smallest item because I thought if I spent money on myself, I would never again have enough.

Take a moment to write in your Esteemable Acts Journal about your earliest memories regarding money. Bring to mind a specific instance in your childhood where the subject of money came up. In exploring this topic please answer the following questions:

- How did it feel to grow up with money? Without it? Or was there just enough?
- How did your parents behave around money?
- Did you have new clothes or did you wear hand-me-downs?
- Did you have to share food/space/clothes with others?
- Did it feel as if there was enough for you?
- Did you want for anything?
- Did you have an allowance? If so, how did that make you feel? If not, how did that make you feel?

Understanding your past experience with money will provide you with additional insight into who you are. And the more you know about who you are, the easier it is to love and accept yourself. By understanding yourself better, it will be easier to define the work you need to do to establish financial freedom.

As you think about your childhood experiences, I also invite you to consider examining those things in your present life that prevent you from experiencing financial freedom. What sabotaging behaviors do you engage in around money? What are you willing to do to change your condition? Write out your answers in your Esteemable Acts Journal.

Your Financial Dream

How do you get from seeing yourself as one of the have-nots to one of the haves? First, you set your intention—that is, you create a dream of where you want to be financially in one year, in five years, in ten years, and in twenty years. Having the courage to dream big dreams is an esteemable act. It can be scary to contemplate something you don't think you'll ever have, especially if you are laden with debt. But go ahead and do it. Stretch yourself. Flex your mind. Take the risk to dream a big financial dream. Then, we'll figure out how to make it happen.

The next step is to create visual support for your financial dream. These are tangible reminders of your financial goals. For example, you might consider creating affirmations on colorful 3 × 5 index cards or construction paper and strategically place them throughout your home, office, and car. Or perhaps you might customize your computer screensaver with a description of your financial goal or a positive statement, affirming where you see yourself. For example, if your goal is to be debt-free, possible affirmations might include:

- I am debt-free.
- I am living a life of perfect financial freedom, emancipated from all debt.
- I effectively manage my finances.
- I have everything I need.
- I have abundance consciousness.

Other visual reminders might be a collage with images and symbols of your financial goal. As you move in, around, and through your life, be open to additional symbols that can and will support your dream. Again, remember, the better you manage your finances, the better managed your life will be.

Steps to Building Financial Freedom

Armed with your dream of financial freedom, here are the steps you need to take to become financially free.

STEP #1:
LEARN THE BASIC PRINCIPLES OF MONEY
AND ACQUIRING WEALTH

There are many resources available—utilize them. The Internet, your local public library, and friends and associates who have walked the path to financial freedom before you are all wonderful places to begin the process. Make friends with the reference librarian at your local library; he or she can guide you to a basic text on accounting and money management. Become familiar with financial terms and concepts. Keep a dictionary close by and use it! Don't be afraid to look up a word you don't understand; if you are afraid to, do it anyway.

If you're really serious, continue your education in financial topics by reading articles in both business and financial magazines and newspapers, such as *Fortune, Forbes, Black Enterprise, Money, Entrepreneur, Fast Company,* the *Business Times,WIRED,* and the *Wall Street Journal.* Also, many nonbusiness periodicals, such as *O* magazine, *Essence, Esquire, Cosmopolitan,* and *Ebony* have financial columns—read them. These and other periodicals will often showcase successful people who are living a life of financial freedom. Study how they got to where they are.

Next, learn all you can about how the stock market works and learn to read the financial pages. If you're a novice, the idea of reading the financial pages can be daunting. This material won't necessarily come easily, but make an effort. Again, utilize your research resources.

Finally, commit to doing one thing today toward your financial education. Perhaps it's reading the finance column in your favorite nonbusiness magazine, instead of skipping over it, or maybe it's making an appointment with that friend of yours who is a financial planner. The idea is to do something. Remember, self-esteem comes from doing esteemable acts and it's an esteemable act to walk through your fear—fear of appearing stupid, fear of not understanding, fear of not getting it the first time, fear of not being able to stick with your new learning.

STEP #2:
KEEP A PIECE FOR YOURSELF

Of all the money you earn or acquire, stash 10 percent away for yourself and just save it. Don't spend it, don't make it a rainy-day fund, just save it. In the beginning, 10 percent may feel like, or actually be, too much to spare; if so, start smaller, but start! Amazingly, wealth starts from saving one penny at a time. My favorite excuse for not saving was "I don't have enough money to live on, how can I save?" And while not having a lot of money can be a valid excuse for not saving a lot of money, you can make a beginning with pennies a day. Think about how many pennies we throw away or leave lying behind on the floor. Pick them up, put them in a jar, and save them. Watch them grow. Some of you may be thinking, "Saving pennies would take me years to have anything of real value." If you saved five pennies every day for a year, you'd have $18.25 at the end of the year. While that might not seem like a lot, it's more than what you started with. And while you can increase the number of pennies saved at any time, five pennies would be your minimum. It's doable. Further, you'll get into the disciplined habit of saving.

STEP #3:
AVOID DEBT: SPEND LESS THAN YOU EARN

Not a novel concept, but one that eludes scores of people as evidenced by the large debt many of us carry. To build financial freedom not only must you have a steady flow of income and save on a consistent basis, you must spend less than you earn. That is the universal law of wealth acquisition and management. In our buy-now-pay-later society, people are encouraged to have debt. For example, credit card companies tantalize students with the promise of a quick fix before they are even capable of supporting themselves. This strategic campaign is not just reserved for graduate students. Credit card companies send appealing invitations to college undergraduates as well. Students learn to say "Charge it!" before they have a job. Spending beyond one's income (especially when there is no income) is a surefire way to financial insecurity, not financial freedom. Debt is not your friend, and neither is the creditor.

Think about it this way: Suppose you put fifty dollars into your savings account every Friday. On Mondays you take out forty dollars and on Wednesday you take out an additional twenty dollars. Then to make ends meet, you borrow a hundred dollars this week and another hundred dollars next week and another hundred dollars the following week. Within a short time, not only have you exhausted your income but you've been forced to borrow money to live—all because you spent more than you earned. By its very nature, debt breeds low self-esteem. When you lose control over your finances, you lose control of your life.

STEP #4:
GRASP THE CONCEPT OF WEALTH

Wealth is not defined by what's in your wallet, your bank account, your stock portfolio, or the size of your house. It's defined by your steady flow of income, how much of it you keep, and your ability to make it multiply. Money is short-lived, changing hands quickly and easily. Wealth on the other hand is everlasting because it keeps growing. If financial freedom is your goal, it's not enough to save, spend less than you earn, and eliminate debt. You must grow your income. The first time I saw this concept at work was with my rental security deposit. The land-lord placed my first and last month's security deposit in an interest-bearing account. When I moved out four years later, my $3,700 investment had increased appreciably.

There are many ways your money can render you a return on your investment, such as stocks, bonds, real estate, a home, rental property, a certificate of deposit (CD), or even a simple bank account. Some of you may be aggressive in your approach to investing in search of the quick win; others of you may be more conservative, preferring to go slowly. Your goals and your disposable income will determine your initial level of invest-ment and your approach. If you're looking for financial free-dom, consider a less aggressive approach in the beginning; then, over time, you can change your strategy.

When I made my first investment in the stock market, I knew I was in it for the long haul. There was no quick-fix strate-gizing for me. I researched several blue-chip companies as well as the dotcoms that were doing quite well at the time. I looked for companies that had shown growth over a few years, com-panies with strong management teams, and companies in in-dustries likely to be around for a while. Then, armed with information, I made my selections, diversifying as I went along. This approach to choosing stocks proved to be a smart move when the dotcoms crashed. People who had put all their money into technology suffered. No doubt tech stocks will once again come around, but the idea of putting your money to work for you in places where it's likely to work over time is the smarter investment.

STEP #5:

WEALTH IS WORTH WORKING FOR AND WAITING FOR

Sometimes that means following through on a commitment even though it seems hard or doesn't yield an immediate result. Do your homework in choosing appropriate investments that will yield a return and allow your money to work for you. The key is doing your part in the process at the beginning, then letting go of the results. If you choose to invest in the stock market, you may from time to time experience what may feel like a roller-coaster ride. If you have made wise choices, it's more likely you will come out on the winning side. But when investing, you must accept that there are no guarantees.

STEP #6:

SEEK COUNSEL FROM A FINANCIAL EXPERT

You wouldn't go to your hairdresser to fix your shoes unless he or she was also an expert in shoe repair. Likewise don't go to nonexperts for financial advice unless they've demonstrated their skill in such matters, such as with a successful business or a life of financial freedom. A caveat: As with choosing a physician, remember that your business is still your responsibility. Regardless of what they tell you, your responsibility is to ask questions, understand what they're doing before they do it, and reserve the right to seek a second opinion.

Financial Responsibility

Financial freedom is about empowerment, about taking control of your life so you can genuinely feel better about yourself. It's easy to turn your financial matters over to someone else—your spouse, your accountant, your parents, your business manager, or your lawyer—but when you do, you do yourself a disservice. It's an esteemable act to walk through your fear of understanding the world of finances. It's an esteemable act to study so you can understand what the terms mean. It's an esteemable act to be ready, willing, and able to take care of yourself financially. It's an esteemable act to be self-supporting through your own effort and not be dependent on your family, your spouse, the government, or a job you hate. What attitudes, behaviors, beliefs, and assumptions surface when you think about being in charge of your finances? What past experiences have made you reluctant to be financially independent? Write out your answers in your Esteemable Acts Journal.

Esteemable Acts

EXERCISE 1

Let's review where you want to be financially. What are your top financial goals? To help you get clear on where you want to be, take a look at what's on your Dreams List as well as your intentions listed earlier in this chapter. Review these dreams and intentions in your Esteemable Acts Journal and next to each, write out your reason for wanting to have these goals.

EXERCISE 2

Now let's look at your sources of income. What is your weekly take-home salary? Do you have a pension? Do you receive Social

Security, stock dividends, alimony, allowances, interest, rental income, royalties, or tax refunds? Record all of this information in your Esteemable Acts Journal. Next, how do you spend your money? For instance, does it go toward housing, car or transportation, eating out, entertainment, health and wellness, education, savings and investments, business-related expenses, or charitable donations? What percentage of your money goes to each category? Record your answers in your journal.

Now, what are your assets? Make a list of everything you own including your car, house, boat, computer(s), and business equipment.

Next, what are your liabilities? Make a list of everything you owe to anyone, from your home mortgage to the five dollars you owe your sister. Do you have balances on your credit cards? Do you have student loans? The quickest and most effective way to find out what you owe is to get a credit report. Credit reporting companies will, for a fee, send you a copy of your report (see Resources, page 203, for more information).

Before you can move ahead, you need to know where you are. This exercise is the most courageous step you'll take regarding your finances, because it involves gathering facts. When you're finished, you should have an accurate snapshot of your financial picture.

EXERCISE 3
Now let's create your plan for success. You know where you are, and you know where you want to be. How do you get there? In your Esteemable Acts Journal, plan out where you want to be financially and by when. Your plan might include a budget. Make

sure you break your goals into small, manageable pieces, making it more likely you'll succeed. For example, if your goal is to be debt-free, you first need to establish what your total debt is. Next, if you are paying high interest rates, explore loan consolidation. Determine, on paper, how much you can comfortably afford to pay toward lowering your debt each month. Based on this figure, how long will it take you to pay off your debt? Next consider ways to reduce your expenses, for example, can you take lunch to work instead of eating out? Can you use a dial-up Internet service provider instead of DSL? If you try, there are lots of ways to shave your expenses. Remember, the key to successfully having financial freedom is taking small steps every day that lead you closer to realizing your financial dream.

Just Do It!

So let's get started. Choose one thing you're willing to do within the next twenty-four hours that will move you closer to your dream of financial freedom. What one action can you take? Perhaps it's as simple as putting your plan in writing, or paying off one small debt. Whatever it is, make the commitment and share it with your Esteemable Acts Buddy. Let him or her know exactly what you agreed to do for yourself financially, and by when. Allow your Buddy to support you on your way to financial freedom.

The gift of choice

It's an esteemable act to be accountable for your choices.

Recently, on a flight home, I sat next to a woman who had just barely made the flight, rushing onto the plane just as the door was closing. It took her a while to settle in, and then once we were airborne, she complained incessantly about how she almost missed the flight because the ticket agent was too slow checking her in and the security agents made her take off her boots and scanned her laptop twice. She even complained that the people in the airport terminal were taking too much time moving to their destinations. She was really mad. And made sure everyone in her immediate area knew it.

When she finished complaining, I asked, "What time did you get to the airport?"

"Thirty minutes before the flight. I gave myself plenty of time," she responded.

"They now recommend you get to the airport at least one and a half hours ahead of your flight, because of heightened security," I replied. "Wouldn't it have been better if you had come earlier?"

"I don't want to hang out at the airport for hours. I have other more important things to do," she said.

"Even if it would relieve your stress?" I asked.

"What, do you work for the airline?" she said.

"No, but if you'd come to the airport earlier, you might not be so stressed."

"You should mind your own business," she said, and didn't talk to me again for the rest of the five-hour trip.

At first I was offended that she was so rude and ungracious. I was only trying to help. Then I realized she was right. I should have minded my own business. Even when she opened up the conversation by complaining, I could have simply smiled, said hello, and continued reading my material. I didn't have to get involved. I made a choice to engage in a dialogue with her. Next time I might not make the same choice. However, there were also different choices she could have made. Perhaps she could have arrived at the airport earlier, thereby alleviating her concern about whether she'd make her flight on time. By giving herself extra time to get to the airport, she would have gotten through the security checkpoints with time to spare, and then could have relaxed. Instead, she was rushed, angry, and had a bad attitude toward everyone she encountered.

We make choices every day about how we want to live, about how we want to behave. We make choices every day about how we want to feel. And every day we and other people feel the effects of those choices. Sometimes, added stress, strained relationships, and fewer desirable opportunities are among the consequences we pay. Referring back for a moment to the above example, the woman on the airplane, by her choice, created stress in her life. She also strained relationships with the people she encountered at the airport from the moment she felt she would be late for the plane until she settled down. Because she was late, she had fewer options. Because she was late, her original first-class seat was released into the general pool for someone waiting for an upgrade. Whatever the outcome, when we choose to do or not do something, we set in motion a domino effect, where each action leads to a reaction.

One of life's greatest gifts comes when we realize we have the power to make our own choices, and therefore direct our lives. The idea that you can control what happens to you is liberating, yet at the same time it can be a powerfully frightening experience, because with choice comes responsibility. Self-esteem is about making choices for yourself and being accountable for them.

How easy it is to see ourselves as victims. How easy it is to do whatever we want in life, and then blame someone else for the outcome. Action #7 is about having the courage to choose wisely and to take responsibility for our choices.

The Right Choice

On any given day we make decisions about everything from what time we wake up in the morning, to what time we go to bed at night; from who we will spend our time with, to what we will spend our time doing; from how we will be treated, to what we won't tolerate. Yes, every day we are faced with a myriad of choices and each choice, regardless of the outcome, moves us closer to or farther away from real and lasting self-esteem.

Sometimes the outcome of a decision we make is exactly what we want, but we still don't feel good about ourselves. Why not? Because some of our choices aren't the right choices for us in the first place. On the other hand, sometimes the outcome we get is not what we want, but ultimately it was the right decision for us.

What's a right choice and how do you know if you're making one? A right choice is a decision you make because your intuition tells you it's the right option for you, regardless of what other people say, or regardless of what your Other Voice tells you. Your Other Voice is the voice that doesn't always have your best interests at heart. That voice is more interested in having fun than in doing what's right for you. It just wants to play, be entertained, and do what's easy. Your Other Voice is sometimes out to get you, and when given half a chance, it convinces you that a right choice is a wrong choice or that a wrong choice is perfectly okay. It's the voice of justification. The Other Voice is skilled at overpowering your intuitive voice, but regardless how loud your Other Voice may be, you always know the right answer. You might pretend not to hear it, but that's the voice that keeps rising to the surface. Has your Other Voice reared its head today? How has it overpowered your intuitive voice? What questions are you battling to which you know the right answer to but are being pulled in another direction? Take a moment and write the answers in your Esteemable Acts Journal.

What Limits Our Choices?

Many things limit your choices to a greater or lesser degree; your feelings, other people's judgments, other people's power, family commitments, lack of money, and restricted time are just a few. But the big three are addiction, sex, and fear.

ADDICTION

Addiction limits your choices. Whether it's a person, a drug, a form of exercise, alcohol, or other habits, your addiction makes decisions for you. When you're addicted to anything, it's the addiction that's in control, not you. All sense of reason disappears. Your thinking is impaired and your decision-making process is hindered. For instance, suppose you're hooked on cigarettes. Isn't it your need for a smoke that controls when you take breaks at work or whether you can take that trip to see Grandma, because you can't smoke in your brother's car on the way there? Or if you are obsessed with a person, how many times will you call him or her, trying to find out where the person is, as opposed to doing something that really needs your attention? Conversely, sometimes even the good and healthy things we're addicted to can be overdone, such as exercise. Addiction limits your choices and has a negative impact on your self-esteem, because when you're addicted you aren't in control of your life. You have turned over to the addiction the power to direct your life and your thinking.

Are there any addictions or bad habits clouding your thinking? If your answer is no, please feel free to bypass this exercise. If your answer is yes, take some time to identify in your Esteemable Acts Journal what that addiction or bad habit is and how you've given it power over you.

SEX

For some people, love is the same as sex. For those folks, everything—absolutely everything—is about sex. They go to any length to have it—it doesn't matter who the person is, or how they feel about him or her, or how they feel about themselves. They rearrange their days and make their life choices based upon their opportunities to have sex. Sex is their addiction, and their lives are ruled by it.

By no means am I suggesting that sex is not an important part of our lives, because it is. But when we make choices that are not good for us because we are afraid we won't get what we need or deserve, or are afraid that someone else will get what we claim as ours, then it becomes an unhealthy dependency.

For other people, sex is used to bind them to their sexual partner. Once we sexually give ourselves to others, we feel we have given them—and they us—the ultimate gift of intimacy, and we feel we have the right to treat them as our possession. We claim them as ours. We want to know every move they make, when they make it, and with whom they make it. If they don't call us at the exact time they said they would, we get angry, sometimes to such an extent that we make fools of ourselves.

Often, sex is mistakenly—and dangerously—used as a substitute for talking. Instead of finding the courage to discuss a problem, particularly if one partner doesn't want to, it sometimes becomes easier to use sex as a temporary salve to a more deeply rooted dilemma. When you make the choice to have sex instead of addressing the relationship problem, the results can be hurtful and ultimately complicate the situation for all involved.

Do you substitute sex for conversation, especially about a difficult topic? Is it easier to jump into the bed than stand up for yourself? Do you feel you are making choices because of your need or desire to have sex or to hold on to your sex partner? Please write out your answers in your Esteemable Acts Journal.

FEAR

Fear, the third of the big three things that limit your choices, is perhaps the most powerful because it is so subtle. As has been discussed throughout this book, fear takes on many disguises. But regardless of how it looks, it reveals itself as something that affects your choices. Fear of risk, fear of pain, fear of failure, fear of success, fear of making a mistake, fear of being held accountable, fear of feeling inadequate, and fear of believing you really can't do what you say you can do are among the fears that surface. When you act out of fear, you inevitably limit your options by making safe and easy choices instead of meaningful ones. Fear compels you to make choices that are designed to keep you out of harm's way. And while these may be the easy choices, they are not necessarily the right ones. I'd like to share with you a parable I heard years ago that fittingly makes this point.

A spy was captured across enemy lines in a foreign land. The spy faced the captain, who was about to sentence him.

"In our country spying is punishable by death," said the captain.

"I know," said the spy.

The captain said, "I'll give you two choices: You can die at the hands of the firing squad at dawn tomorrow or you can walk through that door." The captain pointed to a huge, ugly steel door with old rusty nails and bolts and grotesque carvings imbedded into it.

Taking one look at the door, the spy gasped! "Can you give me until morning to decide? This is a hard choice to make." The captain agreed and sent the spy back to his cell until dawn.

At daybreak, the spy was returned and the captain asked, "Have you made your decision?"

The spy facing the captain said, "Yes, I have. Shoot me, because at least I know what I'm dealing with." The firing squad shot the spy.

Moments later a medical volunteer who had observed the incident asked the captain, "What was behind the door? What could have been worse than death?"

The captain responded, "Behind the door was freedom."

While this is an extreme example, the message is clear; making safe choices in life will not necessarily lead to safe and fruitful outcomes.

Have you made safe choices that didn't lead to the outcome you hoped for? Have you settled for less than you deserve in your life because you were afraid of what was on the other side of the door? Have you ever allowed your fear to convince you that you really didn't want to do something, when in fact you did? Please write out your answers in your Esteemable Acts Journal.

How to Make Right Choices

It's easy to talk about making right choices, but how do you make them when the choices you've always made weren't the best for you? How can you train yourself to solve problems effectively? Below are some suggestions.

IDENTIFY THE PROBLEM

What is the issue that you'd like to solve? What choices are you being asked to make? Sometimes people ask us to make choices, sometimes our situations force us into making choices, and sometimes we're not clear on which is which. There are times when a decision must be made immediately, and there are times when we are given an opportunity to sort it through. Nonetheless, a decision must be made. Often writing, or journaling, is a powerful tool for gaining insight and clarity. Somehow, when you put your thoughts on paper, it makes them more real. Writing also allows you to see what's in your mind. When you keep things in your mind it's easier to deny them. Once your thoughts are on paper, there is no hiding what you really feel.

RECOGNIZE YOU HAVE A CHOICE

Perhaps the most difficult aspect of making right choices is recognizing that *you have the right to choose.* It's often easier for us to see ourselves as victims than empowered men and women who have been given the gift of choice. Recently, I attended a client-sponsored roundtable discussion where the topic was "how to improve the company's morale." In discussing what causes low morale, one person after another cited management as the culprit. In an effort to stimulate a different line of thinking, I asked, "Are employees ever responsible for their actions, or is it always management's fault?" Then I said, "It appears that gossip by employees contributes to low morale." As you can imagine, I kindled strong responses in some people. One man spoke up and said, "I don't want to talk about the individual, I want to talk about management, because if they treated us better, we'd act better and we'd enjoy our jobs more."

Certainly, many organizations need improvement. There are countless books on how organizations can improve their cultures and there are consultants who specifically deal with those issues. But be that as it may, we, too, play a part in the outcomes we experience. If we use the fact that management doesn't treat us kindly as an excuse to treat other people unkindly, then we are no better than our managers. Recognizing we have a choice is a key to making right and different choices.

If you are having difficulty making a decision, be specific in identifying what gets in your way and be as honest as you can in identifying the barriers between you and making the right choice. Write your answers in your Esteemable Acts Journal.

DON'T ACT FROM FEAR

Fear is a real emotion. It is also a limiting factor, and its sole purpose is to keep you feeling miserable about yourself. When you act from fear, you give away your power to the person or thing you are afraid of. When you find yourself giving defensive responses, consider that this first reaction might be grounded in fear.

ASK QUESTIONS

Asking questions will often help you to understand what your choices are. It also puts some time between you and your need to make a decision immediately. But those who ask questions are often perceived as troublemakers. "Why can't you just leave things alone?" "Why do you have to ask so many questions?" "Why do you need to know everything?" are some of the reactions you might get. Or you might be perceived as stupid, unprepared, or not having it all together. No wonder the average person is afraid to ask questions. Yet asking questions for clarification is a surefire way to avoid the misunderstandings that come from making assumptions. Have the courage to walk through the fear of what others will think of you. Ask questions.

It's taken years for me to develop the courage to ask questions about things that are unclear or not right. While at times it's still really hard to do, I do it anyway.

What questions are you afraid to ask? Why? What price are you paying for not asking the questions? What payoff do you get when you don't ask? In your Esteemable Acts Journal, identify a past experience that turned out badly, yet might have been different had you asked a few questions in advance. Identify a situation that turned out okay because you did ask questions. Now identify a past experience that turned out okay, in your mind, because you didn't ask questions? What observations can you make?

DISCUSS YOUR PROBLEM WITH ANOTHER PERSON

Talk over your concerns with a trusted friend who will give you useful, honest guidance. Having an objective perspective can help make sense out of a seemingly senseless situation and alert you to potential roadblocks ahead. In 1981, I purchased my first new car. Having learned how to drive only months earlier, I had little experience with cars. I was advised to do research, shop around before buying, and take a man with me. Afraid to admit I knew nothing about cars, and too arrogant to ask a man for help, I chose to go it alone. With my best cocky, know-it-all demeanor I went to the car dealership ready to buy my first car. Luckily, I only spent fifteen thousand dollars on a car that cost nine thousand. They saw me coming and it could have been worse. Had I listened to those who were trying to help, I would have avoided such a costly mistake.

Also, the very act of sharing your thoughts or problems with another person can make you feel better, because you don't feel alone in the decision-making process. You can share the burden and gain valuable insight at the same time.

TRUST YOUR INNER VOICE

Listening to your inner voice is an esteemable act that requires practice and courage. Be sure to practice, because change doesn't happen overnight. Oftentimes, we must do the same thing over and over for it to be a part of who we are. Almost everything requires courage, first so we are able to receive the messages, and second so we become willing to act on those messages. While your Other Voice may sometimes lie to you, your small inner voice never will. Knowing the difference between right and wrong is not complicated; it just requires a willingness to listen to that inner voice.

Once I received too much change in a grocery store. My groceries came to four dollars and change, and I should have received fifteen dollars and some change back from my twenty-dollar bill. Instead, the cashier mistook my new twenty-dollar bill for a new fifty-dollar bill and gave me forty-five dollars and change. I said nothing. I left the store knowing what I had done, and found cause to justify why I should keep the windfall.

"You need the money," I said to myself. "It was God's will that the cashier made a mistake and God's will for me to keep the money."

But deep inside I knew the right thing to do the moment I counted my change, and that was to give it back. My Inner Voice let me know returning the money was the ethical thing to do. I went to the store the next morning and returned the money.

Think, for a moment, about the choices you have in life. Perhaps your initial reaction is "I don't have many choices at all." If so, I invite you to explore some of the things that could be perceived as choices by others, such as whether or not to get up and go to the gym, whether to allow another driver to cut in front of your car, whether to answer the phone after you missed an appointment knowing that the caller is your missed appointment, whether to confront someone who hurt your feelings, whether to ask that gnawing question, or whether to eat that candy bar.

In your Esteemable Acts Journal, identify three decisions you made in the last month and your reasons for making them. Were they hard decisions to make? Why or why not? Did you listen to your Inner Voice or ignore it? Did addiction, sex, or fear influence your choices? Be as honest as possible when recording your answers.

Sometimes You Just Have No Choice—or Do You?

The Serenity Prayer says, "Grant me the serenity to accept the things I cannot change, the courage to change the things I can, and the wisdom to know the difference." Sometimes it doesn't feel as if we have choices, but in truth we almost always do.

Lara was laid off from her job of fifteen years. She was a loyal employee and was confident her employer would reward her faithfulness with uninterrupted employment and an occasional thank-you. So when she was laid off, she was devastated. "How could this happen to me," she cried, "I've given the company the best years of my life and this is the thanks I get." Lara had a right to be upset. She had a right to be angry. And although she had no choice in being terminated, she did have a choice in how she handled it. She took control of her life. She allowed herself time to be angry. Then, instead of moping around and feeling sorry for herself for weeks and months, she took this seemingly bad situation and turned it into an opportunity to receive training in an area she was interested in. She also used the unscheduled break in employment as a respite, a time for a much needed vacation. Lara chose to work her situation to her advantage.

In your Esteemable Acts Journal, identify a situation in which you feel you didn't have a choice. Explain why you thought you didn't have a choice. Now, go back and think about what you could have done differently. In hindsight, were there other options you could have explored? Is there something you can do now?

Give Up Being the Victim

Victimhood is an appealing place to live. When you're in the victim mode, you get sympathy, you're the center of attention, you have a valid excuse for not taking responsibility for your feelings or your actions, little is expected of you, and you feel justified for being depressed. In truth, it becomes an unhealthy pattern, one that's often hard to break, because you get so accustomed to being the victim. It's the easier, softer way to live for many of us. Yet in truth, it's like digging a hole in the ground and decorating it, making it your permanent living space.

For years I used being black, being female, and growing up poor as excuses for feeling like a victim. Whenever anyone would listen, I'd share my sad sob story. And I used that as an excuse to be angry—all the time. Unquestionably, my life has been challenging, but at what point did I have a responsibility to turn my condition around? At what point did I have a responsibility to recognize that I helped to create some of what happened to me because of the choices I made?

When we choose to relinquish our right of choice, we are making a choice. This is another unhealthy pattern we fall into. Often thinking if we make no decision at all, we're free from responsibility, because someone else will have to make a decision, and be responsible instead of us. But making no decision is making a decision to give someone else the power, and the problem with that is we rarely like the choices others make for us. There is no doubt that the feelings that led you to play the part of the victim are valid, but eventually you must make the decision to move on with your life. It's an esteemable act to make right choices and leave victimhood behind.

Esteemable Acts

EXERCISE 1

Consider decisions to be made in all areas of your life: your work, your family, your health, your social life, your relationships. What choices are there for you to make today? What choices have you been avoiding, hoping they'd go away? Take particular care to focus on an issue that bothers you every time you think about it. How has either addressing the issue or not affected how you feel about yourself?

In your Esteemable Acts Journal, write out your answers. Imagine that you have actively made your choices. How does it feel? It's not uncommon for you to feel uncomfortable doing this exercise. If you're not used to making decisions on your own behalf it will be challenging at first. But with practice, it will become easier. Stick with it. The reward is lasting self-esteem.

Just Do It!

What can you do right now in this moment to move you closer to making better choices? What one action are you willing to take right now? Perhaps it's to talk to your Esteemable Acts Buddy, or go into meditation so you can listen to your inner voice. Maybe it's writing out your feelings about a situation, or asking some questions for clarification. Whatever you do, it's important that you do something. Commit to one thing before moving to the next Action. Just do it!

PART THREE

Giving freely
of what you have
is an esteemable act

And, the greatest of these is love

$\mathscr{I}t's$ an esteemable act to actively love.

*L*ove, as a word, is memorialized in countless books, movies, poems, and musical compositions. While there are many definitions of love, its essence, when used as a verb, can be captured in a few phrases: to care for, to cherish, to respect, to honor, to show an interest in, to value, or to treat with kindness. For some people, love is the feeling you have when you care for someone; for others, it's endearing thoughts about the person who is the object of their affection; and for still others, it's simply saying the words "I love you." But for the purpose of this

Action, love goes beyond the words, the feelings, and the thoughts to the very expression behind the words.

Love is more about how you act than what you say. Think about it; how often have you said something with your words, but your attitude, facial expression, and behavior said something totally different? How often has someone said kind words to you, but their behavior indicated something entirely different? Love is demonstrated through action. When you love someone, you treat them in a way that shows you care for them, cherish them, respect them, and honor them. Action #8 is about how we demonstrate love in our life, going beyond what we say to what we do.

Loving Others Starts with Self-love

For many people, the idea of self-love generates negative thoughts and feelings about narcissistic, ego-driven people. We think of those who care little about others unless they can further their personal or professional goals. That is not the message of this Action or this book. On the contrary, Action #8 suggests that if you genuinely love yourself, you engage in behavior that includes both honest and continual self-care, and kind and generous treatment of others.

There's an age-old theory that you can't love someone else until you truly yourself. This point has been debated by countless experts and the popular answer is, indeed, you cannot love someone else until you truly love yourself. And I agree. How can you care for, honor, or cherish another person if you don't honor or cherish yourself? How can you give away something you don't have? How do you even know what it looks like or feels like if you've never really experienced it? There's a wonderful old saying that is applicable here: Charity begins at home. First love yourself, and then you can love someone else, without judgment and attachment.

For so many of us, men and women alike, our self-esteem is dependent on something outside ourselves, such as our spouse or the man or woman we are dating, the neighborhood or house we live in, the job or career we've chosen, or the amount of money in our bank account or stock portfolio. Without those things, we perceive ourselves as nothing, unless we're taught otherwise or have role models who show us a different example of how to see ourselves.

Make no mistake about it, we are taught how to view ourselves. We learn to value or devalue ourselves as men and women by the examples we see in the movies, on television, in magazines, and at home. And the music we readily listen to reinforces the message of self-care or self-loathing. Sometimes the message is subtle and sometimes it's flagrant. It's always our choice what we do with it.

For years I accepted my role, as was told to me, of being the pretty trophy on the arm of a man. I was the woman with no opinion, particularly if it differed from that of my companion. As a result, the men in my life defined who I was. I behaved in a way that was pleasing and nonthreatening to men. I dressed in a way that was attractive to men. I walked in a way that was sexy to men. And if they weren't impressed, I was devastated, often changing clothes several times before I found something I thought they would like. I was a chameleon, able to change into whatever was expected of me. I believed my role models on television and in the movies who said that my purpose in life was to find and satisfy a man—at whatever the cost. I paid a high price for "at whatever the cost." Not surprisingly, that behavior transcended my relationships with men. I was also that way with everyone I came in contact with—bosses, girlfriends, and family. Over time, the greatest gift I've ever given to myself was learning to become my own best friend.

Learning how to love myself has been a lifetime process and one that will continue. The job is never done. Self-esteem is contingent on what you are willing to do to nurture it. How are you demonstrating self-love in your life? What esteemable acts are you doing today? In your Esteemable Acts Journal write your answers.

Actions Speak Louder Than Words

If love is an action, how do you express self-love? Some people believe that standing in front of a mirror saying "I love you" is an expression of self-love. Others think if you wear beautiful and expensive clothes, that's an expression of self-love. But Action #8 suggests self-love starts with having the courage to be who you are, regardless of what others might think. It is about having the courage to live your dreams, to do what makes you happy in life, so that one day you won't wake up saying, "I wish I had." Self-love is about self-care, making your health a priority. Self-love is revealed in your willingness to stay focused on the things you say are important. It's about having the courage to set boundaries and protect them. When you love yourself, you're willing to make agreements with yourself—and keep them. Self-love is demonstrated in the daily choices you make, in the relationships you have, in your willingness to see yourself clearly, and in how you manage your money. Indeed, self-love is very much about the things you do more than the things you say.

Self-esteem comes from doing esteemable acts. Here are some additional actions you can take that will move you closer to real and lasting self-love.

ELIMINATE NEGATIVE SELF-TALK

Negative self-talk is one of the most destructive behaviors we engage in, because after a while, we start to believe that's who we are. It becomes as much a part of our culture as sex and violence on television, and equally harmful. The injurious process starts with calling yourself derogatory names, such as stupid, idiot, dummy, or whore. Then, before you know it, these words become such a working part of your vocabulary that you're desensitized to their self-negating effect. Because you call yourself names, you consciously or unconsciously give others permission to do the same. It's an esteemable act not to call yourself derogatory names.

In your Esteemable Acts Journal make a list of the negative words you call yourself or have ever called yourself. Be as honest as you can; no one will see this but you. Remember, the more honest you are in seeing yourself clearly, the better you'll be able to change. Now, next to each word, discuss why you label yourself that way. Then replace each word with a more positive description of yourself. The way to really change that old pattern is to practice using the new words whenever you can and behaving in a way that is aligned with those new words.

WALK AWAY FROM UNHEALTHY JOBS AND RELATIONSHIPS

When we don't like ourselves, we settle for seconds in jobs and relationships. Outwardly we say "I matter, I'm important," yet when we look at our lives we see ourselves stuck in jobs we hate and relationships that are abusive. And abuse is not just physical. Often it's easy to become accustomed to emotional and mental abuse, because we don't see the lingering physical scars, but the effects of emotional and mental abuse are just as damaging in the long run. Mental, emotional, and physical abuse eats away at your self-esteem. And if you're living a lie, not only is there abuse, but there is guilt and shame, too. Allowing people to speak to you in a way that is inappropriate (whether in public or at home), turning the other cheek when your spouse or companion has an affair, or allowing someone to take advantage of you in business because you're afraid to speak up are all forms of abuse. How can you love yourself when you tolerate such behavior? There are always excuses for staying in unhealthy relationships and jobs, but after a while the excuses stop working and you're challenged to take action on your own behalf. It's an esteemable act to walk away from unhealthy jobs and relationships.

In your Esteemable Acts Journal make a list of the jobs you've had over the last five years. What did you like about each one? What did you not like? What about your present job? Do you enjoy what you do? Why? If not, why not? Why do you stay in a job you hate, what's the payoff? How does staying in a job you don't like move you further away from self-love?

Now, turn your attention to your relationships and make a list of the most important ones in your life today—for instance, your list might include your spouse, mother, father, teacher, manager, and sibling. Answer the following questions: Describe the kind of relationship you have with each of them. What do you like most about them? What annoys you the most? How does each relationship make you feel good about yourself? How does each relationship make you feel bad about yourself?

SPEAK UP IN THE MOMENT

Speaking up in the moment is another positive step toward real and lasting self-love. It keeps us from holding on to grudges that eventually eat away at us, because our anger at others eventually turns into anger at ourselves for not taking better care of us. Sometimes we're afraid to speak up because we don't think we have anything important to say. Sometimes we're afraid no one will want to hear what we have to say. Sometimes we're afraid of being judged, and sometimes we're afraid of the conflict that is sure to arise when we say what we feel. But if you don't speak up when you have something of value to contribute, you do yourself and the problem-solving process a disservice. Troubles are resolved when there is a diversity of thinking, and some-times that means having the courage to be the one to speak up with a new or different idea. It's an esteemable act to speak up in the moment.

One thing to remember about speaking up: The way you say something is as important as what you say. Most often people will respond positively to thoughtful words rather than words that irritate. So choose your words carefully. It can make the difference between someone hearing and understanding what you're trying to say and someone disregarding you.

In your Esteemable Acts Journal write down five things you wish you had said in the moment over the last three weeks. As you go through this day, make a note of the times you didn't say something you really wanted to say. While you can't go back and change the past, you can make an effort to take better care of yourself in the future by speaking up in the moment.

Three Types of Love

When it comes to the love of others, we can designate three separate types of love: superficial, realistic, and committed. Each is distinct in its own way, and each is characterized by its own set of behaviors and attitudes.

SUPERFICIAL LOVE

Superficial love is surface love, based on nothing of substance. You fall in love with the idea of love or with an image. You are attracted to people because of how they look, their clothes, or their style. You're in love with the people you think they are or with the idea of being in love with them.

When you love superficially, being in love becomes the most important part of living. You're on a mission to find a mate at whatever the cost. But when you're caught up in this type of love, it is virtually impossible for you to truly love someone, because your goal is to find someone to love you. You can't be authentic in a relationship because you're afraid that your mate, once he or she knows who you are, won't like you. So everything you do is designed to make him or her like you at whatever the cost. Your goal is to find someone who can fill the hole inside of you.

REALISTIC LOVE

When you love someone realistically, you see the real person. Their closely guarded character flaws surface during this stage, and sometimes what you see is disappointing, because they are not the people you thought they were. Your loved ones become all too human. While they may have covered up who they are on the first few dates or possibly years, eventually the truth is revealed. Sometimes a relationship can sustain the reality check, and sometimes not.

As humans we all have faults. Sometimes we quickly rush to judgment and don't give other people a chance to prove themselves. We condemn them long before we have all the information, allowing them no leeway for making one or two mistakes. On the other hand, some of us choose to overlook the problem areas. We walk into trouble pretending we don't see it, when in truth we don't want to see it.

COMMITTED LOVE

Committed love is when you see the other person's faults, and you love him or her anyway, or perhaps even because of them. At this stage you identify you and your partner as committed to the relationship. Committed love is when you truly love someone for who he or she is, not who for who you want the person to be.

Recently my husband and I were in the company of four

other couples who had been married much longer than us, twenty-five, thirty-four, fifty-two, and fifty-four years, respectively. You could tell they were married for a long time by how comfortable they were with each other. They seemed to really like one another and share mutual respect, which is not always a trait you witness in those married for a long time. Wanting to know the secret to a long-term marriage, and at the time just barely wedded three years, I asked the couples, "How have you done it? How have you stayed married to the same person for so long?" Lilly and Don said, "Choosing the right partner was the key for us. If you make a mistake in the choosing, you'll suffer for the rest of your life or be in divorce court soon after you tie the knot." Jim and Sally said, "Making a real commitment to be in the relationship." They continued by saying, "Too many couples see divorce as a quick and easy solution and they never give themselves a chance to work through the problems." Pete and Dana said, "Really understanding that a relationship is sometimes eighty-twenty, seventy-thirty, sixty-forty, but rarely fifty-fifty. That when you come into a relationship thinking it's going to be fair, you set yourself up for failure. The key is to see past each other's faults to the good things that work." Lastly, Whitney and Jon told us, "To have a long-term marriage, you have to stay in it for the long term. For example, you don't get to be married for forty years unless you do forty years' worth of work."

Love is a connection between people, a sharing of positive regard that supersedes the rational. It's a feeling of being valued and of valuing. It's when your heart feels good and your spirit expands.

What kind of relationship are you in? In your Esteemable

Acts Journal, identify a relationship you have that falls into each of the three types. Why did you label each of your relationships as you did? Is that what you want them to be? If not, what actions can you take to change your situation? What stops you?

What Happened to the Connection?

For relationships to go to the committed level there must be a willingness to be connected beyond the superficial. In our ever-changing, fast-paced culture it has become increasingly difficult to see others and really be seen by others, because we don't want to. We have found ways to avoid real interactions. Technology is an excellent example. Cell phones, e-mail, Palm Pilots, computers, and faxes provide us with easier, smarter, and faster ways of communicating with one another, without bringing us face-to-face. Not only does technology remove the opportunity for intimacy, it gives us a venue to say things in ways we wouldn't dream of doing but for the technological artifice. Why? Because there's no accountability, you can't see the person. There is no real connection.

Take the idea of seeming love affairs that spring up in chat rooms. Arguably, you can fall in love with a computer image. But think about it; it's easy to fall in love with an image that may or may not be real and an image that can be dismissed with a click of your mouse. The computer relationship can't experience committed or even realistic love because who you are is never really revealed. Indeed, a computer image is the ideal companion for someone who is afraid of intimacy. We often use technological barriers to hide behind and to keep us out of committed love. For true love to exist, we must be face-to-face, present, and willing to give fully of ourselves. Having the courage to see and be seen is the essence of this Action.

What Gets in the Way of Love?

Old emotional baggage is what gets in the way of love 99 percent of the time. It can come in the form of anger and fear, just to name a few.

As far back as I can remember I've been angry at somebody. In one particular case, it was Janine, a friend who stole money from me. I had been mad at her since 1979. It took until 1989 to resolve the conflict. "She was my best friend. I trusted her, and look at what she did to me!" I'd say to anyone who'd listen to me. "I thought she knew if she needed something she could just ask," I cried. But she didn't. After a few years of replaying the story, I knew just how to tell it to get the kind of reaction I wanted. I had an investment in being angry, even though we had been friends since childhood. I was holding on to my emotional baggage.

Have you ever been mad at someone and allowed that anger to last for years? I bet you have. Think about someone you aren't speaking to today and go back to how long it's been. We're not counting bumping into the person in the street, business meetings, or family events, we're talking about really having him or her in your life. I bet it's been a long time, longer than you'd like to admit. Do you remember why you stopped talking? Or how the disagreement even started? Some of you are probably saying, "But it was their fault." Or "They stopped talking to me first."

Perhaps you're right, but you have helped to keep the resentment going. How willing are you to make the world a better place by living love, not just talking about it? How willing are you to start the process right now?

Have you ever gone shopping and returned home with too many bags to carry? Have you ever chosen not to check your bags on the airplane and instead carried all your belongings on the plane with you? How did you feel? Heavy? Weighed down? Excess baggage weighs us down. Anger and resentments are baggage, old stuff that weighs heavily on our hearts and our minds. Our emotional baggage comes when people disappoint us and we don't deal with it in the moment.

People let us down, whether or not they know it. They hurt us with their words, they disappoint us with their actions, and they don't follow through. When they hurt us, we feel justified in holding a grudge—forever. Anger is a powerful intoxicant. You can become so consumed with what someone has done to you that you get angry, the anger gets angry, and the anger gets you.

When I finally resolved the conflict with Janine, it was more for my benefit than hers. I had become more consumed with her than I thought I was or I wanted to be. I realized one day in 1989 while I was attending a retreat that I was still holding on to this old anger and didn't even know it. I thought I had let go of her years earlier, because I said I had. I was quick to say, "I don't care about her anymore, she's out of my life and thank God." But the truth is that she wasn't out of my life, because every now and then she'd come into my mind and I'd be so mad at her. Then for days afterward, I'd replay what she did to me. It would affect everything I did for the next few days. She lived rent-free in my brain. And I allowed it.

I got advice that I didn't want to take—make amends to her. "What do you mean make amends to her, she stole money from me," I cried.

"You played a part in this as well," I was told. "No resentment lives and is nurtured for ten years without all parties aiding in the process. Think about what part you played."

"None," I said. "Janine stole my money." I was told to go back as far as I could to what happened before the money was stolen. Was there something I did that could have been taken the wrong way? And surprisingly to me, but not to her, there was a part I did play. I had invited Janine to visit me in Las Vegas and offered to help her out financially. We argued and in the heat of an argument, I demanded she leave my house immediately, with no place to go. She did, along with my three hundred dollars. Was this justification for her to steal my money? Absolutely not, but my behavior contributed to what happened. I had made a promise and didn't keep it. She was in a strange town all alone and I told her to get out. Perhaps, at the time, I would have behaved the same way that she did. Who knows? All I know is that every problem has two sides. Being willing to see both sides is key to truly living love.

Letting Go of the Baggage

Certainly anger is not the only form of emotional baggage, but anger like fear has the power to destroy more lives, so we've focused on it here.

Letting go of anger is a choice we are free to make. But before we let go, we need to understand why we choose to hold on.

For one thing, holding on to anger is easy. It takes work to move through a conflict and see another person's side, more than most of us want to put out.

Second, anger makes you feel in control. When you're mad at someone you think you are in control of the relationship; actually, it is the other person who is really in command.

Third, you'd rather be right than happy. While it may be that you are correct, consider picking your battles carefully. Not every battle has to be fought and won. Battles, regardless of how small, take their toll on you emotionally. Ask yourself, is it worth it?

Fourth, we also hold on to anger because we're encouraged to do so. Have you ever been in a situation where a friend said, "Don't let that person get away with what they did to you"? Everyone comes to a situation with his or her own agenda; don't let other people's agendas influence your actions.

Fifth, we're angry because we get permission to be that way. Feeling your feelings is one thing, but getting stuck in them is another. Oftentimes we're encouraged to live in the blame rather than move on. I was once seeing a therapist who encouraged me to acknowledge my mother's faults. I loved it! I got permission to bash my mother with absolute impunity.

"It was all her fault," I'd say.

"You're right," my therapist would say. And so it went. For years I lived in the blame, because I had permission to do so. Now I have permission to get past it by seeing my part and moving on. Today I feel my feelings, but I'm not stuck in them.

And finally, expectations, the high demands we place on others, lead us to anger. We judge based on what we think is right or wrong. Yet how often do we expect more of others than we do of ourselves? How often do we expect others to do what we're unwilling to do? Have you ever made a mistake, done something outrageously stupid, or disappointed yourself? Has anything silly, embarrassing, or inflammatory ever come out of your mouth that you wish you hadn't said? Did you stop talking to yourself for days, weeks, months, or even years because you made such a blunder? Of course not. Yet how often have you been disappointed or hurt by someone and you held a grudge—for days, weeks, months, and years? Why do we expect people to be perfect, yet demand our right to be a human being who makes mistakes?

A Word About Gossip

The quickest way to destroy a relationship is through gossip. It seems harmless and we do it because we can, but gossip is a hurtful and damaging force in human relationships.

So what is gossip? Talking about people behind their backs to someone you know doesn't like them. It's a setup for a bad relationship. It's born of anger and fear and is a surefire way to keep the flame going. While it's a part of the human condition to seek out support for our beliefs about others, to do so often sets in motion a series of events that can destroy reputations and backfire on you. Gossip is not just about saying bad stuff, it can even be when the information you pass on is positive. The key to recognizing gossip is your motive. If you are sharing information, are you saying it to compliment the person you're talking about, or because you are jealous and want to get support in making fun of him or her?

Why do we gossip? First, because it's easy to do. Second, when our lives are so uninteresting, we look to the lives of other people to keep us entertained. Third, gossip is the coward's way of dealing with anger. When people have hurt you, instead of having the courage to face them, it is easier to talk about them behind their backs to someone you know will agree with you, thus fueling the flame and garnering support for your anger. When we feel powerless about our conditions, pointing the finger at what's happening with someone else takes the focus off of how bad we feel about ourselves. Fourth, gossip creates camaraderie. When we join in, we become a part of the crowd, and for someone who desperately needs to feel a part of the crowd even at the expense of others, it works. Finally, gossipers don't feel good about themselves and they want others to feel as bad as they do.

The problem with gossip is it hurts the gossiper as much as it does the person being talked about. While it may feel good in the moment to talk badly about someone else, deep down it damages your self-esteem. The energy you could be spending changing your own life is spent trying to destroy someone else's. Gossipers see themselves as victims, and as a victim, you are stuck in a downward spiral. And what goes around comes around. You get back what you put out.

So how do you deal with gossip?

JUST STOP

It feeds off itself until you become willing to just stop doing it. Don't utter the first word. Take it a day at a time.

ASK PEOPLE NOT TO GOSSIP TO YOU

This is easier to say than do, because we all want to be liked. And often we fear that if we don't participate in the gossip, we will become the object of the gossip. Have the courage to just say no.

SPEAK UP IN DEFENSE OF PEOPLE IF YOU KNOW WHAT IS BEING SAID IS UNTRUE

Have the courage to defend the person being gossiped about in a conversation. People rarely talk to me about other people, because I let it be known that I don't want to hear the gossip. But if they do manage to say something in my presence, I'm quick to pose an alternative way of seeing the person they are talking about. Since people who gossip seek out supportive listeners, they are quick to back off when someone challenges their point of view or opinion about someone else.

WALK AWAY

Gossipers need and thrive on willing participants. If no one is there, they won't talk. And even if someone is there, that someone doesn't have to be you.

Esteemable Acts

EXERCISE 1

In your Esteemable Acts Journal make a list of the people you're angry at or not talking to. Next to each name, identify the cause of the conflict or resentment and how it affects your life. Feel free to use the following template if you like:

I am resentful of John because he got the promotion I thought I deserved. His getting that job affected my _____.

The following are examples of how you might be affected.

1. My finances, because I don't have enough money to pay for my kid's college this year
2. My self-esteem, because I make less than my ex-wife, who can pay for our kid's college
3. My relationship with John, because he used to be my friend and now I don't like him

EXERCISE 2
On a new sheet of paper in your Esteemable Acts Journal, rewrite your list created in Exercise #1, then write out what you would say to the person if you could see him and why. Don't be alarmed if your first attempt is filled with harsh and unloving words. You're at the beginning stage of your process; this is only your first draft. At this point, you're just getting your feelings out on paper. Writing allows you to capture them in the moment. It also allows you to step back and observe your anger.

EXERCISE 3
To get past the anger, you must now be willing to see other people as human beings who make mistakes just like you. Next to each name identified in Exercise #1, write out what could have been a valid reason for the person's doing what she did. What could her intention have been? Now in another column write a sentence describing how you would want to be treated if you

were in that position. Since we all want to be seen as loving and kind, why not start attributing the purest motives to others? If you are genuinely able to do this, you will begin to feel a change take place inside. A more loving you will emerge. No, it won't happen overnight, and yes, more work will be needed, but a change nonetheless will become apparent.

Just Do It!

What can you do right now, this moment, to move you closer to loving yourself or someone in your life? What one action are you willing to take right now? Commit to one thing before moving to the next Action.

We get by with a little help from our friends

It's an esteemable act to appreciate those who have helped you along the way.

It was assumed that Corinne, the only girl in a family of boys, would grow up, get married, and have kids—just like her mother. There was no need to train her to do anything else, because her job was to take care of others. So it wasn't a surprise to anyone that Corinne did poorly in school. It was never established as important for her. Through her junior year of high school she consistently got C's and D's and didn't engage in extracurricular activities. Then all of a sudden, in her senior year of high school, her grades jumped from C's and D's to straight A's. What caused the shift? What prompted such a change? What happened was that someone took an interest in Corinne. Someone cared enough to ask the right questions like, "What do you really enjoy doing?" "What would you do with your life if you could?" "Why don't you do well in school?" "What would it take to get you interested in school?" "Do you want to have children right away or at all?" That someone who cared enough happened to be an authority figure at Corinne's school. The authority figure didn't have to be, but he became Corinne's mentor.

Authority Figures, Mentors, and Angels

There's a difference between an authority figure and a mentor. An authority figure is someone in a position of power, someone who can influence your life or influence the direction in which your life is going. Authority figures wield power over you because of their authority. In some cases you give them the power and in other cases they just assume it. Your employer, teacher, therapist, minister, doctor, and parents are all examples of authority figures.

A mentor, on the other hand, is someone who may or may not have authority over you, but who nonetheless cares about your success and is willing to help you reach both your professional and personal goals. Mentors' goals are simply to assist you on your journey, offer helpful feedback along the way, or motivate you into taking some kind of action on your own behalf. Sometimes they motivate you through inspiration, showing you what's possible by their example. Sometimes they motivate you through encouragement, reminding you that you can accomplish whatever you want. Mentors are often invited into your life, and sometimes they just appear in ways you'd never expect. Regardless, they are very special people to be cherished and admired, because they help you discover who and what you really are.

Had I been asked early in life who my ideal mentor would be, I probably would have said "a black female," thus severely limiting my options. It never dawned on me that someone other than a black female could or would take an interest in me. How wrong I was! Over time, I've had mentors like Louise Robertson who share my gender and ethnic background, but I've also been blessed with mentors who are of a different race and gender, such as Hal Marley and Dr. Paul Ohliger.

Who are your mentors? Begin to think about the people who have been there for you in different ways. In your Esteemable Acts Journal start a list. Don't worry if no one comes to mind immediately; this is only the first step.

Now, let's talk about angels—people who do nice things for you without expecting anything in return. Angels give for the love of giving. Perhaps they let your car pass into the next lane without giving you a dirty look. Maybe they were the car ahead of you that paid your bridge or tunnel toll. Perhaps they offered to assist you when you were overloaded with bags. Maybe they helped you up instead of walking by when you fell. Perhaps they gave you their seat on the subway or the bus. Or maybe it was someone who just stopped in the middle of their busy workday to take your call or meet with you for coffee or lunch. All mentors are angels, but not all angels are mentors. They could be those you know or those you met in passing. Whoever they are and whatever the length and extent of your relationship, angels, like mentors, enhance your life.

In this Action you are invited to remember the people who helped you along the way to becoming who you are, who have contributed, in big and small ways, to your life. If you don't yet like who you are, this might feel like a tall order. No need to fret, I'm not asking you to do it all at once. I ask you only to make an effort and do whatever you can at this time, to do the best you can. Begin by saying to yourself out loud, "I see angels everywhere. I am open and receptive to the mentors waiting to assist me."

An Attitude of Gratitude

How do you get started on this journey of acknowledging and appreciating those who've helped you along the way? The first step is to cultivate an attitude of gratitude in which you choose to see the good in all things. The second step is to say "thank you" every chance you get. Being grateful doesn't mean you must always be happy and walk around with a smile on your face. It means that you make an effort to acknowledge what you have to be thankful for. Gratitude lifts the spirit, opens the heart, and nourishes the soul. Think about the times when you've been grateful; wasn't it easier to see the good in others? Also, when you're grateful, it's easier to feel good about yourself because you are willing and able to see the good in others.

Every week I write a gratitude list. There are days when it's so easy to come up with the things I'm grateful for that my pen glides across the paper or my fingers dance over the keyboard. Then there are those days when I can't think of anything to be thankful for. It's not that there isn't anything for me to be thankful for. I just can't—or more honestly, choose not to—see anything. Perhaps it's because I'm angry or hurt or disappointed in the moment, so all I can see is the glass as half empty, rather than half full. The way I get past this block is by writing at least six things I have to be grateful for in that very moment. It could be that I'm willing to write this list. Then, I put pen to paper and just do it! Amazingly, once I begin to write, more things are revealed.

In your Esteemable Acts Journal describe something that happened within the last twenty-four hours that you're grateful for. If you can't think of anything, extend your net a little wider to include the last week, month, or year. Consider also looking beyond the obvious. Perhaps the answer might be something you'd never think about, like being able to see, being able to walk, having a job, or not having a job so you have time to do what you want. For example, at this very moment, I'm grateful you're reading this book.

Whom Do You Thank?

Once you discover what you have to be grateful for, you can turn your attention to whom to thank. Think about people who have consciously or unconsciously helped you along the way. Who are your angels? Your mentors? Who has inspired, motivated, challenged, and/or supported you into doing things you didn't believe you could do? They've often been your most loving and comforting supporters, while at other times, they've been the ones who motivated you through tough love. Consider the following short list as a sampling of people you can thank.

1. Parents, grandparents
2. Stepparents, adoptive parents
3. Husband, wife
4. Ex-spouses
5. Aunts, uncles
6. Teachers, professors
7. School counselors
8. Friends
9. Estranged friends
10. Ex-boyfriends, ex-girlfriends
11. School buddies
12. Employers, employees
13. Shopkeepers
14. Therapists
15. Public figures
16. Strangers you have met that have touched you in some way, regardless of how seemingly small

This is a suggested list only. Arguably, some of you might think your parents don't belong on the list. Perhaps you feel they weren't there for you, they didn't love you, didn't protect you, didn't support you, or didn't give you the space you needed. If you have a block regarding your parents, take them off your list. Perhaps you'll come back to them, perhaps not. I know for myself, until I was willing to see past my mother's faults to her humanity—as I wanted her to see past mine—my heart remained closed and every other relationship was affected as well. Today, as I look back over my life, my mother has been one of my greatest teachers.

In your Esteemable Acts Journal start a list of people you can thank. Having identified some things you have to be grateful for, perhaps this list will be easier to compile. Begin with the last twenty-four hours; who has done something nice for you?

The Forgiveness Factor

If you've gotten this far in this process, you've made a real investment of time and energy in your self-esteem and your relationships with others. But something is gnawing at you. Perhaps you're saying, "Now I know what I'm thankful for and whom I'm thankful for, but what about the people who did horrible things to me? I just can't seem to forgive them." While you may be justified in your anger, it will only destroy you if you continue to hold on to those feelings. As mentioned in Action #8, anger hurts the grudge-bearer far more than it does the object of the fury (see page 153). It's like a slow-acting poison that eats away at a life worth living—*yours*.

The key to forgiveness is a willingness to forgive. Just saying "I forgive you" doesn't rid you of the anger. Think about it: How often have you seen someone who says he's forgiven someone else and yet is still riddled with anger and resentment at the mention of that person's name? Someone who every chance he gets makes hurtful comments aimed at the very person he claims to have forgiven, despite being quick to tell you he's forgiven the person? In these cases, saying "I forgive you" is like making an empty promise, or saying "I love you" when you don't really mean it. If solid action doesn't accompany the words, the words mean nothing.

How Do You Begin to Forgive?

Following is a step-by-step list of suggestions to help you truly forgive:

STEP #1:
PRAY FOR AN OPEN HEART

Even a tiny opening can let forgiveness in. Praying to be willing to be willing often creates a space to allow forgiveness to step in.

STEP #2:
READ INSPIRATIONAL MATERIALS

If prayer is too far out of your reach, or even if it's not, read material that will soften your heart. Sometimes just letting in positive information will create a change of thinking (see Resources, page 203, for a listing of positive reading material).

STEP #3:
ATTEMPT TO UNDERSTAND

Understanding is the foundation of love and love is the basis for gratitude. Grasping why people behave as they do can sometimes help us forgive them. Sometimes, because of someone else's enlightened self-interest, we get hurt. Unfortunately, when people are hurt, they lash out and hurt others. But the truth is that rarely does anyone start out wanting to hurt us. It's not personal, it's just the way it is. This by no means justifies their behavior, it simply explains it.

STEP #4:

SEE YOUR PART

Be open to seeing the part you played in the situation. This is equally as difficult as Step #3, because more often than not, we don't recognize our part. In our minds, we are always the good guy being tormented and abused by the big bad guy. But interpersonal problems almost always involve two or more people. Once you're able to see past your hurt and anger to how you might have contributed to what happened, you're better able to understand that they, like you, are human and make mistakes.

STEP #5:

WHAT YOU PUT OUT IS WHAT YOU GET BACK

Understand that as long as you are unwilling to forgive others, you limit the possibility that others will forgive you. The Universal Law of Karma is alive and well.

STEP #6:

BE GRATEFUL

Write a gratitude list of the things you like about the person or that she or he did well. This might take some effort, but try. By writing this list you create a space for humanity to step in. It is hard to hold on to anger when you see the other person as having done something right.

Gratitude Letters

The essence of Action #9 is to demonstrate the power of saying thank you to people who have, in some way, been there for you.

By now, you probably have a list of potential candidates. What we've done so far is get you ready to write a gratitude letter. But not yet. Below are seven letters I've written to people who have made a significant difference in my life. By no means is this the entire list, it is simply a sampling. Before you embark on writing your own gratitude letters, please read what I've written carefully. There are necessary steps to be taken before you run out and write letters to people you may not have spoken to in a long time or who may not be open to hearing from you.

ROLE MODEL

A role model exemplifies the values and behaviors you admire. Louise Robertson was my first real role model. She was one of the first women to let me know I had choices in how I wanted to behave and be treated. Here's my gratitude letter to Louise.

Dear Louise,

Twenty-three years have gone by fast. It seems like yesterday that I was that snot-nosed, angry young woman off the streets of New York. Thank you for seeing past my tough-girl façade to the scared little kid who just wanted to be loved. How can I ever thank you for all you've given me, for all you've taught me? Perhaps the best I can do is continue to say thank you.

You knew me when. Long before I could stand up for myself, long before there was a self, long before the trappings were so put together, the smile so bright, and the mind so alert. You knew me when, and you loved me anyway. Thank you for letting me know I was more than my body and more than a pretty face; that I was and could be a woman of substance, and that my past didn't have to dictate my future. Thank you for teaching me that self-esteem comes from doing esteemable acts; that I could make of my life whatever I wanted if I was willing to do the footwork.

Thank you for never giving in, for never allowing me to intimidate you, even though God knows I tried. Thanks for having the courage to tell me the truth about my behavior and risk having me walk away when I didn't like what you said. Thank you for teaching me the value of women as friends and showing me how to be one. But mostly, my dear Louise, thank you for guiding me to a God of my own understanding and encouraging me to listen to and to trust my inner voice. Thank you for being my role model. I love you.

Francine

GRANDMOTHER

What can you say about grandmothers? Talk about unconditional love. They're the good guys, sometimes because they just are and sometimes because they missed the mark with their own kids. Whatever the reason, grandmothers are great. Here's my gratitude letter to my grandmother.

Dear Gran,

You were my guardian angel from the very beginning. I'm so glad you were my mother's mother, else I might never have known you. Thank you for loving me unconditionally, and for being there for me when I couldn't be there for myself. Thank you for having the courage to keep praying for my recovery from addiction, even when I appeared hopeless. Your prayers really worked. Thank you for staying alive long enough to see the results of your prayers. Thank you for allowing me to say thank you while you were still alive.

Thank you for teaching me how to sew, knowing it was a valuable and worthwhile skill. Thank you for helping me find my father, when everyone told me he was dead. Thank you for letting me lick the batter from the cake bowl every single time you baked a cake. Thank you for just loving me.

Francine

CREATIVE COACH

A creative coach is a mentor, someone who sees your potential and encourages you to follow through. He is someone you respect and whose opinion you value because you've seen him go through difficulties and get to the other side. He supports the creative side of you by challenging you to take action, even when you don't want to. In the beginning, he is the visionary able to see into the future long before you can. Following is my gratitude letter to my creative coach, Paul.

Dear Paul,

For so long, you were bigger than life, someone I had only read about and quoted from afar. You were an inspiration. You were my inspiration. Then we met, and we became friends. I loved both you and Max from the very beginning and I loved you until the very end. You were there when I failed the California Bar, over and over again, and you gave me strength when I didn't think I could get through it one more time. At the same time, you saw a bigger vision for me, a vision I was afraid to acknowledge. Thank you for your wisdom.

You were the first person to tell me I had a story to share and that I could be a writer. I'll never forget the day I received my first copy of the *Writer's Digest* subscription you got for me. I remember reading it from cover to cover, so excited about the prospect of perhaps being a writer with something to say. You knew my heart's desire long before I did. When you have a dream sometimes it's hard to find people who believe in you and support you before you're a success. You were one of my earliest supporters, particularly at a time when I really needed a friend. Thank you. I love you, Paul. Thank you for allowing me to demonstrate my love for you through my actions and my words.

Francine

TEACHER

Over time most of us grow away from our teachers. They teach us, we grow up, we lose touch. If we're lucky we will have a chance to go back and say thank you to our beloved teachers. This is a letter of thanks to my third-grade teacher, Myra Goldstein.

Dear Myra,

Thank you for being my teacher. Third grade was a painful time for me and you made it easier. My mother, my sister, and I had only been in New York for two years from Atlanta. The kids were cruel. They called me names like "down in the cornfield, hick, and country bumpkin," and I, not knowing how to defend myself against such attacks, just cried a lot and kept to myself. I was a lonely kid looking for a friend. Coming into your class was the best thing that could have happened to me. You gave me the lead in our school play, TheWizard of Oz, and made me feel a part of the class, a part of a world that I usually only wanted to escape from through my books. Thank you for making me feel special by calling me Fran. It meant more than you'll ever know.

Over the years we've become friends. Thank you for sharing many special days with me: both my college and law school graduations, my wedding, and, God willing, many more days. I loved you then and I love you now, because you were nice to me in the third grade. You made me feel like I mattered and for that, I will always be grateful.

Francine

VALUED ELDER

Nowadays people don't seem to value age and wisdom. In our youth-oriented society, we tend to think if someone is old, the person has nothing to say. How sad for us if we, too, hold this view. Our elders have much wisdom to give us. Here's a gratitude letter to my friend and elder, Hal Marley.

Dear Hal,

I remember the first time we met. It was the last Tuesday morning in August 1986. We were in the House Appropriations Room on the third floor of the United States Capitol building. I walked into the room and there you were—the big guy—holding court. Having just moved from New York to Washington, D.C., I was excited to attend my first day of law school. Over the next three years, we were to share many a Tuesday morning together. Had it not been for your guidance and support, I might never have made it through law school.

Every day when the road through Georgetown seemed too hard and treacherous, you reminded me to have an attitude of gratitude. I often thought to myself, "He can't be for real. How can anyone feel grateful all the time?" Yet you did. You taught me that regardless of what happened in life, there was always something to be grateful for. You did more than talk about being grateful, you lived it. I watched you go through many personal trials and tribulations and you always rose above them by seeing a glimmer of something to be thankful for.

And lastly, thank you, Hal, for showing up as an honorable man, for letting me see in you that men could be trusted and respected.

You're getting older and I'm afraid our days together are numbered. All I can say is thank you for the many words, countless phone calls, and love that has spanned sixteen years. In the beginning, it felt like you were my nemesis, then you were my mentor, then you became my friend, and at all times you have been my hero.

I love you, Hal Marley.

Francine

SPOUSE

Sometimes the person the closest to you is the one often taken for granted, the one who is there, day in and day out, the one who has to tolerate the good and bad behavior, the one who loves you no matter what. Here's a letter to my wonderful husband.

Dear Richard,

Our path has been long and, at times, hard. For a while it seemed like we wouldn't make it, but we have, one day at a time.

You didn't know what you were getting into, yet you took on the challenge anyway. You've been stretched, and stretched some more, and consistently, you hung in there. Thank you for not giving up when it would have been so very easy to do so. You are one of the most courageous people I know.

I love you for many reasons, but mostly for what you are and who you've become and for what you have helped me to become. In our safe and loving home, you've created a space for me to become the best person I can be, supporting me to do the things I was destined to do, like write this book.

You are the one I laugh with, cry with, dream with, and have chosen to live my life with. You are my lover, my friend, and my best teacher.

I love you, Richard.

Francine

MOTHER

It may be difficult to see a parent as a mentor, or even an angel for that matter. It may be hard to recognize the good parents do because we may be so invested in hating them for the things they did wrong. But remember, they are charged with the most difficult of all tasks: raising kids into healthy, whole, responsible, and thoughtful adults, as they themselves are learning to do the same. My mother is not the last on the list because she is least important, she is last because she is the most important. This is a love letter to my mother, whom I admire and cherish.

Dear Mama,

I love you for who you are and who you have taught me to be. From you I learned the value of a strong work ethic and discipline. As a kid I resented your not being home because you had to work. Today I understand you did what you did so we could have a better life. You struggled and put yourself through school all the while caring for two small girls. You are my hero. You did the best you could with an arrogant, stubborn, egotistical, and drug-addicted teenager—and you never let go of me, even when I thought you did.

Your strength and your tenacity were powerful examples when I was ready to change my life. When I thought I couldn't do it, I would remember that you had overcome many odds to take care of your family and raise your economic level, and I knew I could do it, too. I love you, Mama. Thank you for being here for me.

Francine

TO SOMEONE WHO DIED BEFORE
I COULD SAY THANK YOU

Some of you are probably thinking, "What do I do when the person I want to thank has died?" "How do I say thank you or I'm sorry when they have made their transition?" In truth, there is no simple answer, because once they are dead, they are beyond reach. But a suggestion I have is to write a letter as if you were writing it to the person. Take a moment and meditate on what you would tell her, making sure you say everything that's in your heart. Don't let the opportunity slip by again. After you've written the letter in your Esteemable Acts Journal, sit with your thoughts and feelings for a while. Allow yourself to truly experience the moment. Then ask for the power to release yourself from your feelings and past actions. This is not a one-shot deal. Sometimes you will have to continually ask for help in letting go. But in time, because you've practiced this discipline, you will feel the sting of your past actions less and less, provided you are living differently today.

Esteemable Acts is a book about having the courage to walk through your fear, so that you don't find yourself one day saying, "I wish I had." Sometimes we're lucky to have another chance to make amends or say thank you, because the person is still alive, even if out of reach. However, when the person is dead, the opportunity is gone—forever.

Many forgiveness experts tell us we can circumvent the feelings that come from having missed that opportunity by saying affirmations such as "I forgive myself." But in truth, we cannot avoid the feelings. Can you recall an opportunity that you missed, a moment that always makes you say to yourself, "I wish I had said what was in my heart and not let what was in my brain control the situation"? If so, you probably know the pain that comes from these feelings. And even though we think we can avoid these feelings with the use of drugs and alcohol, those mind-altering chemicals can only temporarily erase the pain. We, like everyone else, must suffer the consequences for our choices. That is why it's so important now to make right choices that are not motivated by fear.

It's hard to walk through our fear of looking like a wimp when someone has hurt us. It's hard to walk through our fear of not having all the answers when we so desperately want to be seen as smart. It's hard to walk through our fear of giving in when others were the ones at fault. Indeed, taking the high road is hard when your ego is alive and well. But while it may be difficult, I urge you to do it anyway—if not for others, then for yourself. So many people have come to me saddened by how they wish they had just one more moment with their mother, or one more moment with their dad, or one more opportunity to right a wrong, or one more moment to say thank you. Sadly, they will never have the chance.

Don't let the time go by. Say thank you today. Pray for the willingness to get past the stuff that prevents you from doing the right thing. Don't allow another person to make his or her transition without being appreciated by you.

Esteemable Acts

EXERCISE 1

Take a moment and think back over your life once again. This time bring into consciousness the faces of people you knew and once loved—even if you don't love them now. Perhaps it was your best friend from junior high school or high school; maybe it was the owner of the corner candy store or the school bus driver? Identify as many as you can and don't beat yourself up if you can list only four or five. Just try. After you have your list, imagine what you'd say to each person.

EXERCISE 2

The next step is to write the gratitude letter. In some cases, this will be an enjoyable experience and the words will flow from your heart effortlessly. You'll be happy someone gave you permission to put into words what you've been thinking. In other cases, it will prove to be more challenging. Perhaps you'll be writing a letter to someone you've been estranged from for a while and you're not sure how to start the letter. Perhaps the letter is to someone you love but because you never told the person before, you're afraid of how you might be perceived, or maybe you're just afraid because you don't know the right words to say. Just make a start. Write a draft, now! Write it as if no one else will see it, because no one else will. This is only a draft. By the time your letter is ready to go, you will have completed several drafts and come up with the one you are most comfortable with. Don't be in a rush to create the perfect letter. The key components of your letter should be genuine gratitude, warmth, sincerity, and specific instances. Let these be your guide. Then, only when you're ready, really ready, send it off.

Tip: You may want to pray for the right words to flow through you. I often pray for divine guidance, and when I'm receptive, I get it!

EXERCISE 3

And now, the final step is to contact those people from your list in Exercise #1. Is there a way to contact those on your list by phone, e-mail, or snail mail? How can you find out where they are? You may have to do some research. Recently I have been looking to connect with my ninth-grade teacher, Ms. Levy, from Junior High School 80, and with a former school aide, Mrs. Spielmann, from Public School 94, both in the Bronx. I found Ms. Levy but haven't been as successful at locating Mrs. Spielmann, yet I haven't given up. *One caveat:* Please be respectful. Don't go forging ahead to find someone who might not want to be found. Tread lightly and honor the person's boundaries. It's important that you not make yourself feel better at someone else's expense. So tread lightly, but take some action. Get started!

Just Do It!

What action can you take right now that will get you closer to acknowledging those who have helped you along the way? Maybe it's starting your gratitude list, or identifying those you have to thank, or praying to be divinely guided into taking the next right action. Commit to one action before moving to Action #10.

Make a difference
in someone's life

It's an esteemable act to give freely of yourself.

Imagine you've lived a long and full life and now you
find yourself at the "pearly gates." It's been said that
upon arrival, you won't be asked how many cars you had, how
many pairs of shoes you owned, where you went to school, or
even how many children you raised. Instead, you'll be asked,
"Whom did you help? How were you of service to others? How
did you make the world a better place to live?"

Some of you may think of service in terms of money; for
some it will be measured by volunteer hours spent; and still for
others, it will be a tax-deductible, charitable expense. Whatever

your definition, Action #10 invites you to expand your view and consider *service* as whatever you do for the benefit of others. The purpose of this Action is not only that you see giving as an esteemable act, but that you also see it as a desirable way of life, rather than as an intrusion.

Action #10 reminds us that we all have something to give— regardless of how small or how seemingly unimportant the gift may appear. To the beneficiaries, your offering of kindness and generosity is what makes their day. Maybe it's a smile, or an "atta boy!" Perhaps it's the few precious moments you spend in silence with someone, or that you simply listen without judgment. Maybe it's the sharing of valuable information or a skill. Whatever it is, freely giving of yourself makes a difference in someone's life and is an esteemable act.

Why Do We Give?

Self-esteem comes from doing esteemable acts, and while you feel good about yourself when you give to others, there are many more reasons for cultivating a consciousness of giving. Here are a few.

TO HELP OTHERS

One reason for giving of yourself, whether it's your time or your money, is to make a difference in someone else's life. There's something to be said for watching a person's face light up when you help him or her get something the person thinks is impossible to have. My heart warmed the first time I was able to help someone in that way. Mentoring teenage girls is what I love doing most. The feeling that I am able to perhaps make a small difference in someone's life because of my experience and caring is tremendously gratifying. Something magical takes place when you open yourself up to sharing just for the sake of sharing.

In your Esteemable Acts Journal identify some of the ways you help others. If you are not yet doing service, discuss some things you might like to do.

TO MAKE AMENDS FOR PAST MISTAKES

Donny died from AIDS complications shortly after the disease hit epidemic proportions in the mid-1980s. During his last and most painful year, I wasn't there for him, even though I could have been. Instead, I allowed my fear to become more powerful than my friendship. I was afraid to watch him die. I was afraid of how I'd feel. I was afraid to feel. Not only was I not there for my friend, I then allowed people to convince me I did the best I could, even though I know I didn't.

I can never change the past, but I can create a different present, and I have. After he died, I sought opportunities to give in every way I could, especially to people who suffer from terminal illness, including AIDS. Today, I regularly give seminars about walking through the fear of not knowing how to deal with someone who is sick or dying. My commitment is to give a certain number of hours every year of pro bono services to nonprofit organizations, particularly those who provide care and services to the terminally ill.

Are there amends you need to make? Are there ways you can be of service in an effort to make those amends? Write your answers in your journal.

Francine Ward

FOR AN OPPORTUNITY TO MAKE FRIENDS

Like-minded people are drawn to similar places, to do similar things. Rotary International gave me an entry into the world of community service. At first, like so many other people, I had no idea what Rotary was really all about. I thought it was where old, retired men got together to have lunch once a week. What I found instead was a place where people who love to be of service connect with other people who love to be of service. At my first meeting of the Marin Sunrise Group, in Corte Madera, I knew I was home. I recall hearing the group's president say, "This is not your father's Rotary." And indeed, it was not. That statement, coupled with a genuine friendliness toward me, made me want to keep coming back. Today, some of my closest friends are in that group, and I look forward to my Wednesday-morning meetings.

TO GET THROUGH THE ROUGH TIMES

When times are tough, sometimes the only thing that helps you get through them is to help someone else get through her pain. None of us can escape the tough times. They are a part of life. But being there for someone else helps you cope with your own hurt. In 1997 I put Athena, my feline friend and companion of nineteen and a half years to sleep. She had been with me through many of my own challenges in life. When she died, it felt as if a piece of me died with her.

That day was a hard day to show up for anyone or anything. Yet the only way I was able to survive the experience was by showing up for others and having the courage to tell the truth about my feelings. I had previously scheduled a speaking engagement for that day, and while the meeting planner probably would have understood had I canceled, I knew I was supposed to be there—and I was. I cried in front of my audience and made no apologies for my tears. Not only did I help myself by sharing my pain, I also helped others. There were many people in the audience who had recently lost loved ones, and my courage and willingness to be there and share my experience gave them courage, too.

In your Esteemable Acts Journal, take a moment and identify your reasons for giving. Don't worry if your motives don't seem altruistic. Just be as honest as you can.

What Gets in the Way of Giving?

For all the reasons to give, we nonetheless find excuses not to. We think that we don't know how to give, or that we're too busy, or we're afraid of being rejected, or we just don't like the person we're asked to help. There are many more reasons for not giving, but the chief motivator behind them all is, you guessed it, fear.

NOT KNOWING HOW TO GIVE

Some of us get trapped in the limiting belief that giving requires big actions, such as paying someone's rent, buying dinner, sharing your personal belongings, giving thousands of dollars to charity, or volunteering many hours of your precious time. While indeed it can mean those things, it's the mere act of giving that is big. Knowing how to give is not an art and requires no skill or talent. It simply requires a willingness to give. To give means to do something, to take some action, regardless of how small. Doing the laundry, running an errand, or preparing a meal for someone who's infirm, is an act of giving. Taking out the garbage without being asked, volunteering to help out a neighbor who works long hours, or offering to pick up the kids are all examples of things we can do in the name of helping another person.

Maybe your act of giving is spending time with a friend who wants your company. Maybe it's listening to someone who needs to be heard, even if it's hard to hear her. Maybe your gift is not giving someone the finger or cutting him off in traffic. Maybe it's having the courage to love instead of hate. Maybe it's treating people with kindness even when there's no crisis. Maybe your gift is not participating in gossip, and maybe it's even going to the next step of being a voice against gossip.

Remember, the easiest thing in the world is to do what's easy. Sometimes your greatest gift is doing something for someone when it's hard, when you're not predisposed to doing it, or when you just don't want to do it. Perhaps your gift is forgiveness. Maybe you've been holding a grudge against someone not just for days and weeks, but for years. Maybe the greatest act of service could be to free that person and yourself from the grip of resentment.

Maybe your act of giving is being an example of courage. How easy it is to live in fear, and when you do, you give others permission to do the same—whether or not you know it. Once at a meeting I had a desire to speak, yet I was afraid. I realized early in life that for every action I took, there was always a price to pay. Consequently, I learned to edit my words so people would like me. I learned to keep my mouth shut so as not to shake up the status quo. Further, to reinforce the idea that honesty doesn't pay, I saw daily examples of how adults lived in fear of being seen for who they really were. They were afraid to say what they really felt for fear of paying a price, whether it was losing a job, a friend, or something else that was important.

The world is full of examples of living in fear. But an act of service is having the courage to be yourself, to speak your truth even when you're afraid. Eventually, I spoke up in that meeting, and I did pay a price. But the price would have been greater had I not been true to myself. As well as feeling good about myself, I helped someone who was also afraid to speak up but did so because I did.

There are many opportunities to give of yourself. All you need is an open mind and the right opportunity will appear. When you're not sure what to do, think of what's needed in the moment. In your Esteemable Acts Journal identify some need in your community, on your job, or in your life where you can give of your time, money, or talent. Now, identify specific ways you can be of service to others. What can you do to give?

NO TIME TO GIVE

Some of you may believe that giving to others takes up too much time, and since you're already overcommitted, the last thing you want is another obligation. No doubt there *are* commitments that require a lot of time. But the good news is you get to pick and choose how you want to serve. You give in the way you're able to. When I first went back to school in 1981, my biggest complaint was "I don't have time to be of service. I have

a full-time job and a heavy class load." At the time, two classes
and a full-time job were more than I could handle. It was then
that my friend and mentor, Louise, helped me realize that there
were many different ways to be of service that would suit my
lifestyle.

I started small. One of my first service commitments was
visiting the children's ward in a local hospital every Christmas.
With a group of like-minded friends, I gathered toys and food
to take to the children. Then I started to visit the patients at the
Veteran's Hospital every Sunday. I'd feed them, talk to them, and
listen to them, because most had no family or friends who
would come to visit. While at times my short visits didn't seem
like a lot, looking back I know the patients were grateful. They
knew they could count on seeing me every Sunday. Once a week
was all I could fit into my schedule at the time. But it was a beginning.

Gradually I added more things to my commitment list. Every
Thanksgiving and Christmas I cooked dinner and invited people
over who didn't have a place to go. Since for most of my early adult
life I was either estranged from my family or living far from them,
this was also my way of creating a family. I didn't have a lot of
money, nor did I have a lot of time, but what I had was a warm
heart and a home. The key was my willingness to serve.

Are you using not having enough time as an excuse for not being of service? In your Esteemable Acts Journal explore some ways
that you can fit service into your schedule. Remember, there are
lots of ways to give. Be creative. Think of where there might be a
need, even a small one. What one thing can you do today?

REJECTION

Fear of rejection stops some of us from giving to others. How often is our heart in the right place when we give, only to have our loving gift not appreciated? At one time or another it's happened to all of us. But that's no reason not to try again, and again.

I learned early on that what the person does with what I give is none of my business. During college I made friends with a woman who, like me, was a returning student. Often she came to class physically bruised, insisting she fell.

"Is there something I can do to help?" I'd ask.

"No, nothing is wrong," she continually said.

I recognized the signs of physical abuse and I wanted to help, even if she didn't want my help. Finally, one day after class, she told me her husband beat her.

"I'll do whatever I can to help you," I said, "if you're willing to help yourself."

"I'll do anything, anything to stop the pain," she cried.

I made her an appointment at a women's shelter. She never showed up. The next time I saw her at school she said, "He's really a good guy. He doesn't mean to hurt me, it's just when he drinks he gets out of control. I really love him. I'm better off staying with him, because he's my husband."

For weeks I was angry at her for not being stronger. I thought to myself, "Doesn't she understand what's she's doing to herself and to her kids? Can't she see the example she's setting? Can't she see I'm trying to help?" I took her actions as a personal affront to me, which they weren't. After that, I didn't want to help another woman for fear she'd reject my efforts.

What I really wanted was an excuse and permission not to be of service anymore, and I found it. So I gave myself permission to feel sad and angry. Eventually I found the next person to help.

In your Esteemable Acts Journal discuss a time when you felt your kind actions were rejected. How did you feel? How did you handle the situation? Have you allowed that incident to stop your giving? Explain.

One of the best ways to deal with such seeming rejection of your gift is to walk through your feelings. Do you know someone who is in need of a kind word today, an offer of friendship? Who appears ungrateful and angry? Sometimes those who seem not to need or want our help need it the most. Don't give up on them; perhaps just try a different approach. One of the girls I mentor is right off the streets of San Francisco and tough—just like I was. It's easy to see her anger as rejection. But in truth, it's a cry for help. My job is to see past the "seeming" problem to the solution.

WHY SHOULD I HELP THEM?

Another thing that gets in the way of giving is not liking the person who needs your help. It's easy to help people who either don't need your help or with whom it's a pleasure to work. You give, then look good for having given. On the other hand, it's not so easy to help those you don't like. Maybe you think they don't deserve your gift, maybe you think they'll squander it, maybe you don't like what they stand for, or maybe their beliefs differ from yours. Whatever the reason, it's easy to place limits on our gifts, providing us with yet another reason not to give.

By no means am I suggesting there should be no limits placed on giving or that you shouldn't be selective in whom you give to. I'm just inviting you to consider the criteria you use for defining those limits. What opportunities have presented themselves to you where the receiver of the gift is someone you don't like or would rather not help? Why the hesitation? Are you using not liking the person as an excuse for not being of service? What will it take to get past it? Or can you? What do you have to lose if you give the person what she needs? What will you gain by not giving? In your Esteemable Acts Journal write about an opportunity to give that you let go by because you didn't like the person to whom you were asked to give. What were the circumstances? How did you handle it? Did the person need your help? What are your observations about your behavior?

Getting Past the Obstacles

How do you get past the obstacles that prevent you from giving to others? Before you are ready to take action, you must first create an open space in your heart that allows you to see the act of giving as a good thing, as a useful thing, as a beneficial thing. By creating an open space, you can see the need for change and then become willing to take action. When we feel touched by someone or something, we become receptive to assisting in whatever way we can. When we feel a connection to the person or to the cause, we're more readily able to give. So the idea is to feel that connection. Open yourself up to the degree that you can feel connected to someone who needs your help.

How do you open your heart, how do you feel that connection? For starters, bring to mind something that touches you emotionally. Perhaps it's something that makes you cry, such as a song, a commercial on television, your pet, your child, a greeting card, or a letter you've received in the mail. If you can access the feeling, then recall what about it makes you feel. If you can't access it without assistance, locate the card or play the music. Then reflect on what is it about the experience that softens your heart. In your Esteemable Acts Journal, write out your answer, being careful to allow yourself to feel your feelings. You may be tempted to bypass or rush through this feeling exercise. I encourage you not to.

Then, think of something you are passionate about. What do you love? What makes your hair rise? What gets you mad? What gets you excited? Refer back to Action #1 (page 15) where you were asked to identify your passions. Often thinking of the things we are passionate about gives us a place to begin the conversation of where and how to be of service. What project or cause would you work on if you could? In your journal, make a list of causes you are passionate about.

Some Suggestions for Giving

There are many ways to give. It all starts with a desire.

BE OPEN TO THE OPPORTUNITIES

When your heart is open, there will be an outpouring of opportunities for you to give. Pray for the willingness to see what they are. You could be walking down the street and see an opportunity to give. You could be at work and see an opportunity to serve. You could be in traffic or in the line at the supermarket and come face-to-face with an opportunity to be of service. They are everywhere, people and situations that cry out for your gift of caring.

DO SOMETHING

Start small, but do something. If you're really interested in giving in some way, look for something small to do. It is better that you start with a little kindness and get in the habit than wait to do something big and do nothing. Waiting to give the perfect gift is sometimes an excuse not to give. Are you looking for an excuse not to give? What small act of kindness can you perform?

STRETCH YOURSELF

When you can, do what you normally wouldn't do. Stretch yourself. Go beyond your comfort zone and give just a little more than you'd normally give. If giving money is not an issue for you because you have plenty of it, consider also volunteering your time. Spend the day with a child you wouldn't normally have access to, and expose him or her to something different. For example, take an inner-city child to the museum or the opera or the ballet. What a treat it would be for the child, and you. If you like to get your hands dirty, volunteer to clean someone's lawn or plant their garden. Stretch yourself.

BE A RECEIVER-CENTERED GIVER

Give with the person you are giving to in mind. For example, if you give a gift, give what the recipient might like to receive, not what you think the person should receive. Often we give a gift because it's what we want the other people to have, then get upset when they are not as happy as we think they should be. Have you ever given a birthday present to someone who was less than thrilled, and you got angry thinking she was an ingrate? While no doubt the recipient could have practiced kindness and gratitude, you could have given a gift the person could use and would want. There are lessons for us all.

GIVE WITHOUT STRINGS ATTACHED

If you give, let it go. How often do we give and then reserve the right to dictate every detail about the giving, including how the gift will be used? If you give, give for the love of giving, and let go of the outcome. Years ago, before I really understood the importance of freely giving of what I had, I was walking down the street with a friend when a beggar asked us for money. In my most cavalier tone, I said to him, "Why don't you get a job?"

My friend, on the other hand, took three dollars from her purse and gave it to him. I was horrified. "Why did you do that?" I asked.

"Because he asked for it and I had it to give."

"He'll only use it for drugs and booze," I said.

"So what if he does? If I give a gift, I need to let go of the strings I've attached to it." I thought to myself, "This woman is crazy," but it was the first esteemable act I was to witness that demonstrated the power of giving without strings attached.

FOLLOW THROUGH

When you say "yes" to a commitment, follow through. People are relying on you to do what you said you'd do and if you can't do it, give sufficient notice. Recently, I agreed to speak for a non-profit even though the date conflicted with another engagement. Why? Because my need to have people like me was more powerful than my need to be responsible. I had months to rectify my irresponsible action by notifying one of the parties that I had to cancel. But I chose not to. Finally, the day before the event, I canceled. The meeting planner was livid and I got defensive saying, "I have a right to take care of myself."

Fortunately for me, one of my mentors set me straight.

"It's wonderful that you took care of yourself," she said, "but you had no right to do it at the expense of others, particularly when you could have avoided this outcome."

She was right, of course. First, I never should have accepted the engagement, but once I did and knew I couldn't do it, there was plenty of time to cancel, which would have given the meeting planner a chance to get another speaker. It was fear, pure and simple, that got in my way—fear of not being liked, fear of what they would think of me if I said no. Now, because of my behavior, the very thing I feared has come true. They don't like me and will never use me again. Hopefully in time I'll be able to make it up to them.

KEEP YOUR BALANCE

The other side of doing nothing is doing too much. Sometimes we tend to overdo even a good thing, and after a while we're so focused on helping others that we forget to tend to our own needs. We support our kids and our spouse, we take care of our friends, our customers at work, and we are always volunteering to help others. Eventually, if we don't take the time to be there for ourselves, we burn out. Don't let doing too much for others translate into neglect of yourself. While it's easier to say than to do, with practice, you can take better care of yourself. Enlightened self-care is an important element in building self-esteem.

Esteemable Acts

EXERCISE 1

Now that you have an idea of what you might like to do to be of service to others, it's time to create a plan. Start with where you are now, where you want to be, and how to get you there. In your Esteemable Acts Journal, on a page entitled "Ways I Give," make a list of all the things you do that are giving acts. Don't be bashful. If you haven't written this out yet, this is your time to really look at the many ways you give to others. Then, on another page entitled "Ways I'd Like to Give," make a list of things you'd like to do, would consider doing, or that you find interesting. On a third page entitled "How I Get There," identify all the steps you think might be required to get you from where you are to where you want to be.

EXERCISE 2

Select one thing from your list that you can do in the next twenty-four hours to be of service to someone. It might simply be to get the telephone number or visit the Web site of your local hospital volunteer's office. This is where it starts. Perhaps one small action will lead to another.

EXERCISE 3

Finally, let's keep track of your activities. In your Esteemable Acts Journal make a journal entry for every service activity to do, starting now. The idea is to simply keep a running journal of your volunteer service activities so that over time you can see how far you've come. This also strengthens your commitment to yourself, because you'll see what you are really capable of doing if you try. That, in and of itself, is an esteemable act.

Just Do It!

What can you do right now to move you closer to embodying a conciousness of giving? What one action are you willing to take right now?

ꞳFTERWORD

Congratulations, you've made it! If you've gotten this far and made an effort to do at least some of the exercises in this book, you've given yourself the most incredible gift—the gift of self-love. By moving past your limitations, you already have a new and more appealing picture of your life. Bravo, for starting this journey. But don't stop now. You've only come to a pause in your work—not a close.

Esteemable Acts is a book to be studied, not just read. I hope it will become a working part of your life and that you will refer to it from time to time. The practicing of esteemable acts is an ongoing experience. Perhaps you will want to recommit yourself to working through the steps in this book annually. Perhaps you might consider making it a birthday present to yourself, or maybe you'll create study groups, big or small, around the book. Be kind to yourself, support and encourage yourself, and remember that self-esteem comes from doing esteemable acts!

$\mathscr{R}$ESOURCES

Recommended Books

DREAMS

The *Artist's Way*, by Julia Cameron and Mark Bryan. J. P. Tarcher Books, 1992.

Building Your Field of Dreams, by Mary Manin Morrissey. Bantam Books, 1996.

How to Write a Book Proposal, by Michael Larsen. Writer's Digest Books, 1997.

The Shortest Distance Between You and a Published Book, by Susan Page. Broadway Books, 1997.

FOCUS

First Things First, by Stephen R. Covey, A. Roger Merrill, and Rebecca R. Merrill. Simon & Schuster/Fireside, 1994.

How to Say No Without Feeling Guilty, by Patti Breitman and Connie Hatch. Broadway Books, 2000.

The Power of Focus, by Jack Canfield, Les Hewitt, and Mark Victor Hansen. Health Communications, 2000.

FAILING

Each Day a New Beginning, by Karen Casey. Hazelden, 1982.

Feel the Fear and Do It Anyway, by Susan Jeffers, Ph.D. Fawcett
  Columbine, 1987.
For the Inward Journey, by Howard Thurman. Friends United Meet-
  ing, 1981.
Meditations to Heal Your Life, by Louise Hay. Hay House, 1994.

INVENTORY

Don't Sweat the Small Stuff, by Richard Carlson, Ph.D. Hyperion, 1997.
The Four Agreements, by Don Miguel Ruiz. Amber-Allen Publishing,
  1997.
Life's Little Instruction Book, by H. Jackson Brown, Jr. Rutledge Hill
  Press, 1991.
The Precious Present, by Spencer Johnson, M.D. Doubleday, 1984.
The Road Less Traveled, by M. Scott Peck. Touchstone Books, 1978.

HEALTH

The Big Book, by Bill Wilson (AA Basic Text), Alcoholics Anonymous World Services Publication (4th ed), 2001.
Creating Health, by Deepak Chopra, M.D., Houghton Mifflin, 1991.
The New Our Bodies, Ourselves, Boston Women's Health Book Collective. Touchstone Books, 1992.

FINANCES

Let's Talk About Money, by Barry Spilchuk. Let's Talk, 2001.
The Richest Man in Babylon, by George S. Clason. Plume, 1955.
Spiritual Economics, by Eric Butterworth. Unity Books, 1998.

CHOICES

Empowering Women, by Louise Hay. Hay House, 1997.

Lessons in Living, by Susan Taylor. Anchor Books, 1995.

Life Makeovers, by Cheryl Richardson. Broadway Books, 2000.

Life Strategies, by Phillip McGraw, Ph.D. Hyperion Press, 1999.

Nathan, by Jacqueline L. Clarke. Matou Communications, 1998.

LOVE

The Healing of America, by Marianne Williamson. Simon & Schuster, 1997.

No Less Than Greatness: Finding Perfect Love in Imperfect Relationships, by Mary Manin Morrissey. Bantam Books, 2001.

Prospering Power of Love, by Catherine Ponder. De Vorss Publications, 1983.

Real Moments, by Barbara DeAngelis, Ph.D. Dell Publishing, 1994.

A Return to Love, by Marianne Williamson. HarperCollins, 1996.

Worthy of Love, by Karen Casey. Harper & Row, 1985.

MENTORS AND ANGELS

Angel Voices, by Karen Goldman. Simon & Schuster, 1993.

A Grateful Heart, edited by M. J. Ryan. Conari Press, 1994.

Women Make the Best Friends, by Lois Wyse. Simon & Schuster, 1995.

GIVING

Chicken Soup for the Soul, by Jack Canfield, Mark Victor Hansen, and Patty Hansen. Health Communications, 1996.

40-Day Mind Fast, Soul Feast, by Dr. Michael Beckwith. Agape Publishing, 2000.

The Generosity Factor, by Ken Blanchard. Zondervan Publishing, 2002.

Seven Spiritual Laws of Success, by Deepak Chopra, M.D. Amber-Allen Publishing, 1994.

As Bill Sees It, by Bill Wilson. Alcoholics Anonymous World Services Publications, 1967.

The Infinite Way, by Joel Goldsmith. De Vorss & Company, 1956.

The Science of Mind, by Ernest Holmes. G. P. Putnam's Sons (50th anniversary ed.), 1988.

This Thing Called Life, Ernest Holmes. Tarcher/Putnam Publishers, 1997.

This Thing Called You, by Ernest Holmes. Tarcher/Putnam Publishers, 1997.

Until Today, by Iyanla Vanzant. Fireside Books, 2000.

You Are Always Your Own Experience, by Tom Johnson. Los Arboles Publications, 1995.

Magazine Web Sites

Black Enterprise: www.blackenterprise.com

Essence: www.essence.com

Fast Company: www.fastcompany.com

Forbes: www.forbes.com

Fortune: www.fortune.com

GQ: www.gq.com

O magazine: www.oprah.com/omagazine

Wired: www.wired.com

Worth: www.worth.com

Associations and Organizations

AIDS Hotline: (800) 342–2437

AIDS Quilt Project: (800) 872–6263

Alanon: www.al-anon-alateen.org

Alcoholics Anonymous: www.alcoholics-anonymous.org

Children with AIDS: (800) 866–AIDS

Covenant House: www.covenanthouse.org

Literacy Volunteers of America: www.literacyvolunteers.org

Make a Wish Foundation: www.wish.org

National Committee for Prevention of Child Abuse: (312) 663–3520

National Speakers Association: www.nsaspeaker.org

Optimum Health Institute: www.optimumhealthinstitute.com

Rancho la Puerta: www.rancholapuerta.com

Rotary International: www.rotary.org

Weight Watchers: www.weightwatchers.com

The
Conscience
of the
Constitution

TIMOTHY SANDEFUR

The
Conscience
of the
Constitution

THE DECLARATION
OF INDEPENDENCE AND
THE RIGHT TO LIBERTY

CATO
INSTITUTE
WASHINGTON, D.C.

Library of Congress Cataloging-in-Publication Data

Sandefur, Timothy.
    The conscience of the Constitution: the Declaration of Independence and the
right to liberty / Timothy Sandefur.
        pages cm
    Includes bibliographical references and index.
    ISBN 1-939709-03-2 (hardback : alk. paper)
        1. Civil rights--United States. 2. Due process of law--United States.
    3. Political questions and judicial power--United States. 4. Liberty--Philosophy.
    I. Title.

    KF4749.S26 2014
    342.7308'5--dc23

                                                                    2013032221

Cover design by Jon Meyers.

Printed in the United States of America.

CATO INSTITUTE
1000 Massachusetts Ave., N.W.
Washington, D.C. 20001
www.cato.org

Dedication

To Christina

Contents

Acknowledgments

My thanks to Roger Pilon, Deborah J. La Fetra, and Christina Sandefur, who offered many detailed and thought-provoking suggestions on the manuscript. Portions of these chapters are based on material that appeared in *Cato Unbound*; the *Chapman Law Review*; the *Harvard Journal of Law and Public Policy*; the *Journal of Law & Politics*; the *New York University Journal of Law & Liberty*; the *Notre Dame Journal of Law, Ethics, & Public Policy*; and *Reason Papers*, and are used with permission. My thanks also to Samantha Dravis, Daniel A. Himebaugh, David B. Kopel, Trevor Burrus, Jason Kuznicki, Tibor R. Machan, R. S. Radford, and Ilya Shapiro. This book is partly the result of more than a decade of work with the Pacific Legal Foundation, for which I am immensely grateful. But the opinions expressed herein are not necessarily those of the foundation, its staff, supporters, or clients.

Introduction

American constitutional history has always hovered in the mutual resistance of two principles: the right of each individual to be free, and the power of the majority to make rules. The dynamic tension of these two ideas has generated some of our most persistent and complicated debates. Yet they are not just forces moving in opposite directions. Rightly understood, liberty and order are profoundly interrelated: without order, liberty is not actually liberty, but a chaos in which every person is vulnerable to being violated and controlled by others: "For who could be free," asked John Locke, "when every other Man's Humour might domineer over him?"[1] On the other hand, order without liberty is not really order at all; it is a terrifying void in which the will of the ruler becomes the ultimate reality, and the citizen must stand constantly on guard for shifts in the ruler's mood. When the relationship between liberty and order is perverted, the entire political system can be thrown out of sync, resulting in abuses of power that undermine the legitimacy of government itself. In 1864, Abraham Lincoln articulated this point with a typically well-chosen metaphor:

> We all declare for liberty; but in using the same *word* we do not all mean the same *thing*. With some the word liberty may mean for each man to do as he pleases with himself, and the product of his labor; while with others the same word may mean for some men to do as they please with other men, and the product of other men's labor. Here are two, not only different, but incompatible things, called by the same name—liberty. . . . The shepherd drives the wolf from the sheep's throat, for which the sheep thanks the shepherd as a liberator, while the wolf denounces him for the same act as the destroyer of liberty. . . . Plainly the sheep and the wolf are not agreed upon a definition of the word liberty.[2]

Lincoln understood that while the power to make rules is important, it is not the most basic principle of our constitutional system.

1

The wolf is wrong to imagine that he has a fundamental right to rule others, or that the sheep's rights are simply whatever the wolf decides to allow. America's constitutional order is premised on the opposite principle: on the basic right of each person to be free. People are born with liberty; their rights are not privileges that government gives to them as it pleases. Legitimate government is based on, and bound by, their rights, and nobody—no king, no legislature, no democratic majority—has any basic entitlement to control them. Freedom is the starting point of politics; government's powers are secondary and derivative, and therefore limited.

That principle—the primacy of liberty—was most eloquently expressed in the Declaration of Independence. That document, which created the United States as a political unit and defines the terms of its sovereignty, is the light by which we must guide our understanding of our political and legal institutions. More than a merely rhetorical statement, the Declaration sets the framework for reading our fundamental law. It is, in short, the conscience of the Constitution. Together, the Declaration and the Constitution hold that all people are naturally born free, and may use their freedom to create a political and legal order that respects and protects their rights. But because government can be perverted and endanger liberty, the people must take care to design it in such a way that it is both strong enough to secure their freedom, and limited so as not to threaten that freedom. Liberty is the goal at which democracy aims, not the other way around.

Nevertheless, people often misconstrue the relationship between liberty and order, attempting to elevate "democratic" power above the individual rights it is supposed to protect, or to assert that the majority has some fundamental right to rule. The most obvious example of this perverse understanding of political order is slavery. Nineteenth-century defenders of slavery and states' rights rejected the Declaration's principles, and advocated instead what Lincoln called the wolf's notion that political power is primary, and freedom only a secondary privilege conferred by society. "It is a great and dangerous error to suppose that all people are equally entitled to liberty," wrote the champion of this "States' Rights" school, John C. Calhoun. Freedom, he said, "is a reward to be earned, not a blessing to be gratuitously lavished on all alike—a reward reserved for the intelligent, the patriotic, the virtuous and deserving."[3]

The collision of this wolfish doctrine with the nation's founding principles of equality and liberty put America on the path to civil war; the nation could not permanently endure while divided over such a basic matter. In the years leading up to that war, anti-slavery leaders who remained faithful to the Declaration's principles developed a constitutional interpretation that would counter that argument and give real effect to the primacy of liberty. These men— including Congressman and former president John Quincy Adams, Senator Charles Sumner, Representative John Bingham, future chief justice Salmon P. Chase, and former slave Frederick Douglass—laid the groundwork for the great constitutional revolution that the war ushered in. When peace came, they sought to ensure that the primacy of liberty would be permanently enshrined in the nation's fundamental law. They drafted the Fourteenth Amendment to re-dedicate the nation to the ideas of the Declaration.

But new challenges soon arose—first with the Supreme Court's shocking refusal to enforce one of the central guarantees of that amendment, and then, in the 20th century, when new political theories emerged that once again upended the relationship of liberty to order. Led by Progressive Era–thinkers such as Oliver Wendell Holmes, John Dewey, and Louis Brandeis, that effort was so successful that today the leaders of political and legal opinion generally hold that order comes before liberty, and that democratic rule is the basic premise of our institutions, with individual freedoms regarded essentially as privileges given to people by government. Today's debates over the perceived danger of judicial activism, or over legal theories like substantive due process, often take for granted this modern wolf's conception of the relationship of liberty to order.

This book is an attempt to revive the conscience of the Constitution. Chapter 1 looks at the Declaration of Independence—source and charter of our nationhood, which established the centrality of liberty to our constitutional order—and at how Progressive intellectuals reversed its principles to prioritize democracy over liberty. The Declaration sets forth not just general aspirations but a logical argument about the relationship of government to the governed. And because it is part of our fundamental law, it gives us a guide for understanding and interpreting the Constitution. But today, intellectual leaders mainly reject its propositions about natural rights, arguing instead that rights are only privileged spaces of autonomy that the government gives to people whenever doing so serves government's needs. This inversion warps our understanding of the Constitution and leads to absurd and dangerous consequences.

Chapter 2 explores how the Fourteenth Amendment was meant to recommit the United States to the Declaration's principles and how the Supreme Court's decision in the 1873 *Slaughter-House Cases* hampered that effort. In Chapter 3, we look at substantive due process—the controversial legal doctrine that has played a leading role in protecting individual rights against state interference. Although condemned by both left and right, that theory is a legitimate—even crucial—element of our constitutional law, as a protection against government arbitrariness. Finally, Chapter 4 examines the ongoing debate about "judicial activism"—the charge that our democracy is being sabotaged by unelected judges who ought to be more deferential toward legislatures and less inclined to pronounce laws unconstitutional. In fact, a vigorous, independent judiciary is essential for a legal order that is dedicated, as ours is, to securing individual rights.

In short, this book examines what Supreme Court Justice Benjamin Cardozo called our system of "ordered liberty."[4] That system saw the relationship between order and liberty in a particular way: liberty comes first, and order arises from it. We have gone astray in our constitutional understanding because we have upended that relationship. Lawyers, judges, law professors, political leaders, and commentators largely believe that the power of government, or of the democratic majority, is primary and that the freedom of the individual is only secondary. The growth of government power at the expense of individual rights—the abuse of eminent domain, the censorship of speech, the exploitation of entrepreneurs through licensing laws and similar regulations, intrusions on rights of personal privacy and freedom of choice—all have their origin in this basic reversal of priorities. To secure again the blessings of individual freedom, we must restore the primacy of liberty and heed once more the conscience of the Constitution.

1. Democracy and Freedom

When Supreme Court Justice Stephen Breyer was asked in a 2006 interview what he thought was the most important part of the United States Constitution, his answer was simple: "Democracy."[1] This surely struck many as unremarkable, even as clichéd. But it is curious when we recollect that the word democracy is nowhere to be found in either the Constitution or the Declaration of Independence.

On the contrary, the Founders had different priorities. In the very first sentence of the Constitution, they pronounced unambiguously that liberty is a "blessing." They did not say the same about democracy. The Constitution they wrote imposes manifold limits on the power of the majority, some quite severe: two separate houses must pass a bill; some bills must get a supermajority vote; the president can veto legislation; only certain subjects can be addressed by Congress. The Framers saw majority rule as a useful but dangerous device, to be employed sparingly in order to protect freedom.

It is now commonplace to attribute the Founders' skepticism toward democracy to their elite biases. Their motives, we are told, were corrupt and personal, or their political understanding was limited by the times and by their class parochialism; the Founders did not appreciate, as we moderns do, the self-evident legitimacy of democratic rule. But this is a myth, formulated in the early 20th century, when Progressives were in the process of radically transforming American institutions.[2] Foremost among their aims was to reverse America's constitutional priorities, making *democracy* primary and *liberty* secondary in American law. They were largely successful in that effort. In what can only be called a complete reversal of the Founders' perspective, judges, lawyers, political scientists, politicians, and journalists today generally see democracy as the *source* of liberty, and hold that the most basic principle of our Constitution is not that each person deserves to be free, but that we all have a right, collectively, to govern each other. The "right to rule" now comes first—the freedom of the individual second. This is what Lincoln called the wolf's understanding of liberty: that those with power—whether they be a democratic majority or a legislature or a regulatory agency—have a basic right to do as they please with other people and the product of their labor.

For many on both left and right today, this is a basic assumption. Consider Cass Sunstein, a liberal law professor at the University of Chicago who served in a prominent regulatory post in the Obama administration. In many books and articles over the years, he has argued that individual rights are, at bottom, only privileges given to us by the government.[3] Property rights and freedom of speech, he contends, are simply spaces of privacy that the state has chosen to carve out and protect. Political leaders could just as well decide tomorrow to implement some different system of rights and privileges, or to abolish or rearrange those rights and privileges. A newcomer might be surprised to discover that the same argument was endorsed by the conservative judge Robert Bork in his book *The Tempting of America*. Bork assailed "[t]he attempt to define individual liberties by abstract moral philosophy," arguing that "our freedoms" (Bork always used the plural) "depend upon their acceptance by the American people."[4] And the majority is not bound by any principles when it decides whether to create such rights and privileges.[5]

Bork's and Sunstein's view of the nature of individual rights—a view that is today called "positivism"—is the opposite of the classical liberalism of America's Founders, who believed individual rights were primary and that government power was only secondary and derivative. To the Founding Fathers, individual freedom was the essential starting point for any proper understanding of government, which in their view was only deputized or hired by the people for the purpose of protecting that freedom. Government was therefore justified by the same principle by which it was limited: the consent of the governed gives government legitimacy, but the people's power to consent is itself limited. Because people have no right to commit unjust acts, they may not ask government to commit unjust acts on their behalf, or excuse such violations by appealing to the people's consent. "[T]he Sovereignty of the Society as vested in & exerciseable by the majority," wrote James Madison, "may do any thing that could be *rightfully* done, by the unanimous concurrence of the members," but "the reserved rights of individuals (of conscience for example), in becoming parties to the original compact" are "beyond the legitimate reach of Sovereignty."[6] In other words, people are born with rights, and then delegate certain powers to government—not the other way around. Because rulers—whether kings, presidents, legislatures, or voting majorities—derive their authority from the consent of people who are entitled to freedom, that authority is limited. Freedom is more basic than government power, and it sets the terms that rulers must respect.

This principle was well understood by the Founding Fathers. In 1768, Boston patriots, led by Samuel Adams, wrote that "the supreme Legislative derives its Power & Authority from the Constitution, [so] it cannot overleap the Bounds of it without destroying its own foundation. . . . [T]he Constitution ascertains & limits both Sovereignty and allegiance."[7] In the summer of 1776, the Virginia Declaration of Rights proclaimed that "all men are by nature equally free and independent, and have certain inherent rights, of which, when they enter into a state of society, they cannot, by any compact, deprive or divest their posterity"; that all government powers are "derived from the people"; and that government officials are the people's "trustees and servants, and at all times amenable to them."[8] Weeks later, the Continental Congress boiled this argument down to an elegant expression in the Declaration of Independence: all men are created equal, with certain inalienable rights, and governments are instituted to secure those rights. Liberty is the source of, the justification for, and the protection against political rule.

Today, we are prone to read the Declaration as political rhetoric or a general pronouncement of aspirations. But it is more: it is a legal document—a part of the nation's organic law and the inspiration for America's Constitution. The Declaration helps make constitutional priorities clear—that rights come first and government power only second—and thus it anchors our legal and political system on a firm philosophical ground.

Equality, Liberty, Consent

The foundation begins with the Declaration's premise that all men are created equal. This obviously does not mean that they enjoy equal endowments but rather that the starting point for political analysis is that no person is fundamentally entitled to rule another. Normal, mature adults are ultimately responsible for their own survival and flourishing: our actions typically depend on our own choices, which is why we are rightly praised or blamed for our voluntary decisions. Although others may at times assist us in achieving our goals, they can neither fully assume responsibility for our choices, nor experience the consequences, good or bad, as directly as we ourselves can. We cannot absolve ourselves of responsibility for our actions by becoming instruments of some other person. In everything we do, we retain at least *some* element of responsibility, even when acting on behalf of another, and many things are simply nondelegable. No other person can eat for us, or learn for us, or believe for us, for instance. Thus, we cannot entirely alienate either our capacity or our responsibility for free, independent choice. It is this quality of indefeasible personal responsibility—of rule over ourselves—that the Declaration refers to when it speaks of all people being created equally free and of our basic rights being inalienable. Shortly before his death, Jefferson explained the connection between equality and liberty when he wrote that "the mass of mankind has not been born with saddles on their backs, nor a favored few booted and spurred, ready to ride them legitimately, by the grace of God."[9]

Contrary to what is often claimed, the argument for individual liberty does *not* require one to adopt an optimistic view of human nature—on the contrary, if one believes that people are too ignorant, careless, or corrupt to make good decisions in their *own* lives, that is all the more reason not to trust them with power over others.[10] Due to what social scientists call the "principal-agent problem," whenever one person purports to act on another's behalf, that person—subject to normal human frailties and temptations—is liable to make mistakes, or to abuse that trust. Yielding our self-responsibility to another is therefore a dangerous proposition. Whether one has an optimistic or pessimistic view of human nature, the conclusion is the same. Each of us is rightly entitled to run his own life. No other person is better suited than oneself to know one's needs and priorities, and nobody else can be trusted to run our lives for us. (This is not entirely true of, say, parents and children: parents are the obvious rulers of minor children because parents have the experience, knowledge, and skills that children lack, and upon which children must depend for survival. But even that rule is a limited one—parents do not *own*, and thus are not free to abuse, their children.[11])

It is unfortunate that by using the plural word "rights," the Declaration leads some readers to imagine freedom as broken up into discrete acts, each of which a person may have the particular right to undertake: the right to speak, the right to own property, and so forth. But the Declaration goes on to describe human rights as including "life, liberty, and the pursuit of happiness"—that is, an indefinite range of freedom, rather than a list of specific liberties. Liberty does not come in discrete quanta; it is a general absence of interference. It is, in Jefferson's words, "unobstructed action according to our will, within the limits drawn around us by the equal rights of others."[12]

If no person is *entitled* to rule another, then those who would impose rules on others must justify their doing so; they cannot appeal to "divine right" or to any inherent right to command. They must obtain some kind of consent from the governed, as the Declaration says—perhaps not actual consent in each instance, but something like it. So long as the government follows the predetermined rules, and respects the people's right to change their government, and so long as the people actually do choose to abide by its rule, then the government can claim to be justified by this tacit consent. This idea is problematic, and people have debated it for centuries.[13] But such discussions tend to obscure the most important reasons for the consent requirement. First, by likening the people's acceptance of the ruler's authority to an agreement, the classical liberal argument is meant to draw attention to the people's right *not* to consent—that is, the analogy of government to a contract is designed to emphasize that people are fundamentally free, and that rulers possess only delegated authority as servants, not masters. If the relationship between the ruler and the ruled is something like a consensual agreement or contract, then the ruler cannot enforce his mere whims. Instead, he must give, or at least be able to give, reasonable justifications for his actions, reasons sufficient to convince a citizen that the ruler is acting within his delegated authority.

Second, if government is justified by something like consent, then it is simultaneously justified *and limited.* Just as an employer cannot rightfully command an employee to commit a crime, so the citizen cannot delegate to the ruler the power to commit an injustice. The principle of consent inherently restricts government: the ruler can tell the citizen, "I did this because in some sense you told me

I could," but the citizen can answer, "I didn't tell you to do that," or even "I *could not have* told you to do that, because I had no right to do it myself, and hence no right to ask you." In descriptions of classical liberalism, consent is often treated as some etiological myth intended to rationalize the state. But the consent analogy is far richer: instead of seeing government and individual rights as wholly distinct realms, it accounts for government's existence and legitimacy in the moral vocabulary of the rights of individuals. The same arguments by which we know that we have the right to create a government also erect a fence around government that protects us from it. As Jefferson said, "the people in mass . . . are inherently independent of all *but moral* law."[14] Or, in the words of the Declaration, government may do "all other Acts and Things which Independent States may *of right* do"—not everything, but only those things that states may do *of right*. Political authority is justified only within the realm of legitimacy established by justice.[15]

The Constitution reflects the same understanding. Nowhere does it take the wolf's view that the majority has a preeminent right to govern. Rather, its language consistently reflects the primacy of liberty and the government's obligation to explain and justify any limits on individual freedom. The Constitution promises to "secure" liberty—not create it. It provides that no laws shall be passed "impairing" contractual agreements, that Congress shall have no power to "abridge" the freedom of speech or to "violate" the people's "right" against unreasonable searches, and so forth. Most important of all, the Ninth Amendment provides that the mere fact that some rights are specified in the Constitution must not be interpreted as meaning that people have no other rights. As Professor Randy Barnett, the nation's leading authority on the Ninth Amendment, has observed, this idea would make no sense to one who assumes that government has a fundamental entitlement to rule; on the contrary, the fact that individual rights are not, and cannot be, exhaustively listed indicates that freedom is the general rule, and government restrictions are the exceptions to that rule that must be justified.[16] To presume that government has a primary right to command would mean that a person must articulate and justify the existence of his right to engage in every specific act he proposes to undertake. "Enumerate all the rights of men!" said James Wilson during a debate over ratifying the Constitution. "I am sure, sir, that no gentleman in the late Convention would have attempted such a thing."[17] On the contrary, the Framers expected government, and not the individual, to account for its acts. Even the requirement that a bill must receive a majority vote in both houses before it can become law makes sense only if the Constitution's authors intended a presumption in favor of liberty, with restrictions only permitted for good reasons.

The Innovation of the Declaration

The Declaration of Independence marked an important innovation in how Americans thought about their freedom. Until the Continental Congress issued the document in July 1776, arguments about British policies in North America had focused primarily on the colonists' traditional rights as Englishmen, rights derived from the British constitution and English common law. But with the Declaration, the colonists announced that they were no longer Englishmen. While American lawyers, judges, and politicians would continue to cherish the heritage of the common law and rely on its precedents, the Declaration cut Americans loose and forfeited claims to "the rights of Englishmen" in exchange for arguments based on the rights of all mankind.

Nowhere is that innovation clearer than in the Founders' transition from a belief in religious *toleration* to a belief in religious *liberty*. Religious *toleration* had long been a feature of British institutions; in the 1689 Act of Toleration, for instance, Parliament allowed religious freedom to Protestants who refused to join the Church of England so long as they pledged oaths to the crown and rejected the Catholic doctrine of transubstantiation. Later laws even made Protestants who refused to join the Church of England eligible to hold public office. The jurist Sir William Blackstone, whose four-volume *Commentaries on the Laws of England* had a profound influence on American law, admired his country's "just and christian [*sic*] indulgence" toward nonconformists, and even hoped that someday the proscriptions against Catholics would be lifted.[18] But as Americans came to reject allegiance to the British constitution, they also questioned the basis of this toleration.

Toleration is a privilege accorded to an inferior. It is, wrote Thomas Paine, only a "counterfeit" of freedom, not the opposite of intolerance. Both tolerance and intolerance "are despotisms," he argued. "The one assumes to itself the right of withholding liberty of conscience, and the other of granting it."[19] James Madison and Thomas Jefferson, too, saw freedom of religion not as a mere matter of government favor but as a natural right to which all people are entitled. In 1775, when Virginia was preparing a bill of rights, the brash 24-year-old Madison served on the drafting committee alongside the patriarch George Mason, and he successfully urged the older man to eliminate the word "toleration" from the draft and replace it with "the free exercise of religion, according to the dictates of conscience." This substitution, Madison later wrote, was significant because it "declared the freedom of conscience to be a *natural* and absolute right."[20] Jefferson, too, rejected the argument that government merely tolerated religious diversity, and, only months after completing the Declaration, drafted a Statute for Religious Freedom for his home state that overthrew the toleration principle. As he explained in his book *Notes on the State of Virginia*, religious liberty was not a matter of government indulging differences that it could not extinguish. Rather, religious freedom is a natural right over which government has no legitimate claim in the first place. "[O]ur rulers can have authority over such natural rights only as we have submitted to them," he wrote, but "[t]he rights of conscience we never submitted, we could not submit."[21]

Patrick Henry and other conservatives opposed Jefferson's efforts, believing that government must superintend the people's religious views in order to "correct the morals of men, restrain their vices, and preserve the peace of society."[22] But in Jefferson's view, the role of government was not to restrain vice, but simply to protect individual rights and allow people to run their own lives. "The legitimate powers of government extend to such acts only as are injurious to others. But it does me no injury for my neighbour to say there are twenty gods, or no god. It neither picks my pocket nor breaks my leg."[23] Obviously, anyone who *did* break another person's leg or steal his money should be prosecuted—but there was no crime in merely believing or disbelieving a religious creed. If one's beliefs are false, one will suffer for that mistake without any need for government intercession. Moreover, officials entrusted with the power to combat vice were more likely to abuse that power than to succeed in making people good. Already the church was being corrupted by political manipulators, Jefferson wrote, and if the state were to prohibit religious differences, these corruptions would be "protected, and new ones encouraged." Government had performed poorly when overseeing other areas of life, often enforcing foolish restrictions and refusing to permit healthy innovations. "Galileo was sent to the inquisition for affirming that the earth was a sphere: the government had declared it to be as flat as a trencher, and Galileo was obliged to abjure his error. This error however at length prevailed, [and] the earth became a globe."[24]

Finally, in 1786, Jefferson and Madison overcame Henry's obstructions, and Virginia adopted the Statute for Religious Freedom. It rejected the toleration model entirely and enacted instead the clear pronouncements of natural rights. "Almighty God hath created the mind free," it began. While the government may "interfere" when necessary to preserve "peace and good order" against "overt acts" of lawbreaking, it could have no legitimate power to intrude into private decisions "on supposition of their ill tendency." That would obliterate "all religious liberty" because government officials would "make [their] own opinions the rule of judgment."[25] Government existed to protect individual rights, not to police private behavior and beliefs, and allowing it power over the latter would endanger the liberty it was supposed to secure.

The overthrow of toleration and its replacement with religious liberty signaled a crucial change in how Americans viewed their rights.[26] Although government establishments of religion would linger in the United States for decades afterwards, Americans came to agree that each person has a basic right to form his own religious beliefs and to practice according to his conscience without being dictated to by political leaders. This victory was only one manifestation of a more profound departure from the monarchical idea that rights are privileges given out by rulers. Like John Locke, the Founders saw that government exists to protect the rights of individuals, not to oversee society in general, or to extend and withdraw privileges to the people as it sees fit. "In Europe," wrote Madison, "charters of liberty have been granted by power. America has set the example . . . of charters of power granted by liberty."[27]

Why the Declaration Is Law

Are the Declaration's philosophical pronouncements about natural rights and human nature still relevant? This may seem a

13

strange question, since the Declaration plays such a prominent role in American life. Yet it is frequently treated with disrespect in certain intellectual circles today. On the left, it is seen as an exercise in hypocritical, self-righteous fraud. Some, including even Supreme Court Justice Thurgood Marshall,[28] have agreed with Chief Justice Roger Taney's dreadful assertion in *Dred Scott v. Sandford*[29] that the Declaration really only meant that *white* men are entitled to liberty. "[E]ven by its own language," wrote the fashionable radical Howard Zinn, the Declaration "was limited to life, liberty, and happiness for white males."[30] The Founders' references to self-evident truths, he claimed, were only a ruse to manipulate the working classes into joining a struggle that was really about protecting the privileges of elites.[31] (One might have thought the Founders would have avoided the inflammatory language of equality and liberty if this was their goal, but since Zinn built his class-warfare interpretation on the blueprint of a conspiracy theory, he had a ready answer: the Founders were just clever enough to create a foolproof disguise.)

Meanwhile, on the right, conservatives regard the Declaration with suspicion because natural rights provide a warrant for radical efforts to reform or overthrow traditional social structures. If conservatism is an "anti-ideology" that prizes traditional hierarchy and social stability,[32] it is little wonder that the Declaration's doctrines of universal law and the right to rebel even against longstanding institutions would make conservatives squirm. Prominent figures such as Russell Kirk and Irving Kristol downplayed or denounced the Declaration, calling it an empty rhetorical exercise or a ploy to lure the French into supporting the American army.[33] (In reality, the Revolutionary generation took the Declaration's abstractions quite seriously, and notwithstanding their compromises over slavery and women's rights, made enormous strides in abolishing class hierarchy and privilege.[34])

Contempt for the Declaration would be less shocking if it were only an advertising poster, or a campaign speech, or the manifesto of a defunct political party. But the Declaration is more than that. It appears at the front of our law books, at volume one, page one, of the United States *Statutes at Large*, and at the head of the United States Code.[35] As a resolution approved unanimously by the Continental Congress, a body whose other resolutions have never been regarded as anything less than law,[36] the Declaration obviously

14

had legal consequences, separating the United States' legal system from that of Great Britain. American law still takes July 4, 1776, as the starting point of the nation's political autonomy. Lawyers of the Founding Era, such as Thomas Jefferson, James Wilson, and others regarded the Declaration as law—"the fundamental act of union of these States," Jefferson called it[37]—as did later lawyers and government officials, including Abraham Lincoln. In fact, beginning with Nevada in 1864—the first state admitted after the Southern states seceded—every new state has been required, as a condition of admission into the union, to draw up a constitution consistent not only with the federal Constitution but also with the Declaration of Independence.[38] It is hard to understand why we would deny the Declaration standing as law.

Nevertheless, modern leaders of political and legal opinion, including such professed constitutional "originalists" as Justice Antonin Scalia, regard it as something less. Indeed, Scalia has said that the Declaration "is not part of our law" at all, only a political statement, not particularly relevant when interpreting the Constitution.[39] In a 2000 case challenging a state law that forced unwilling parents to allow grandparents and others visitation rights with their children, the Supreme Court declared that the parents' right to direct the upbringing of their children is one of the fundamental rights that the Constitution protects; Justice Scalia disagreed, declaring that while that right may be among those the Declaration calls inalienable, "the Declaration of Independence . . . is not a legal prescription conferring powers upon the courts." Judges must not "deny legal effect to laws that (in my view) infringe upon what is (in my view) [an] unenumerated right."[40]

Elsewhere, Scalia has made clear his disdain for the broader principles of the Declaration. In a dissenting opinion rejecting First Amendment protection for nude dancing, he derided the "Thoreauvian 'you-may-do-what-you-like-so-long-as-it-does-not-injure-someone-else' beau ideal," because there was "no basis for thinking that our society has ever shared" that principle, "much less for thinking that it was written into the Constitution."[41] Yet the Declaration of Independence *does* incorporate this ideal by providing that government exists to secure the freedom to which every person is naturally entitled—as does the Constitution, with its reference to the rights of "liberty" and to the "other rights

15

retained by the people."[42] The primacy of liberty means that the majority has no preeminent right to rule; it must justify any limits it imposes on individual freedom by reference to some genuine public principle, such as preventing people from harming one another. If the majority fails to make that justification, it has no grounds to complain when courts invalidate restrictions on freedom. By giving government power to secure individual rights, and requiring it to respect the more basic liberty of individuals, the Constitution does indeed implement the rule that one may act as one pleases so long as one does not hurt others. In the traditional Latin phrase, *sic utere tuo ut alienum non laedas*—one may do what one wishes if one harms no other person.

Of course, Scalia is right that the Declaration is not a detailed framework of government in the same way that the Constitution is, and it would do little to resolve most ordinary legal cases. But it *is* a part of our organic constitution—that is, one of the fundamental laws that constitutes our legal order and makes the American people a political unit. Like any written document, its meaning has sometimes been misrepresented. But properly understood, the Declaration instructs our political and legal institutions, and it ought to guide courts interpreting our basic law. Some judges have regarded it as such. Consider *Grutter v. Bollinger*, the 2003 case upholding the constitutionality of race-based admissions policies at the University of Michigan Law School. There, Justice Scalia joined Justice Clarence Thomas in denouncing the policy as a violation of the Fourteenth Amendment. But Scalia made a point of refusing to sign on to the short concluding paragraph of Thomas's dissenting opinion. That was the paragraph in which Thomas supported his denunciation of government racial discrimination by invoking "the principle of equality embodied in the Declaration of Independence."[43]

Does It Make Any Difference?

Why should it matter whether we regard the Declaration as part of our law? It matters for two reasons. First, judges and lawyers tend to ignore whatever falls outside the category of law. After all, the practice of law depends on honoring the difference between those pronouncements entitled to obedience and those that are not, and much of a lawyer's time is spent figuring out which documents are so entitled, and why. Reflexively dismissing the Declaration as "not law" is a crude way of depriving it—and the principles it articulates—of respect in constitutional discourse. And this leads to the second reason why it makes a difference. The Declaration helps to orient our political and legal order and to coordinate the constitutional scheme in terms of justice. If we deem it out of bounds, our understanding of the Constitution itself may be distorted.

Today, the legal profession is dominated by adherents to varieties of legal positivism—realists, critical race theorists, postmodernists—who think of law only in terms of power, and of moral principles as disguised power gambits. To these thinkers, the Declaration's principles are simply anathema. To regard it as law would undercut the legitimacy they assume for many of the legal doctrines they favor. If the Declaration—which says that all people have certain rights that no government may legitimately disparage—is a part of our fundamental law, then it would become clear how far beyond the orbit of the Constitution stands the work of such figures as Oliver Wendell Holmes, Robert Bork, or Cass Sunstein.

To emphasize: if the Declaration is a part of our law, it sets forth an explanatory principle for our legal institutions. Obviously, it will not tell us whether, say, the *Miranda* warning is the best way to ensure that a suspect's Fifth Amendment rights are protected, or whether execution by electric chair is cruel and unusual punishment. But it gives us a direction in understanding the limits of government power, and helps us interpret such broad constitutional phrases as "privileges or immunities of citizens of the United States" or "due process of law" or "equal protection of the laws." That the Declaration provides a philosophical framework rather than particular limits on personal behavior or instructions to government agencies does not make it any less a part of our Constitution. Some parts of the Constitution itself are also more like guideposts than specific commands for official enforcement.[44] The Ninth and Tenth Amendments, for example, command nothing—but they serve as guides for understanding the rest of the document. Like them, the Declaration establishes a presumption—a legal pole star for interpreting constitutional language. Chief Justice John Marshall once observed that Congress's authority to pass laws "necessary and proper" for effectuating its powers could not allow legislation inconsistent with "the letter and spirit of the constitution,"[45] and in his recent decision in the case challenging the constitutionality of the

Obama Administration's health insurance legislation, Chief Justice John Roberts reiterated that "laws that undermine the structure of government established by the Constitution" and "reach beyond the natural limit of [Congress's] authority" are not "proper."[46] The Declaration's principles of equality and liberty help judges to understand the spirit of the Constitution, the structure of government it creates, and the "natural limit" of government power, and can therefore guide interpretations of the Necessary and Proper Clause. In short, as Senator Charles Sumner said, the Declaration is "the illuminated initial letter of our history . . . the national heart, the national soul, the national will, the national voice, which must inspire our interpretation of the Constitution, and enter into and diffuse itself through all the national legislation."[47]

It is apt to mention Sumner, the Massachusetts abolitionist whose fiery speeches condemning slavery once provoked a South Carolina congressman to bludgeon him with a cane on the floor of the U.S. Senate. If the Declaration is relevant to any constitutional problem, it is particularly relevant to understanding the great legal achievement of Sumner's generation: the Fourteenth Amendment. Ratified in 1868, that amendment, more than any other federal law, was meant to institutionalize the principles of the Declaration. The grueling civil war that Sumner and his fellow Republicans had just won centered on a controversy over those principles; so, too, during the debates over the writing of the amendment, its advocates repeatedly invoked the Declaration, as when Senator John Sherman told his colleagues that courts interpreting the amendment's Privileges or Immunities Clause should refer to the Declaration of Independence to help define the rights of Americans,[48] or when Senator Luke Poland explained that the amendment would ensure enforcement of "the very spirit of our system of government, the absolute foundation upon which it was established . . . in the Declaration of Independence."[49]

The Declaration sets forth what we may call the *regime philosophy* of the nation. American institutions have a higher calling than those of mere kinship groups or tribes, which are governed by what Alexander Hamilton termed "accident and force."[50] The Constitution makes reference to the Declaration's principles, both explicitly— as in its opening invocation of the "Blessings of Liberty" and "the People of the United States," who make their first appearance as "one People" in the Declaration—and implicitly, as in the Ninth

Amendment's reference to rights "other" than those specified in the Bill of Rights. It is obviously true, as Justice Scalia has said, that the Declaration does not define the powers of federal courts. But when they are called upon to decide whether a person has been deprived of the "privileges or immunities of citizens of the United States," or whether the government has violated the constitutional promise that it will accord people "due process of law," courts should refer to the Declaration's explanation of the nature of rights, and the limits of government legitimacy. It is only a slight exaggeration to say that, as ancient Athens was consecrated to Athena, so the United States is consecrated to the principles enunciated in the Declaration of Independence. Disregarding those principles can sever our understanding of the Constitution from the wider political order of which it is a part.

Modern legal thinkers, pursuing that illusion of objectivity that consists of refusing assent to any moral propositions, often do just this. They endeavor to interpret the law without reference to the ends it aims to achieve, and even claim that the Constitution is compatible with whatever purpose political leaders choose to pursue. Thus, Justice Oliver Wendell Holmes famously said that the Constitution is "not intended to embody a particular economic theory, whether of paternalism and the organic relation of the citizen to the State or of laissez faire. It is made for people of fundamentally differing views."[51] If that is true, then the Constitution presents no obstacle to political movements or government programs that alter the landscape of rights in dramatic and dangerous ways. If the Constitution is made for people who differ on fundamental matters, then those fundamental matters—including rights that the Constitution was written to fortify against political interference—are vulnerable to a political realm that can be irrational and unpredictable, influenced by prejudice, hatred, corruption, or demagoguery. On the other hand, if the Constitution is part of a larger set of principles, then some proposals are out of the question entirely. As Justice Robert Jackson put it, the purpose of the Constitution was to insulate our rights against "the vicissitudes of political controversy."[52]

The Declaration makes clear that government is established to secure those rights. It is an employee, hired to protect the people—like a guard employed to prevent a bank from being robbed. The problem is that the government has such extensive powers that those in charge might pervert it and use it for foolhardy, destructive, or self-interested purposes, just as a bank guard might be tempted to rob the bank himself. This confronts the author of a constitution with a dilemma: in designing a government which is to be administered by fallible human beings, wrote Madison, "the great difficulty lies in this: you must first enable the government to control the governed; and in the next place oblige it to control itself."[53]

Here we see again the importance of respecting the philosophical orientation that the Declaration of Independence provides: the reason for checks and balances within the constitutional order is to ensure that government serves its overall purpose of securing individual rights. If government existed for no purpose at all, or simply to benefit the ruler, there would be no reason to "oblige the government to control itself." The Constitution's careful separation of powers would be pointless. But the Founders understood their purpose well. Madison described the Federalist system as a "compound republic" with the states in tension against the federal government, which would in turn be divided into different branches to provide "a double security" to "the rights of the people"[54]—a deliberate echo of the Declaration's reference to "securing rights." And he made a crucial observation about the connection between liberty and order: "In a society under the forms of which the stronger faction can readily unite and oppress the weaker, anarchy may as truly be said to reign as in a state of nature, where the weaker individual is not secured against the violence of the stronger."[55] A government that enables a single tyrant or a powerful group of influential insiders to exploit power to benefit themselves would expose citizens to the same dangers of violence and oppression that would exist in a country ruled only by warlords and strongmen. In other words, the extremes touch: a world without lawful protection, and a world in which government has become too powerful, both lead to the same evil consequences.

This is not a rhetorical flourish. It is an observation about the rational mechanics of lawful rule, which might be rephrased in economic terms: in a world without regular, enforceable guidelines and institutions to define and enforce private rights (that is, in a state of nature), individual actors will strive to gain as much control over resources as they can.[56] Take, for example, a fish pond.[57] Each will try to hoard access to it, investing heavily in fencing it off and otherwise defending it against rivals, or in discovering ways to confiscate their rivals' gains. Such investments divert attention away from more productive undertakings and are thus economically wasteful.[58] Each person will also tend to overexploit the resource, taking as many fish as possible because they cannot trust that others will not grab the remaining fish. In the absence of any authority to police each person's rights, the race will go to the swift and the battle to the strong. But if the people agree to a system of rules to govern legitimate claims—a contract, a set of *mores*, or a police system that protects every person's right to fish in the pond—each will gain because he can reduce his inefficient investments (in predation or defending against predation) and can instead focus his energies on productive activity. Each fisherman is also less likely to overexploit the resource since the police will guarantee the claims of rivals who are too poor or too weak or otherwise unable to enforce their own claims. Thus, in theory, a common system of rational rules improves economic efficiency by reducing wasteful expenditures in obtaining and defending resources. This is what makes the social compact rational.[59]

But imagine that the rules regulating the fishing pond become so complicated and confusing that they cannot be understood without expensive legal representation, or cannot be understood at all. Now, fishing rights can be obtained only by bribing the officials who guard the fishing hole. Those who are too poor or too weak to enforce their rightful claims are once again barred from access, or are again made vulnerable to predation. A convoluted system of rules riddled with unprincipled exemptions can become so arbitrary that it is as bad as having no meaningful rule at all—or worse. "It will be of little avail to the people that the laws are made by men of their own choice," wrote Madison, "if the laws be so voluminous that they cannot be read, or so incoherent that they cannot be understood; if they be repealed or revised before they are promulgated, or undergo such incessant changes that no man, who knows what the law is to-day, can guess what it will be tomorrow."[60]

Rules that become so complicated essentially transform the pond back into a kind of common resource, to which access is gained not by force but by corruption, cleverness, or arbitrary political influence. This encourages the fishermen to switch their efforts to rent seeking—that is, finding ways to confiscate fish from others, or to

21

fence off their own gains. Although these inefficiencies take the form of lobbying, payoffs, and complicated paperwork, instead of turf wars with weapons, they are in substance the same: rightful claims go unenforced, each actor wastes resources jostling with rivals,[61] and the "the weaker individual is not secured against the violence of the stronger."[62] This is why government must be limited in scope and extent. The more complex and pervasive it gets, the more counterproductive it can become. By reminding us of government's purpose and limits, the Declaration of Independence helps us to keep in mind the reasons for both creating and restricting political authority.

Sneering at the Rights of Man

Attacks on the principles of the Declaration began at an early point in American history. In the four decades before the Civil War, defenders of slavery explicitly rejected it, even calling it, as Senator John Pettit did in 1854, "a self-evident lie."[63] Horrified by this, antislavery politicians rallied to the Declaration. They developed a constitutional interpretation that emphasized liberty and equality, and they denounced slavery as incompatible with the Constitution.[64]

While their arguments seemed extreme at the time, events proved at last that the stop-gaps and compromises by which slavery had been perpetuated could no longer be sustained. That was because neither the Constitution of 1787 nor any other constitution can exist among people of "fundamentally differing views." Like a marriage, a constitution represents a fundamental *agreement* on shared principles, which leaves other, more mundane decisions to be settled through negotiation. A constitution provides a political framework for formulating specific policies, but it is built upon a basic assent to the moral precepts that underlie that framework, and these precepts are not the proper subject of democratic vote. The Constitution's foundation is the Declaration of Independence, and as slavery's defenders were increasingly forced to reject its principles, and to defend racial inequality and hierarchy as good things, they found it increasingly difficult to maintain allegiance to the Constitution.

As we will see, the Union's victory in the Civil War gave antislavery leaders the opportunity to permanently rededicate the Constitution to the Declaration's principles. But their efforts were only partly successful. The reaction against the classical liberal doctrines described in the Declaration, which began before the war and climaxed with the pro-slavery cause, survived the war and exerted a powerful influence on the next generation of intellectuals. In his 1903 book, *A History of American Political Theories,* Charles Edward Merriam, the University of Chicago's first professor of political science, observed that the war's end had *not* meant the triumph of anti-slavery arguments about the basic right to freedom—quite the opposite. "The Abolitionists thought that liberty is the birthright of all men," he wrote, while "defenders of slavery thought it the possession of those only who are fit." Forty years after the Gettysburg Address, Merriam was prepared to say that "[f]rom the standpoint of modern political science the slaveholders were right in declaring that liberty can be given only to those who have political capacity to use it."[65] The profession of political science, he claimed, had "abandoned" the Declaration's premise "that liberty is a natural right," and had come to hold that freedom is created by government as a sort of privilege: "rights are considered to have their source not in nature, but in law."[66]

It seems remarkable that one of the leading saboteurs of the anti-slavery effort to vindicate the nation's commitment to liberty would be Oliver Wendell Holmes, son of a prominent Massachusetts family and an opponent of slavery, who volunteered for Union service in the war and was wounded more than once in that cause. But Holmes's experience in the war taught him not that all people have a right to freedom, but rather that claims about right and wrong are really only illusions.[67] Ethical principles, he believed, are subjective, emotional commitments that cannot be judged right or wrong. Ideas such as justice or moral good are only the expressions of arbitrary personal preferences and are no more rational than a person's preference for one kind of beer over another.[68] The real foundation of all politics is the willingness of people to back up such nonrational personal tastes with physical force. What we call laws or rights are just arbitrary preferences enforced by violence, in just the same way that "a dog will fight for his bone."[69] A constitution is simply an effort to render that process less violent by subjecting the inevitable clashes to majority vote instead of battle. But in the end, politics is just war by other means.

One may observe that Holmes's metaphorical dogs had a better grasp of political philosophy than did Holmes himself. A dog's willingness to fight for its bone is not an arbitrary emotional preference. Dogs value bones not for subjective or conventional reasons but because dogs are mortal beings who live in a world of limited resources and limited time, and, unlike humans, they cannot create wealth. They have good reasons to value bones, and it is natural and rational for them to fight for bones when they must. Indeed, it is *right* for them to do so, since not doing so would presumably lead to starvation and death.[70] Human beings, by contrast, can create wealth, communicate their preferences, negotiate, and make bargains. They have a much different method of survival. But they, too, have a nature, and therefore a natural (i.e., not merely subjective, conventional, or socially constructed) standard of goodness. It is naturally right for them to engage in those behaviors—discovery, creativity, productivity, cooperation—that are appropriate to human flourishing, just as it is naturally right for dogs to act in ways that enable them to flourish.[71]

In his book, *The Common Law*, Holmes used another dog example: "even a dog," he wrote, "distinguishes between being stumbled over and being kicked."[72] But this suggests that the difference between these two things is real—that is, natural—rather than purely conventional, since dogs do not have conventions.[73] And if there is a natural difference between the intentional wrong of kicking and the accidental injury of being tripped over, then why can a human society not recognize other distinctions of justice, as the Declaration does, that are based on the laws of nature and not on mere convention? And since no dog *enjoys* being either kicked or tripped over, and will take steps to avoid both, why can we not extrapolate from this (and from other known facts about dogs) that their aversion to being kicked makes good, objective sense, and that dogs would benefit from rules against kicking them? If we can draw such conclusions about dogs, we should be able to draw similar conclusions about human beings.

In any event, Holmes believed that law is nothing more than the commitment to use force in the service of collective norms, which are merely the subjective preferences of a majority of the people. There are no "transcendental" principles of law, because law "does not exist without some definite authority behind it."[74] To suppose that it has any deeper meaning than the ruler's arbitrary command, he said, is "churning the void in the hope of making cheese."[75] The idea that people have certain rights at all times and in all places is

24

absurd: rights are only what a society's power-wielders choose to allow. "All my life I have sneered at the natural rights of man," he told a friend, and he meant it.[76] His judicial writings were guided by the view that law is only an expression of power in a universe devoid of other meaning.

In one of his most infamous opinions, *Buck v. Bell*, he ruled that states may force mentally "deficient" women to undergo sterilization operations against their will, concluding that "three generations of imbeciles are enough."[77] In *Kawananakoa v. Polybank*, he ruled that a person cannot sue the government because "there can be no legal right as against the authority that makes the law on which the right depends."[78] In another case, *Abrams v. United States*,[79] Holmes wrote a dissenting opinion that many today regard as a classic defense of free speech[80]—indeed, it originated the metaphor of the "marketplace of ideas."[81] But reading the opinion, one soon encounters a chilling line: "Persecution for the expression of opinions seems to me perfectly logical."[82] The only reason we do not persecute people, Holmes went on, is because it is good for *society* to allow debates. Thus, government gives people the privilege of free speech—for its own purposes, not for the individual's purposes—and it can withdraw that privilege when it chooses. And so Holmes also wrote *Shenck v. United States*, upholding the conviction of a man who distributed pamphlets protesting the military draft—an act Holmes likened to falsely yelling fire in a crowded theater.[83]

Here we see in miniature what Holmes and his allies effected on a massive scale in the American constitutional scheme: they reversed the Founders' understanding in which individual rights such as free speech were primary, government regulation was secondary, and government's legitimacy was compared to a baseline of individual freedom. Instead, Holmes and his contemporaries held that government power was primary and was the source, rather than the guardian, of rights; the legitimacy of rights would now be tested in terms of their suitability to the state. Holmes had adopted the wolf's conception of liberty: the basic principle of politics is the right of some people to do as they will with others and with the product of their labors. Indeed, he regarded the Declaration's principle of the primacy of liberty as a mere "shibboleth," writing that "the word 'liberty'" is "perverted" when it is interpreted "to prevent the outcome of a dominant opinion" or when it obstructs the majority's "right" to "embody their opinions in law."[84]

Holmes's rejection of the concept of justice and his enthusiastic attitude toward raw political power may seem stark and cruel—indeed, he seemed to enjoy playing Thrasymachus, the antinomian cynic[85]—but leaders of the legal community today continue to make these arguments, in politer terms. Harvard professor Laurence Tribe argues that, when called upon to decide whether a law unreasonably restricts liberty, judges cannot compare that law to some abstract notion of freedom because there is no such thing: "[T]he law is inevitably embroiled in the dialectical process whereby society is constantly recreating itself,"[86] meaning that there is no "neutral, 'natural' order of things."[87] The "'freedom' of contract and property" is "an illusion."[88] There is no baseline of natural freedom against which political or legal institutions can be contrasted; there is only a fluctuating "dialectical process" in which rules and rights are constantly created and destroyed by the state.

Sunstein, too, views rights as privileges created by the government. During the New Deal, he writes, political thinkers realized that the "private or voluntary sphere" is "actually itself a creation of law, and hardly purely voluntary. When the law of trespass enabled an employer to exclude an employee from 'his' property unless the employee met certain conditions, the law was crucially involved. Without the law of trespass, and accompanying legal rules of contract and tort, the relationship between employers and employees would not be what it now is; indeed, it would be extremely difficult to figure out what that relationship might be, if it would exist in recognizable form at all."[89] Arguing in favor of a "New Deal for free speech," Sunstein believes that "American constitutionalism has failed precisely to the extent that it has not taken the New Deal reformation seriously enough. . . . Instead, we simply assume that government 'intervention,' reflexively understood in a distinctive, pre–New Deal way, is the intrinsic evil to be eradicated through constitutional law."[90]

Contrast this perspective with the logical order described in the Declaration of Independence. There, all people are seen as born equally free, meaning that each is presumptively at liberty to act, until those who would limit a person's freedom give good reasons for such limits. This presumption of liberty is not just a rhetorical device or an arbitrary preference for a convenient starting point in philosophical debates. Rather, it makes clear that those who claim the right to rule others have the burden *themselves* to justify that claim. That is what the right to equal freedom means: just as the person who asserts a claim in any argument has the responsibility to prove that claim, so one cannot be expected to prove he ought to be free. But the positivist view presumes that individuals have no rights until they propose such rights and persuade others to give them such rights. If they can do that, then the government may choose to protect or subsidize realms of individual autonomy—thus giving them "rights" that are really just privileges. "[R]espect for private rights, the private sphere, and limited government should themselves be justified by publicly articulable reasons," writes Sunstein. "In the United States, any particular conception of the private sphere must be defended by substantive argument."[91]

There are serious problems with this theory. First, it reduces all rights to potentially conflicting assertions with no guiding principle for resolving the conflicts that arise. If the state chooses to create one right for me and a different, contradictory right for my neighbor, how is this conflict to be settled? Do we have any right to be treated equally? Not if the state declines to give us that right. And yet the whole purpose of rights, and of law, is to limit the power of the state, at least pursuant to some comprehensible standard that treats like cases alike and allows people to understand and predict how the state will treat them.

Second, it is not clear how one could meet a burden of justifying a right to be free, or even how to describe what that burden of proof really entails. Forcing someone to prove that the government should *not* restrict his freedom means forcing him to prove a negative—a task that is literally impossible because the person must then disprove an infinite series of potential reasons for denying him the right/privilege he seeks.[92] Of course, the state could set some lower standard as sufficient to establish a proposed rights claim, but such a lower standard would then be arbitrary. One can hardly imagine a weaker definition of a right than a privilege that the state gives to citizens for arbitrary and unpredictable reasons.

There are other ways in which the Sunstein-Tribe model collapses into an infinite regress. If a person must prove that he deserves to be free, then that person must first be free to make such a proof. Yet where does he get *this* freedom? The person would then be required to prove that he should have the right to prove the other right, and that would require another level of freedom, which the person must also prove—and so on, calling for an endless series of proofs. This may seem a strange observation, but abolitionists faced this exact problem during the Petition Crisis of the 1830s. For almost a decade, Congressman John Quincy Adams and others were forced to combat the Gag Rule, under which Southern representatives barred Congress from even receiving, let alone considering, petitions against slavery. Adams's heroic struggle against this rule was a fight for the right of *petition*, one step removed from any debate over slavery.[93] He was forced to argue that he should have the right to argue against the "peculiar institution."

What's more, as Tom G. Palmer has observed, if rights are only realms of freedom that the state positively enforces, then there would have to be an endless series of government enforcers. One could have a right not to be tortured by the police, for instance, only if there is a secondary police force charged with enforcing that right. But there must then also be a third set of monitors to ensure that the second set faithfully polices the police, and then another layer of monitors over them. Sunstein's theory would require "an infinite hierarchy of people threatening to punish those lower in the hierarchy. Since there is no infinite hierarchy, we are forced to conclude that [this is] actually . . . an impossibility theorem of rights in the logical form of *modus tollens*: If there are rights, then there must be an infinite hierarchy of power; there is not an infinite hierarchy of power, therefore there are no rights."[94]

In addition, under the positivist view, the state cannot grant individuals any *morally legitimate* rights or privileges. If there is no prepolitical theoretical basis for individual rights, then the legislature cannot give legitimacy to the rights/privileges it hands out: those rights/privileges have no more moral value than a resolution proclaiming Tuesday to be National Bacon Day. Nor can the legislature itself claim legitimacy or justify any demand for respect. According to the social compact tradition articulated in the Declaration of Independence and the Constitution, government is legitimate because the people consent to it, thus agreeing in some sense to respect its determinations. But people can consent only because they have a basic right to decide whether or not to consent, a right that is *not* a mere privilege from the government. One who rejects the existence of prepolitical rights cannot rely on this argument to give legitimacy to the government's decisions any more than a kidnapper might excuse his crime by saying that he has chosen to use violence to make himself the child's guardian. A person who denies that rights preexist the government cannot argue that the rights/privileges the state gives out are entitled to respect without first showing why any of the state's decisions are entitled to respect. If the answer is, as Holmes thought, that the state deserves respect only because it has a military and a police force, or because it is an historical inevitability, as Tribe's reference to the dialectical process implies, then the state-created rights/privileges are not really principles at all. Government could do whatever it pleases, because politics is then basically an act of will, not of reason. This way of seeing things makes it impossible to distinguish free states from tyrannies, just rulers from unjust rulers, or healthy regimes from abusive regimes. In practice, it would mean that whatever political group happens to wield power, by arms or by propaganda, is, ipso facto, legitimate. Yet the whole point of the Declaration and the Constitution was to found a government on something more than accident and force. If rights and political legitimacy are *created* by accident and force, then there is no moral difference between the dictatorship of a military strongman and a free state governed by fair laws; whatever the political authorities choose to call "just" is so, by definition.

This suggests a final problem with the idea that rights are privileges parceled out by the state. If political leaders choose which rights to give citizens, then there must be a caste of leaders who enjoy greater freedom than do the citizens who are the recipients of these "rights." That is, the rulers must stand on a higher plane from which they can hand down judgments about what rights are to be given to or withheld from the people below. In making their decisions, they must have access to principles of justification that are beyond the comprehension of the citizen, or they must enjoy some fundamental, special authority to make those decisions however they wish, an authority that puts them outside the sphere inhabited by the mere citizen. Either way, this conception of rights implies that rulers enjoy a degree of freedom withheld from ordinary people, at least the right to decide when to grant people the requested rights/privileges. The people themselves have no such freedom, since all rights are privileges given by the rulers. So where did the rulers get it? Evidently they gave it to themselves, or they enjoy it by some inherent principle of superiority such as divine right. In other words, they must be a class of Platonic guardians, contrary to the American conception of a government of equal people, by equal people. Despite their appeals to principles of democracy, therefore, Tribe, Sunstein, and their allies end up denying the premise of equality upon which democracy is supposed to rest. Without prepolitical principles to guide the lawmakers' actions, all of the citizens' rights are trumped by the rulers' mere will. And this must mean the rulers are, as Orwell put it, more equal than others. Whatever this theory is, it is not what the Founders envisioned. Nor is it true democratic rule; indeed, it brings to mind the tribulations of those groups—blacks in the 19th century, women in the 20th, gays in the 21st—who have learned through struggle that freedom is not given, only claimed.

The characteristic difference between rights and privileges is that rights are *not* held at the mercy of another person, or of the state. We *deserve* rights; we cannot be made to pay for them, and are not answerable to our neighbors or to the state when we exercise them. But privileges are given to us by one in a superior position, who retains authority to restrict or to eliminate those privileges. One cannot *deserve* a privilege, and one *can* be required to pay for it. To obscure this distinction and contend that rights are permissions issued by the state is to reject the basic proposition of equality articulated in the Declaration, and to presume that some people are fundamentally entitled to decide how much freedom others should enjoy.

What Would It Mean if the State Did Create Freedom?

The danger of confusing the state's protection of prepolitical rights on one hand, with its creation of rights/privileges on the other, becomes clear when we ask whether the state creates, say, a woman's right not to be raped. According to the positivist argument, a woman has no fundamental human right not to be raped; her so-called private or voluntary sphere is only a creation of law, and hardly voluntary. Without the criminal laws against rape, or legal rules relating to marriage, divorce, and child-rearing, and the regulation of contraceptives, maternity care, or abortion, the relationship between men and women would not be what it now is. Indeed, it would be extremely difficult to figure out what that relationship might be, if it would exist in recognizable form at all. If a woman wants the right not to be raped, then according to this argument she must advance and justify that right in a public forum. The state might *give* it to her by promulgating and enforcing rules against rape, but only if the lawmakers—who stand in a superior position to her, not in a position of equality—choose to create such a realm of freedom for her.[95]

This example might appear extreme. But Robert Bork used the same example to make just this argument. In a democracy, he argued, the majority has a boundless power to outlaw whatever conduct it finds objectionable, including conduct that takes place in private, harms nobody, and is not witnessed or overheard by anyone else. This is because all law is simply the enforcement of the majority's subjective, nonrational prejudices. Just knowing that some activity is taking place and being "outraged" by it entitles the majority to proscribe that activity.[96] Presumably, this would even include criminalizing private religious beliefs—because "[a] change in [the] moral environment . . . may surely be felt to be as harmful as the possibility of physical violence."[97] But it certainly would include rape, because laws against rape are based on nonrational emotional impulses: "[t]here is, indeed, no objection to forcible rape in the home . . . except a moral objection,"[98] and morality has "no objective or intrinsic validity."[94] Thus, while Bork claimed to recognize a "moral distinction between forcible rape and consenting sexual activity between adults," such a distinction could only be his own personal idiosyncrasy.[100] There is "no objectively 'correct' hierarchy" of ethical values, and therefore "no way to decide" whether "sexual gratification [is] more worthy than moral gratification." So we must "put such issues to a vote," and "the majority morality prevails."[101]

That, of course, means that a woman's right not to be raped is only a subjective preference—and one the majority may override at will. So, notwithstanding Bork's belief that there is a difference between rape and consensual sex, "the subject for discussion is not *my* morality. . . . If a majority of my fellow citizens decide that [rape and consensual sex], while not alike, are nevertheless similar enough so that both actions should be made criminal," then one must comply with that decision regardless of one's own opinion; "while I may disagree . . . it is in the polling booth that my moral views count."[102] Obviously, it would follow from the same premises that the majority may also *permit* rape by *revoking* a woman's rights/privileges. Women would then need to resort to the ballot box to request that protection—assuming the majority sees fit to give them the right/privilege to vote.

We see here the horrifying consequences that follow from the notion that rights are benefits created by the state. That contention empties the word "right" of any real content, and replaces it with a permission extended by the superior state to the inferior individual, when and how the state chooses.

The Founding Fathers were familiar with this argument, and they rejected it. John Locke, the intellectual progenitor of the American Revolution, is most famous for his *Second Treatise of Civil Government,* passages of which Jefferson paraphrased in the Declaration of Independence. But in his *First Treatise,* Locke focused on refuting the arguments of Robert Filmer, a monarchist whose view of rights was remarkably similar to the modern positivism of Tribe, Sunstein, and Bork. Filmer claimed that government owns citizens, and that it may give them rights or withhold rights from them whenever it sees fit. So, Locke asked in his rejoinder, can princes also *eat* their subjects?[103] If we recognize that rights are *not* just government-created permissions, we also can recognize that there are limits to what rulers may justly do to us. But to argue, like Filmer, Tribe, Sunstein, and Bork, that government comes first, and that it gives people freedom when it wills, and for its own purposes, is, as Locke concluded, the same as saying "that no man is born free."[104]

2. The Civil War and the Incomplete Reconstruction

Noble as the ideas of the Declaration of Independence were, it was obvious before the ink was dry that they clashed with a central fact of everyday life in America: slavery. Americans grappled with this conflict for almost another century, and in the process they confronted even more directly the dilemma of which takes precedence: the individual's right to freedom, or the power of the majority to govern.

Only after four dismal years of war did the nation add three new amendments to its Constitution, rededicating itself to the primacy of liberty and the other principles of the Declaration of Independence.[1] Once slavery was abolished, the core of the changes that followed was found in the Fourteenth Amendment, which for the first time defined the terms of American citizenship and declared that no state could deprive people of their natural rights or the traditional rights inherited through the common law. Yet shortly afterwards, that amendment was crippled by a Supreme Court decision known as *The Slaughter-House Cases*. Although parts of the amendment still provide real security for individual freedom today, the wrong done in that 1873 precedent still hampers protections for liberty today.

In the decades leading up to the Civil War, two parties formed with competing views of the Constitution. These parties went by various names, but we will call them the States' Rights Party and the Republican Party. Their differences focused on two issues: the nature of federal-state relations and the scope of government's power to rule. Republicans believed that the people of the United States make up a single sovereign nation. The States' Rights Party held that sovereignty resides primarily in each separate state and that the federal government's powers are delegated to it by the states, not by the people. Second, Republicans held that all Americans enjoy protections for their natural and traditional common-law rights through their federal citizenship, not through their state citizenship. The

States' Rights theory, on the other hand, held that states possess almost limitless power to define, protect, and limit individual rights. When, at the war's end, Republican leaders drafted the Fourteenth Amendment, they hoped it would resolve these controversies and ensure that their constitutional theory—which Jacobus tenBroek called "paramount national citizenship"—would forever be preserved in the nation's supreme law.[2]

National or State Sovereignty

The authors of the Fourteenth Amendment believed that either the Declaration of Independence or the Constitution itself had made the people of the United States into a single unified nation. National sovereignty—limited, of course, to those specific powers enumerated in the Constitution—prevailed over the autonomy of states. This meant that the states had no authority to secede from the union, but it also meant that the Constitution guaranteed rights to all Americans that overrode any provisions of state law.[3]

This theory was faithful to the constitutional structure the Founding Fathers created. The most striking difference between the 1787 Constitution and the Articles of Confederation that preceded it was that, while the Articles operated like a treaty among separate states, the Constitution set out a framework for an independent federal authority exercising its own powers directly. The Articles were explicitly signed by the states as a "league of friendship," and provided that "each state retains its sovereignty, freedom, and independence." But the new Constitution was not a league; it was a constitution, and the Preamble made clear that it was ordained not by states but by "the People of the United States."

In the *Federalist Papers*, Alexander Hamilton put the point succinctly: the "great and radical vice" of the Articles of Confederation was that it only allowed Congress to legislate "for STATES or GOVERNMENTS, in their CORPORATE or COLLECTIVE CAPACITIES"[4] and was therefore "a mere treaty, dependent on the good faith of the parties, and not a government."[5] The Constitution would cure this defect by deriving its authority directly from the people, who acted as a unified national sovereign. When Patrick Henry warned his colleagues at the Richmond ratification convention that "the language of *We the People*, instead of *We, the States*," signaled "an alarming transition, from a confederacy to a consolidated government," James Madison coolly answered that this was among the Constitution's best features.[6] The Articles had been based on "the dependent derivative authority of the legislatures of the states," he said, but the Constitution would draw its authority "from the superior power of the people."[7] Although it did not consolidate the states in every way, the Constitution, once ratified, would create "a government established by the thirteen States of America, not through the intervention of the Legislatures, but by the people at large."[8]

Madison, Hamilton, and other delegates had debated the question of federal sovereignty at Philadelphia months earlier. On June 19, 1787, Maryland's Luther Martin told the Constitutional Convention that he "considered that the separation from Great Britain placed the thirteen states in a state of nature towards each other."[9] Apparently alone among the delegates, he thought each state was a politically independent unit, and he later opposed ratification on the ground that uniting the whole people of America into a sovereign union trespassed on the sovereignty of the states. "[E]very thing which relates to the formation, the dissolution or the alteration of a *federal* government over States equally free, sovereign and independent is the *peculiar* province of the *States* in their *sovereign* or *political* capacity."[10] But Pennsylvania's James Wilson refuted Martin's argument. Wilson "could not admit the doctrine that, when the colonies became independent of Great Britain, they became independent also of each other."[11] Citing the Declaration of Independence, he contended that "the *United Colonies* were declared to be free and independent states, and infer[red], that they were independent, not *individually*, but *unitedly*, and that they were confederated, as they were independent states."[12] True, the Articles' reference to the states' separate sovereignty seemed to contradict that view, but the Constitution would eliminate that confusion. The new federal government would rest "upon the supreme authority of the people alone."[13] The sovereignty of the whole nation was "the rock on which this structure will stand."[14]

Many other opponents of the Constitution joined Martin in arguing against ratification because it would replace the league of sovereignties with a single national sovereignty. The writer "Brutus," for instance, warned that, if ratified, the Constitution "will not be a compact entered into by the States, in their corporate capacities, but an agreement of the people of the United States as one great body politic." The federal union would no longer be "a union of states or bodies corporate," but "a union of the people of the United States considered as one body."[15] Likewise, the "Federal Farmer" warned that the Constitution would be agreed to "not by the people of New Hampshire, Massachusetts, &c., but by the people of the United States."[16] Nobody ever said otherwise, or sought to allay the fears of anti-federalists by promising states that they could secede later if they wanted.[17]

Thus, at the time of ratification there was a broad national consensus—one that included even the Constitution's opponents—that ratification would vindicate the sovereignty of the American people as a whole and that the new federal government would derive its powers directly from the whole nation and not from the states. The U.S. Constitution would not be a coalition or treaty, as the Articles had been, but would be the supreme law of the land. Probably no intellectual of the post-ratification period expressed this idea more effectively than Chief Justice John Marshall, who observed in *Gibbons v. Ogden* (1824) that, while the Articles of Confederation had only established "a league" of "allied sovereigns," the Constitution "converted their league into a government," causing "the whole character in which the States appear" to "under[go] a change."[18] Likewise, in *McCulloch v. Maryland* (1819), he wrote that the federal government "proceeds directly from the people. . . . It required not the affirmance, and could not be negatived, by the state governments. The constitution, when thus adopted, was of complete obligation, and bound the state sovereignties."[19]

It was not until long after ratification, under the influence first of Thomas Jefferson's 1798 Kentucky Resolutions and then John C. Calhoun's philippics during the Nullification Crisis of the 1830s, that Southern political leaders devised a states' rights theory that resurrected the idea of a league of sovereignties.[20] Writing anonymously, Jefferson contended that "each State acceded as a State, and is an integral party" to the Constitution, so each state could "judge for itself" whether the Constitution had been violated, and decide on "the mode and measure of redress."[21]

At first, this argument was rejected or ignored, but shortly after Jefferson's death, when the Jackson administration's policies provoked Southern states' anger, spokesmen for this new states' rights theory became bolder. Ignoring the ratification debates of a half-century before, they argued that the federal union was still only a treaty among sovereign states. Upon separating from Great Britain, they reasoned, the states had become "distinct, independent, and sovereign communities" and thus the basic units in the American federation.[22] In 1776, the sovereign power that Parliament once wielded had been transferred to each state individually, and not to the American union, as Wilson and others had said. Those states had ceded some of their power to the federal government by joining the union, but they still remained the principals, and the federal government was their agent.[23]

Among the most eloquent opponents of this states' rights theory was Massachusetts Senator Daniel Webster, who in his famous 1830 debate with South Carolina Senator Robert Hayne argued that federal authority was "not the creature of the State governments,"[24] as Hayne claimed; it was instead "made for the people, made by the people, and answerable to the people."[25] Webster also hinted at the implications of national sovereignty when he observed that, "if the whole truth must be told," the American people had established the federal government "for the very purpose, amongst others, of imposing certain salutary restraints on State sovereignties."[26]

Webster's argument became a classic of American oratory, but it did not convince the South Carolinians. Following his mentor, Calhoun, Hayne contended that the states enjoyed "the right to the fullest extent of determining the limits of their own powers," a right that was "full and complete," indeed, "plenary."[27] In 1832, when the state legislature issued its Ordinance of Nullification, purporting to invalidate a federal law, it simultaneously published an explanatory *Address to the People*, which embraced the most extreme form of the states' rights theory. Quoting William Blackstone's *Commentaries*, the *Address* asserted that states enjoyed "'irresistible, absolute, uncontrolled authority'" and "absolute control 'over the lives, liberties, and properties of the people, and the internal order, improvement, and prosperity'" of the community. A state could not "suffer any other restraint upon her sovereign will and pleasure, than those high moral obligations, under which all Princes and States are bound before God and man, to perform their solemn pleasure."[28]

The Reach of Sovereignty

As this language of "plenary" authority suggests, the States' Rights and Republican parties differed not only over the *location* of sovereignty but also over its *nature and limits*. states' rights leaders tended to rely on Blackstone, who had argued that every government contains a "despotic power"—an irreducible kernel of authority that entitles it to make law.[29] This right to obedience was boundless. It was "supreme, irresistible, absolute, [and] uncontrolled"[30] and could do "every thing that is not naturally impossible."[31] Blackstone rejected the arguments of "Mr. Locke, and other theoretical writers," who held that government had only the powers people gave it, and therefore that there were some things the king or Parliament had no right to do. Government, Blackstone wrote, does not hold delegated or limited authority—it has a basic right to do as it pleases with people and to give them rights or withdraw those rights whenever it sees fit. This meant that "the power of parliament is absolute and without control."[32] And if each state now wielded that same power, as states' rights partisans held, they too now enjoyed unlimited and irresistible authority.

Blackstone's arguments disturbed some of the Founders; Thomas Jefferson and James Wilson both explicitly rejected his writings because of his belief in absolute sovereignty, and when Virginia judge St. George Tucker published an edition of Blackstone's *Commentaries* in 1803, he added almost a thousand pages of footnotes and clarifications, refuting or qualifying the Englishman's views of government power.[33] The "essential difference between the British government and the American constitutions," wrote Tucker, is that while "parliament is unlimited in it's [*sic*] power, or, in their own language, is omnipotent," American legislatures are "altogether different."[34] More important, Blackstone's notion of sovereignty was irreconcilable with the principles of the Declaration of Independence. If government can possess only those powers delegated to it by the people, and people can have no fundamental right to rule over others, then government cannot rightly claim absolute power, let alone a basic right to rule. Citing the Declaration, Tucker declared that Blackstonian "supreme, irresistible, absolute, uncontrolled authority . . . doth not reside in the legislature, nor in any other of the branches of Government, nor in the whole of them united."[35]

Nevertheless, Blackstone's books became the basic text of American law students at the beginning of the 19th century,[36] and by the time of the Nullification Crisis, his doctrine of absolute sovereignty was growing increasingly popular. In 1840, Virginia politician Abel Upshur, who later served in President John Tyler's cabinet, published a book arguing that states possess "absolute, unqualified, unconditional, and unlimited sovereignty."[37] A few years later, St. George Tucker's son, Henry, delivered a series of lectures at the University of Virginia endorsing absolute state sovereignty,[38] and Henry's brother, Beverley, published a book arguing that states, and only states, possessed "this right to command, to be obeyed, and to protect; the right to hold the individual responsible to the community and to interpose the collective responsibility of the community between him and any foreign complainant—this it is which constitutes sovereignty."[39]

Southerners were not the only ones to endorse the Blackstonian model of sovereignty. One of its most outspoken advocates was a Pennsylvanian, Jeremiah Sullivan Black, who, as the state's Chief Justice, wrote the 1853 decision in *Sharpless v. Mayor of Philadelphia*.[40] That case upheld the constitutionality of an ordinance that transferred money from taxpayers to a private corporation to build a railroad. The plaintiffs argued that this was an abuse of power, inconsistent with the basic premises of constitutional rule, but Black disagreed. States possess absolute, Blackstonian sovereignty, he declared, and can do whatever they like with citizens' money. When the United States declared itself independent of Britain, Parliament's "transcendant [*sic*] powers" were transferred to the states, who therefore enjoyed "supreme and unlimited" power.[41] This meant that, "[i]f the people of Pennsylvania had given all the authority which they themselves possessed, to a single person, they would have created a despotism as absolute in its control over life, liberty, and property, as that of the Russian autocrat."[42] Although Black conceded that the states had given up some of this limitless power to the federal government, he believed they retained "a vast field of power . . . full and uncontrolled," and their use of that power "can be limited only by their own discretion."[43] States could do anything not expressly prohibited by their own constitutions, without regard to principles of justice or the purposes for which the people entrust government with power.[44]

Justice Ellis Lewis dissented: the idea that states possess *"all the powers of sovereignty not expressly withheld from them"* was a legacy of the "absolute despotisms of the old world," and deserved no respect in a free state where government exercised delegated powers. Despots alone thought that government was limited only by "the arbitrary will of usurping tyrants." A constitution, by contrast, imposed laws on rulers in order to protect individual rights. Those rights took precedence over the majority's authority to rule. The legislature could not claim unlimited power to redistribute property or restrict other individual rights because this would contravene the very reasons for establishing government in the first place. Black's analogy to the Russian czar was singularly wrongheaded, Lewis wrote. The state "has no more right to abandon the liberty and prosperity of any portion of her citizens to the will of others than she would have to transfer them to a Russian or an Austrian Despot."[45]

But such arguments went unheeded, as defenders of state's rights continued to assert that government had a basic right to rule and that freedom was essentially a privilege given to the individual by the all-powerful state. "Order is a moral duty," wrote Henry Hughes in his 1854 *Treatise on Sociology*. No person has a "right to use his mind and body as he will"; people are given that right as a "social use only . . . to use it as a social being ought."[46] William Harper attacked the Declaration of Independence section by section in his *Memoir on Slavery*, arguing that "no man was ever born free" and that freedom was "no matter of natural right." Instead, freedom is "settled by convention as the good and safety of society may require."[47] Calhoun, the arch champion of states' rights, agreed. It was, he said, "a great and dangerous error to suppose that all people are equally entitled to liberty."[48] Building on Blackstone's premise that government has a basic right to rule, which does not depend on the consent of the governed or the fundamental liberty of individuals, Calhoun argued that rights are privileges given by states as "a reward reserved for the intelligent, the patriotic, the virtuous and deserving."[49] The Declaration's propositions about equality and liberty were falsehoods, and were "inserted" into the Declaration "without any necessity."[50] The truth was that mankind was created inherently *unequal*, with the superior race ruling over the inferior, and the American Revolution was not fought to vindicate the basic right of each person to be free but to protect the "chartered privileges" of colonial governments. Each colony broke from Britain as a separate unit to preserve its autonomous power, and that autonomy remained when they became states. Each state therefore had full power to dictate the terms of citizenship, expand or contract the sphere of individual freedom,[51] and, if necessary, to defend its sovereignty by seceding from the union.[52]

Alarmed at the growing popularity of these anti-liberty doctrines,[53] the elderly James Madison wrote in 1835 that "the sovereignty of the society" was inherently limited; the majority or the legislature had power to do only things "that could be *rightfully done*," which meant that "the reserved rights of individuals" were "beyond the legitimate reach of sovereignty."[54] States had no right to trample on individual freedom or to defy federal law. But Southern leaders paid little heed. Instead, Madison's strongest supporters were Massachusetts politicians, including Edward Everett, Daniel Webster, and former President John Quincy Adams, now a Congressman and a pivotal but often overlooked figure in American constitutional law.[55] Like Madison, Adams believed that no sovereign was entitled to intrude on natural rights, and this meant that state authority was limited by the principles of justice articulated in the Declaration of Independence. In his 1848 pamphlet *The Jubilee of the Constitution*, he emphasized that Americans' rights were protected not because they were citizens of states, but because they were citizens of the union, which originated in the Declaration.[56] The colonies declared independence collectively, Adams contended, so that on July 4, 1776, Parliament's authority over American subjects—and its duty to protect their rights—was transferred to the union, not to each individual state.[57] And this was not the absolute parliamentary sovereignty Blackstone postulated: the same terms by which the Americans declared their independence also limited government power. The nation was justified in exercising authority only insofar as it respected the primary value of individual liberty. Americans were "proclaimed to be *one people*, renouncing . . . all claims to chartered rights as Englishmen. Thenceforth their charter was the Declaration of Independence. Their rights, the natural rights of mankind. Their government, such as should be instituted by themselves, *under the solemn mutual pledges of perpetual union*, [was] founded on the self-evident truths proclaimed in the Declaration."[58]

The Declaration was therefore not just a call to arms, but part of the binding, organic law of the United States; it separated the American from the British nation, by pledging to protect individual rights from government. American national identity was not an ethnic or historical happenstance but the product of a covenant to respect individual liberty. The Declaration "proclaims the natural rights of man, and the constituent power of the people to be the *only* sources of legitimate government. State sovereignty is . . . a mere reproduction of the omnipotence of the British parliament in another form, and therefore not only inconsistent with, but directly in opposition to, the principles of the Declaration of Independence."[59] Blackstone's idea "that *sovereign* must necessarily be uncontrollable, unlimited, despotic power"[60] stood "in direct contradiction to the Declaration of Independence, and [was] incompatible with the nature of our institutions."[61] If that "hallucination" were not promptly discarded, he warned, it would render the Declaration's promise "a philosophical dream," and "uncontrolled, despotic sovereignties" would then "trample with impunity, through a long career of after ages, at interminable or exterminating war with one another, upon the indefeasible and unalienable rights of man."[62] Adams thus took literally Daniel Webster's famous phrase, "Liberty and Union . . . one and inseparable!"[63] Political union and protection for individual rights reinforced each other.[64]

Adams exerted a lasting influence on the rising generation of anti-slavery politicians and lawyers. His leading protégé, Charles Sumner, became the greatest of all abolitionist political leaders.[65] William Seward published the first biography of Adams before becoming the leading anti-slavery presidential candidate and eventually secretary of state in the Lincoln administration.[66] And Lincoln himself was a devotee of Adams's writings and served with him in Congress.[67] Like Adams, these men believed that the Declaration had created the American nation, a nation whose sovereign identity depended upon the truth of the principles articulated in the Declaration.

The connection between national sovereignty and the limits that natural rights imposed on government power was never more clearly expressed than by another Adams admirer, Ohio lawyer Salmon P. Chase, whom Lincoln later named chief justice. In 1847, Chase joined William Seward to argue before the Supreme Court in *Jones v. VanZandt*[68] that the Fugitive Slave Law was unconstitutional because it deprived people of due process, a jury trial, and other rights. But it was unconstitutional for another, deeper reason: the Constitution was

> mainly designed to establish as written law, certain great principles of natural right and justice, which exist independently of all such sanction. [It] rather announce[s] restrictions upon legislative power, imposed by the very nature of society and of government, than create[s] restrictions, which, [if] erased from the constitution, the Legislature would be at liberty to disregard. No Legislature is omnipotent. No Legislature can make right wrong; or wrong, right. No Legislature can make light, darkness; or darkness, light. No Legislature can make men, things; or things, men. Nor is any Legislature at liberty to disregard the fundamental principles of rectitude and justice. Whether restrained or not by constitutional provisions, there are acts beyond any legitimate or binding legislative authority. There are certain vital principles, in our national government, which will ascertain and overrule an apparent and flagrant abuse of legislative power. The Legislature cannot authorize injustice by law; cannot nullify private contracts; cannot abrogate the securities of life, liberty, and property, which it is the very object of society, as well as of our constitution of government, to provide; cannot make a man judge in his own case; cannot repeal the laws of nature; cannot create any obligation to do wrong, or neglect duty. No court is bound to enforce unjust law; but, on the contrary, every court is bound, by prior and superior obligations, to abstain from enforcing such a law.[69]

Unsurprisingly, Chase failed to persuade Chief Justice Taney and his colleagues. But over the next two decades, the ideas he expressed continued to gain adherents. Sovereign power limited by natural rights, national sovereignty superseding state autonomy, and a paramount national citizenship which entitled all Americans to protection of their common law and natural rights—these were the basic principles of anti-slavery constitutionalism that would eventually find expression in the Fourteenth Amendment.

Citizenship

Before the Civil War, Congress usually sought compromises to evade, rather than resolve, touchy debates over states' rights and

THE CONSCIENCE OF THE CONSTITUTION

sovereignty. These attempts were not limited to matters of slavery and race. Until 1872, for example, the federal government never used the power of eminent domain to take property for federal needs.[70] This was because eminent domain—government's power to force people to sell property to the government for public uses— is considered a fundamental attribute of sovereignty, and although the Constitution itself implicitly allows the federal government to use eminent domain, any attempt to do so would have triggered a showdown over whether the union was sovereign and rouse the suspicion of Southern leaders, who could foresee the power being used to take slave property. Thus, until almost a century after the Constitution was written, the federal government depended upon state officials to use eminent domain and then transfer the land for federal uses.

Another power inherent in sovereignty is the power to determine citizenship. Here, again, a critical vagueness afflicted the Constitution of 1787. Although it gave Congress power to enact naturalization laws, and made passing references to national citizenship,[71] nothing in the document defined the word "citizen." Congress enacted naturalization laws to enable immigrants to become citizens, but the citizenship status of the native-born was left unaddressed, and states assumed authority to determine who was eligible. States' Rights partisans saw this as proof that the states, and not the federal government, were the real sovereigns. Republicans answered that the federal government had, even if it had not yet used, its own independent power to determine citizenship for federal purposes. Neither side could point definitively to constitutional language to resolve this dispute. And since the qualifications for citizenship differed from state to state, a person eligible for citizenship in, say, Massachusetts, might not be eligible for citizenship in South Carolina. Article IV of the Constitution declared that "[t]he Citizens of each State shall be entitled to all Privileges and Immunities of Citizens in the several States," meaning ostensibly that a Massachusetts citizen—even a free black man—was entitled to travel to South Carolina and do business or reside there unmolested. Yet state laws made clear that they were not welcome.

In 1820, Missouri sought admission to the union and asked Congress to approve a state constitution that would give the legislature power to bar the immigration of free black citizens of

44

other states. Slavery's opponents in Congress, particularly Adams, denounced this as a violation of the Privileges and Immunities Clause. To allow a state to close its borders to American citizens, Adams said, would be "a dissolution of the Union. If acquiesced in, it will change the terms of the federal compact—change its terms by robbing thousands of citizens of their rights. And what citizens? The poor, the unfortunate, the helpless, already cursed by the mere color of their skin."[72]

After an angry debate, Congress dodged the issue again, adopting a euphemistic resolution that admitted Missouri into the union on the condition that its constitution not be interpreted as allowing it to violate the Privileges and Immunities Clause. What this meant, nobody knew. But it sufficed to postpone debate on the question of whether blacks could be citizens of the United States. Disgusted, Adams confided to his diary that slavery's advocates had "threatened and entreated, bullied and wheedled, until their more simple adversaries have been half coaxed, half frightened into a surrender of their principles for a bauble of insignificant promises."[73] Eighteen years later, Tennessee's highest court upheld that state's law barring free blacks. This did not violate the Privileges and Immunities Clause, the court ruled, because they could not be citizens. The logic was, to say the least, remarkable: "either the free negro is not a citizen in the sense of the Constitution; or, if a citizen, he is entitled to 'all the privileges and immunities' of the most favored class of citizens. But this latter consequence, will be contended for by no one. It must then follow, that they are not citizens."[74]

Conflict over the question of citizenship flared up again shortly after the Missouri crisis, when, in 1822, South Carolina passed a law called the "Negro Seaman's Act," or the "Police Bill." It required all black sailors on ships landing in the state's ports to be jailed at the captain's expense, and released only when the ship returned to sea. If the captain failed to pay the costs of their detention, the sailors would be "deemed and taken as absolute slaves."[75] Supreme Court Justice William Johnson declared the law unconstitutional in 1823,[76] and the following year President Monroe's attorney general, William Wirt, agreed.[77] But the state defied these decisions and continued to enforce the law.[78] Foreign countries, particularly the British, protested that the act violated American treaty obligations, and their complaints were echoed by Northern states. Free blacks could legally become citizens of Massachusetts, a state whose economy depended heavily on shipping. This meant that Massachusetts sailors were liable to be imprisoned and sold into slavery when their ships stopped at Charleston or in the ports of other Southern states that enacted similar laws. But, thanks to the rise of the States' Rights doctrine, Andrew Jackson's attorney general, Roger Taney, rejected Wirt's and Johnson's opinions and proclaimed the act valid.[79] In language that eerily presaged the *Dred Scott* decision that he would write 16 years later, Taney wrote that members of the "African race" were

> a degraded class—& exercise no political influence. The privileges they are allowed to enjoy, are accorded to them as a matter of kindness & benevolence rather than of right. They are the only class of persons who can be held as mere property—as slaves. And where they are nominally admitted by law to the privileges of citizenship, they have no effectual power to defend them, & are permitted to be citizens by the sufferance of the white population & hold whatever rights they enjoy at their mercy. They were never regarded as a constituent portion of the sovereignty of any state. But as a separate and degraded people to whom the sovereignty of each state might accord or withhold such privileges as they deemed proper. They were not looked upon as citizens by the contracting parties who formed the constitution. They were evidently not supposed to be included by the term *citizens.* . . .
>
> This view of the subject is illustrated by that article of the constitution which gives to citizens of each State the "privileges & immunities of citizens in the several States.["] Was this intended to include the coloured race? Did the slave holding states when they adopted the constitution intend to give within their own limits to a free coloured person residing in Massachusetts or Connecticut all the rights and privileges which they allowed to the white citizens of those states? The article has never been so construed. . . . Every slave holding State . . . has prohibited their migration & settlement within their limits. . . . Did the slaveholding states mean to surrender their right to enact such Laws? It is impossible to imagine they could have so intended, and the uniform course of their legislation since the adoption of the Federal Constitution shows that they did not so understand that instrument. The slave holding states could not have surrendered this power, without

> bringing upon themselves inevitably the evils of insurrection
> & rebellion among their slaves, & the non slave holding states
> could have no inducement to desire its surrender.[80]

By 1844, so many Massachusetts citizens were being imprisoned under the Police Bill that the governor appointed a prominent Boston politician named Samuel Hoar to travel south and serve as a local agent overseeing the legal defense of jailed Bay State sailors. The South Carolina legislature responded by instructing the governor to throw Hoar out of the state the moment he arrived. "Has the Constitution of the United States the least practical validity or binding force in South Carolina?" Hoar asked in a report to Massachusetts' governor when he returned home. "She prohibits, not only by her mob, but by her Legislature, the residence of a free white citizen of Massachusetts within the limits of South Carolina, whenever she thinks his presence there is inconsistent with her policy."[81]

South Carolina's mistreatment of Hoar helped illustrate the problems created by the Constitution's ambiguity about citizenship and federal precedence over state power. Black Massachusetts citizens should have been entitled to the rights of American citizenship—the "privileges or immunities" to which Article IV of the Constitution referred—and no state had authority to infringe those rights. Yet South Carolina was not only ignoring this protection for black sailors; it was also violating the rights of white citizens who wanted to hire or do business with them. And it purported to do so on the ground that *it* was the true sovereign, with supreme authority to "protect" its native population against the nefarious plots of abolitionists. In the case in which Justice Johnson ineffectually declared the Police Bill unconstitutional, the state's lawyers had argued that "South Carolina was a sovereign state when she adopted the constitution; a sovereign state cannot surrender a right of vital importance; South Carolina, therefore, either did not surrender this right, or still possesses the power to resume it, and whether it is necessary, or when it is necessary, to resume it, she is herself the sovereign judge."[82]

Six years after Hoar was thrown out of South Carolina, Wisconsin Senator Isaac Walker made the episode a central feature of a blistering denunciation of slavery's defenders. Southern politicians had long portrayed themselves as victims of Northern anti-slavery agitators, he noted, but it was actually they who had committed aggression against the North by mistreating Yankee citizens in violation of the Constitution. "Suppose that a citizen of Wisconsin or of Massachusetts, colored though he may be, but being a citizen, is entitled to all the privileges and immunities of citizenship in the several States, should visit, in the pursuit of his business, the shores of South Carolina—what hospitality awaits him there? It is imprisonment in the dungeon. Suppose the State from which he goes . . . sends another citizen—a white citizen—equally entitled to all the immunities of citizenship, to South Carolina, to inquire why they allowed this . . . what treatment does he meet with? Why, sir, if *he* is not imprisoned—if *he* is not deprived of *his* liberty—it is because he can make tracks fast enough."[83]

South Carolina Senator Pierce Butler replied that the law protected his constituents against the presence of free blacks who might encourage slave uprisings. But he went further. Free blacks could not be American citizens. They were "a species of persons" who enjoyed only those rights that states chose to give them. "[T]hey have no federal eligibility, or federal recognition, as citizens of the United States." The slave states were not obliged to regard them as citizens,

> and a free man of color in Massachusetts—call him a citizen of Massachusetts if you choose—can have no higher grade of political existence, under the Constitution, than a free negro in South Carolina, when he comes to South Carolina. Their condition must be assimilated under the law that operates on them. A free man of color in South Carolina is not regarded as a citizen by her laws . . . or Federal laws.[84]

If Walker's argument prevailed, Butler warned, "a Wisconsin free negro, made a citizen there," would automatically become "a citizen of the other States, so far as he may avail himself" of the Privileges and Immunities Clause. And this was unthinkable—why, it might even make a black man "eligible to the Presidency!"[85]

This did not scare Walker. Not only were black citizens of free states entitled to the protections of national citizenship, he argued, but slavery was confined to state law only; federal law could take no cognizance of slavery: "in the UNITED States there is no such thing as a slave. Within the geographical limits of the United States there are slaves; but there are no slaves in the UNITED States—or, to transpose it, there are no slaves in the States

UNITED. It is confined . . . to the States in which it exists."[86] And this, of course, was exactly what slave owners feared. If slavery were confined within Southern boundaries, the new states that grew from the fallow western territories would be free states whose senators would eventually outnumber their own. At the same time, the free black populations of other states would have a federally protected right to travel to, and do business in, the slave states, breeding resentment among the native slaves, encouraging escapes, or even provoking revolts. Slavery must expand to the west, or it would be doomed. And such expansion seemed imminent. In 1850, the year of Walker and Butler's debate, Congress superseded the Missouri Compromise with a new compromise, and four years later, replaced that with a third: the Kansas-Nebraska Act, which allowed the (white) people in western territories to "decide for themselves," democratically, whether or not to incorporate slavery into their new state constitutions. Slavery was no longer confined.

Antislavery Constitutionalism

All the while, the citizenship controversy festered. In the spring of 1835, the Antislavery Society of Ohio published a report that inferred the definition of American citizenship, not from the Constitution's Preamble, but from its "Three-Fifths Clause." That clause apportioned representation on the basis of the "free" population, plus three-fifths of "all other persons." The Antislavery Society argued that this language, along with the fact that other countries classified freedmen as citizens, strongly suggested that "all *free* persons born in and residents of the United States," except for Indians, were American citizens "entitled in every state to all the privileges and immunities of citizens of these states."[87] State laws prohibiting the immigration of free blacks were therefore unconstitutional.

At about the same time, the prosecution of abolitionist schoolteacher Prudence Crandall became a cause célèbre in Connecticut, where her all-star legal team argued that free blacks were citizens of the United States and that state laws restricting their access to education were unconstitutional. That court managed to dodge the question,[88] but in a book published shortly thereafter, New York judge William Jay—son of America's first Chief Justice—reiterated the arguments of Crandall's attorneys to make the case that free blacks were entitled to federal citizenship and thus to the protection of the Privileges and Immunities Clause.[89]

Of course, slavery's opponents had to explain away many legal ambiguities that seemed to contradict their arguments. It would be anomalous for the nation's fundamental law fully to protect the rights of free black Massachusetts citizens, while simultaneously allowing South Carolina to brutalize and rob the same people of all their liberty. If a slave escaped into a Northern state where slavery was prohibited, would he or his children suddenly become citizens of the United States—even though the Constitution explicitly promised that escaped slaves would be returned to their owners? Could a slave owner, by emancipating a slave, thereby make him a citizen of the United States, with no intervening act by government, and contrary to state law? It seemed far-fetched to argue that the Constitution's authors meant to make slaves into citizens, let alone that a person could be both a slave and a member of the body politic at the same time.

Yet some of the nation's brightest legal minds made just this argument.[90] They developed a broader theory of citizenship according to which Americans were primarily citizens of the nation and only secondarily of states. All Americans, regardless of race, could be equal members of the people of the United States. Indeed, some argued that ratification of the Constitution in 1789 made slaves citizens by operation of law, and that it was therefore already illegal to hold them as slaves. Among these thinkers was Frederick Douglass, who argued that "the Constitution knows all the human inhabitants of this country as 'the people,'"[91] and that black slaves were therefore federal citizens just like free whites, regardless of what state law might provide.[92] Because the Fifth Amendment promises that no *person* shall be deprived of life, liberty, or property without due process of law, laws supporting slavery—which accorded people no process of law whatever—must be unconstitutional.[93] The notion that the Founding Fathers meant constitutional protections to apply only to whites, Douglass said, "is Judge Taney's argument" in *Dred Scott*, but "it is not the argument of the Constitution. The Constitution imposes no such mean and satanic limitations upon its own beneficent operation."[94] Federal citizenship entitled slaves, along with everyone else, to protection for their natural and common-law rights.

Among the most penetrating of the anti-slavery constitutionalists was New York lawyer Joel Tiffany, who believed that "[s]overeignty, as an attribute of the people of the United States as a nation, excludes the like sovereignty of the people of a single State, as State citizens merely. Hence, the authority of a citizen as a constituent of the nation, is superior to his authority as a constituent of a mere State."[95] Neither state nor national sovereignty could include the power to override fundamental natural rights: society "must establish its foundations in natural justice" and "permit no necessary liberty or right of the individual to be abridged."[96] The American nation, "in virtue of its inherent sovereignty, has ordained and established a constitutional government, which in its authority, as the representative of the nation, is supreme over all." Thus, every citizen of a state is "also a citizen of the nation" and "has national rights" that states must respect.[97]

As to whether slaves could be citizens, Tiffany explained in his 1849 treatise, *The Unconstitutionality of American Slavery*, that there were three ways to become a citizen. First, people residing in the United States when the Constitution was ratified were citizens; second, people born in the United States after ratification were citizens, and third, people naturalized pursuant to laws enacted by Congress were citizens. All residents at the time of ratification had become citizens because the Constitution was "*'ordained and established' by the people*, not by the States, not by the white people, or black people, not by the rich people, or poor people . . . not by one class, as opposed to any other class in the United States; but expressly, and emphatically by all. . . . There were no citizens, or aliens, to it, before its adoption, but all became citizens by its adoption."[98] The Constitution protected all Americans in their rights to life, liberty, and property. The adoption of the Constitution must therefore have automatically prohibited slavery, since slavery countermanded all these rights.

Massachusetts attorney Lysander Spooner agreed. The Constitution's Preamble, he wrote, "has told us in the plainest possible terms" that "'We, the people of the United States,' 'do ordain and establish this constitution,'" but it did not say who this "people" was. "It does not declare that 'we, the white people,' or 'we, the free people,' or 'we, a part of the people'—but that 'we, the people'—that is, we the whole people—of the United States, 'do ordain and establish this constitution.'" If this did not mean to make citizens of all Americans, but to leave the determination of citizenship exclusively to states, then "the consequence would [be] that the constitution established a government that could not know its own citizens."[99]

51

The fact that the Constitution made no distinctions among "the people of the United States" could have one of three consequences, argued Spooner. Either every person enjoyed federal citizenship, including slaves; or there simply were no such things as federal citizens; or states enjoy absolute authority "to determine who may, and who may not be citizens of the *United States government.*"[100]

The first option would necessarily bar slavery, since states could have no authority to reduce free citizens to slavery without due process of law. The second would mean there is no such thing as the United States, which was absurd. The third option was inconsistent with federal sovereignty, and with the Constitution's Supremacy Clause. The only possible conclusion, therefore, was that slaves were citizens—made such by the adoption of the Constitution—and that slavery was an illegal violation of their rights. Spooner admitted that the Framers may not have personally intended this result, but the law did not consist of their subjective intentions—it consisted of the actual words on paper. To say that the Framers *meant* to authorize slavery was "palpably a mere begging of the whole question," because if that had been their intent, they would have written that into the document.[101] On the contrary, they took pains to avoid even using the word "slave."

Provisions like the Three-Fifths Clause or the Fugitive Slave Clause were a bit harder for Tiffany and Spooner to account for, but they formed plausible interpretations even of these. The Fugitive Slave Clause, said Spooner, applied only to persons held to labor "under the laws" of a state, such as criminals convicted after being given due process of law. But states could not reduce to slavery people whose freedom was federally guaranteed. After all, nobody claimed that the Constitution's guarantees for property rights extended to property acquired by theft, robbery, murder, or other crimes. Similarly, if slaves were part of "the people of the United States," then states could claim no lawful authority to subject them to slavery.

Today, the proposition that slavery was already unconstitutional strikes many as outlandish. Yet some of slavery's defenders took a position no less extreme. Spooner had thought it absurd to deny that there were such things as American citizens, yet John C. Calhoun and other Southerners did just that. "There is," Calhoun wrote, "no such community, *politically* speaking, as the people of the United States." Nor was there any such thing as "one people or nation."

The "people" referred to in the Constitution's Preamble "neither could, nor ever can exercise any agency,—or have any participation, in the formation of our system of government."[102] In an 1833 speech, Calhoun insisted that "every citizen is a citizen of some State or territory" primarily, and only derivatively of the United States. "If by citizen of the United States [one] means a citizen at large, one whose citizenship extends to the entire geographical limits of the country . . . all I have to say is, that such a citizen would be a perfect nondescript; that not a single Individual of this description can be found in the entire mass of our population."[103] After the war, former Confederate Vice President Alexander Stephens published a lengthy constitutional defense of secession and states' rights in which he still maintained that there was "no such thing as a general citizenship of the United States."[104] And in his own memoir, Jefferson Davis argued that "no such political community as the people of the United States in the aggregate exists at this day or ever did exist."[105]

What Tiffany and Spooner recognized—and what Calhoun and his allies emphatically denied—was that the Constitution did implicitly assume two different categories of citizenship: state and federal. And if federal citizenship existed, they believed, then federal protection for the rights attendant upon that citizenship must preempt state laws, including those that policed the institution of slavery. The American nation, argued Tiffany, "in virtue of its inherent sovereignty, has ordained and established a constitutional government, which in its authority, as the representative of the nation, is supreme over all."[106]

While radicals scoped out clear positions at either pole, practical political leaders groped for some compromise, only to see their efforts worsen the crisis. As late as 1862, President Lincoln's attorney general, Edwin Bates, confessed that he had "often been pained by the fruitless search in our law books and the records of our courts for a clear and satisfactory definition of the phrase citizens of the United States. . . . Eighty years of practical enjoyment of [the rights of federal] citizenship, under the Constitution, have not sufficed to teach us . . . the exact meaning of the word."[107] In fact, the dual citizenship model that anti-slavery thinkers were developing fit snugly with the dual sovereignty contemplated by the Constitution's Framers. During the ratification debates, Madison, Hamilton, and other advocates of the proposed Constitution had explained that it would establish a new union, with its own separate system of laws, elections, and courts—a system that did not depend on state sovereignty and would secure federal rights as the supreme law of the land. This implied that Americans would be citizens of two distinct, but overlapping, polities: the state and the federal union. Calhoun, in effect, conceded this point when he denied the existence of both the American nation and federal citizenship. If, as he professed, the Constitution was a mere treaty among sovereign states, then the term "citizens of the United States" could only be a meaningless figure of speech, and the union was not really a government at all. But if there was an American nation, there could be no denying the primacy of national citizenship, and with it, federal power to block states from depriving Americans of their rights.

Dred Scott

If black Americans qualified as citizens—as members of "the People of the United States" who ordained the Constitution—then holding them in bondage was legally absurd and morally outrageous. And if a slave who entered free territory suddenly became a citizen of the United States by operation of state law, slave property could never be secure. Thus it was that the most important court decision on the question of slavery centered primarily on the question of whether descendants of "the African race" could become citizens of the United States.

Dred Scott was a slave who sued his owner, Sanford (the Supreme Court reporter misspelled his name Sandford) for his freedom. Scott argued that he was freed by operation of state law when he was taken for a time into a free state. The Supreme Court rejected this argument in a long, rambling decision, announced on March 6, 1857. Chief Justice Taney refused to allow the dissenting justices to read his draft opinion beforehand, one reason Justice Benjamin Curtis resigned from the Court in protest—the only Supreme Court justice ever to do so.[108] Taney's opinion ranged far beyond what was necessary to resolve the legal dispute. He seemed to hope that the decision would silence what he considered the frivolous arguments of anti-slavery constitutionalists. That hope was disappointed.

Taney began with a proposition on which he and the anti-slavery lawyers agreed: "The words 'people of the United States' and 'citizens' are synonymous terms, and mean the same thing."[109] But slaves and their descendants could not possibly be "people of the United States," he continued, because at the time of the Constitution's ratification they were "considered as a subordinate and inferior class of beings, who had been subjugated by the dominant race."[110] Taney did not take the extreme route that had led Calhoun to deny the existence of an American nation, but he ruled that "no State can, by any act or law of its own . . . introduce a new member into the political community created by the Constitution of the United States. It cannot make him a member of this community by making him a member of its own."[111] Slaves and their descendants could become citizens only if a federal act gave them that opportunity.

It was at this point that Taney introduced his infamous language that at the time America declared independence, black men and women were considered "unfit to associate with the white race," and were "so far inferior, that they had no rights which the white man was bound to respect."[112] Since the Founders believed in black inferiority, he claimed, they could not possibly have meant to include slaves or freedmen as members of the American political community. Taney was inverting the anti-slavery argument: where Tiffany and Spooner had used federal supremacy to argue that slavery was unconstitutional, Taney was arguing that, on the contrary, federal supremacy protected slavery throughout the land.

Taney's proof that the Declaration of Independence applied exclusively to whites was startlingly weak.[113] Indeed, he provided only one relevant piece of evidence: the fact that the men who signed the Declaration and the Constitution, and who owned slaves, failed to free them at that time. Of course, each slave owner had his own reasons, hypocrisy being just one of them, for failing to abide by the principles of equality and liberty for which he pledged his life, fortune, and sacred honor. But this fact, in addition to the Three-Fifths Clause and the clause temporarily protecting the slave trade, persuaded Taney that neither slaves nor their descendants were among the "people of the United States" who had ordained and established the Constitution. In the years since ratification, Congress had never asserted authority to make blacks citizens. The naturalization laws it had enacted allowed only free white foreigners to become citizens— a statutory distinction that "followed out the line of division which the Constitution has drawn between the citizen race, who formed and held the Government, and the African race, which they held in subjection and slavery, and governed at their own pleasure."[114] Since Dred Scott was not, and could not be, a citizen, he had no power to file a lawsuit in federal court.

Justice Curtis objected. The Constitution had made any person who was a citizen of a state in 1787 into a citizen of the United States, he argued, and according to the laws of New Hampshire, Massachusetts, New York, New Jersey, and even North Carolina, that included all free persons, regardless of color.[115] Indeed, although South Carolina had once tried under the Articles of Confederation to confine American citizenship solely to white persons, that proposition had been rejected. This made it clear that in at least some states, free blacks could qualify for citizenship at the time of ratification, and thereby become American citizens; in some states, they had even been allowed to vote on whether to ratify the Constitution! It was therefore "not true, in point of fact, that the Constitution was made exclusively by the white race."[116]

But just as Taney had not fully adopted Calhoun's extreme pro-slavery theory, neither did Curtis endorse the entire position of the anti-slavery constitutionalists. Instead, he believed that citizenship was determined solely by state law. Since the Articles of Confederation had given this power to states, and no provision of the Constitution overrode that grant, they must still have that power. Pointing to Article IV, he observed that the Constitution guaranteed the enjoyment of certain "privileges and immunities . . . throughout the United States," but did so on the condition that the person was a citizen of a state. This complicated paragraph of his opinion would have lasting consequences:

> here, privileges and immunities to be enjoyed throughout the United States, under and by force of the national compact, are granted and secured. In selecting those who are to enjoy these national rights of citizenship, how are they described? As citizens of each State. It is to them these national rights are secured. The qualification for them is not to be looked for in any provision of the Constitution or laws of the United States. They are to be citizens of the several States, and, as such, the privileges and immunities of general citizenship, derived from and guarantied [sic] by the Constitution, are to be enjoyed by them.[117]

In other words, Article IV's Privileges and Immunities Clause speci-fied only the category of *rights* that were guaranteed nationwide—not the category of *persons* who held those rights. On the contrary, state governments held the exclusive power to determine who qualified as citizens. Once a state made a person a citizen, that person was entitled by the federal constitution to the "privileges or immunities of citizens of the several states." The word "several" here is signifi-cant—it means "discrete," or "considered separately," or "respec-tively." When the Fourteenth Amendment was written, it would employ a more unitary, nationalistic phrase: "the privileges or immunities of *citizens of the United States*." Its protections would not depend on state authority at all, but would shift the responsibility for citizenship and security to the nation instead.

Bingham on the Oregon Bill

Dred Scott did not resolve the controversy, as Taney had hoped, not even temporarily. Only a few days later, justices on the Maine Supreme Court issued an opinion rejecting it, holding 7-1 that blacks could be citizens of Maine and therefore of the United States.[118] New York's highest court followed with a decision in *Lemmon v. People*, emphatically rejecting *Dred Scott* and holding that a slave brought into New York was automatically freed.[119]

Two years after *Dred Scott*, Ohio Congressman John Bingham delivered a clever and important speech on the nature of federal citi-zenship. He did not begin with an attack on racial discrimination; rather, he opposed the admission of Oregon to the union because its proposed state constitution expanded civil rights too *broadly*. Specifically, Oregon's draft constitution extended voting rights both to citizens and to foreigners who pledged that they intended to become American citizens. This, Bingham argued, was unconstitu-tional; states could not grant federal citizenship rights to aliens, let alone those who simply claimed that they would become citizens at some future date. The right to vote "is the sovereignty of America," and was not susceptible of transfer to noncitizens. To extend the fed-eral franchise to aliens was, in effect, to recognize state power to override federal naturalization laws.

But in the process of making this argument, Bingham reiter-ated his belief that states could not deny citizenship to those who *were* entitled to it: "All free persons born and domiciled within the jurisdiction of the United States, are citizens of the United States from birth" regardless of race.[120] The proposed Oregon Constitution, like Missouri's decades earlier, also allowed the state to exclude nonwhite Americans. But citizens of the United States included "all persons born and domiciled within the United States—not all free white persons, but all free persons."[121] Reiterating the points made by the *Dred Scott* dissenters, Bingham pointed out that blacks were citizens of several states at the time the Constitution was adopted, and had even fought in the Revolutionary army. No subsequent law deprived them of the citizenship they had gained, and thus four years after the Revolutionary War ended, when the Constitution invoked the "People of the United States," it must have meant eligible people of both races. And this meant that federal citizenship could not be confined to whites. "This government rests upon the absolute equality of natural rights amongst men."[122]

For states to exclude nonwhite citizens would violate the Privileges and Immunities Clause, Bingham continued. This clause guaranteed a panoply of rights that were federal in nature: it did not protect those rights "which result exclusively from State authority or State legislation," but it did protect the rights "of citizens of the United States in the several States." There was "an ellipsis in the language employed in the Constitution," he said, "but its meaning is self-evident that it is 'the privileges and immunities of citizens of the United States in the several States' that it guaranties [*sic*]."[123] The dual character of American citizenship limited state sovereignty and overrode state laws that infringed on the rights guaranteed to all Americans.

Thus Congressman Bingham and Justice Curtis, like their more extreme allies Spooner and Tiffany, formulated a model of dual citizenship grounded in the Founding Fathers' design of dual sovereignty. Federal citizenship and federal authority were independent of, and superior to, the states' power to define citizenship or govern individuals—and the federal realm was ultimately incompatible with slavery, because it rested on the inalienable rights articulated in the Declaration of Independence. This was enough to rebut the states' rights theory, which could not account either for the fact that nonwhites were admitted as citizens at the time of ratification, or for the Constitution's clear language of supremacy. In response, some Southerners had gone to the untenable extreme of arguing that there was no such thing as an American nation in the first place. The anti-slavery view—that there was an American citizenship independent of state citizenship, which brought with it a category of rights protected against state governments—was a critical insight. But as historian Jacobus tenBroek observed, this doctrine of paramount national citizenship "could not simply be read into the Constitution; it had to be written into it."[124]

Paramount National Citizenship and the Privileges or Immunities Clause

By the time the Civil War ended, Roger Taney was dead; he was succeeded by anti-slavery Chief Justice Salmon Chase. Slavery had been dealt a practical death blow by the Emancipation Proclamation and the collapse of the slave power. Congress quickly followed by writing the Thirteenth Amendment to prohibit slavery. Elated, Lincoln signed that amendment upon its passage, even though presidents are not required to sign constitutional amendments to make them valid.[125]

But freeing the slaves was not enough. *Dred Scott*, after all, had declared not only slaves, but all persons of "the African race" ineligible for federal citizenship. Some Radical Republicans argued that the Thirteenth Amendment automatically made the former slaves citizens under federal law—"no longer a slave, he is a common part of the Republic, owing to it patriotic allegiance in return for the protection of equal laws,"[126] said Charles Sumner—but most Republican leaders believed a new amendment was needed to provide stronger, more explicit security for individual freedom and equal treatment. Thus, in 1868, they ratified the Fourteenth Amendment to constitutionalize the principles of paramount national citizenship and federal protection for natural and common law rights, thereby resetting the constitutional priorities in accordance with the Declaration of Independence.[127] By establishing the primacy of federal citizenship and federal sovereignty, the amendment overthrew the states' rights vision of proud, autonomous states, and replaced it with a system in which people are American citizens first, and citizens of states only derivatively, and in which their rights are protected by federal law.

"All persons born or naturalized in the United States, and subject to the jurisdiction thereof," declares the Fourteenth Amendment, "are citizens of the United States and of the State wherein they reside. No State shall make or enforce any law which shall abridge the privileges or immunities of citizens of the United States; nor shall any State deprive any person of life, liberty, or property, without due process of law; nor deny to any person within its jurisdiction the equal protection of the laws."

The structure of the amendment's first section makes its intent clear. The first clause defines federal citizenship, making it primary, with state citizenship secondary and derivative.[128] Indeed, it deprives states of power to determine who their own citizens are, the most basic power of any true sovereign. The next sentence then asserts that states shall not make or enforce laws that abridge the rights all American citizens enjoy. And the final two clauses assure all people that they will not be deprived of life, liberty, or property without due process of law, or denied the equal protection of the laws. The amendment echoes the Declaration of Independence in both its wording and its argument. Where the Declaration announced that people are born free, and can choose to create a government to protect their rights—thereby becoming "one people"—the new amendment, too, is grounded on a national body politic, which prioritizes individual rights over government power. All Americans are entitled to security for the rights that belong to the citizens of all free governments—and that security is valid against the state governments as well.

Republicans did not think of this as *altering* the Constitution so much as *rescuing* it from the perversions of the states' rights theorists and the Taney Court. The 1787 Constitution, Sumner argued, had been written "to remove difficulties arising from State Rights."[129] From its inception, it had recognized only one sovereignty: that of the nation. States retained "special local control which is essential to the convenience and business of life," but the United States "as Plural Unit" possessed "that commanding sovereignty which embraces and holds the whole country within its perpetual and irreversible jurisdiction."[130] State authority was subordinate "[c]onstantly, and in everything."[131] This predominant federal sovereignty brought with it the power to protect the rights of federal citizens.[132] Bingham also saw the amendment less as an innovation than as a recommitment to an old promise. A decade earlier, he had explained that the rights of citizens were based in national, not state citizenship.[133] States had no authority, he said, to "restrict the humblest citizen of the United States in the free exercise of any one of his natural rights; those rights common to all men, and to protect which, not to confer, all good governments are instituted."[134] Indeed, if states did violate these rights, the people would have "sufficient cause" for the "reconstruction of the political fabric on a juster basis, and with surer safeguards."[135] Now, he and his friends would make good that reconstruction, adding surer federal safeguards for the natural and common law rights to which all Americans were entitled by virtue of their membership in the national body politic.

But what were these rights? Anti-slavery thinkers answered by pointing to the Declaration of Independence.[136] That document had inextricably connected the doctrine of natural liberty with the basis of citizenship. Since the Declaration premised government's legitimacy on its protections for individual rights, the questions of who citizens were, and what rights they were entitled to, could not be regarded separately. Rather, the principles of equality, liberty, and consent were the basis of both political authority and citizenship. Sovereignty was not a basic right to rule, combined with some discretionary benefits handed down to the subject: it was the product of an agreement that the government would respect and protect each person's fundamental right to freedom. Citizenship was not a system of subordination and obedience, as the slaveholders had claimed, but a reciprocal, contractual relationship in which the citizen yielded loyalty in exchange for protection for his rights. Allegiance could not be separated from the truthfulness of the Declaration's claims about rights, any more than one could consider oneself a Christian while denying the doctrines of Jesus, or a Republican while rejecting the party platform. "By incorporation within the body-politic," said Sumner, the former slave "becomes a partner in that transcendent unity. . . . Our rights are his rights; our equality is his equality; our privileges and immunities are his great freehold."[137] Americans became "one people" by subscribing to its propositions about rights and the source of political authority. To now add the former slaves to that people meant signing them on to those fundamental principles.

The Fourteenth Amendment's authors frequently defined privileges or immunities as referring to natural rights, and cited the 1823 decision in *Corfield v. Coryell*, in which Supreme Court Justice Bushrod Washington defined the privileges and immunities of Americans as the "fundamental" rights "which belong, of right, to the citizens of all free governments."[138] Washington specified the right to travel from state to state for work, the right of habeas corpus, the rights to sue, to dispose of property, and to vote in compliance with state law. But privileges and immunities also included "[p]rotection by the government; the enjoyment of life and liberty, with the right to acquire and possess property of every kind, and to pursue and obtain happiness and safety; subject nevertheless to such restraints as the government may justly prescribe for the general good of the whole."[139]

More than four decades later, as Republicans sought to clarify the contours of federal citizenship, they adopted that decision's catalogue of the rights to which citizens of any free *state* are entitled, and used it to describe the rights that in their view belonged to citizens of a free *nation*. Senator Jacob Howard quoted from *Coryell* when he explained that the amendment's new Privileges or Immunities Clause would provide for "'protection by the Government, the enjoyment of life and liberty, with the right to acquire and possess property of every kind, and to pursue and obtain happiness and safety'" as well as "the personal rights guarantied and secured by the first eight amendments of the Constitution."[140] Senator John Sherman, too, explained that the new clause would protect the "privileges, immunities, and rights (because I do not distinguish between them, and cannot do it,) of citizens of the United States, such as are recognized by the common law, such as are ingrafted [sic] in the great charters of England, some of them ingrafted [sic] in the Constitution of the United States, some of them in the constitutions of the different States, and some of them in the Declaration of Independence." Courts applying the clause would "look first at the Constitution," and "[i]f that does not define the right they will look for the unenumerated powers [sic] to the Declaration of American Independence, to every scrap of American history, to the history of England, to the common law of England," where they would find "the fountain and reservoir of the rights of American as well as of English citizens."[141] The new amendment would nationalize *Coryell*.

Its authors did not interpret the privileges or immunities of citizenship merely as benefits given in exchange for loyalty. Instead, Republicans believed that the primacy of individual liberty was the foundation of all legitimate government, and its fair protection the only basis for the citizen's allegiance. They believed that when, in 1776, sovereignty was taken from the British crown, it was transferred to the nation as a whole, making Americans primarily members of the new nation and only secondarily citizens of states. At the same time, the sovereignty that was transferred was also recharacterized in accordance with the Declaration's self-evident truths. It was therefore not the absolute parliamentary sovereignty Blackstone hypothesized, but the limited government described in the Declaration. This was why John Bingham contended that the new amendment would "take[] from no State any right that ever pertained to it." According to the Republican constitutional theory, "[n]o State ever had the right, under the forms of law or otherwise, to deny to any freeman the equal protection of the laws or to abridge the privileges or immunities of any citizen of the Republic."[142] States had flouted those principles in the past, leading to "flagrant violations of the guarantied [*sic*] privileges of citizens of the United States, for which the national Government furnished and could furnish by law no remedy whatever."[143] The new amendment would provide that remedy by giving the federal government "power . . . to protect by national law the privileges and immunities of all the citizens of the Republic and the inborn rights of every person within its jurisdiction whenever the same shall be abridged or denied by the unconstitutional acts of any State."[144]

Slaughter-House's Errors

Yet resistance boiled under the surface. A war-weary public was increasingly reluctant to enforce civil rights in the South, where states were persecuting freedmen and mobs were rioting and torturing former slaves and their friends. Even in the North, defenders of the old system worked to undermine the new constitutional protections.

One of the most strident of these was Jeremiah Sullivan Black, the Pennsylvania "doughface" who had so fervently endorsed the absolute sovereignty of states in the *Sharpless* case.[145] Black had resigned from the Pennsylvania Supreme Court in 1857 when President James Buchanan appointed him attorney general, and in that position he reiterated his states' rights views in a magazine article criticizing Illinois Senator Stephen Douglas for taking too moderate a view of state power. "Sovereignty" he wrote, "is in its nature irresponsible and absolute. . . . Mere moral abstractions or theoretic principles of natural justice do not limit the legal authority of a sovereign. No government *ought* to violate justice;

but any supreme government, whose hands are entirely free, *can* violate it with impunity."[146] After the war, Black continued to argue that the states "were sovereign before they united" and that they retained "all the sovereign rights not granted in the [Constitution to the federal government]."[147] The notion that national citizenship took precedence over state citizenship and that states must respect all Americans' natural or common-law rights was nefariously "inserted in the creed of the abolitionists because they supposed it would give a sort of plausibility to their violent intervention with the internal affairs of the states."[148]

Black's hostility to the principle of paramount national citizenship and to federal efforts to enforce that doctrine through civil-rights laws led him into a personal crusade against Reconstruction. He considered military occupation of the South a travesty on a par with the English occupation of Ireland or the Russian occupation of Poland[149] and thought Reconstruction was responsible for an "infamous combination of Yankee and negro thieves who now have the government of the Southern States in their hands."[150] As an adviser to President Andrew Johnson, Black drafted Johnson's veto of the 1867 Reconstruction Act,[151] and after Congress overrode that veto he devoted his legal talents to defeating civil rights legislation in court.[152] In such prominent cases as *Ex Parte McCardle*,[153] *Ex Parte Milligan*,[154] and *Bylew v. United States*,[155] he challenged federal power to protect civil rights, and he even helped defend Johnson at his impeachment.[156]

Thus, when he was asked to represent the state of Louisiana in the *Slaughter-House Cases*, Jeremiah Black saw a unique opportunity to undo Reconstruction. As his fawning biographer acknowledged, the Fourteenth Amendment had "[u]ndeniably" been "written with the deliberate intention to nationalize all civil rights [and] to make Federal power supreme over the States." But Black sought a way to destroy that provision and "smash the intent of the Radicals."[157] A Supreme Court decision fatally undercutting the amendment's strength "would leave Louisiana free to deal with Carpetbaggers in her own way as soon as military force should be removed."[158] The states' rights theory that he would articulate on the state's behalf was the opposite of the doctrine of paramount national citizenship; indeed, it was precisely the states' rights theory that Republicans tried to destroy when they drafted the Fourteenth Amendment less than five years before.

The *Slaughter-House Cases* involved a Louisiana statute that required all cattle slaughtering in New Orleans Parish to be done at a single, privately owned abbatoir, called the Crescent City Livestock Landing and Slaughtering Corporation. Although framed as a sanitary measure, the law put hundreds of small-scale butchers out of business to benefit a single, politically powerful corporation. The butchers sued, arguing that this violated the Fourteenth Amendment's Privileges or Immunities Clause because it deprived them of their right to earn a living without interference by government monopolies. This right had been a centerpiece of Anglo-American common law for almost three centuries by that time and had long been regarded as one of the basic rights referred to by the phrase "privileges and immunities."[159]

Nevertheless, the Court upheld the law in a 5-4 ruling on the ground that, with "few" exceptions, "the entire domain of the privileges and immunities of citizens of the States" was still left to the state governments to enforce, or not, as they saw fit.[160] Justice Samuel Miller, who wrote the decision, acknowledged a difference between federal and state citizenship, but he failed to honor the Republican principle that federal citizenship brought with it the whole spectrum of natural and common law rights that for so long had been relegated to state supervision. Declaring that most individual rights still "belong[ed] to citizens of the States as such" and were "left to the State governments for security and protection,"[161] Miller's decision essentially repeated the states' rights theory that sovereignty and, with it, common law protections for individual freedom, rested primarily with the states, and not the federal government. In other words, the Court embraced the very theory of federalism and citizenship that the amendment was designed to overthrow. Miller denied that the amendment was meant to "radically change[] the whole theory of the relations of the State and Federal governments to each other and of both these governments to the people,"[162] even though that was *exactly* its purpose: to constitutionalize the Republican doctrines of paramount national citizenship and natural rights.[163]

The way Miller regarded the *Coryell* precedent was especially telling. That case had defined the phrase "privileges and immunities" to include the basic rights of citizens of all free governments, and the Fourteenth Amendment's Framers had used it as a reference point for the rights that they believed *federal* citizenship also guaranteed. Yet the *Slaughter-House* Court ignored this innovation, regarding the *Coryell* list of rights as still "belonging to the individual as a citizen of a State" rather than as a citizen of the nation.[164] These rights, the Court proclaimed, "have always been held to be the class of rights which the State governments were created to establish and secure."[165] That may have been true before the Fourteenth Amendment was ratified, but Republicans had always considered that a grave error, and they wrote the amendment to undo the legal precedents that had so confined citizens' rights. By disregarding the constitutional changes that anti-slavery leaders had wrought, Justice Miller's opinion perverted the amendment's model of citizenship. Republicans regarded citizenship and protection for individual rights as inseparable, mutual covenants, but after *Slaughter-House*, Americans owed their primary allegiance to the nation, while their rights were still primarily confided to the care, and often neglect, of the states.

That paradox echoes through *Slaughter-House*'s most revealing passage: "Was it the purpose of the fourteenth amendment," asked Miller, "to transfer the security and protection of all the civil rights which we have mentioned, from the States to the Federal government?"[166] He immediately answered his rhetorical question in the negative. But the real answer was *yes*—at least insofar as states did not protect those rights. That had been the primary goal of anti-slavery advocates for 40 years. It was the centerpiece of the constitutional argument against slavery and states' rights, and the culmination of the struggle of people like Joel Tiffany, Frederick Douglass, Charles Sumner, and Salmon Chase. Yet the Court brushed this aside because enforcing a federal check on state power would "degrade the State governments by subjecting them to the control of Congress," which would be "a departure from the structure and spirit of our institutions."[167] Whatever validity such a concern might have, it was hardly a good reason for denying effect to the amendment's plain language. As one contemporaneous critic of the decision wrote, "If such was to be the effect of the amendment, it was so because the American people had so decreed, and it was not the province of the court to defeat their will."[168] Moreover, that concern was exaggerated: *legitimate* state autonomy was not threatened by the amendment's change to federalism. States still retained most of the routine responsibilities of government, including the protection of individual rights. The amendment simply required states to exercise their power consistently with those rights.

Justice Stephen Field, who dissented in the *Slaughter-House Cases*, rightly held that the Fourteenth Amendment "recognized, if it did not create, a National citizenship." The amendment declared that the privileges and immunities of all persons, "which embrace the fundamental rights belonging to citizens of all free governments," should not be violated by state laws. By ignoring the amendment's basic premise that "[n]ational citizenship is primary, and not secondary," Field complained that the *Slaughter-House* decision had "shorn" the amendment of its power and nullified its promise that all Americans would be protected against abuse by state governments.[169]

If there were any doubt that the Court had washed its hands of paramount national citizenship, that doubt evaporated two years later when, in *United States v. Cruikshank*,[170] it threw out the federal prosecution of the perpetrators of the Colfax Massacre, the bloodiest of the Reconstruction race riots. On April 13, 1873, coincidentally the very day that the *Slaughter-House* decision was announced, local government officials in Colfax, Louisiana, descended upon a group of black citizens who had gathered to protest fraudulent election results and brutally murdered about 80 of them. Because the victims had been peaceably assembling to protest grievances, as well as bearing arms and exercising other Bill of Rights freedoms, federal prosecutors charged the officials with depriving citizens of federal privileges and immunities.[171] But the Court rejected this argument. The right to petition *Congress* may be "an attribute of national citizenship . . . under the protection of, and guaranteed by, the United States," the Court said, but the right to assemble to petition *state* government was not.[172] Likewise, the right to bear arms "is not a right granted by the Constitution," but a pre-existing common law right not "in any manner dependent upon [the Constitution] for its existence."[173] And while it may be true that "[t]he rights of life and personal liberty are natural rights of man," and that "[t]he very highest duty of the States" is to protect those rights, "[s]overeignty, for this purpose, rests alone with the States. . . . That duty was originally assumed by the States; and it still remains there."[174] Because the justices held, in accordance with obsolete, pre–Fourteenth Amendment precedents, that most individual rights appertained to state, rather than national, citizenship, the Court advised people to "look to the

States" for protection.[175] Sadly, this meant that Americans of all races were abandoned to the mercies of the same state governments that were oppressing them—in direct contravention of the intent of the Fourteenth Amendment's Framers.[176]

Jeremiah Black's victory in *Slaughter-House* warranted his niece's boast that "the modification and at length the practical abandonment" of Reconstruction "was in no small measure due to the merciless assaults of Judge Black."[177] The *Slaughter-House* Court's withdrawal of the protections promised by the Fourteenth Amendment was a calamity for civil rights, and along with similar rulings it prepared the way for what historian Douglas Blackmon calls "a torrent of repression" and the practical reestablishment of slavery.[178]

After *Slaughter-House*

Since 1873, the Supreme Court has virtually never enforced the Privileges or Immunities Clause.[179] In one case in 1999, the justices did use it to strike down a California law that restricted the welfare payments available to people who moved in from other states, but they stayed carefully within the stifling confines of the *Slaughter-House* precedent. Writing for the majority, Justice John Paul Stevens acknowledged that legal scholars had "fundamentally differing views" about what rights the clause protects, but he found no need to resolve that question because he concluded that a state law limiting benefits for people who move from other states burdens their right to travel, and even *Slaughter-House* held that the clause protects that right.[180]

In the 2010 case of *McDonald v. Chicago*, the Court was asked directly to overrule *Slaughter-House*. That case challenged a city ordinance restricting gun possession—only a year after the justices had declared that the Second Amendment bars the federal government from depriving individuals of the right to own guns.[181] The Chicago case required the Court to decide whether that right was one of the privileges or immunities of federal citizenship that states, too, must respect. But the justices ducked the question of whether the Privileges or Immunities Clause protected that right, holding instead that "[f]or many decades, the question of the rights protected by the Fourteenth Amendment against state infringement has been analyzed under the Due Process Clause of that Amendment."

The Court therefore "decline[d] to disturb the *Slaughter-House* holding."[182] Only Justice Clarence Thomas would have revived the amendment's full strength.

It is shocking that the Court refused, with no stronger justification, to rectify what an overwhelming consensus of legal scholars on both left and right agree was an embarrassing mistake. It is true that courts have employed the Due Process Clause to protect many of the same rights that the amendment's authors expected the Privileges or Immunities Cause to protect, but that is no reason to leave a wrongly decided precedent on the books, where it will continue to warp our constitutional interpretations. During the oral argument in *McDonald*, Justice Antonin Scalia challenged the plaintiffs' attorney: why bother with the Privileges or Immunities Clause rather than relying on the existing theory of substantive due process?[183] But the question misses the point. There can be no better reason for overruling a wrong decision than the fact that it is wrong. Persisting in error simply because it is old is no solution. Nor has the *Slaughter-House* precedent generated a significant body of case law, as Justice Stevens implied when he said he was unwilling to "dislodge 137 years of precedent."[184] On the contrary, that case so effectively nullified the Privileges or Immunities Clause that even Stevens acknowledged that it has left the clause "a clean slate" ever since.[185]

The real reason the justices refused to reconsider the question was that doing so would force them to reexamine many of the foundations of the modern regulatory welfare state. Today, state governments intrude on so many of our freedoms and interfere with so many of our choices that courts have had to improvise a set of rationalizations and exemptions to constitutional principles and turn a blind eye to many of the rights that the authors of the Constitution—and of the Fourteenth Amendment—intended to protect. To disturb the edifice of today's intrusive administrative state by rethinking the amendment's meaning—let alone by taking seriously the ideas of natural rights and the primacy of liberty—would threaten the viability of much of modern government.[186] Yet, as one scholar has written, the Constitution's meaning "will elude us unless we put aside modern conceptions of law and surrender ourselves to the naturalist vision that guided the nineteenth century."[187] The Progressive legal theories that have prevailed in the decades since the New Deal are incompatible with that vision, and the *McDonald* Court was making clear that it is not willing to face that conflict—at least for now.

The consequence is that state governments continue to enact laws that violate a wide swath of individual rights that the authors of the Fourteenth Amendment meant to shield. By reviving an obsolete conception of states' rights, the *Slaughter-House* decision deprived Americans of the amendment's critical innovation: a federal guarantee against state overreaching. True, state autonomy is sometimes a benefit because it allows states to try different approaches to public problems and keeps political decisions at a local level where officials are more knowledgeable and voters can monitor them more carefully. But the type of autonomy that *Slaughter-House* endorsed went beyond this healthy notion of federalism, removing the critical counterbalance of federal security promised by the amendment. Although in the years since that decision, federal courts have sometimes protected people against state oppression under other constitutional clauses, they have done so only in a haphazard and confusing way, and some rights—particularly the right to earn a living, or the right to own and use private property—have gone largely unprotected.

When explaining the original Constitution, James Madison said that striking an appropriate balance between federal and state power would give citizens "a double security," because "the different governments will control each other."[188] Eighty years later, Congressman John Bingham argued that the Fourteenth Amendment's Privileges or Immunities Clause would "protect by national law" the "inborn rights of every person" against "the unconstitutional acts of any State."[189] But the *Slaughter-House* Court removed the most potent protection against state overreaching and threw that double security out of balance.

3. In Defense of Substantive Due Process

Many scholars argue that after the 1873 *Slaughter-House Cases* obliterated the Fourteenth Amendment's Privileges or Immunities Clause, the Supreme Court began utilizing the next clause in the amendment—which promises that no person will be deprived of life, liberty, or property without due process of law—to protect the rights that the Privileges or Immunities Clause was meant to secure. This, they claim, was the origin of what is today one of the most controversial of all legal doctrines: the theory of "substantive due process." Although (or because) courts have often used this doctrine to protect individual rights, prominent intellectuals on both the left and right have denounced it as illegitimate—as a myth or a trick by which judges enforce their own idiosyncratic political views under the mask of law.

But all of that is wrong. Substantive due process is a legitimate part of our constitutional system, one with roots that reach back far before 1873. Although courts used the Due Process Clause to protect individual rights in the post–*Slaughter-House* era, they were not merely conjuring it as a substitute. The Due Process Clause, rightly understood, prohibits all arbitrary government action, including unjustified restrictions of individual liberty.

First, though, a point about terminology: the phrase "substantive due process" is relatively new.[1] Nineteenth-century judges who developed the doctrine called it simply "due process of law." The term "substantive due process" implies a rigid separation between *substantive* and *procedural* due process that has become a mainstay of American constitutional law, but, as we will see, that distinction makes little sense. Also, the modern habit of referring to "the Due Process Clause" worsens the confusion by leaving out two crucial words: "due process *of law*." This clause promises that government will deprive us of life, liberty, or property only in accordance with *law,* and the question in such famous "substantive due process" cases as *Loan Association v. Topeka*[2] or *Lawrence v. Texas*[3] was whether the deprivations in those

71

cases qualified as *law* or merely lawless exertions of government force. To understand what it means for the government to promise to act lawfully, we must start with basic principles.

The Law of the Land

The Due Process Clause originated in the Magna Carta, which declared that "no free man shall be seized or imprisoned, or stripped of his rights or possessions, or outlawed or exiled, or deprived of his standing in any other way, nor will [the king] proceed with force against him, or send others to do so, except by the lawful judgement of his equals or by the law of the land."[4] The phrases "law of the land" and "due process of law" are synonymous, and they mean that the ruler will treat citizens in accordance with the law, and not his mere will.

This distinction between law and mere will reverberates throughout the history of due process of law. The 17th-century jurist Sir Edward Coke built on it his belief that law essentially *is* reason; a law is a directive that derives its obligatory force from its underlying rightness, and not from the fact that failing to obey will incur punishment.[5] This means that for a government act to qualify as law, it must comply with certain preexisting principles. That was what Coke meant when he said that the king is "not under any man, but under God and the law."[6] His contemporary, and sometime rival, Francis Bacon agreed: "In Civil Society, either law or force prevails," Bacon wrote. "But there is a kind of force which pretends law, and a kind of law which savours of force rather than equity. Whence there are three fountains of injustice; namely, mere force, a malicious ensnarement under colour of law, and harshness of the law itself."[7]

If there is a difference between law and mere force, then there must be some qualities or criteria that law possesses and that mere force lacks. It is these qualities, and not the simple fact that the ruler issues a command, that makes a command into a law. If this logic seems familiar, that is because Plato employed the same argument in his dialogue, the *Euthyphro*, in which Socrates asks whether the gods value a good thing because it is actually good, or whether it is only good because the gods value it.[8] If the latter, then goodness is essentially arbitrary; the gods might just as easily value any other thing. But if the gods consider something good because it actually *is* good, according to some objective criteria, then those criteria should also be comprehensible to us, meaning that there really is such a thing as goodness, regardless of whether or not the gods value it. Likewise, if the ruler's acts are law merely because the ruler chooses to act that way, then all law is essentially arbitrary. The king's promise to comply with "the law of the land" would be meaningless, because anything he does would automatically be law anyway. But if there are objective criteria for determining which of the ruler's acts are really *law*, then we can use those criteria to enforce the constitutional promise that government will act only in lawful ways.

The idea that not all of the ruler's acts are law is a necessary condition of what we call the rule of law. Today, many legal scholars attribute the lawfulness of a government act either to its compulsory quality or to the simple fact that government has chosen to do that thing. But "law of the land" or "due process of law" make sense only if lawfulness is something other than the ruler's say-so—if the lawful quality of a statute or a government action depends on its correspondence to independent criteria, and not on mere force. Whenever a society recognizes that not all of the ruler's acts are *law*, then it must develop a way to determine which governmental acts are and are not lawful—and there must be a role for someone other than the ruler (a class of priests, an independent legislative body, or lawyers) to deliberate over whether or not the ruler has acted lawfully. That deliberation accounts for the rule of law because it implies that there are rules that bind the rulemaker; that the ruler's acts are not law ipso facto.

Non-arbitrariness

The promise that government will not deprive a person of life, liberty, or property except through lawful actions is most fundamentally a prohibition against arbitrariness. "Arbitrary" is not an easy word to define, but we can recognize certain basic outlines. An arbitrary act is one that does not accord with a rational explanatory principle: one that has no connection to a legitimate purpose or goal. It may lack reasons to explain it, or be supported by illegitimate reasons, or reasons that would, with equal plausibility, justify the opposite act. An action is rational if it is a cost-efficient means toward some legitimate end. But an arbitrary action does not fit within a reasonable schedule of goals and methods; it is not really a means to any end. It exists of itself, with no (or with only an illusory) guiding

73

principle or purpose. Arbitrariness is to law as mere will is to reason. It is not susceptible of persuasion, but depends only on force. It is essentially ipse dixit—the ruler says "because I say so." The Due Process Clause is a promise that government will not take away the people's rights simply because it says so, but only in accordance with principles that we recognize as marking the difference between lawful and arbitrary rule.

As Madison observed in *The Federalist*, people subjected to arbitrary, lawless rule are no better off than they were "in a state of nature, where the weaker individual is not secured against the violence of the stronger."[9] Consider two classic literary depictions of arbitrary political rule: Shirley Jackson's short story, "The Lottery,"[10] and Jerome Bixby's "It's a *Good* Life"[11] (made into a famous *Twilight Zone* episode starring Bill Mumy). Jackson's story is set in an unnamed village, a pastoral hamlet in a timeless alternate universe, where the people assemble every year for the ritual of stoning to death a randomly chosen citizen. The system is *procedurally* even-handed—victims are picked by drawing names from an old wooden box—but what makes the story so chilling is precisely the fact that there is no reason for the execution. It has just *always been that way*, and the villagers go on, year after year, enforcing the fundamentally arbitrary rule, annually killing a villager for no reason whatsoever.[12] When Tessie Hutchinson's name is drawn, and her neighbors close in upon her with rocks in their hands, the horror is not that there has been some formal or procedural mistake, but that there is no point to any of it. The people are subjected to a rule that deprives them of life arbitrarily. "It isn't fair, it isn't right," are Tessie's last words.[13] But she is not the only victim. The other villagers are also vulnerable; they are haunted by the risk of inescapable, regular, utterly pointless annihilation. Life in the village may not seem unstable or unpredictable. But there is no rationale for the use of force, and the people can never know when or why their lives are to be sacrificed. They live under the lawless rule of mere power.

A different kind of terror dominates Bixby's story. There, 10-year-old psychic Anthony Fremont has used his mind to vaporize all the world except 46 residents of a nondescript Midwestern town. Able to read the villagers' minds and to punish them telekinetically for their bad thoughts, Anthony presides over a reign of terror: the townspeople must think only pleasant things, and praise him even when he tortures animals, kills loved ones, and destroys the crops on which their lives depend. His rule has no reason whatsoever to it, and one of the cruelest aspects of life in the village is each person's hopeless effort to figure out what Anthony approves, or will approve—when, of course, his moods are childishly fleeting and incomprehensible. There is no guiding principle, and therefore no safety; every day is different and unpredictable—Anthony might make it snow, or make the television work, or transform animals into startling monsters. There is no hope of revolution, only the paranoia of unpredictable fear.

Different as Bixby's and Jackson's stories are, they are both visions of arbitrary rule, in which power is wielded according to no sensible principle. In "The Lottery," the senselessness is regular, and violence comes every year; in "It's a *Good* Life," the terror is random and unpremeditated. But in both, power is wielded according to no principles, no explicable order; the rulers can provide no rational account for why they should be obeyed. Both villages are realms of utter arbitrariness, and though ruled with an iron fist, they are not ruled by law.

Rule by the Ruler's Self-Interest as an Illusory Principle

It is easy to see how being governed by the ruler's mere whim is arbitrary. But so, too, is government that serves the ruler's self-interest. This is arbitrary because there is no reason why the ruler's self-interest ought to be privileged over everyone else's.[14] Instead, rule for the self-interest of the ruler is rule according to "because I say so"—rule by ipse dixit.

In *Politics*, Aristotle distinguished between governments aimed at the benefit of the ruled and those that aim only to profit the ruler.[15] Those ruled for the benefit of all he classified as monarchies, aristocracies, or polities, depending on whether they are ruled by one, or a few, or the many. He likened these governments to a family, which is governed "for the sake of the ruled"—that is, for the better flourishing of all concerned. But states that ruled for the ruler's *own* benefit he classified as tyrannies, oligarchies, or democracies. These he likened to slavery because just as the master rules the slave for his own benefit, not for the good of the slave, so these societies are governed for the sake of the ruler—whether it be a single tyrant, a cadre of oligarchs, or a vulgar, self-interested mob.

Aristotle's pejorative use of the word "democracy" seems strange to modern eyes, but his point was to distinguish healthy majority-rule societies from lawless mob rule. Governments "that look to the common benefit" are "correct," meaning they are actually *governments*—"whereas those which look only to the benefit of the rulers are mistaken and are deviations from the correct constitutions" and are not really governments at all. In other words, the basic ground for distinguishing between these types of political rule is whether they abide by a rule of law that respects the values of equality and individual autonomy. Corrupt governments are "like rule by a master," in which the people, like slaves, are considered inferior to the ruler, and the ruler asserts a right to rule others for his own benefit. But a "correct constitution" is "a community of free people." It is a group of basic equals who associate for the benefit of all—to enable each to flourish. Their commonwealth is not premised on any primordial hierarchy in which some have the right to obedience from others.[16]

Although Aristotle was not a classical liberal like America's Founding Fathers, both he and they started with the same basic principle:[17] that legitimate, lawful rule depends upon a community of basic equals who agree in a sort of contract to submit to reasonable rules for protection against violence and fraud. Law is not submission to arbitrary command for the ruler's benefit. Each person's basic right to freedom entitles him to an equal say in the formation of the state and to equal treatment by that state. This baseline of equal liberty is not a mere assertion, but a logical presumption from which deviations are allowed only when justified by rational argument.[18] And the presumption against deviations means that the ruler cannot simply demand compliance with his whims. Where no good reason justifies treating people unequally, such treatment is arbitrary, and where no good reason entitles the ruler to limit a person's freedom, he may not do so.

If the ruler's power is legitimate only insofar as he can give good reasons for rule, then what is a good reason? John Locke answered this with a reasonable-person argument: it would be unreasonable for people to subject themselves to arbitrary rules or to agree to become mere tools for the king or the majority. This would put them "into a worse condition than the state of Nature, wherein they had a Liberty to defend their Right against the Injuries of others."[19] The minimum conditions of legitimate, lawful rule are that the state's coercive powers must be used according to general guidelines, and must rationally promote the public good, which means government must protect the people's rights regularly and fairly. The rule of law establishes an order that deserves compliance because it respects everyone's freedom: the purpose of law "is not to abolish or restrain, *but to preserve Freedom*," Locke wrote. "For *Liberty* is to be free from restraint and violence from others which cannot be, where there is no Law." Contrary to what some people claim, freedom does not mean "*Liberty for every Man to do what he lists:* (For who could be free, when every other Man's Humour might domineer over him?)" Instead, it means "a *Liberty* to dispose, and order, as he lists, his Person, Actions, Possessions, and his whole Property, within the Allowance of those Laws under which he is; and therein not to be subject to the arbitrary Will of another, but freely follow his own."[20]

While the dystopian fantasies of Jerome Bixby and Shirley Jackson depict memorable examples of lawless rule, an even more jarring picture of a society ruled for the ruler's self-interest is found in Freidoune Sahebjam's book, *The Stoning of Soraya M.*, based on a true story and made into a film in 2008. The village of Kupayeh is governed by a perverted mullah, Sheik Hassan, and a complaisant mayor, Ebrahim, who together allow Soraya's abusive and hypocritical husband, Ghorban-Ali, to frame her for adultery and execute her so he can marry another woman.[21] Unlike in "The Lottery," this execution does serve a purpose, but that purpose is merely to satisfy the desires of the men in power. Soraya and the other women in the village cannot navigate the patterns of rule because there are none— and thus no safety.

After making a fortune in blackmail by exploiting his job as a prison guard, Ghorban-Ali becomes bored with Soraya and makes a pact with Sheik Hassan: Hassan will see to it that Soraya agrees to a divorce, allowing Ghorban-Ali to marry the girl with whom he is now infatuated. In exchange, Hassan will have Soraya for his own wife. When Soraya refuses, the two frame her for having an affair with another man and execute her. Sheik Hassan is a murderer and thief whose "master[y] at the art of obsequiousness and the art of scheming"[22] has given him a "visible ascendancy over the mayor."[23] Unchecked by the cowardly Ebrahim, Hassan becomes the village's ruling power, and his house becomes "a kind of law court where the mullah played all the roles, those of both prosecutor and public defender. And since any service rendered had its price, it was not long before the sheik had managed to acquire a few acres of land, half a dozen head of cattle, some poultry. . . . All this was done by perfectly legal means, with the full accord of the mayor and his deputies."[24] With nothing more than truth on her side, Soraya cannot hope to resist the power of these men; robbed of the opportunity to defend herself, she retreats into silence and dies for no good reason at the hands of the brutal villagers, all "according to the rules of law."[25] Here we see the realization of Locke's and Madison's warnings. In a society like Kupayeh, where coercive power is wielded arbitrarily, people like Soraya have gained none of the benefits that are supposed to emerge from the establishment of political rule. On the contrary, she is worse off than she would have been in a state of nature, because she is intimidated by the emblems of apparent legitimacy and disarmed by the government's official powers.

It is Soraya's aunt Zahra, the village's female elder, who stands as the symbol of lost lawfulness in the village. It was she who once selected Ebrahim to be mayor. Now it is she who confronts him, charging that his willingness to let Hassan and Ghorban-Ali exploit authority for their own purposes renders him unfit for that trust. "[Y]ou've lost everything," she cries, "everything that gave you the right to be the head of our community: authority, honesty, courage, independence, goodness."[26] In other words, Ebrahim's acts are no longer truly lawful because the qualities that would make his decisions law instead of mere words are absent. He is now only the shell of authority—the form of law, without substance. Now he may wield power and may sign legal documents purporting to legitimize "the illicit commerce that Sheik Hassan was carrying on in league with Ghorban-Ali,"[27] but his signatures cannot make that commerce any less illicit, and "the vocabulary of officialdom" cannot make Soraya's death lawful. It is Zahra who stands for the substantive principles of law, but without the authority to put them into practice, she is rendered an impotent witness as the political order degenerates into a "diabolical machine."[28] It is "the law of men, the law that men make and say it is the law of God," she tells Soraya. "They have found you guilty, whereas you are not."[29] Like Sophocles's Antigone, Zahra does not mistake the fiction of men's will for the actual lawful order, and after the execution she defies Sheik Hassan's decree that Soraya shall not be buried.[30]

The Elements of Law

Phrases like "true law" or "higher law" sound like mysticism to modern ears. But the idea does not rely on supernatural claims. It merely asserts that there are rational principles that limit the kinds of rules we can adopt, and those limits cannot rightly be overridden by fiat. This is a familiar idea. Principles of mathematics inhabit a realm of logical abstraction that cannot be observed in physical reality but nevertheless apply to our lives, limiting and guiding our choices. The logic of lawful rule similarly limits the kinds of things that government may do. For example, as Francis Bacon observed in 1620, a lawmaker cannot declare a law unrepealable, since a provision barring repeal could itself be repealed. Any attempt to create an unchangeable statute would be "void ab initio & ipso facto" simply "by the impertinency of it."[31] This restriction on the legislator's power is not imposed by any statute, of course, but by the logic of lawfulness itself.[32] And there are many similar abstract natural laws that restrict the power of lawmakers. For instance, the commonplace rule that a later-enacted law takes precedence over an older, contrary law is, as Alexander Hamilton wrote, "not derived from any positive law, but from the nature and reason of the thing."[33] Or consider a statute that was simply an unintelligible gibberish of symbols. Would it in fact be a law? How would we know? We could answer this question only by reference to abstract principles that limit and guide the legislator's power.[34]

This means that law is a thing with certain qualities, and an enactment lacking these qualities cannot be fairly described as law. In other words, like all human institutions, law is a combination of descriptive and normative: a convergence of "is" and "ought." As philosopher Philippa Foot observed, knowing *what* a manmade thing is means knowing what a *good* thing of that kind would be.[35] A bartender who leaves out the pineapple juice has made a *bad* piña colada—and if bad enough, it is not really a piña colada at all. In the same way, a law that lacks certain elements is a bad law, and if bad enough, is not even really a law at all.[36] And the ingredients of law include generality, regularity, fairness, rationality, and public orientation.[37] In other words, a law is a general rule that realistically serves some public, not merely private, goal.

Daniel Webster put this point eloquently in his famous argument in the 1819 case of *Dartmouth College v. Woodward*—in words the

Supreme Court quoted time and again throughout the 19th century as the best definition of the term. Law, Webster said, is

> "a rule; not a transient sudden order . . . to or concerning a particular person; but something permanent, uniform and universal. . . ." By the law of the land, is most clearly intended, the general law; a law, which hears before it condemns; which proceeds upon inquiry, and renders judgment only after trial. The meaning is, that every citizen shall hold his life, liberty, property and immunities, under the protection of the general rules which govern society. Everything which may pass under the form of an enactment, is not, therefore, to be considered the law of the land. If this were so . . . decrees and forfeitures, in all possible forms, would be the law of the land. Such a strange construction would render constitutional provisions, of the highest importance, completely inoperative and void. . . . There would be no general permanent law for courts to administer, or for men to live under. The administration of justice would be an empty form, an idle ceremony.[38]

We know that these are the ingredients of a law by considering what law is supposed to accomplish—just as the ingredients of a cocktail are determined by what it is meant to taste like. To know whether a law is a good one or not, we must know the reason for establishing a law-making body. That reason is to give security and stability to individual rights, protecting them against the intrusions of others and against the interference of the government itself. Webster hinted at this when he paraphrased a passage from Edmund Burke: "'Is that the law of the land,' said Mr. Burke, 'upon which, if a man go to Westminster Hall, and ask counsel by what title or tenure he holds his privilege or estate, according to the law of the land, he should be told, that the law of the land is not yet known; that no decision or decree has been made in his case; that when a decree shall be passed, he will then know what the law of the land is?'"[39] When government acts according to no limit but its own discretion—when the citizen can only know what the rules are after the ruler announces them, and only for that moment, until the ruler changes them again—then the citizen's rights are insecure; he is vulnerable to the self-interested or abusive acts of the ruler. He cannot make plans or deal with others safely and rationally. These evils follow regardless of whether the arbitrary power is wielded by a monarch or by a democratic voting majority.

Webster's definition of law was borrowed from William Blackstone, who explained in his *Commentaries* that law differs from a specific command, because a command is only "a transient sudden order from a superior, to or concerning a particular person," whereas law is a "rule," and therefore "permanent, uniform, and universal."[40] A statute that confiscates a particular person's goods or purports to convict him of treason is not a law, because "the operation of this act is spent" upon that one person, and "has no relation to the community in general." Such an enactment would be "rather a sentence than a law."[41] The same holds for statutes that confiscate the goods of a *group*, or deprive a group of liberty.[42] If the legislature can violate their rights for no other reason than that they have too little political influence to defend themselves, then the legislature would have power to alter or destroy rights at will, contrary to the purposes for which the entire apparatus of legal procedure was established.

Previous generations of lawyers called enactments whereby the majority enriched itself or vented its displeasure on politically disfavored groups "legislative deprivations," and regarded them as quintessential violations of the due process of law requirement.[43] As the Tennessee Supreme Court observed in an influential 1836 decision, a statute that seizes a person's property "does not partake of the character of a law, for it forms no rule of action of that permanent, uniform and universal character which Blackstone . . . says constitute the fundamental principles of municipal law."[44] Instead, such a statute is more like a judicial decree. It takes a person's property away and gives it to someone else in the manner of a court judgment, but without weighing evidence or legal precedent as courts do. Yet the point was not merely that such statutes violate the principle of separation of powers by intruding on the province of the courts, it was that if legislatures could deprive individuals or groups of their rights simply by voting to do so, then the people would be exposed to lawless rule and would be no safer than they were in a state of nature. The legislature could erase their rights whenever it saw fit, for any reason or no reason. Rights would then be held not by lawful tenure, but simply by permission from the ruling majority.

In his 1967 masterpiece *The Morality of Law*, legal philosopher Lon Fuller described eight ways in which the government can fail to make *law* even while claiming to do so. If it passes bills that do not create rules, for example, but only implement ad hoc policies without reference to general principles, then it is not enforcing a rule of law. If it abuses retroactive legislation so as to punish acts that were legal when they were committed, or if it passes contradictory or incomprehensible statutes, it would not be rightly regarded as a government of laws. A citizen living under such rule could not predict how the government would operate, or whether private agreements and rights would be enforced. On the contrary, such lawless rule would undermine whatever rules did exist and deprive them of their power to guide action and facilitate citizens' choices. If the government fails to actually enforce or abide by the rules it announces, or changes those rules suddenly and without reason, it is not successfully producing law.[45]

The 2010 report of the World Justice Project agreed with this argument, recognizing that "the rule of law must be more than merely a system of rules" because "positive law that fails to respect core human rights" is "at best 'rule *by* law,' and does not deserve to be called a rule of law system." That report identified four universal principles recognized across all cultures as inherent in the rule of law: First, the government is subject to, and not superior to, the law; second, the laws are clear, public, stable, evenhanded, and protect fundamental rights such as persons and property; third, the procedures of enactment and enforcement are accessible, fair, and efficient; and fourth, the laws are actually enforced by independent, competent, and ethical officials.[46] The law must be rational and comprehensible—so as to avoid the arbitrariness of "The Lottery" or "It's a *Good* Life"—and must be general and oriented toward public goals—so as not to become a trick for predatory rulers as in *The Stoning of Soraya M.* But its rules must also be regular and basically fair. A purported law that lacks these requirements would not be a law at all, just as Alice's "trial" before the Red Queen in *Alice in Wonderland* is too absurd to deserve the name "trial."

True, generality, fairness, and equality describe broad ideals that might be difficult to define and apply in any specific case,[47] and they must accord some degree of discretion to the lawmaker. For example, an unyielding generality requirement that would bar the legislature from passing statutes applicable only to particular groups or individuals would be unworkable, since there are circumstances in which distinctions are appropriate. On the other hand, a monarch or a legislature that frequently resorts to specific commands rather than general rules is more likely to be ruling arbitrarily, or to be abusing power to serve private interests instead of the public interest. Likewise, regularity is an elastic concept. In some cases, a special rule for a special case is proper, and it is not easy to draw a line that excludes inappropriate special rules but also allows lawmakers sufficient discretion to react to unusual circumstances. Yet the fact that these principles are not mathematically precise does not render them invalid, nor does it mean that courts are incapable of applying them. Courts routinely employ abstract concepts like "the reasonable man," "foreseeable under the totality of the circumstances," "due diligence," and "necessary and proper." And courts applying the concepts of generality or regularity have developed a rich and useful body of case law to enforce constitutional limits.

Consider, for example, the prohibition on "special laws" contained in many state constitutions. Special laws, which confer unique benefits on some discrete subset of the populace, violate the principle of generality and betray the inherent principle of lawfulness unless there is some legitimate reason for singling out a case as unique. Difficult as it may be to define special laws, it is still clear that they are an abuse of the lawmaking power. They are symptomatic of a government that legislates for the ruler's self-interest or for the benefit of his cronies. As one court explained:

> The inherent vice of special laws is that they create preferences and establish irregularities. . . . [They thus replace] a symmetrical body of statutory law on subjects of general and common interest to the whole people . . . [with] a wilderness of special provisions, whose operation extends no further than the boundaries of the particular school district or township or county to which they were made to apply. . . . A public law is a measure that affects the welfare of the state as a unit; a private law is one that provides an exception to the public rule. The one is an answer to a public need, the other an answer to a private prayer. When it acts upon a public bill, a legislature legislates; when it acts upon a private bill, it adjudicates. It passes from the function of a lawmaker to that of a judge. It is transformed from a tribune of the people into a justice shop for the seeker after special privilege.[48]

Such legislation is not, strictly speaking, *law* at all. It is a command or a dictate. It violates the principles of lawfulness from, as it were, both the internal and external point of view. By granting localized benefits to specific persons, special laws employ state power in an irregular manner not justified by any broader public purpose. But they also do violence to the democratic process of deliberation and public decisionmaking, thus encouraging "improvident and ill-considered legislation." A law that concentrates benefits or burdens on constituents in one county will not be weighed or considered by legislators who represent different counties. And the legislature will "fritter[] away" its time "in the granting of special favors to private or corporate interests or to local communities," instead of addressing problems of general importance.[49]

How Substantive Due Process Works

If a legislative enactment that fails the tests of generality, regularity, fairness, rationality, and public orientation is not a *law*, then enforcing it against a person would violate his or her right to due process *of law*. Under the Constitution, government may only deprive people of their rights if it acts within the principles of lawfulness. These principles are both procedural and substantive, and they distinguish *lawful* from *unlawful* state action. For the government's acts to qualify as lawful, they must comply with formal procedures (e.g., the "rules of promulgation"), and they must also include the substantive elements like regularity, generality, and fairness. Form and substance cannot be separated here any more than they can be in the realm of physical reality, and the effort to treat "substantive due process" and "procedural due process" as separate categories collapses upon examination. Consider some examples.

First, imagine that Congress were to pass a bill (say, requiring ship captains to maintain a list of passengers) but the president vetoes it. Having been vetoed, the bill does not become law, but this is only for procedural or formal reasons, not for substantive reasons or any objections relating to the bill's content. Had the president signed it, nobody would deny its validity. But now that it has been vetoed, a harbor master who tries to enforce it by arresting a captain who fails to keep a list of passengers would be acting unlawfully—without the necessary legal authority. He would be depriving the captain of liberty without due process of *law*.

The same reasoning applies where a purported law fails for substantive, and not for procedural, reasons. Thus, suppose Congress were to pass a bill, and the president were to sign it, which established an official religion for the United States. That bill would not be a law, even though it complied with the *formal* steps required to make a law, because the First Amendment denies Congress power to make any such law, regardless of the formalities: "Congress shall make no law respecting an establishment of religion." And since that statute could have no claim to status as law, a sheriff who arrested a dissenter for violating it would be depriving that person of liberty without due process of law, just as in the first hypothetical. The arrest would be *unlawful*, not because of any formal or procedural shortcoming, but because the sheriff could not point to any duly constituted *substantive* authority to justify his actions.

These two examples are relatively easy to follow since they rest on explicit constitutional limitations on government power. But there are also *implicit* or inherent limits on government power. These implicit limits are part of the very idea of law itself. No constitution or contract could hope to spell out the infinite commonsense principles that it presupposes or implies. Even the most airtight contract assumes certain unspoken elements, either because the parties consider them too obvious to require specification, or because the background laws create "gap fillers" that clarify the meaning of the terms. Implicit limits on lawmaking play a similar role in constitutional law. For example, in *Clinton v. City of New York*,[50] the Supreme Court ruled that the Constitution did not allow Congress to give the president a line-item veto power. The Constitution does not *explicitly* prohibit the line-item veto, but the Court's logic was irresistible: the Founders wrote down the entire procedure for making a bill into a law. They did not provide any alternative methods, but were "silent on the subject of unilateral Presidential action that either repeals or amends parts of duly enacted statutes."[51] The Founders' "constitutional silence" was "equivalent to an express prohibition"[52] against Congress devising any alternative methods of lawmaking. In other words, by specifying one procedure for making and vetoing laws, the Constitution implicitly bars Congress from creating others. It logically followed that Congress had no power to give the president a line-item veto, and the statute doing so could not be regarded as a law. In short, if the legislature passes a statute it lacks the authority to make, that statute has no standing as law, even if its fatal weakness is that it contradicts generally understood principles or the logical implications of the Constitution's provisions, instead of any explicit prohibition.

By forbidding the government from depriving a person of life, liberty, or property except through due process of *law*, the Constitution bars legislators, presidents, or other government officials from going beyond the limits—whether explicit or implicit—on their authority. If the Constitution is a kind of contract among the people, then government is an agent, "hired" for the purpose of protecting individual rights. And inherent in its "employment contract" is the principle that it may not *violate* those rights, or act in ways that only serve the rulers' own self-interests.

This argument is familiar from the realm of arbitration law. An arbitrator can settle a dispute between two parties only because the parties have chosen to let him. But their agreement to submit to his decision limits his powers, both explicitly and implicitly. It is not unusual for the parties to a dispute to later go to court seeking to challenge the validity of the arbitrator's decision. In such a case, as the Seventh Circuit Court of Appeals once observed, "the plaintiff normally will be pointing to *implicit or explicit limits that the contract places on the arbitrator's authority*—principally that he was to interpret the contract and not go off on a frolic of his own—and arguing that the arbitrator exceeded those limits."[53] Where an arbitrator acts in ways that the arbitration agreement does not authorize, his decision is invalid. One might even say that such an arbitrator has deprived the parties of their right to the "due process of their contract." In the same way, government actions that the Constitution does not authorize violate the Due Process of Law Clause.

Classical liberals such as the Framers saw government not only as an arbitrator but also as a security guard. The people, anxious to protect their resources and freedoms, hire the government to protect them, just as the owner of a bank might hire an armed guard. But while this solves the problem of robbery, the bank owner now has a new problem: he has allowed the guard to enter his bank with a gun, and the guard might very well give in to temptation and rob the bank himself. If this were to happen, the guard's actions would obviously exceed the terms of his employment contract and would lack legitimate authority.

This actually happened in a Florida case in 1986.[54] A bank contracted with a detective agency to provide a guard, but the guard then conspired with third parties to help rob the bank. The bank sued the detective agency, arguing that the agency was responsible for its employee's wrongdoing. But the court rejected this argument because the guard's actions were a "classic case of an employee acting outside the scope of his employment. . . . [W]e think the employee was plainly off on a frolic of his own, [and] was in no way furthering the interests of his employer."[55] In other words, the guard's authority as an employee existed only within the boundaries of the employment contract, so when he stepped beyond those limits, his acts lacked validity. This conclusion is obvious even though the contract contained no *explicit* provision against holding up the bank. That prohibition was *implicit*, because the whole point of the owner hiring the guard was to ensure against robbery. The owner need not write out a rule against the guard robbing the bank, because the contract contains both explicit and implicit, common-sense terms; acts that exceed those implicit limits are *ultra vires* and deprive him of his status as an employee just as surely as do acts that violate the contract's explicit provisions.

When a court is asked to determine whether the government has violated the due process of law guarantee, it must approach the question the same way. It must decide whether the government has obeyed both the explicit and the implicit limits on its authority. As *The Federalist* explains, the Constitution is the instrument by which the people delegate power to the legislature, and when the lawmakers go beyond their bounds, courts must intervene to keep them "within the limits assigned to their authority" by pronouncing their illegal acts unenforceable and void.[56] This is how courts ensure that the people's "bank guard" does not fall prey to the temptation to rob the bank for himself.

How Implicit Limits Apply in Due Process Cases

What are the Constitution's implicit limits on government authority? As with an employment contract, we can answer this question only by asking what the Constitution is designed to accomplish. And this requires us to address questions of political philosophy. It is not surprising that this obligation has generated so much debate throughout American history. Yet this is not, as many have claimed, an invitation to judges to do whatever they please: the principles of the Constitution's political philosophy are not left up to the judges to invent, but are stated in the Declaration of Independence.

Justices James Iredell and Samuel Chase began the argument in *Calder v. Bull*,[57] a 1798 case involving a state law that tried to set aside a trial court's verdict in an inheritance lawsuit. That statute was a specific command, rather than a general law, and it sought to change the rules of litigation in the middle of the game. The Supreme Court justices had to decide whether this violated the Constitution's prohibition on ex post facto laws, and although Chase and Iredell agreed in the end that it did not, their reasoning differed. Chase thought the Constitution imposes certain inherent restrictions on legislatures that bar them from "revis[ing] and correct[ing] . . . a decision of any of its Courts of Justice."[58] Even where the Constitution imposes no "express[] restrain[t]" on lawmakers, "[t]he nature, and ends of legislative power will limit" their powers.[59] In other words, there are implicit restrictions on what government may do, and those implicit limits can be understood by considering the purposes of government, just as a bank guard's authority is implicitly limited by the nature of his task:

> The purposes for which men enter into society will determine the nature and terms of the social compact; and as they are the foundation of the legislative power, [those purposes] will decide what are the proper objects of [government authority]. . . . There are certain vital principles in our free Republican governments, which will determine and overrule an apparent and flagrant abuse of legislative power; [such as if the legislature tries] to authorize manifest injustice by positive law; or to take away that security for personal liberty, or private property, for the protection whereof the government was established. An ACT of the Legislature (for I cannot call it a law) contrary to the great first principles of the social compact . . . cannot be considered a rightful exercise of legislative authority. The obligation of a law in governments established on express compact, and on republican principles, must be determined by the nature of the power, on which it is founded.[60]

Justice Iredell disagreed, arguing that courts should not be in the business of interpreting the implicit limits on legislative authority.

"The ideas of natural justice are regulated by no fixed standard: the ablest and the purest men have differed upon the subject."[61] In the absence of express constitutional prohibitions, courts must acquiesce even in legislation they think "inconsistent with the abstract principles of natural justice."[62]

Justice Iredell's hesitancy is certainly understandable; it would be easy for judges to exploit their power to interpret the Constitution's implicit principles to nullify laws they simply dislike. Judges are often accused of doing just that. But this is a prudential concern, not a legal argument. Judges infer inherent principles all the time—as in *Clinton v. New York,* or in ordinary arbitration decisions, or cases interpreting employment contracts. They might abuse their authority when doing so, or reach incorrect decisions, but that does not show that the undertaking itself is improper. Wise as Iredell's warnings might have been, they do not refute Chase's logical position that governments are formed for certain purposes, and that their authority must be implicitly limited by those purposes. Judges must resort to political philosophy in making their decisions because the Constitution is not a morally neutral framework for empowering lawmakers. But the philosophical propositions on which the Constitution rests are set forth in the Declaration, which tells us that government exists to preserve the blessings of liberty and to secure individual rights by establishing lawful, non-arbitrary rule.

Nevertheless, Chase's invocation of the principles of political philosophy has been condemned by many, especially in recent decades. Justice Scalia, who has scoffed at such ideas as "vague ethico-political First Principles,"[63] has declared that the Constitution gives judges no power to define what rights are, or to "enforce the judges' list [of rights] against laws duly enacted by the people."[64] Yet courts have done just this throughout legal history. Before the Revolution, common-law judges enforced individual rights by invalidating laws that clashed with basic principles of lawfulness or traditional protections. Even under the lenient rational-basis test of modern times—the "paradigm of judicial restraint"[65]—courts must still determine whether a challenged law rationally relates to a *legitimate government interest*, which obviously implies that some government interests are not legitimate. While courts have done a poor job of explaining which interests do and do not qualify, they have still ruled some things out of bounds. For example, they have made clear in a series of cases that government may not use its powers simply to burden or exclude disfavored groups as a sign of disapproval.[66] This even applies to groups that have not traditionally received protection under the civil rights laws. As the justices explained in *Romer v. Evans*,[67] the constitutional requirement that a law must "bear a rational relationship to an independent and legitimate legislative end" exists to "ensure that classifications are not drawn for the purpose of disadvantaging the group burdened by the law."

In other words, when a court is asked to rule whether a challenged statute is lawful or arbitrary, it must be prepared to look past that statute's form and examine its substance. The judge must determine whether the principle that the ruler purports to be advancing is genuine or only illusory. This will always be a normative question, but it is not up to the judges' personal views. They must enforce the principles of the Constitution and the Declaration.

As long as judges are in the business of "saying what the law is,"[68] they must enforce the substantive distinction between lawfulness and arbitrariness. A statute under which the government takes away a person's life, liberty, or property without constitutional authority, or for no genuine public reason, or simply because the government wants to, is not a *law* as far as the Due Process of Law Clause is concerned, even if the majority supports that act. As the Supreme Court put it in 1884, law is "something more than mere will exerted as an act of power. . . . Arbitrary power, enforcing its edicts to the injury of the persons and property of its subjects, is not law, whether manifested as the decree of a personal monarch or of an impersonal multitude."[69]

Some Examples of Substantive Due Process Cases

Because the question of whether or not the government has acted lawfully in a particular case necessarily involves considerations of political philosophy, substantive due process lawsuits have often become arenas for the clash between the wolf's and the sheep's definitions of liberty. Consider two 19th-century cases about government funding for railroads. In 1871, in *Stockton & Visalia Railroad v. Common Council of Stockton*,[70] California's progressive Chief Justice William T. Wallace upheld the constitutionality of a city ordinance that spent tax money to subsidize a privately owned railroad. Citing

Jeremiah Black's decision in the 1853 *Sharpless* case, Wallace began with the premise that, except where the Constitution explicitly limits the state's power, the legislature "is politically omnipotent,"[71] and its authority "embraces in its ample range whatever can be supposed to promote the interest of the body politic."[72] Since the Constitution did not explicitly bar the government from funneling tax dollars to private businesses, Wallace presumed that lawmakers may do what they like with the citizens' earnings. True, the Constitution prohibited the taking of property except for public use, but it did not define "public use," so the legislature could ascribe to that term nearly any meaning it chose.[73] And anyone who argued that the Constitution *implicitly* barred the government from transferring tax money to politically influential corporations was just using legal arguments as a "mask" behind which to "oppose the right of the people to vote upon the question of local taxation."[74] Wallace would not allow such a "usurpation" of democratic power.[75]

His colleague, Justice Joseph Crockett, disagreed. Although he, too, upheld the ordinance, he thought Wallace's extreme pronouncements about legislative power were dangerous. They would put the people "wholly at the mercy of the Legislature,"[76] which "the framers of the Constitution could not have intended."[77] Where Wallace adopted the wolf's premise that the legislature had a basic right to rule, Crockett held that it only had power to promote the genuine public good.

Three years later, the U.S. Supreme Court rejected Wallace's approach when it struck down a similar ordinance in *Loan Association v. Topeka*.[78] One of the archetypical substantive due process cases, *Loan Association* concluded that an ordinance which invested tax-payer money in a privately owned railroad was unlawful because it merely took property from some people and gave it to others for their own private benefit. A law is by definition public oriented, the justices explained, and "tax" means an assessment for public purposes, not for private ones. Although in some cases it might be difficult to draw the line between private benefits and public goods, using government power just to seize some people's wealth for the benefit of others could not qualify as a genuine tax law, because it violated the principles of generality and public orientation:

> There are limitations on [government] power which grow out of the essential nature of all free governments. Implied reservations of individual rights, without which the social

> compact could not exist, and which are respected by all
> governments entitled to the name. No court, for instance,
> would hesitate to declare void a statute which enacted that
> A. and B. who were husband and wife to each other should
> be so no longer, but that A. should thereafter be the husband
> of C., and B. the wife of D. or which should enact that the
> homestead now owned by A. should no longer be his, but
> should henceforth be the property of B.[79]

Since government was designed to protect these rights against
arbitrary or wrongful deprivation, any government act which violated such rights, or used government power for private benefit
rather than to accomplish the purposes for which government was
instituted, would only be an act of force, and not of law. "This is
not legislation. It is a decree under legislative forms."[80] The individual's basic right to his earnings could not be intruded upon by
government without legitimate justification. If the government took
a person's property for an invalid reason, then it did not matter
whether it did so "under the forms of law"; such an act was "none
the less a robbery."[81]

A more recent example, *Lawrence v. Texas*,[82] illustrates the continu-
ing split between those who prioritize *liberty* and those who prioritize *democracy* in constitutional interpretation. In that 2003 case, the
Supreme Court invalidated a Texas law that criminalized private,
consensual sexual acts between adults of the same sex. If one adopts
a constitutional interpretation oriented toward liberty, that decision
is sensible. The statute was not a means of protecting individual
rights, and its defenders made little effort to justify it in terms of
liberty. They did not pretend that it ensured against innocent people
being harmed in any way—it did not apply to rape, public inde-
cency, or prostitution; it did not protect minors, or "persons who
might be injured or coerced or who are situated in relationships
where consent might not easily be refused."[83] Nor did it involve
same-sex marriage or adoption by same-sex couples. At times, the
state claimed that the law promoted public morality, but the justices
found this argument implausible, since the law applied to private
conduct that was not witnessed by anyone.

Yet this did not matter to the statute's supporters, because they
did not believe that government power is limited to public conduct,
or to acts that affect nonconsenting people. Instead, they believed

the state could impose a burden on a disfavored minority simply to express disapproval, without having to account for its acts in terms of individual rights, because the state has a basic entitlement to dictate how people may act. "The State of Texas," fumed Republican Congressman Ron Paul, when the Court ruled the law unconstitutional, "has the right to decide for itself how to regulate social matters like sex, using its own local standards."[84] A spokesman for Concerned Women for America said that the decision "is further evidence that 'We the People' have virtually lost the right to govern ourselves because of judicial activists."[85] University of Texas law professor Lino Graglia was even more explicit. "The three basic principles of the Constitution," he wrote, "are democracy ... federalism ... and separation of powers"—not individual freedom.[86] The *Lawrence* precedent, he warned, would "presume unconstitutional all laws limiting 'liberty,'" and this would "put on the states or national government the burden of justifying them," which Graglia deplored.[87] In short, *Lawrence*, like many other due-process cases, pitted those who think government has a fundamental right to rule, and that individuals seeking freedom must politely ask the majority to give them that freedom, against those who hold that individual liberty is an indefeasible right, which government may limit only when necessary to protect the rights of others.[88] As Justice Kennedy observed in his *Lawrence* decision, if people are not hurting each other or seriously threatening the public, "[t]heir right to liberty under the Due Process Clause gives them the full right to engage in their conduct without intervention of the government."[89]

"Substantive due process" simply enforces the Constitution's promise that government will not arbitrarily infringe individual rights, or act in ways that exceed the implicit limits on lawmakers' authority. But because arbitrariness or the rightful limits on government power are matters that cannot be understood except by reference to moral considerations, enforcing the Due Process of Law Clause requires courts to address controversial principles of political philosophy. While this may a complex undertaking, it does not entitle either judges or legislators to impose their subjective preferences on the citizenry. Instead, the Due Process of Law requirement puts legally enforceable boundaries around the power of government, and those boundaries are built on the foundation of equal liberty articulated in the Declaration and the Constitution.

4. The Critics of Substantive Due Process

For decades, conservatives and liberals have lambasted the doctrine of substantive due process, characterizing it as an oxymoron or a trick by which judges cynically write their own policy preferences into the Constitution while pretending to engage in constitutional analysis. According to Robert Bork, "[t]here could be no intellectual structure to support this concept."[1] He and other critics contend that the Due Process Clause guarantees only certain *procedural* formalities—a hearing or a trial—before a person may be deprived of life, liberty, or property. It does not bar the legislature from eliminating rights altogether, nor does it impose any broader requirements of fairness. As long as the legislature provides *some* sort of procedure before it takes away a person's life, liberty, or property, it has met its constitutional obligation.

This argument is deeply flawed, and it dissolves when we examine it carefully. Assume, for instance, that the Due Process Clause requires only a trial or hearing of some sort. Would this requirement be satisfied if the "trial" consisted of a coin toss, or a consultation of the zodiac, or the drawing of lots as in "The Lottery," or the shenanigans of Alice's trial in *Alice in Wonderland?* The answer is obviously no, because these procedures are not guided by rational principles and therefore are not actually *trials* or *hearings* at all. The concept of a legal proceeding itself presumes certain standards of fairness.

A memorable scene in the 1980 film *Gideon's Trumpet*—based on Anthony Lewis's book about the Supreme Court's *Gideon v. Wainwright* decision—expresses this idea succinctly. Henry Fonda, playing Clarence Gideon, is asked by a fellow prisoner if he really thinks the Constitution guarantees an accused person the right to a lawyer in a criminal proceeding. Fonda begins his answer by reading from the Fourteenth Amendment: "'No state shall deprive any person of life, liberty, or property without due process of law,'" he says. "I asked them for a lawyer and they wouldn't give me one. Means I was deprived of liberty without due process of law. . . . They can't put you in jail without they give you a fair trial." Note the necessary

95

overlap between procedure and substance: if a trial lacks the elements of fairness, it is not really a *trial* in the first place. Gideon's contention was that courtroom procedure is so complicated that if a defendant is forced to represent himself without an attorney, he is in a position analogous to one whose fate is decided by a coin toss. The procedural due process requirement therefore incorporates substantive rights.

The distinction between form and substance recedes from our grasp as we approach it. The two are inseparable in physical reality: all substances exist in some form, and no form can be expressed except in a substance. The same is true in law. A legal procedure is comprised of substantive rules. But procedure is also a substantive right in itself. In one sense, a trial is a procedure—it is a process through which a person goes before being sentenced or acquitted. But anyone who demands a trial is regarding it as a substantive right—as a particular thing to which he is entitled, and without which it would be arbitrary to punish him. A trial can also be subdivided into many substantive rights: the right to cross-examine a witness, for example, or the right not to be compelled to testify against oneself. Taking another step back, the right to a trial can be seen as one substantive component of the accused person's broader right not to be treated arbitrarily. It is not possible to neatly categorize a trial or any other aspect of these rights as procedural or substantive. The attempt to divide due process of law into "substantive" or "procedural" is misguided.

Moreover, the commitment to abide by fair *procedures* only makes sense if we are first committed to *substantive* fairness. Justice Clarence Thomas recently declared that the Due Process Clause "is not a secret repository of substantive guarantees against 'unfairness,'"[2] but this is wrong: fairness *is* required by the clause's explicit commitment to *law*. There is nothing secret about it. It would be pointless for the government to give defendants trials or other procedural protections unless it is committed to ensuring the accused person's more general right to be treated impartially. Why require an unbiased judge, or allow the accused to cross-examine witnesses, or to obtain a competent attorney, unless we are committed more broadly to protecting against unfairness? What we call procedural due process is only a *subset* of the Due Process Clause's more general guarantee against arbitrary rule.

True, the *term* "substantive due process" does seem at first to be an oxymoron. But that phrase was not invented by the lawyers who developed these ideas; to them, it was simply due process of law. They understood that the formal and substantive aspects of law cannot be divided. And this also helps explain the word "due" in the Due Process Clause. The Constitution does not require just *any* process but *due* process—the people have a right not to be treated arbitrarily by the government. The Thirteenth Amendment repeats this word; it holds that no person shall be subjected to involuntary servitude unless he has been *duly* convicted of a crime. Not all convictions are due, and those that are not due are arbitrary, baseless, or flawed in some other way. Someone who is convicted because the judge is biased, or on the basis of insufficient evidence, is not *duly* convicted. On the other hand, if the Due Process Clause guarantees citizens the right only to some procedural ritual, without regard to its content, there would be no reason to guarantee "due" process of law—because any process whatever would suffice.

An approach to law that focuses exclusively on process cannot explain the foundations of those processes themselves; it can only take them as arbitrary givens. This process-only approach, which today dominates the legal academy, holds that a statute is lawful simply because it is passed according to rules of promulgation. But the rules of promulgation are also laws, so what justifies *them?* The Framers did not regard the rules of promulgation as arbitrary assumptions; they established those rules for specific reasons, in accordance with certain standards of political philosophy. For example, the Constitution requires that bills for raising revenue must originate in the House of Representatives, because the Framers thought the taxing power was best left with those legislators who are closest to the people. The Constitution also limits military appropriations to two-year increments, out of fear that an independent standing army would endanger freedom. The requirement that treaties must receive a two-thirds vote in the Senate was adopted in order to ensure careful deliberation over important matters of foreign affairs. A purely formalistic approach to the law cannot offer this kind of holistic account of constitutional structure—instead, it takes the rules of lawmaking as unquestioned postulates, hovering like "skyhooks" without intellectual foundation.[3]

But if the rules of lawmaking cannot be justified by reference to more basic principles, then there is no particular reason why legislators should honor one set of promulgation requirements rather than another. Suppose a legislature passes a bill in a way not permitted by the Constitution—say, it enacts a statute by a bare majority where the Constitution requires a two-thirds supermajority. Does this violate the rules of promulgation, and render the measure invalid? Or is the legislature just creating a new rule of promulgation which is now entitled to respect? And why should a court prioritize the constitutional rule over this new procedure? It is no answer to say that the courts are obliged to follow the Constitution; so is the legislature, after all. If rules of promulgation are just arbitrary assumptions, then neither courts nor legislatures have any reason to view the rules listed in the Constitution as more binding than the more convenient new rules that the wayward legislature has now announced.[4] In short, a theory by which something is law simply because it is issued according to some rule of promulgation is a useless theory, since it cannot account for those rules. Unless officials are committed to a broader *substantive* conception of good government, they have no reason to abide by a Constitution that imposes procedural limits on the legislature.

On the other hand, a natural-law theory like that endorsed by the Framers of the Constitution and the authors of the Fourteenth Amendment can account for the existence of the Constitution, the limits it imposes on lawmakers, and the way that it treats individuals. It sees procedural due process protections as only one element of the Due Process Clause's overall guarantee that the state will deal with everyone in a non-arbitrary manner. If we disregard the principles of political philosophy, and declare that law is whatever the ruling power enacts according to the rules of promulgation, then the constitutional guidelines that control lawmakers and courts begin to look like pointless rituals that cannot obligate the rulers or the ruled.

Not Everything the Legislature Does Is Law

The Constitution itself makes clear that "due process" means something more than the legislature's decision to pass a bill. For example, Article VI declares that only laws "which shall be made in Pursuance" of the Constitution "shall be the supreme Law of the

Land." Called upon to explain this language, Alexander Hamilton wrote that government acts "which are *not pursuant* to its constitutional powers . . . will [not] become the supreme law of the land. These will be merely acts of usurpation, and will deserve to be treated as such." But this would have been true, Hamilton observed, even if the Constitution had not said so explicitly. The Supremacy Clause's wording was "merely . . . an instance of caution" because "that limitation would have been to be understood, though it had not been expressed."[5] In other words, Congress's lawmaking powers would be limited by both the explicit and implicit principles of the Constitution. This "truth . . . flows immediately and necessarily from the institution of a federal government."[6] The Founders well understood that the question of whether a statute was truly *law* or only an unauthorized, illegitimate use of force was to be resolved in terms of logic and abstract principle, not just by asking if the bill received the required number of votes.

Abstract principles are unavoidable in any case. Suppose the legislature were to pass an unintelligible statute, or one containing a self-contradiction: one which simply declares, "This is not a law," or a statute that simultaneously requires and forbids the same act. Would this be a law? In a 1677 decision, England's Chief Justice, John Vaguhan, said no—"a law which a man cannot obey, nor act according to it, is void, and no law: and it is impossible to obey contradictions, or act according to them."[7] It seems obvious that to call such a thing a law would be absurd. A self-contradiction is nothing; it is null; it is no more a law than it is a pigeon or a sneeze, and a court is justified in regarding it as void, even if the legislature passed it with full procedural formalities. This is true, even though the Constitution does not expressly forbid self-contradictory statutes. Such enactments are void on account of what Francis Bacon called their "impertinency," or what Hamilton called "the nature and reason of the thing."

If one concedes this much, then one must admit that mere promulgation is not enough to make something a law. Instead, the legal status of a promulgated rule must be determined partly by its content—that is, by its substance. We must ask *what* a law is, and determine whether a particular thing purporting to be a law meets that definition. Even William Blackstone, who thought government possessed "supreme, irresistible, absolute authority," still admitted that it could not do things that are "naturally impossible,"[8] even if it tried to do so in ways that complied with Parliamentary procedures. The theory of "substantive due process" means just this.

The due process of law guarantee makes no sense if everything the legislature passes automatically qualifies as a law. As Justice Greene Bronson of the New York Supreme Court once observed, if everything the legislature does is a law for purposes of the Due Process of Law Clause, then that clause would be "absolutely nugatory. . . . The people would be made to say to the [legislature], *You shall be vested with 'the legislative power of the State' but no one 'shall be disfranchised, or deprived of any of the rights or privileges' of a citizen, unless you pass a statute for that purpose.* In other words, *You shall not do the wrong, unless you choose to do it.*"[9]

In an article arguing against substantive due process, law professor John Harrison calls Bronson's argument "circular" because the "conclusion can follow only if the clause is indeed designed to prevent legislative deprivations."[10] In Harrison's view, the due process of law requirement only "require[s] compliance with existing law"[11] or "imposes the rule of law and does nothing else."[12] But this does not overcome the force of Bronson's point. To begin with, the tradition within which Bronson was working did indeed hold that "legislative deprivations"—arbitrary restrictions or confiscations imposed by the legislature—were among the things that the due process requirement was written to prevent. Bronson's words were a straightforward application of the constitutional requirement that the legislature respect the principles inherent in lawfulness. This is not circular reasoning, because those principles are ontologically prior to legislative acts—they exist whether or not the legislature recognizes them—and they explain, justify, and limit what qualifies as law. On the contrary, the proposition that everything a legislature does qualifies as law *really is* circular: it assumes its own premises, since it would mean something is law just because it purports to be. By that reasoning, a statute is lawful because the ruler promulgates it—which means everything government does automatically satisfies the due process of law requirement.

This cannot be what the authors of the Fourteenth Amendment meant. As Harrison admits, they were primarily concerned with mob violence against former slaves and the Black Codes that Southern states adopted at the Civil War's end, which sought to deprive

Americans of their rights to travel, vote, run businesses, or own firearms. The Due Process Clause thus imposed "a federal requirement of legality," aimed largely, though not exclusively, at overturning the South's "unwritten constitution" of social segregation and terrorist oppression.[13] Yet Harrison maintains that the clause is not offended if the legislature restricts individual rights through a duly enacted statute. The problem with this is that the post–Civil War Black Codes *were* statutes, and thus legal in this sense, just as the stoning of Soraya M. or of Tessie Hutchinson in "The Lottery" are legal in this sense. It is implausible that the amendment's authors considered promulgation by a corrupt or rebellious legislature—or by a sham legislative process—sufficient to satisfy the Due Process Clause. A legislature could easily pass a statute giving lynch mobs (perhaps euphemized as "the militia") unlimited discretion to adjudicate and punish perceived wrongs, or a statute assigning the automatic death penalty for vague crimes such as being "uppity."

That is not far different from what did happen in the decades following the Civil War. In a 1923 case, *Moore v. Dempsey*, the Supreme Court overruled the convictions of five black defendants who, after a show trial, were condemned for having sparked an Arkansas race riot.[14] The all-white jury heard testimony from black witnesses who had been tortured into implicating the defendants, and the defendants were not allowed to consult with the lawyer appointed for them before the 45-minute trial opened. The neighborhood and the courthouse were surrounded by an armed mob whose efforts to lynch the defendants had been mollified only by local officials' promise that the defendants would be convicted and sentenced to death. "[I]f, in fact, a trial is dominated by a mob so that there is an actual interference with the course of justice," declared the Supreme Court, in reversing the convictions, "there is a departure from due process of law." If "the whole proceeding is a mask" in which "counsel, jury and judge were swept to the fatal end by an irresistible wave of public passion," the principles of due process would be offended even if the procedural "machinery" had operated with "perfection."[15]

In other words, a substantively arbitrary procedure cannot be made any less arbitrary just because it receives the blessing of public officials. If a statute is passed specifying *how* officials are to toss coins, consult the zodiac, or convene lynch mobs, those things would still be arbitrary. And even if, as in the *Moore* case, a mob mimics the superficial *procedures* of a trial, it is still a lawless mob. In short, Justice Bronson was right: if the legislature has unrestricted power to designate as "law" whatever it likes, the promise of due process of law makes no sense.

The Due Process Clause does, as Harrison says, impose a rule of law requirement. But that requirement is not satisfied by the legislature enacting statutes. The statutes themselves must also consist with the principles inherent in the concept of lawful order: generality, regularity, fairness, rationality, and public orientation. These principles are what make an official pronouncement *law*, rather than mere force. When a ruler disregards those principles, he acts unlawfully—beyond the limits of his delegated authority. His actions are then arbitrary and unauthorized, like the bank guard who robs the bank, or the arbitrator who exceeds his chartered powers. The constitutional promise that government will act in a *lawful* way inherently limits what the executive, legislature, or judiciary may do, because legislative approval cannot transform an arbitrary act into a non-arbitrary one, or make an unauthorized action authorized. This is what Justice Chase meant when he said in *Calder* that legislatures "cannot change innocence into guilt; or punish innocence as a crime."[16]

Original Intent and Substantive Due Process

Another persistent criticism of substantive due process is that the authors of the Constitution did not intend the Due Process Clause to bar lawmakers from depriving people of rights—they only meant to require courts to abide by traditional procedures. For judges to restrict legislators' powers through the Due Process Clause is a modern idea, it is often said, and not a part of the Founders' original intent. But this is also wrong.

First, the historical evidence shows that the Constitution's authors were familiar with what we today call substantive due process. In fact, when the Constitution was written, common-law courts protected individual rights almost exclusively through this theory. Then, as now, Britain had no written constitution. The 1628 English Petition of Right and the English Bill of Rights of 1689 were considered mere statutes, which articulated some—but not all—of the principles of lawfulness. Courts relied upon them when determining whether or not a government action qualified as the "law of the land." When British courts protected individual rights under the unwritten constitution, they did so by holding that violations of those unenumerated rights did not qualify as "law" and therefore could not be enforced.

Such decisions were commonplace in the 17th century, when colonization of North America was under way. In 1615, for example, an English court ruled that a Parliamentary act allowing certain cases to be tried without a jury was void because "an Act of Parliament made against natural equity, as to make a man Judge in his own case, is void in it self, for *jura natruae sunt immutabilia* [the laws of nature are unchangeable] and they are *leges legum* [laws that limit legislation]."[17] Courts in America applied the same principles. In one remarkable 1657 case—130 years before the Constitution was written—Justice Samuel Symonds of Massachusetts Bay Colony invalidated a town's attempt to force people to pay for the construction of a home for the town's minister. According to the "rules of the learned in the lawes of England," wrote Symonds, an ordinance "repugnant to the fundamentall law . . . is voyd." That fundamental law gave officials only "a derived power in trust," and "not such an unlimited domination over other mens estates or persons." If town leaders could, "by pretence of authority or without," give away citizens' property "when in their prudence" they thought it appropriate, then "no man hath any certaynty or right to what he hath." This would be "against a fundamentall law in nature," since "noe man is come to New England to have his goods given and taken from him, unto, or for what good end, or under what pretence soever." Any "lawes positive" that exceed the legislators' derived power or that violate the basic premises of lawfulness "lose their force and are noe lawes at all." While general taxes were legitimate—since they were voted upon by the general public, applied alike to all, and funded public services—an ordinance that simply took property from some people and gave it to another person for his own private benefit was not. "Noe, noe, lawyers would have blushed to give such a construction of lawes; and suddenly their faces would have waxed pale."[18]

Justice Symonds was not the only early American judge to employ the logic of substantive due process. Professor Frederick Gedicks has assembled a mass of evidence showing that the founding generation generally agreed with the proposition that the ruler's powers were "under the law"—meaning that government's actions were entitled to respect as law only if they were consistent with deeper principles such as generality, public orientation, and respect for individual rights, that made a government act *lawful* rather than a mere exercise of power. "By the early 1770s," he writes, the law of the land provision of Magna Carta "had merged with the broader concept of higher-law constitutionalism, which held king and Parliament alike to limitations prescribed by the natural and customary rights recognized at common law. By then, the colonists had also adopted the 17th-century tenet that English common-law liberties reflected and reinforced natural law and natural rights."[19]

Revolution-era lawyers, raised on the writings of Edward Coke, were quite comfortable with this idea. In 1792, a South Carolina court declared that a statute taking property from one person and giving it to another was "against Magna Carta."[20] A Rhode Island court in 1786 struck down a statute that required people to pay their debts in banknotes and deprived any person accused of violating the statute of any right to a trial by jury. The court ruled that law void even though the state lacked any state constitution at the time because it violated the law of the land provision of Magna Carta.[21]

The law of the land theory of the common-law lawyers was strengthened by the transition to natural rights during the Revolutionary period. Having gone beyond religious toleration to adopt the idea that religious liberty was a natural right, they cherished the British tradition of rights inherent in common-law reasoning, but they went further by grounding their constitutions on the precepts of universal, natural rights articulated in the Declaration of Independence. This means that not only would a statute have to conform to the principles of generality, public orientation, and so forth in order to qualify as law, but it would also have to consist with constitutional provisions that incorporated the standards of natural rights. "To call a legislative act a 'law' during that era did not mean that the act merely satisfied constitutional requirements for lawmaking," writes Gedicks, "but rather signified that it conformed to substantive limitations on legislative power represented by natural and customary rights. Legislative acts that violated these limitations would not have been considered 'laws,' even when they satisfied the constitutional requirements for lawmaking."[22]

Professor Robert E. Riggs agrees, observing that the Constitution's authors understood the phrases "law of the land" or "due process of law" as providing both procedural and substantive protections against government abuses. "This was true in colonial times; it was true during the early decades of the new republic; it has always been true of the fifth amendment due process clause."[23]

Originalist opponents of substantive due process often quote the following line from *Federalist 78* as proof that the Framers meant the courts to exercise a minimal role in the federal scheme: "The courts must declare the sense of the law; and if they should be disposed to exercise WILL instead of JUDGMENT, the consequence would equally be the substitution of their pleasure to that of the legislative body."[24] But the noteworthy part of this passage is that Hamilton was *not* arguing for "judicial restraint" but for a vigorous, engaged judiciary that would patrol constitutional boundaries against legislative encroachments.[25] Indeed, the purpose of his essay was to defend a high degree of judicial independence. The distinction between *judgment* and *will* was central to his argument, because whereas *will* is a dangerous, proactive force, which must be kept on a close leash, *judgment* is the faculty of dispassionate interpretation, which must be insulated from outside influences. It would be improper to constrain the faculty of judgment by considerations of political expediency—and thus improper for courts to abstain from defending the Constitution against legislative overreaching. Hamilton would have had little sympathy for the modern notion of judicial restraint or judicial modesty; he would have agreed with the Supreme Court's statement in *United States v. Butler*:

> It is sometimes said that the court assumes a power to overrule or control the action of the people's representatives. This is a misconception. The Constitution is the supreme law of the land ordained and established by the people. All legislation must conform to the principles it lays down. When an act of Congress is appropriately challenged in the courts as not conforming to the constitutional mandate, the judicial branch of the Government has only one duty; to lay the article of the Constitution which is invoked beside the statute which is challenged and to decide whether the latter squares with the former. All the court does, or can do, is to announce its considered judgment upon the question.[26]

Nevertheless, some originalists have argued that the Constitution's authors meant the Due Process Clause to restrict only the actions of the *executive* or *judicial*, not the *legislative* branch. This argument relies on similarly flawed logic and historical misconceptions. For one thing, the due process of law or law of the land guarantee originated in Magna Carta at a time when there was only a rudimentary understanding of separation of powers, and the wording of that document makes no such distinction. Not only did the king exercise what we would consider judicial and legislative powers, but until relatively recently, Parliament was more like a court than a legislature.[27] Magna Carta's Law of the Land Clause was not directed to one branch or another. Neither are its modern descendants, the Fifth or Fourteenth Amendments' Due Process of Law Clauses; they simply declare that no person shall be deprived of rights without due process of law— not that no person shall be deprived *by the judiciary* or *by the executive* without due process of law.

Nor is it clear how the Due Process Clause *could* restrict only the executive or judicial branches without also applying to the legislature. Lawsuits virtually never involve just one branch acting alone. Consider the example of the sheriff who arrests a dissenter under an unconstitutional law that establishes a national religion. The arrested person would argue that the sheriff violated his constitutional rights: the arrest deprived him of liberty without due process of law. The sheriff would answer by pointing to the statute as giving him the authority to arrest. Since the sheriff is an executive officer, and thus admittedly bound by the Due Process Clause, a court must resolve the case by determining whether he acted with lawful authority, but that would compel the court to inquire into the constitutionality of that law, which means inquiring into the legislature's actions. If the Due Process of Law Clause applies to the executive, it must necessarily also apply to the legislature because it makes the laws that executive officials execute. On the other hand, if the sheriff could cut off the inquiry simply by saying that the legislature passed the statute in question, then the result would again be what Justice Bronson predicted: the Constitution would bar the government from doing wrong—except when it chose to.

There is no proof that the Framers believed in such paradoxes. On the contrary, they understood that the Constitution restricted the legislature as well as the executive and the judiciary. In the nation's early years, members of the Federalist Party argued that the Sedition Act of 1798—which criminalized certain forms of political expression—did not violate the First Amendment. They reasoned that the amendment was modeled on the British common law, and under that law, freedom of speech and the press were protected against violation by the king but not by Parliament. James Madison refuted this by observing that the American Constitution differed fundamentally from that of Great Britain: there, the legislature was considered sovereign, and "the danger of encroachments on the rights of the people is understood to be confined to the executive magistrate." But in the United States,

> [t]he people, not the government, possess the absolute sovereignty. The legislature, no less than the executive, is under limitations of power. Encroachments are regarded as possible from the one as well as from the other. Hence . . . the great and essential rights of the people are secured against legislative as well as executive ambition . . . not by laws paramount to prerogative, but by constitutions paramount to laws. This security of the freedom of the press requires that it should be exempt, not only from previous restraint of the executive, as in Great Britain, but from legislative restraint also. . . .[28]

Alexander Hamilton agreed. Some critics claim that Hamilton thought the Due Process Clause would not apply to the legislature and quote from a speech Hamilton delivered in the New York state house in 1787, in which he said, "The words due process of law have a precise technical import, and are only applicable to the process and proceedings of the courts of justice; they can never be referred to an act of the legislature."[29] According to Professor Raoul Berger, this was proof that Hamilton thought the Due Process of Law Clause related "solely to procedure in the courts, not to legislative acts."[30]

But consult the actual speech, and a different picture emerges. The question under debate was whether the legislature could exclude certain former British Loyalists from voting, a proposition Hamilton opposed on the grounds that this would be a "legislative disqualification" that violated the due process of law guarantee. To disqualify someone from voting, or to impose any other punishment on him, the government must first give that person due process of law— and the mere enactment of legislation imposing that punishment could not suffice: "Some gentlemen hold that the law of the land will include an act of the Legislature," said Hamilton—that is, some people argue that the law of the land guarantee is satisfied by the legislature passing a statute—but

> Lord Coke, that great luminary of the law, in his comment upon a similar clause in Magna Charta, interprets the law of the land to mean presentment and indictment. . . . [And] if there were any doubt upon the Constitution, the bill of rights enacted in this very session removes it. It is there declared that no man shall be disenfranchised or deprived of any right but by due process of law or the judgment of his peers. The words "due process" have a precise technical import, and are only applicable to the process and proceedings of courts of justice; they can never be referred to an act of the Legislature. Are we willing, then, to endure the inconsistency of passing a bill of rights and committing a direct violation of it in the same session? In short, are we ready to destroy its foundations at the moment they are laid?[31]

In other words, the due process of law requirement could not be satisfied by the mere fact that the legislature approved a deprivation. For lawmakers to take away a person's rights, including the right to vote, simply by passing a statute to that effect, would be a lawless act, which courts should set aside.

In the decades that followed the Fifth Amendment's ratification, courts frequently endorsed "substantive" readings of the Due Process Clause. The North Carolina Supreme Court ruled in a 1794 case that the legislature could not pass a statute declaring certain people, without any hearing, to be liable for debts to the state. The state constitution's law of the land clause did not allow the legislature simply to proclaim that people were delinquent: since elected officials are "deputed only to make laws in conformity to the constitution, and within the limits it prescribes," a law that violates its principles "is not any law at all. Whenever the Assembly exceeds the limits of the constitution, they act without authority, and then their acts are no more binding than the acts of any other assembled body."[32]

The justices repeated this point in an 1833 case, *Hoke v. Henderson*.[33] "In other countries," wrote Justice Thomas Ruffin, the "will of the governors" was "admitted to be the supreme law." But in America, where "written Constitutions, conferring and dividing the powers of government, and restraining the actions of those in authority" have been "established as securities of public liberty and private right," judges must often make a "comparison between what the representatives of the people have done, with what the people themselves have said they might do, or should not do; and if upon that comparison it be found that the act is without warrant in the Constitution, and is inconsistent with the will of the people as there declared, the Court cannot execute the act." If the legislators "pass an act upon a subject upon which the people have said in the Constitution, they shall not legislate at all," or if they were to "enact that to be law which the same instrument says shall not be law," judges would be bound to regard that legislation as something other than law—as an unauthorized act.[34]

Courts in New York and other states used the Law of the Land or Due Process Clauses of their state constitutions to strike down legislative efforts to take property from one person and give it to another.[35] And the U.S. Supreme Court did likewise, concluding in *Terret v. Taylor* (1815) that "the great and fundamental principles of a republican government" limited legislative power.[36] And in the 1829 case of *Wilkinson v. Leland,* the Court declared that "[t]he fundamental maxims of a free government" implicitly restricted what kinds of laws the government could enact. "[N]o court of justice in this country," wrote Justice Joseph Story, "would be warranted in assuming that the power to violate and disregard" the principles of generality or public orientation "lurked under any grant of legislative authority, or ought to be implied from any general expressions [in the Constitution]."[37] Given this history, it is unsurprising that Daniel Webster's explanation of substantive due process in his 1819 argument in the *Dartmouth College* case[38] was celebrated for its eloquence, not its originality.

Substantive due process was already widely accepted by 1857 when the Supreme Court referred to it in a single sentence of the *Dred Scott* decision.[39] In fact, the doctrine was so pervasive that none of the dissenters, and not even the most strident abolitionists, criticized that part of the ruling. And in 1868, when the Fourteenth Amendment added a second Due Process of Law Clause to the Constitution, this time to restrict state legislatures, the doctrine was so conventional that the amendment's supporters referred to it only in passing, and always with approval. In a 2010 article in the *Yale Law Journal*, Professor Ryan C. Williams—who has argued that Madison, Hamilton, and their contemporaries did *not* believe in the doctrine of substantive due process—nevertheless acknowledged that it had become commonplace by the time the Fourteenth Amendment was written.[40] Lawyers at that time were familiar with decisions like *Wilkinson, Hoke,* and *Terret,* as well as Webster's *Dartmouth College* argument and the writings of scholars such as Thomas Cooley, all of which interpreted the Due Process Clause as protecting substantive rights against legislative interference. Supporters of the amendment even cited many of these cases in their speeches explaining what the amendment would mean.[41] Thus, even if one denies that the Founding Fathers believed the Due Process of Law or Law of the Land Clauses would protect individual rights against legislative interference, that idea had become so widespread by the end of the Civil War that "the overwhelming weight of authority would have supported a broader interpretation" of the new amendment's due process guarantee.[42]

Did Substantive Due Process Lead to *Dred Scott?*

It is often claimed that the concept of substantive due process was first employed in *Dred Scott,* the infamous case in which the Supreme Court barred Congress from outlawing slavery in the territories and declared that black Americans had no rights that whites were bound to respect. This assertion appears to have originated in John Hart Ely's 1980 book *Democracy and Distrust,* and while not entirely false, it contains only enough truth to be misleading. *Dred Scott* was not the origin of substantive due process; while that case contains many faults, its brief, single-sentence reference to substantive due process (on page 450 of the decision) is not one of them.

As we have seen, *Dred Scott* was a long and complicated decision, with many objectionable points. But its basic logic goes as follows: First, for the government to deprive an owner of slave property under a statute that exceeds Congress's lawmaking authority would be a deprivation of property without due process of law. Second, Congress has no constitutional authority to ban slavery in the Western territories, which is what it attempted to do by enacting legislation that had the effect of depriving Mr. Sanford of his slave. Therefore, that legislation deprived Sanford of property without due process of law.

110

As a logical matter, this argument was valid. But it was unsound because the minor premise was false: the Constitution quite clearly *did* give Congress power to ban slavery in the territories, by providing that Congress may "make all needful Rules and Regulations respecting the Territory or other Property belonging to the United States." Taney's elaborate attempts to deny this—which take up the bulk of the opinion—were denials of plain fact. But his major premise—that *ultra vires* legislative action cannot count as a law and therefore violates the due process of law guarantee—was correct, and was well established and noncontroversial by 1857.[43] Indeed, anti-slavery leaders had been making the same argument for many years by that time. Abraham Lincoln, and others who railed against the *Dred Scott* decision in speeches and pamphlets, did not dwell on this aspect of the case; they focused instead on showing that Congress did, indeed, have the lawful authority to ban slavery in the territories.[44] Today, legal historians acknowledge that substantive due process was not a novelty in 1857 and that, whatever other well-deserved criticisms were leveled at the *Dred Scott* decision when it was issued, nobody at the time—not even the dissenting justices—seems to have regarded that aspect of the case as problematic.

Thus while substantive due process played a role in *Dred Scott*, it is misleading to characterize it as a "substantive due process case," let alone as the source of that theory, and it is devious to use the infamy of that decision to disparage substantive due process. It would be akin to saying that the problem with *Korematsu v. United States*[45] was that it was "a Supremacy Clause case," or that the problem with *Plessy v. Ferguson*[46] was that it was "an Equal Protection case"—and then to disparage those clauses for having been so used. It will not do to smear substantive due process with the stain of *Dred Scott*. Substantive due process is an analytical test; a legal theory. Judges can misunderstand or misapply legal theories, or even abuse them to reach corrupt decisions. But that is an argument for choosing judges carefully—not an argument for discarding the law itself.

The Redundancy Argument

Many opponents of substantive due process have argued that the Due Process Clause cannot have been meant to prohibit legislative abuses that are already forbidden by other constitutional provisions because this would make the Constitution redundant.

If the due process of law requirement bars special legislation or arbitrary treatment, it would seem strange that the same Constitution would also have other clauses aimed at those same wrongs. A traditional rule of legal interpretation holds that lawyers should avoid reading a law in a way that renders any of its parts redundant. Therefore, these critics argue, the authors of the Constitution would not have added the more specific guarantees if they had thought that their concerns were already resolved by the Due Process Clause.

But as Professor Gedicks has observed, this redundancy critique is a weak argument,[47] given that "'lawyers say everything at least twice.'"[48] Constitutional guarantees often overlap: frequently, a law that violates the Due Process Clause will also violate, say, the Equal Protection Clause, or the Just Compensation Clause, or provisions that protect freedom of expression. In fact, the Bill of Rights is itself a redundancy. During the ratification debates in 1787 and 1788, the Constitution's leading authors, including Madison,[49] Hamilton,[50] and James Wilson,[51] argued persuasively that a Bill of Rights was unnecessary because the Constitution gave the federal government only certain limited powers: people therefore need not fear for the security of their rights. Still, they agreed to add the amendments as an additional precaution, "provided," Madison said, "it be so framed as not to imply [government] powers not meant to be included in the [Constitution]."[52] The Bill of Rights really only reiterates, in a different way, the limitation on federal power that was built into the Constitution to begin with; it is thus redundant, but it would be absurd to say that it should be disregarded on that account. Moreover, the Bill of Rights is also internally redundant: its provisions specify such basic *procedural* rights as the right to a jury, or to a trial, which are already part of due process of law. Under the redundancy argument, one would have to conclude that these provisions do not really mean what they say.[53]

A better reading of "due process of law" would see it as being a general prohibition against all government arbitrariness. Given how old that prohibition is, it is not surprising that a constitution would include other, more recent provisions that overlap with it. As different types of government abuses have appeared through history, people have added more specific constitutional protections, even where they thought those abuses should have been barred already by the existing Due Process of Law Clause. They would certainly have had no reason to remove or whittle down the older guarantee. Thus, during the 19th century, as Westward expansion and the growth of railroad corporations gave rise to new constitutional problems—such as the abuse of eminent domain to benefit private companies, or government subsidies to politically influential industries—the delegates to state constitutional conventions would naturally frame additional protections against these abuses without thereby reducing the power of the existing Due Process Clause.

As Justice John Harlan Jr. wrote, the "full scope" of "due process of law" must not be sought in "the specific guarantees elsewhere provided in the Constitution," but instead in legal principle and historical experience.[54] It should be seen as "a rational continuum which, broadly speaking, includes a freedom from all substantial arbitrary impositions and purposeless restraints, and which also recognizes, what a reasonable and sensitive judgment must, that certain interests require particularly careful scrutiny of the state needs asserted to justify their abridgment."[55]

Is Substantive Due Process Undemocratic?

Probably the most common complaint about substantive due process is that it is anti-democratic: unelected, life-tenured judges, the argument goes, exploit that doctrine to impose their will on a democratic society. But this argument misunderstands the nature of our constitutionally limited democracy, and the role of our judicial system.

The Constitution does not provide that whatever the majority decrees is law. Instead, it carefully limits the power of the majority by drawing a legal boundary around it, restricting what voters and elected officials may do.[56] Since the Constitution takes precedence over the will of the majority, it is proper for courts to enforce the Constitution—which is the supreme law—even against the majority. Courts do not stand *outside* of the constitutional structure, they are a *part* of that structure, the purpose of which is to restrict political power. The people, knowing that they and their legislators are sometimes led astray, chose to erect a system of separated powers, including a judiciary entrusted with the job of ensuring that the democratic process stays within the boundaries of the nation's fundamental law.

The Founders were well aware that in a democracy, the majority can often confuse the genuine social good with its own self-interest, and can exploit and hurt minorities or individuals for this purpose.[57] In a society where the majority makes the laws, Madison wrote, abuses typically originate "not from acts of Government contrary to the sense of its constituents, but from acts in which the Government is the mere instrument of the major number of the constituents."[58] In *Federalist* 10, he warned that the majority is just as likely as a monarch or a small elite to pervert power for its own gain—and possibly more so. He used an illuminating metaphor to explain. Proposed laws are a lot like lawsuits in which the majority is both the plaintiff and the judge. "[W]hat are many of the most important acts of legislation, but so many judicial determinations, not indeed concerning the rights of single persons, but concerning the rights of large bodies of citizens . . . ?"[59] But unlike in a court case, where the parties can seek adjudication by a disinterested arbiter, democratic legislatures are more likely to be biased by the self-interest of the voters.

Suppose a group proposes to abolish all debts, which would benefit the private self-interest of the majority, but would commit an injustice against the lenders and harm society in general by ruining credit and destroying the chances for future prosperity and progress. This "wicked project" is like a legal dispute: "the creditors are parties on one side, and the debtors on the other. Justice ought to hold the balance between them. Yet the parties are and must be themselves the judges; and the most numerous party, or, in other words, the most powerful faction must be expected to prevail."[60] This is the central problem for any democracy: "[n]o man is allowed to be a judge in his own cause; because his interest would certainly bias his judgment, and, not improbably, corrupt his integrity,"[61] yet the majority in a democratic society is responsible both for passing laws and determining their constitutionality. This creates a risk that the majority will exploit its power to serve its own self-interest, instead of the general good—or might even become so confused about the relationship of liberty and order that it can no longer understand the difference between these two things. For a democracy to be legitimate, therefore, it is not sufficient that the majority approves of a bill; instead, the government must be run in a way that keeps the distinction between arbitrariness and lawful rule constantly in mind.

The Constitution represents the people's effort to restrict their representatives' acts within legal limits. The judiciary, no less than the other branches of government, is charged with maintaining and enforcing that distinction, by policing the boundary of lawfulness against legislative majorities tempted to act unlawfully. A judge may sometimes err, as can any government official. But by resisting the majority, the judge does not contradict the principle of lawful democratic order; he plays an important part in representing the people's interests. True, federal judges are not elected, but they are chosen by the people through the same indirect, appointment-and-confirmation process whereby cabinet secretaries or ambassadors are chosen. Nobody would say that a decision by, say, the secretary of labor lacks democratic legitimacy; the same goes for decisions of judges. In fact, many voters pick presidential candidates exclusively on the basis of the judges the candidate is likely to appoint.

This critical factor is often ignored in critiques of substantive due process. One author, for example, argues that the "central problem" with the Supreme Court's power of judicial review is that "federal judges do not represent the community, and can only exercise carte blanche power at the expense of the community's authority."[62] But federal judges *do* represent the community; they are chosen by the people, through a process designed to protect their independent judgment against prejudice or bias. Federal judges do not exercise their power at the expense of the community's authority, because the community cannot rightfully claim *lawless* authority. When the community or its elected officials act in ways that exceed constitutional boundaries, those acts have no more weight than the acts of an arbitrator who goes beyond the arbitration agreement, or of the bank guard who decides to rob the bank. Indeed, since the Constitution—and not any particular piece of legislation—reflects the *true* intent of the people, a court that invalidates an unconstitutional piece of legislation is actually *enforcing* the true will of the people.[63]

But the "democracy" critique of substantive due process often goes deeper. It is typically premised on the Progressive Era–notion that moral or ethical values are products of the majority's arbitrary will. Courts have no business addressing questions about justice, or individual rights, or the implicit limits on government power, because these matters are determined by majority vote. In Bork's words, moral or ethical values have "no objective or intrinsic validity"[64] but are only a collection of the majority's personal tastes. Chief Justice William Rehnquist expressed this view, in words that demonstrate how the critique of substantive due process rests on a combination of political majoritarianism and moral relativism. There is "no basis other than the individual conscience of the citizen that may serve as a platform for the launching of moral judgments," he wrote, and "no conceivable way in which I can logically demonstrate to you that the judgments of my conscience are superior to the judgments of your conscience, and vice versa." Thus, when the majority enacts laws, it aggregates the people's subjective preferences—which then become both morally right and legally valid. "The laws that emerge after a typical political struggle in which various individual value judgments are debated," he argued, "take on a form of moral goodness because they have been enacted into positive law." But it is only "the fact of their enactment that gives them whatever moral claim they have upon us . . . not any independent virtue they may have."[65]

This inverts America's constitutional foundations, which rest on the principles of the Declaration of Independence. According to those principles, majority rule is legitimate only within the boundaries of individual rights—rights that are not created by the government but are objectively related to human nature and can be rationally defended and understood. Human nature defines the contours of morality, which limits what the majority may legitimately do. "The people in mass," wrote Jefferson, "are inherently independent of all *but moral* law."[66] That is why the Declaration provides that states may do only things "which Independent States may *of right* do." But Rehnquist's formulation reverses this: the will of the majority *creates* moral law, so that *states* decide what *individuals* may, of right, do.

Relativists like Bork and Rehnquist see the courts' power to declare laws invalid as an intrusion on the majority's right to rule. Because they see reasoning about natural rights as foolish abstraction, they think the major problem in constitutional interpretation is confirmation bias—the tendency to read into the Constitution whatever the reader wants to see. Since judges cannot be trusted to be objective about questions of fairness or justice—no such judgments *can* be objective—judges should defer as much as possible to the will of the majority. But this argument holds a hidden contradiction: it assumes that imposing normative views in the law is wrong, yet this is itself a normative position. A commitment to majoritarian democracy is an abstract principle. If moral principles are arbitrary, the decision to defer to the majority's will is just as arbitrary as the decision to do the opposite. If moral priorities are irrational preferences, one cannot claim to be objective by prioritizing the will of the majority, because that, too, would be an irrational preference.

Consider two prominent positivists, law professors Nelson Lund and John McGinnis, who argue that legislatures "have always been" in the business of "adjusting the substantive contours of [fundamental] rights, and must continue to do so" without judicial interference.[67] Lund explicitly "denies that the existence of natural or inherent rights is self-evident, no matter how strongly we may desire it to be true,"[68] because "political philosophers have engaged for centuries in sharp and unsettled debates" about these rights.[69] This difference of opinion means there must be no truth of the matter, and the issue should be left in the hands of the majority. Rights are simply privileges that "arise from human institutions"[70]—privileges granted to individuals on the basis of the majority's subjective preferences, not rational principles rooted in human nature. This argument unashamedly erases the dividing line between law and arbitrariness.

Yet at the same time, Lund and McGinnis call judges who employ substantive due process "lawless judges"[71] and accuse them of "judicial disobedience."[72] This is strange, considering that the Founders deliberately chose to create an independent, not an "obedient," judiciary. But Lund and McGinnis evidently mean that judicial decisions that are poorly reasoned, or in which judges act beyond their legitimate powers, are not *lawful*—that they are not actually the *law*. This raises a paradox. The judges who write such opinions do so according to traditional court *procedures*. How, then, can their decisions be "lawless"? The answer must be that the *substance* of their decisions makes them not law, regardless of how those decisions were promulgated. But if it is possible to accuse a *judge* of acting arbitrarily or "lawlessly," even when that judge complies with procedural formalities, then why is it not also possible to say that a *legislature* that acts unjustly, or beyond its legitimate authority, is acting lawlessly—and thus violating the Due Process of Law guarantee—even if *it* abides by procedural requirements?

In short, like all positivists, Lund and McGinnis try to adopt a descriptive, value-free view of law, and leave all normative questions to the majority—yet doing so is still taking a position on how the law *ought to be*. To say that courts *should* defer to the majority is a prescription, and to recommend it to a judge is to make a claim about what is right. Positivists cannot say that it is an abuse to impose (allegedly subjective) normative commitments in the guise of constitutional interpretation, since they do precisely the same thing. Worse: while the authors of the Constitution and the Declaration of Independence could root their normative claims about how law and government ought to work in objective propositions about human nature, positivists can do neither of these things. Their appeal to the value of democracy rests on no foundation: by their own confession, it is a baseless, arbitrary, emotional preference. They endorse democracy, not because it is good but just because they feel like it.

The positivist critique of substantive due process is misguided in another way. It is *not* clear that judges use substantive due process to rationalize their own policy preferences and read them into the Constitution. On the contrary, a person's policy preferences and constitutional interpretations typically have a much more complex relationship—best described as "potential congruence."[73] A good-faith reader of the Constitution will likely be attracted to those constitutional interpretations that will allow for his preferred policy outcomes, but he also is drawn to policies that he considers constitutional. A person will typically jostle these two perspectives—policy and constitutionalism—against each other in his mind until they reach a basic equilibrium, generally discarding policies he cannot reconcile with his constitutional views, and vice versa. But there are also plenty of examples of judges acknowledging that their preferred policy outcomes are unconstitutional.[74] And whenever a person calls for amending the Constitution, he is admitting that his preferred policy is not constitutional. Aside from cynical prejudice, there is no reason to think that people generally read the Constitution to endorse their preferred policy outcomes.

Moreover, people are typically drawn to study the Constitution in the first place because they approve, at least in general, of the Constitution as they understand it. That initial opinion might be biased by their instructors, and people will refine their understandings as they learn more, or might even reject the Constitution if they conclude that it does not actually live up to their initial approval. People go through such phases of intellectual exploration and ideological refinement all the time. But nothing about this process of learning, debate, and elaboration means that there is no fact of the matter to be apprehended, or that all interpretive methods are equally valid. Nor does it render constitutional interpretation or the doctrine of substantive due process suspect. Government is a human enterprise, liable to human failings. That is one reason the Founders provided powerful checks that Congress and the president can use against the courts if they go too far. But the Framers did expect judges to apply normative criteria to their interpretive tasks.

Does this mean a judge should shamelessly impose his personal views as law? Of course not. As a constitutional officer, sworn to uphold the Constitution, a judge is bound to impose the normative views, both express and implied, that are *part of the Constitution*.[75] The Constitution is not a neutral document "made for people of fundamentally differing views,"[76] and it is not equally compatible with whatever political or economic perspectives voters or legislatures choose to adopt. It incorporates a classical liberal political philosophy rooted in individual rights and the promise of lawful, non-arbitrary rule. Courts are bound to enforce these principles even against the majority. Deviating from these standards—either by adding new constitutional rules that do not exist, or by refusing to enforce existing constitutional strictures—is wrong.

This should not be controversial. Nobody would deny, for example, that the Constitution incorporates the English common-law system. Yet the Constitution does not *explicitly* adopt the common-law system—it incorporates the common law *implicitly*. We infer as much from its textual references to "suits at common law," "cases in law and equity," and the writ of habeas corpus. Courts interpreting these terms are right to employ outside sources to understand how habeas corpus and other devices operate.[77] In the same way, the Constitution's text implicitly incorporates the classical liberal political philosophy of the Founders, and of the anti-slavery leaders who recommitted the Constitution to those ideas in the Fourteenth Amendment. We can see this by the document's references to "liberty," "property," and "other" rights. The Preamble declares that "liberty" is a "blessing." And in the Due Process Clauses of the Fifth and Fourteenth Amendments, the Constitution incorporates a promise that government will treat individuals in a lawful, non-arbitrary manner.

In short, the Constitution has a specific normative direction, and it incorporates substantive political values. A judge interpreting the Constitution may not be able to avoid ideological biases in every case, but as a deputy chosen by the people to interpret and apply its text, he is faithful to his task when he orients his judgments by principles found both explicitly and implicitly in the instrument itself.

Implicit principles are commonplace in constitutional law. The phrase "separation of powers," for example, is nowhere to be found in the Constitution, and it is sometimes difficult to apply in particular cases because the Constitution does not precisely define the boundaries between the three branches. Yet the principle of separation of powers is part of our law because it is inherent in the structure described by the Constitution's words and is echoed throughout other founding-era documents. It would be perverse to abandon this principle just because it is not explicitly stated in the text, or to ridicule the logic on which it stands as being a set of subjective value judgments. The same holds true for substantive due process.

The Due Process of Law Clause's prohibition on arbitrary action may be complicated to apply; it may respond to difficult and overlapping demands of law and political philosophy. But it is part of our law. In a way, it just *is* law. Breezy rejections of substantive due process as an "oxymoron," or as a simple trick for judges to do whatever they wish, are superficial and unserious, and should not be indulged by mature lawyers. Substantive due process might be a nuanced area of constitutional law; it is certainly among the most hotly contested. But by promising the people that government will obey law rather than enforce arbitrary dictates, the Constitution incorporates basic principles of generality, regularity, fairness, rationality, and public orientation. We should not hastily disregard, attack, or ridicule such principles—and we should cherish the clause's protections.

5. Judicial "Activism" and Judicial Abdication

If the left and right agree on nothing else, they share a conviction that judges—particularly unelected federal judges—frequently exceed the scope of their office and impose their own political views from the bench, an evil called "judicial activism." Condemnation of "activist courts" has become a regular feature of presidential elections, and the press has been swamped with books about supposedly extremist judges—with such foreboding titles as *Men in Black: How the Supreme Court Is Destroying America*, by Mark Levin; *Radicals in Robes: Why Extreme Right-Wing Courts Are Wrong for America*, by Cass Sunstein; *Coercing Virtue: The Worldwide Rule of Judges*, by Robert Bork; and *The Rehnquist Court: Judicial Activism on the Right*, by Herman Schwartz. But for all their anxious language, few such books seriously address the role of the judiciary in our constitutional system or ask whether activism is really as dangerous as political leaders claim.

Among the crowd, three figures stand out: liberal Supreme Court Justice Stephen Breyer has authored two books about courts and democracy; conservative judge Robert Bork also wrote at length on the subject, focusing on what he saw as the threat "judicial activism" poses to the moral stability of society; and University of Pennsylvania law professor Kermit Roosevelt, author of the 2006 book, *The Myth of Judicial Activism*, stands in the center, as a specimen of the mainstream of legal scholars today. For all their differences, these three together demonstrate that the controversy over judicial activism is really a debate over the relationship between liberty and democracy in the American Constitution.

The authors of our fundamental law meant for it to protect individual liberty—the right to act freely without interference by, or violence against, others. But Breyer, Bork, and Roosevelt see the Constitution as concerned primarily with fostering democracy and enabling the majority to create its preferred society through legislation. In their

121

eyes, even cherished individual rights are worthy of protection not for the individual's sake, but only because they aid the majority in making decisions and implementing its will. This again gets the constitutional priorities backward. Focusing on democracy instead of liberty as the basic constitutional value not only reflects a surprising naïveté about how legislatures actually operate, but it takes for granted the wolfish perspective that lawmakers or the majority of voters have the right to "do as they please with other men, and the product of other men's labor."[1]

The Constitutional Role of the Judiciary

Before discussing "judicial activism," we must first understand the role that judicial review plays in the American Constitution, since it is impossible to know whether "activism" is an abuse without first knowing what judges ought to do.

Judicial review existed long before 1803, when Chief Justice John Marshall wrote the famous opinion in *Marbury v. Madison*.[2] Alexander Hamilton had explained the idea more than 15 years earlier in *The Federalist*.[3] The Constitution, he wrote, embodies the genuine will of the people, whereas a statute only embodies the will of a particular legislative majority at a particular time. When a statute conflicts with the Constitution, therefore, the judge, far from subverting the will of the people, is actually *enforcing* it by declaring that statute unconstitutional and void. This is why Justice Stephen Field called the judiciary "the most Democratic of all" the federal government's branches: it enforces the true popular will against incursions by temporary legislative majorities.[4] The Constitution is a high wall, or "bulwark," broadly encircling the majority's authorized discretion, and one job of the judiciary is to ensure that the parties in democracy's often hectic debates do not breach that wall. The people may, of course, amend the Constitution—but they must not subvert it.

From America's founding, the courts were seen as a limitation on democratic decisionmaking, created out of a distrust of majority rule and aimed at preserving the Constitution,[5] rather than facilitating the majority's power to impose its wishes. What motivated this distrust? James Madison answers this question in *Federalist* 10 and 51: the problem with any popularly elected government is that it can be captured by private-interest groups seeking to use government power for their own private benefit. These "factions"—a term

Madison defined as "a number of citizens, *whether amounting to a majority or minority* of the whole [populace], who are united and actuated by some common impulse of passion, or of interest, adverse to the rights of other citizens, or to the permanent and aggregate interests of the community"[6]—can breach the limits that the Constitution places on their power and enact laws that deprive people of their private property, abridge religious freedom, or implement other "improper or wicked project[s]."[7] When this happens—when either a small faction uses government to harm the majority, or where the majority uses government to harm the minority—the rights of individuals are placed at risk, just as they were before the establishment of government. Such a society is governed not by law, but by the unaccountable will of the majority.[8] Madison rejected the notion that "the interest of the majority is the political standard of right and wrong," because unless it was "qualified by every *moral* ingredient," that notion would be "only reestablishing under another name and a more specious form, force as a measure of right." After all, "it would be in the interest of the majority in the community to despoil and enslave the minority."[9]

Contemporary economists specializing in public-choice theory have renamed the problem of faction "rent seeking."[10] As these writers explain, rent seeking occurs when interest groups devote their energies and resources to persuading government to pass laws that will profit them. Because government's power to redistribute wealth and opportunity is worth a lot of money, and because that power will increase in value as the scope and frequency of redistributions increase, the result is a spiral effect: the more valuable the redistributive power becomes, the more time and money lobbyists will invest in trying to exploit that power for their own benefit.[11] The exploitation of government by "the private interests" is not simply a symptom of society's moral failings; it is a product of the economic incentives that political institutions put in place.

The *Federalist* offers at least three cures for the "mischiefs of faction."[12] The most famous is the system of checks and balances, which pits groups against one another, ensuring that none can gain a permanent and menacing ascendancy.[13] Another is to limit the power of the state in an absolute sense: where the government is unable to censor the press, or to take one person's property away and give it to another,[14] or to force people to buy a product or service,[15] there will be little danger that factions will try to use government power to plunder others, or to threaten the public safety.[16] Finally, a separate and independent judicial branch can "introduc[e] into the government a will not dependent on" the will of the majority, which is therefore able to resist the majority's inappropriate ambitions without being swayed by popular passion.[17]

These two judicial roles—enforcing constitutional limits on legislative power and preventing the "mischiefs of faction"—share an important attribute: both aim at protecting individual liberty. Enforcing the constitutional will of the people, including its safeguards for freedom, is important not because the majority wants it—indeed, doing so in particular cases is often quite unpopular[18]—but because, as Hamilton wrote, constitutional limits secure "the rights of individuals from the effects of . . . ill humors which . . . designing men . . . sometimes disseminate among the people."[19] It is important to emphasize that the "mischiefs of faction" can only be recognized as *mischiefs* if one is committed to values other than democracy itself. If one is concerned simply with ensuring that majorities can enforce their will, there is little reason to fear factions; self-interested intrusions on individual rights would then just be the outcome of the majoritarian free-for-all, and there would be nothing mischievous about them. But if one regards democracy as an instrumental good, serving the goal of protecting individual liberty, then one must take precautions to protect people against the abuses of majority rule.

Not only the Declaration's language, but also the very logic of a written constitution supports this view. Majorities, after all, have little need for constitutions. A pure democracy like ancient Athens needs no written constitution because the majority's will is the supreme power, trumping individual rights or traditional protections.[20] The purpose of a written constitution is to channel and restrict the majority's power so as to reap the benefits of democratic rule while preventing it from endangering the rights that government is instituted to protect. As Jefferson put it, "An *elective despotism* was not the government we fought for; but one which should not only be founded on free principles, but in which . . . no [branch] could transcend their legal limits, without being effectually checked and restrained by the others."[21]

Breyer and the Progressive Critique of Judicial Review

This original conception of the judicial role contrasts sharply with the modern views of Justice Breyer and Judge Bork. In his books *Active Liberty* and *Making Our Democracy Work,* Breyer lays out an approach to the Constitution that is centered not on liberty but on democracy[22]—or what Breyer calls "the people's right to 'an active and constant participation in collective power.'"[23] One should always keep in mind that the power to which he refers is *power over individuals*—the power to force people to do things or refrain from doing things against their will. Justice Breyer's "active liberty," in short, is the liberty of the majority to do to people what it likes.

According to Breyer, the "need to make room for democratic decision-making" requires judges to exercise "modesty,"[24] meaning that they must defer to legislative decisions in virtually every case, striking down laws only in order to further promote "participatory self-government."[25] Thus he regards the courts' power to review the constitutionality of statutes as an "anomaly," which can be explained only in terms of "[t]he Constitution's efforts to ensure a *workable* democracy,"[26] and not by any overriding commitment to liberty. Indeed, for Breyer, liberty is valuable principally, if not solely, when it aids the majority in making decisions: freedom of speech, for example, is valuable not because each person has the right to utter his opinions as he likes but because free speech "helps the voters exercise an informed democratic choice."[27] This means Breyer has a hard time justifying legal protection of "rights that have little to do with the preservation of democracy,"[28] and he ultimately even rejects the word "rights" in favor of "values," because the latter word "better describes the deep, enduring, and value-laden nature of the Constitution's protections."[29] Although he never explains how courts discern these values, it is clear from the context that by transforming rights into values, Breyer means to blur the distinction between the individual's inherent right to autonomy and the privileges that the government gives to people. This allows courts to manipulate and reshape the amount of each person's freedom in order to "further some other comparably important interest."[30]

Of course, the Framers believed that even important interests were not sufficient to justify violating individual rights (with, of course, such embarrassing exceptions as slavery). But for Breyer, judges should decide constitutional cases by "ask[ing] whether the

125

restriction" on a constitutionally protected right "is proportionate to, or properly balances the need" of society against the "constitutionally protected interest."[31] By describing human rights as "constitutionally protected interests," Breyer's wording emphasizes his view that rights are privileges granted by the majority—a collective choice to hold back the collective's powers—not a basic aspect of each person's individual value. Thus, the balancing he prescribes does not mean comparing society's needs with the value of individual freedom; it means balancing one majority preference against another: is society's interest in this particular case more or less than society's interest in giving citizens the privilege at issue? Genuine individual rights, as opposed to Progressive rights/privileges, play no significant role.

Not only does this vague "balancing" approach maximize the power of judges—replacing legal safeguards for liberty with a judge's notion about what is convenient to society as a whole—but it conflicts with the Constitution's basic commitment to the protection of individual rights—protections that were adopted not because they facilitated the majority's decisionmaking powers but because individuals need and deserve a shield against democracy, *especially* when legislators or the majority claim that they "need" to violate people's rights.

Breyer's view is straight out of the Progressive Era. Rejecting the Founders' focus on individual freedom, the Progressives sought ways to expand government's power over private life and to overthrow legal precedents that they saw as obstacles to social progress. On one hand, Progressive political scientists proposed fundamental changes in the definition of the word "liberty."[32] Rather than referring to the right of the individual "to dispose, and order, as he lists, his Person, Actions, Possessions, and his whole Property, within the Allowance of those Laws under which he is; and therein not to be subject to the arbitrary Will of another, but freely follow his own,"[33] as Locke had characterized it, the Progressives defined freedom as an individual's ability to participate in collective decisionmaking— and more. According to the leading philosopher of Progressivism, John Dewey, liberty meant the individual's "effective opportunity to share in the cultural resources of civilization."[34] Writing in 1935, Dewey acknowledged that the Founders believed individuals should be protected from government intrusion, but that view, he claimed, was now obsolete. In today's world, lawmakers must create "favorable institutions, legal, political and economic," so as to shape the souls of citizens. "An individual is nothing fixed, given ready-made," he wrote, but "something achieved," and achieved *by the government*, "with the aid and support of conditions ... including ... economic, legal, and political institutions as well as science and art." Government must redistribute wealth and redesign society so as to mold the mind and character of each person. As historian Eric Foner puts it, Dewey and his allies "repudiated liberal individualism in favor of an organic vision of the good society."[35]

Progressive politicians presided over a dramatic expansion of government programs—everything from minimum-wage legislation to laws banning alcohol and segregating people by race—aimed at transforming people's very nature.[36] At the same time, Progressive legal thinkers sought to make room for new forms of social engineering by abolishing long-standing constitutional restrictions on government.[37] Repudiating the classical liberal principles of the Declaration in favor of the primacy of government power, judges like Oliver Wendell Holmes, Louis Brandeis, and others substituted *democracy* for liberty as the central constitutional value, although this was a special kind of democracy, often overseen by unaccountable expert administrative agencies and social planners.[38] This meant emphasizing the idea of judicial restraint, which would give legislators broader discretion and allow constitutional boundaries to erode.[39] It also meant focusing not on whether the policies lawmakers implemented were just or fair but rather on the *procedures* whereby the majority forms and expresses its will.[40] As historian Louis Menand writes, Progressives came to hold that "if the legal process was adhered to, the outcome is just,"[41] regardless of what that outcome might be. In fact, Progressive legal theory was so morally agnostic that some leading judges and law professors hoped to devise a theory of law that would be entirely separate from ethics—a *wertfrei*, or value-free, law that would not depend on such messy, unscientific notions as individual rights.[42] Their attitude is perhaps best summarized by contrasting Alexander Hamilton's understanding of the role of courts—as "an intermediate body between the people and the legislature, in order . . . to keep the latter within the limits assigned to their authority"[43]—with that of Holmes. "If my fellow citizens want to go to Hell," Holmes once told a friend, "I will help them. It's my job."[44]

In a Progressive world of process and moral agnosticism, judicial review exists not primarily to protect substantive rights, or to promote pre-political ideas of justice, but to sustain the machinery of collective decisionmaking. Unsurprisingly, this collectivist approach regards individual rights as justified only as a tool for honing the majority's power.[45] This is why freedom of speech receives protection, not as an essential right of all people, but because it helps resolve political disputes and form a social consensus. And it is why individual rights may be constricted or abolished when a judge thinks society's "needs" outweigh them. The Founders saw liberty as the right of individuals to be left "free to regulate their own pursuits of industry and improvement."[46] The Progressives understood liberty as the right of the majority to enact its preferences into laws binding on individuals.

Bork and Conservative Progressivism

Although Progressive theories are usually seen as politically liberal, one of the most influential conservative critics of judicial activism, Robert Bork, wholeheartedly embraced those theories in his book, *The Tempting of America*. The "temptation" to which he referred is the temptation of judges to implement their political preferences as constitutional law and thus intrude on the power of the majority. This is deplorable, because in the "Madisonian system," which is the American Constitution, "in wide areas of life majorities are entitled to rule, if they wish, simply because they are majorities."[47] The majority need not enunciate any practical, general purpose for its commands, nor are its powers limited to the protection of individual rights, since "[m]oral outrage is a sufficient ground for prohibitory legislation."[48] Although Bork claimed to recognize that courts have a duty to protect the individual against the majority, he provided no recipe for doing so, and he believed individual liberties should be strictly limited to those specified in the Bill of Rights.[49] Of course, the Ninth Amendment declares that this is the wrong way to read the Constitution: it says that the fact that some rights are specified must *not* be interpreted to deny the existence or importance of other rights. But Bork tried to dodge the import of the Ninth Amendment by claiming, falsely, that there is "almost no history that would indicate what the ninth amendment was intended to accomplish,"[50] and even likening that amendment to an indecipherable "inkblot."[51]

Actually, Madison, Hamilton, and others wrote at length about what that amendment was intended to accomplish, making clear that it was designed to ensure that nobody would think the Bill of Rights lists all individual rights.[52]

Bork's Progressive-style rejection of the idea that rights precede the state and limit its powers was rooted in his Progressive-style moral agnosticism. "There is no principled way to decide that one man's gratifications are more deserving of respect than another's or that one form of gratification is more worthy than another," he wrote.

> There is no way of deciding these matters other than by reference to some system of moral or ethical values that has no objective or intrinsic validity of its own and about which men can and do differ. . . . The issue of the community's moral and ethical values, the issue of the degree of pain an activity causes, are matters concluded by the passage and enforcement of the laws in question. The judiciary has no role to play other than that of applying the statutes in a fair and impartial manner.[53]

Thus, despite his reputation for moralistic conservatism, Bork was actually a relativist: the majority has virtually unlimited freedom to adopt its (entirely subjective) moral preferences as law, and to impose those preferences on others.[54] There is no way to judge the rightness or wrongness of the majority's decisions in this matter, because the fact that a majority has adopted something just makes it right.[55]

This argument is an updated version of the wolf's view of political authority: legislative majorities have a basic right to do whatever they want with the citizen and the product of his labor, and those protections that are accorded to individual rights are only matters of legislative grace. In fact, Bork indignantly rejected Justice Harry Blackmun's statement in a 1986 case that individual rights are protected because "a person belongs to himself and not others nor to society as a whole."[56] Such "extreme individualism," Bork contended, would lead to a world in which "morality is completely privatized and society may make no moral judgments that are translated into law."[57] Thomas Jefferson wrote that each of us is "made for ourselves," and that it would be "slavery" to "suppose that a man had less right in himself than one of his neighbors or indeed all of them put together,"[58] but in Bork's view, the notion that each person belongs to himself and not to society "can hardly be taken seriously." Nobody, he wrote, "should act on the principle that a 'person belongs to himself and not to others.' No citizen should take the view that no part of him belongs to 'society as a whole.'"[59]

The real target of Bork's assault was not "activism," but judicial review itself. He was surprisingly open about this, calling the Supreme Court's landmark *Marbury v. Madison* decision, in which it first declared an act of Congress unconstitutional, an "intellectually dishonest"[60] example of judicial "misbehavior[]."[61] Of course, this is only consistent. If the majority has the right to rule simply because it is a majority, and judges may not impose their own values by interfering with the majority's arbitrary choices, then there can be no sensible justification for constitutional limits on the majority—except that the majority has temporarily chosen to tie one hand behind its back. Without a grounding in natural rights, even these limits make little sense. Why should a 200-year old constitution, written for a nation of 3 million people, bind a Congress that today represents a hundred times that number? If the majority is entitled to obedience simply because it is a majority, then it seems pointless to prevent today's majority from enforcing its political preferences just because they conflict with the words of an antique document written by men long dead. Bork's majoritarianism is too extreme to support judicial review or even loyalty to a written Constitution.

Activism and Abdication

We can put some flesh on these abstract principles by examining two Supreme Court decisions that are often at the center of debates over "judicial activism" and the role of the judiciary: *Lochner v. New York*[62] and *Kelo v. New London*.[63] Decided in 1906, long before the Progressive revolution in constitutional law was complete, *Lochner* involved a New York law that limited the number of hours that bakers could work per day. When Utica bakery owner Joseph Lochner allowed his employee, Aman Schmitter, to work more than 10 hours per day, Lochner was charged with violating the statute, and he appealed his conviction to the Supreme Court.[64]

It struck down the law. Although it acknowledged that states have broad power to protect "the safety, health, morals and general welfare of the public," and can even "prevent the individual from making certain kinds of contracts"[65] when necessary to protect the public's interests, the Court found no reason to believe the maximum-hours rule actually protected the public or the bakery workers. Bakers, wrote Justice Rufus Peckham, are generally "equal in intelligence and capacity to men in other trades," and are "able to assert their rights and care for themselves without the protecting arm of the State."[66] Nor was the bread they baked unhealthful or of poor quality due to their choice to work overtime. Therefore, since the law restricted their freedom without advancing any public goal, it was a "mere meddlesome interference[]" with the rights of employers and employees "to make contracts regarding labor upon such terms as they may think best."[67]

Lochner was a textbook application of the classical liberal principles embodied in the Declaration of Independence and the Constitution. "The general right to make a contract in relation to his business is part of the liberty of the individual protected by the Fourteenth Amendment," and while states may restrict that liberty when necessary to prevent injury to workers or the general public, they may not simply limit people's freedom at will.[68] Courts must ensure that any such limits are "fair, reasonable and appropriate exercise[s] of the police power," rather than "unreasonable, unnecessary and arbitrary interference with the right of the individual to his personal liberty or to enter into those contracts . . . which may seem to him appropriate or necessary for the support of himself and his family."[69] If courts were to look the other way any time the legislature asserts that its laws promote the public good, the Fourteenth Amendment would become a sham, "and the legislatures of the States would have unbounded power." Lawmakers could then deprive people of liberty by "a mere pretext." Any time the legislature violated a person's rights, it could claim that doing so was somehow good for the public, and courts would have to regard the legislation as valid, "no matter how absolutely without foundation the claim might be." This was unthinkable, since the Constitution guarantees to each person due process of *law,* thus forbidding arbitrary interference with freedom. The Constitution was meant to protect liberty, not to allow the legislature to alter or revoke rights at will.

Although the *Lochner* decision received little attention at first, it gradually came to symbolize what Progressives considered an outdated, individualist view of the Constitution and of the judiciary's role. Professor Roscoe Pound denounced it as "mechanical jurisprudence,"[70] meaning that the Court was excessively concerned with abstract rules and deaf to the practical hardships faced by workers. Justice Holmes, who dissented in the case, argued that the justices were forcing their own private opinions about economic policy on the country in the guise of constitutional interpretation. President Theodore Roosevelt attacked the decision as an instance of "stick-in-the-bark legalism, the legalism that subordinates equity to technicalities" and is thus "a potent enemy of justice."[71] He wanted to "emancipate the people" from "the iniquity of enforced submission to a doctrine which would turn Constitutional provisions which were intended to favor social justice and advancement into prohibitions against such justice and advancement."[72]

Few of these criticisms had merit. Contrary to Pound's implications, the *Lochner* Court did consider the complexities of industrial life when writing the opinion.[73] Notwithstanding Justice Holmes's assertion, the other justices did not rely on any economic theory at all, but on the principle that people are presumed free unless the government has sufficient reason to limit their freedom.[74] And whatever the value of President Roosevelt's comments, they simply had nothing to do with the questions about the legitimacy of the restrictions on liberty that were at issue in the case.

It was not until the 1930s that the Progressive outlook came to dominate the legal world. In the 1934 case of *Nebbia v. New York*,[75] the Supreme Court abandoned the vigilant, *Lochner*-style protections of substantive due process and adopted a new legal theory, called the rational-basis test, under which courts would defer to the decisions of legislatures in virtually every case on the theory that elected officials and bureaucrats are better suited to address the subject matter in question than are courts. This test is extremely deferential to political bodies—according to some precedents, a court must uphold legislation even where it serves no public good, so long as the judge can imagine that a legislature might have thought it would be a good idea.[76] The Court backtracked somewhat in 1938 when it announced in notorious Footnote Four of *United States v. Carolene Products*[77] that it would still give some rights meaningful protection. But at the same time, the Court subtly changed the way it described those rights. No longer were they the basic protections for individual autonomy to which all free people are entitled; instead, the justices protected primarily those rights that enhanced the majority's decisionmaking powers. Judges should apply "more exacting judicial scrutiny" to "legislation which restricts those political processes which can ordinarily be expected to bring about repeal of undesirable legislation" or that "curtail the operation of those political processes ordinarily to be relied upon to protect minorities."[78] The New Deal Court viewed the protection of freedom in terms of how it served democracy, rather than seeing democracy as a device for protecting freedom.

In this new atmosphere, the name *Lochner* became an epithet for "undemocratic," and the case came to symbolize an out-of-control judiciary bent on imposing its political will in the guise of interpreting the law. This meant the case could stand for practically anything—a bogeyman instead of a Supreme Court decision. The tradition of invoking *Lochner* to represent whatever the speaker dislikes continues today, leading to what Professor David E. Bernstein calls a "simplistic discourse" that obscures what the case was really about.[79] Bernstein, the nation's leading *Lochner* expert, notes that even in recent debates over the constitutionality of the Obama administration's health insurance legislation, the law's defenders repeatedly invoked *Lochner* as a codeword for "activist judges," even though the two cases had absolutely nothing in common.[80] Considered on its own merits, *Lochner* was an unremarkable use of judicial power to invalidate a law that deprived people of liberty without reasonable justification. But today's liberals condemn the case out of an indifference, if not a hostility, to economic freedom—in alliance with conservatives who want to downplay natural rights and the role of abstract ideas in constitutional interpretation.

Yet both sides also rely on the judiciary's power to protect rights that they *do* consider important. Following the *Carolene Products* footnote, the Court now distinguishes different kinds of rights, protecting some with *Lochner*-style skepticism, while leaving others to the mercy of legislative whim. For example, the right to travel and the right to political speech are now considered "fundamental" rights, which means they are given a strong type of legal protection, called "strict scrutiny." In these cases, courts presume that the individual is free and then require the government to justify the challenged law by showing that it is "narrowly tailored" to serve a "compelling government interest." But other rights, including the right to build a home on one's property or to negotiate various employment and commercial transactions free from governmental interference, are considered nonfundamental. These rights are still subjected to the ultra-deferential rational-basis test, under which the Court presumes that the legislature has vast regulatory powers and the individual is required to prove that the challenged law has no rational foundation at all, which is usually impossible to do.[81] This well-known "double standard"[82] has no basis in the Constitution, which makes no distinction between kinds of rights. It is instead the offspring of a Progressive political theory that prioritizes some rights over others, usually based on whether they are seen as promoting collective ends or only individual goals.[83] This scheme has often been criticized by lawyers, law professors, and even federal judges, but it remains the framework within which constitutional cases are decided today.[84]

The result is a case like *Kelo v. New London*, the notorious 2005 decision allowing states to condemn private property and transfer it to private developers for the developers' private profit, notwithstanding the Fifth Amendment's requirement that takings be "for public use." Susette Kelo and several neighbors challenged an attempt by their Connecticut hometown to boost the local economy by bulldozing their homes and giving their land to a developer to construct luxury condominiums. Kelo and her friends argued that, although states may use the power of eminent domain to build government installations such as military bases, or provide public services like roads or schools, they may not take property from one person and transfer it to another simply because politicians think doing so might result in greater tax revenue, or improve the overall look of the neighborhood. This would be a *private* use and not the *public* use the Constitution requires. Yet the Court rejected this argument in a decision that represents an almost perfect distillation of Progressive legal theory.

Using the rational-basis test devised in *Nebbia*, Justice John Paul Stevens emphasized that legislatures need "broad latitude in determining what public needs justify the use of the takings power."[85] Since "[p]romoting economic development is a traditional and long-accepted function of government," government officials may take private property whenever they think that doing so would benefit the community.[86] In dissent, Justice Clarence Thomas pointed out the ironic consequences of legal precedents that accord strong, *Lochner*-style protection to some rights, and apply *Nebbia*-style pro-government deference to others: "Though citizens are safe from the government in their homes, the homes themselves are not." This absurd consequence reveals that "[s]omething has gone seriously awry with this Court's interpretation of the Constitution."[87] After *Kelo*, owners of homes, businesses, churches, farms, and other property hold their property essentially as a privilege, at the mercy of the government.

By indulging political leaders in cases like this, the Supreme Court betrays its obligation to enforce constitutional guarantees for individual rights. The result is just what the *Lochner* Court warned would happen: government now has practically "unbounded power" because it can just assert that its acts are meant to serve the public good, and courts will regard those acts as "valid, no matter how absolutely without foundation the claim might be."[88] Remarkably, Justice Stevens himself was once a sharp critic of the rational-basis test he used in *Kelo*. In an earlier case, he argued that it "sweeps too broadly, for it is difficult to imagine a legislative classification that could *not* be supported by a 'reasonably conceivable state of facts.'" Such an approach "is tantamount to no review at all."[89] His reliance on that test in *Kelo* proves that the Progressive theory leaves it to judges to decide when to enforce constitutional protections and when not to, in the service of political, rather than constitutional, goals.

Lochner and *Kelo* represent opposite views of the role of the judiciary, views that rest in turn on opposing theories about the relationship between liberty and order. If people are basically free, with government created to secure their rights, then laws restricting their freedoms can be justified only if they actually serve some general *public* benefit, not if they only benefit some at the expense of others. As Justice George Sutherland put it, *Lochner* recognized that freedom is "the general rule and restraint the exception; and the exercise of legislative authority to abridge it can be justified only by the existence of exceptional circumstances."[90] This view respects the primacy of liberty articulated in the Declaration of Independence, on which the Constitution is premised. On the other hand, if democracy takes priority, and individual freedoms are given to people by the government to serve the goals of political leaders, courts should avoid "judicial activism" by presuming in favor of government, as the *Kelo* Court did, and should allow elected officials virtually free rein.

Justice Stevens' statement that "[p]romoting economic development is a traditional and long-accepted function of government" is especially telling. According to the Constitution's Framers, the function of government was not to foster government plans for economic development but to protect individual rights against violation by the state. The *Kelo* decision reverses the constitutional priorities, placing government power first, and individual rights second. It presumes that government has a fundamental right to rule—to do what it pleases with people and the product of their labor. More than 80 years ago, one of *Lochner*'s loudest critics, law professor Thomas Reed Powell, looked forward to this when he rejected Justice Sutherland's admonition that freedom is the general rule. "[R]egulation has long since become the rule, and freedom the exception," he retorted. "Whence, then, comes the rule that Mr. Justice Sutherland reveals? Needless to say, it comes from Mr. Justice Sutherland. It represents his personal views. . . . Against this presumption in favor of individual freedom from legislative restraint, we may set the presumption in favor of legislative freedom from judicial restraint."[91]

Is There Such a Thing As "Activism?"

In *The Myth of Judicial Activism*, Kermit Roosevelt resoundingly claims that there is no such thing. That term is only "a rhetorically charged shorthand for decisions the speaker disagrees with,"[92] and it stems from a misconception about the nature of judicial work. In Roosevelt's view, those who accuse judges of activism wrongly assume the Constitution contains an unambiguous meaning which can be applied directly to cases without any interpretive gloss. But most constitutional provisions are actually general, especially the most important and far-reaching ones, such as the Equal Protection or Due Process Clauses. These require some intermediary between the facts of the case and the general constitutional language to determine whether or not a government action has violated the Constitution. This gap is filled by "doctrine"—the body of law that interprets the general language and applies it to particular circumstances. But doctrine must never be confused with the actual meaning of a constitutional provision, Roosevelt continues. The doctrine that grows around a constitutional provision over the years may end up being either overinclusive or underinclusive, accomplishing either more or less than the actual aim of the provision.[93]

There may be several reasons that courts adopt a doctrine that does not precisely fit the meaning of the Constitution's words, but for Roosevelt the most important is institutional competence. If other branches of government are better suited to address a given topic than is the judiciary, then courts should leave that matter generally to the other branches, even where doing so means that the other branches will sometimes act unconstitutionally. But where no other branch is more qualified, courts should take a firmer position and limit the discretion of the others, even if they might have acted properly without judicial oversight. This happens when courts employ a high standard of review like strict scrutiny, which curbs the power of Congress or the president. This "over-enforce[s]" the Constitution by restricting lawmakers more than necessary. But when courts use a lower-level standard such as rational basis, they "underenforce" the Constitution and give legislatures more leeway than its words really authorize.

Roosevelt acknowledges that both paths have their risks, but in his view courts should normally choose the underenforcing path and defer to legislatures because "a decision erroneously striking down a law is harder to correct than one erroneously upholding a law."[94] Only where history or institutional handicaps demonstrate that the democratic process cannot be trusted to "balanc[e] the costs and benefits" of legislation should courts apply a higher level of scrutiny.[95]

Roosevelt's argument fails for four reasons. First, it is premised on a fatally simplistic notion of how legislatures work. Elected officials do not simply weigh the costs and benefits of legislation: they are subject to pressures that put minorities—and sometimes even majorities—at an inherent disadvantage. Political entrenchment and personal influence, the benefits of incumbency and name recognition, and many other factors tilt the legislative process against minorities and individuals in ways that have nothing to do with the merits of legislative proposals. Faithful enforcement of the Constitution can help redress these problems. Second, it is not true, as Roosevelt claims, that the dangers of wrongly annulling a law exceed the dangers of wrongly upholding it. The risks are at least equal, and underenforcing the Constitution may pose unique problems that do not exist when a court "overenforces." Third, the role of the judiciary is to determine whether a law is constitutional—not, as Roosevelt would have it, to decide when legislatures are "competent" enough that their constitutional infractions can be treated leniently. Finally, one cannot determine whether a legislature is capable of making proper decisions without reference to underlying moral and political values—yet Progressive constitutionalism is built on avoiding such questions.

Underenforcing the Constitution can be extremely dangerous. Courts can wreak havoc by ignoring the primacy of liberty and allowing the legislature too much leeway in the name of democracy. Indeed, this can do violence to democratic procedures themselves. Consider *Guinn v. Legislature of Nevada*.[96] In that 2003 case, Nevada governor Kenny Guinn, unable to wrangle the constitutionally required two-thirds vote in the state legislature to support his proposed tax increase, asked the state supreme court to issue a writ forcing lawmakers to approve his budget. Reasoning that without a budget the state could not fund its schools, and that the state constitution guaranteed citizens a system of free public schools, the Nevada Supreme Court granted the writ and ordered the legislature to disregard the two-thirds requirement imposed by the state constitution and "proceed expeditiously . . . under simple majority rule."[97] The justices declared that "[w]hen a procedural requirement that is general in nature prevents funding for a basic, substantive right, the procedure must yield."[98]

This conclusion flies in the face of centuries of constitutional law. Lawyers have developed principles of constitutional interpretation—including the rules that more recently enacted or more specific laws take precedence over older or more general ones—in part to limit the power of courts.[99] Yet the justices ignored these rules and, in a decision that echoes Justice Breyer's balancing approach, ordered the legislature to put aside the constitutional procedures so as to "preserv[e] the democratic process" and allow the "majority of legislators, representing a majority of the citizens of this state, [to] make decisions on the services to be provided."[100] They erased an explicit limit on lawmaking power because they considered democratic majoritarianism more important than the Constitution's actual language—language the people adopted in order to protect the rights of minorities against that very majoritarianism.

By forsaking the two-thirds rule as a mere "technicality," the judges gave themselves discretion to "balance the interests" they considered relevant and ultimately to control the outcome of the political process, all in the name of democracy and deference to the legislature.

That decision—which was quietly overruled only a few years later—is just one extreme example of the way judges can abuse their power by failing to enforce limits on democratic processes as well as by wrongly interfering with those processes. They can corrupt the constitutional order not only by being too "active" but also by underenforcing constitutional restraints in the name of democratic objectives.[101]

Public Choice and Factions

Roosevelt's basic argument for judicial deference is that the legislature, whatever its imperfections, is better suited than are other branches that weigh the costs and benefits of proposed legislation, to craft statutes that satisfy more members of the public, and to solve problems with the least amount of trouble. This is probably true, but we should not ignore the significant dangers of representative government. Legislators are agents who exercise delegated power, and they are often self-seeking or biased in ways that betray their trust and harm the people. Public-choice theory demonstrates that when a legislature has the power to redistribute resources between groups in society, that power will become a valuable commodity over which private interest groups will struggle for control. The greater the potential rewards from favorable legislation, the more time and money these factions will invest in trying to persuade lawmakers to act in ways that benefit them—the rent seeking discussed in Chapter 1. Meanwhile, the costs of wealth redistribution are widely dispersed among taxpayers, and its benefits are highly concentrated on a few lucky recipients of government favors. When each taxpayer loses a few pennies to support a program that grants tens of millions to a small class of beneficiaries, there will be far more lobbying in favor of that program than against it, regardless of its merits or demerits.[102]

Roosevelt is silent about rent seeking. Although he acknowledges that there are "cases in which there are reasons to doubt that the legislature is acting in good faith,"[103] he does not suggest a way to detect such cases. This is a critical matter, because rational-basis scrutiny, with its extreme deference to the legislature and its disregard for facts, blinds courts to the self-seeking or bad faith of legislative decisions. Consider *Dukes v. New Orleans*,[104] in which the Court employed an extreme version of rational-basis scrutiny to uphold an ordinance that banned the sale of food from vending carts in the Crescent City's French Quarter, but grandfathered in a single existing vendor, Lucky Dogs, Inc.[105] The ordinance bore all the traits of special-interest lawmaking, designed to benefit a single firm at the expense of competitors and the consuming public. Lucky Dogs was not required to maintain the current appearance of its vending stands or to stay in the same location,[106] and the ordinance did not impose any other kinds of regulations on its performance or appearance. The restriction merely conferred a monopoly on a single business. Although recognizing that city governments have broad discretion to regulate the economy for the public welfare, the court of appeals struck the ordinance down as an arbitrary deprivation of liberty. It acknowledged that grandfathering in existing businesses may be appropriate in some instances,[107] but not here, because the grandfather provision bore no relationship to the ordinance's stated purpose of preserving the small-town atmosphere or the aesthetic experience of visiting the tourist destination. There was "simply no suggestion that eight years' experience in the pushcart hot dog business . . . is necessary or helpful to better hot dog salesmanship, or that it instills in the licensed vendors (or their likely transient operators) the kind of appreciation for the conservation of the Quarter's tradition that would move them to refine their methods of operation."[108]

But none of this mattered when the Supreme Court reviewed the case. Classifying the ordinance as "solely an economic regulation"[109]—as if that rendered it or the rights of the city's job-seeking merchants insignificant—the Court upheld the law, manufacturing a set of irrelevant or wholly speculative justifications for it. For example, the justices imagined that the city might have taken this as a first step toward gradually eliminating all the street vendors, or that the grandfather provision was meant to compensate Lucky Dogs for its sunk costs in hot dog vending.[110] But there was no reason at all to believe these things; indeed, if the city had been concerned about the latter, it would not have created the grandfathering rule, since newcomers in a market are more in need of recouping their investments than are long-established, successful firms. The justices also speculated that the city might have "ma[de] the reasoned judgment that street peddlers and hawkers tend to interfere with the charm and beauty of a historic area" and might have sought to curtail them.[111] Even if that were true, it was irrelevant. The question was whether those concerns were rationally advanced by a law that allowed a single business to remain without imposing on it any aesthetic guidelines or performance regulations, and without regard to whether potential competitors might do a better job. The Court did not merely imagine "the flimsiest reasons" to support the New Orleans ordinance; it also consciously ignored the actual facts in the record, to which the lower courts had paid scrupulous attention, and which showed that the law was simply a special-interest enactment designed to create a monopoly benefitting a single vendor.[112] As one article noted shortly after the decision came out, *Dukes* is "the kind of case that gives economic regulation a bad name."[113] Indeed, it is the most extreme kind of legalistic formalism. The justices sidestepped their obligation to realistically evaluate the facts and rubber-stamped the ordinance by invoking magic words: "solely an economic regulation."[114] In accordance with Progressive "Footnote Four" legal theory, this meant that the statute was subjected to rational-basis scrutiny, and the city was given almost carte blanche.

Roosevelt contends that courts should defer to legislatures in cases involving economic freedom and property rights because legislative choices "are subject to review and correction through democratic politics in a way that judicial decisions are not."[115] But this is what Professor Robert McCloskey called "the amiable fiction"—the myth that victimized minorities can persuade the majority to "throw the bums out."[116] In fact, most victims of eminent domain (like Susette Kelo) and most workers whose right to earn a living is violated by economic regulations (like Joseph Lochner's employee, Aman Schmitter, or the would-be hot dog vendors of New Orleans) are relatively powerless, and can only rarely hope for legislative protection—or even attention.[117] The fiction becomes even less amiable when we reflect on the many ways in which elected officials entrench themselves—through gerrymandering, campaign finance regulations, and other devices that protect incumbents against challenge.

Worse still, most of the rules and regulations that affect the rights of ordinary Americans are not laws written by elected lawmakers but regulations imposed by unelected administrative agencies that wield broad authority to interpret their own commissions, write their own regulations, and enforce their own rules in hearings overseen by their own agents. These bureaus are not accountable to the voting public in any realistic sense; they are generally beyond the control even of an affected citizen's elected representatives. Yet courts review their actions with a lenient, deferential attitude, under the doctrine of *Chevron, U. S. A. Inc. v. Natural Resources Defense Council*, a precedent that gives agencies power to interpret their mandates as expansively as they want except in the most extreme cases.[118] In short, the modern administrative state has outstripped the quaint model of conscientious legislators deliberating about the public good, which might have justified a court in leaving citizens to the political process for protection. The idea that the people can "vote the bums out" if they dislike government policy is simply unrealistic. And the Founders foresaw this, at least enough to design a constitutional separation of powers and a system of checks and balances.

Advocates of "Footnote Four" jurisprudence have identified certain classes of legislative behavior that do not deserve judicial deference, but they have done so less out of a concern for advancing the primary constitutional value of individual freedom than out of a belief that some legislative acts pervert the democratic process. Roosevelt identifies racially discriminatory laws[119] and laws that discriminate against people born out of wedlock[120] as examples of biases that should invoke more effective judicial protection. But those prejudices are only the most obvious examples of the broader problems of rent seeking. In such instances, legislative majorities have burdened disfavored groups through the legislative process for their own benefit or out of simple pique. If judicial skepticism is warranted in those cases, then why not in cases involving other disfavored minorities, such as private property owners, entrepreneurs, or bakers who want to work overtime? If courts should refuse to defer whenever the legislature is subject to biases that put particular minorities at a disadvantage, the same should apply to other forms of discrimination. The would-be hot dog vendors in New Orleans, or landlords in New York or San Francisco,[121] are every bit as vulnerable to exploitation and unjust exclusion as are, say, religious minorities—possibly more so, given the greater profits that politically influential groups stand to reap by burdening them.[122] To deny them judicial protection and throw them on the mercies of the democratic process is essentially to deprive them of the security of law. This is just what the Constitution, with its basic principle of the primacy of liberty, was written to prevent.

Roosevelt's failure to address these issues is particularly glaring in his discussions of *Lochner* and *Kelo*. Although he sees *Lochner* as "a good faith mistake rather than a deliberate one,"[123] he goes on to argue that the Court should have sustained the maximum-hours legislation because in a modern, industrialized society, "government regulation might be necessary to avert clashes between labor and capital."[124] This is done in the name of "equalizing" the "bargaining power" between employer and worker; and "once the question becomes whether redistribution of bargaining power serves the public good, the superior competence of legislatures becomes evident, suggesting the modern deferential approach."[125]

But this makes no sense. Legislatures can be expected to say that *anything* they do serves the public good.[126] If a court does not take account of the rent seeking that warps the legislative process, its deference will render the judge powerless because legislatures will merely declare that their unconstitutional acts benefit the general public, and thus escape constitutional constraints. This is just what happened in *Kelo*.[127] Roosevelt believes that that case was correctly decided because "the question of whether the benefits of a particular government act exceed its burdens is one that legislatures are generally better at answering."[128] But the Constitution does not allow legislators to approve whatever law they think has greater benefits than costs, let alone to "do good" in whatever manner they see fit. Rather, it gives government a limited authority to promote the public good within boundaries—boundaries that include the Fifth Amendment's Public Use Clause, which forbids government taking private property for private use.

Roosevelt's attitude toward *Lochner* and *Kelo* raises the inescapable question: why should courts apply strict scrutiny in some cases and deferential rational basis in others? If deference is good enough for economic liberty and private property rights, why is it not acceptable in cases involving religious liberty or racial discrimination? What factors indicate that a court should distrust the legislative process sometimes, but not other times? Roosevelt's answer here is unsatisfying. Laws infringing the rights of women or of blacks were enacted by legislatures that "contain very few blacks and women," he writes, and given the long history of discrimination against these groups, it is likely that such laws were motivated by "reprehensible" attitudes. Further, "the political power of blacks and women may be insufficient to prompt correction" of such decisions.[129] Also, lawmakers are typically immune from such discriminatory legislation themselves.

These iniquities are serious, to be sure, but the same could be said of the condemnation in *Kelo* or the restriction on employment contracts in *Lochner* or the hot dog monopoly in *Dukes*. Legislatures tend to be dominated by lawyers, intellectuals, and activists, rather than practicing businessmen; legislators' homes are rarely threatened with the use of eminent domain, and none of them are struggling to make a living selling hot dogs on the sidewalk. The history of politics is replete with legislative action targeting businessmen or private property owners, and their relative political power is unlikely to prompt the correction of wrongful legislation—particularly given the effects of rent seeking.[130] *Lochner, Kelo,* and *Dukes* cannot be shrugged off by claiming that the laws challenged in those cases advanced the public welfare—since legislatures that persecuted blacks and women said the same thing about their acts.

Roosevelt's legislative-bias theory weakens still further when he begins fiddling with the relevant minorities. In explaining why courts should protect abortion rights against legislative interference, for example, he writes that

> [t]he question is how well the legislature can be expected to represent the interests of pregnant people. . . . If we focus the inquiry more narrowly on those who actually seek abortions, the case for deference becomes even weaker. These people . . . are . . . generally speaking, younger women. And, again speaking generally, they tend to be poor and unmarried. So the question comes down to whether we trust legislatures to weigh appropriately the interests of young, poor, unmarried women.[131]

But if we can manipulate the categories of affected persons in this way when deciding whether a legislature can be trusted, then the scope of judicial discretion becomes indefinitely flexible. Opponents of abortion, after all, would be quick to argue that the relevant minority is not pregnant women, but *unborn children*, who are not members of any legislature on earth and have no realistic opportunity to defend themselves in the legislative process. The question could plausibly be put: whether legislatures can be trusted appropriately to weigh *their* rights, assuming they have any.[132]

The same problem applies to Roosevelt's other examples. Prohibitions on working more than 10 hours a day in a bakery, or against opening new hot dog stands, are likely to fall hardest on poor, underrepresented immigrant workers who need the work to make money to support their families. How well can a legislature be trusted to weigh *their* interests? The use of eminent domain for private development tends to fall hardest on the poor and members of racial minorities, who have insufficient political weight to defend their property rights against wealthy developers and ambitious local politicians.[133] Virtually every plaintiff challenging the constitutionality of a law might be classified into any number of minority groups by race, sex, income, occupation, or otherwise. By defining the relevant characteristics one way or the other, it is possible to describe almost any litigant as a powerless minority—or, with equal plausibility, to deny that claim. Roosevelt does not explain why one classification should take priority over another, and therefore gives no guidance as to why courts should defer in some cases but not in others. What makes some types of legislative intrusions "reprehensible" and others not?

Of course, none of this is meant to suggest that judicial intervention is the all-purpose solution for rent seeking.[134] Courts cannot stop every instance of special-interest legislation, nor should they try. But the classical justification for an independent judiciary has *always* been that it adds an extra layer of security against this lamentable tendency of representative government.[135] As the Supreme Court has put it, the judiciary has a "special role in safeguarding the interests of those groups that are 'relegated to such a position of political powerlessness as to command extraordinary protection from the majoritarian political process.'"[136] This should include not just racial minorities or women—courts also ought to protect businessmen, property owners, and any other group that lacks the influence necessary to convince lawmakers to respect their rights.

145

Wrongly Upholding Laws Is Just as Dangerous as Wrongly Invalidating Them

Roosevelt posits that more danger results when courts overzealously strike down laws than when they allow unconstitutional laws to stand. But this is dubious. Legislatures are well armed to defend themselves from mistaken judicial decisions. They can check the courts by rejecting judicial appointments, stripping judges of jurisdiction, or creating new, more sympathetic administrative bodies to review disputes. In the last resort, they can simply ignore judicial decisions they dislike. Presidents and Congress have done this more than once in American history.[137] More significantly, lawmakers can re-enact a law that the courts have invalided after removing or revising the invalid elements. This is far easier than Roosevelt seems to think. In 2003, after federal judges held that the Federal Trade Commission's "do-not-call" registry[138] exceeded the agency's statutory mandate,[139] Congress enacted legislation the same day to grant it this authority. The president signed that bill only four days later. Such legislative celerity may be unusual, but it shows that legislatures can clear judicial obstacles, particularly where their policies actually do enjoy widespread support.

By contrast, when the Massachusetts Supreme Judicial Court held in *Goodridge v. Department of Public Health*[140] that the state Constitution required Massachusetts to permit same-sex marriages, many reacted furiously to the court's "activism" and legislation was introduced to overturn it.[141] But that legislation never passed. This inaction, Roosevelt contends, is part of "a gradual process of acceptance by the general public,"[142] as it learns that same-sex marriage will not bring about social catastrophe. Roosevelt is right that one reason for the failure to overturn *Goodridge* was because the decision was well thought out, but another reason is that legislation to overturn it would seriously infringe on the rights of a significant minority of Massachusetts citizens. While legislatures can rapidly correct wrongful court decisions—or decisions they perceive as wrongful—it is not so easy to overrule a judicial decision when doing so would endanger the rights of a significant part of the citizenry. Nor should it be. Legislatures *ought* to be hindered in their attempts to violate individual rights. By forcing lawmakers to rethink questions and meet a higher burden, courts can help promote the protection of liberty. Thus, the risk of an overly active judiciary is often outweighed by its benefits.

Wrongly upholding an unconstitutional law is at least as hazardous as wrongly striking down a valid one. Compare any two cases from the list of infamous cases, one from each category. *Lochner*, for example, is widely regarded (though not by Roosevelt) as among the Supreme Court's worst decisions—allegedly an example of judicial activism that struck down legislation that ought to have been upheld. But whatever one thinks of the decision, it is hard to see why it is categorically worse than such notorious instances of excessive judicial restraint as *Buck v. Bell*[143] or *Kelo v. New London*. The consequence of *Lochner* was to block a particular attempt by the state of New York to forbid bakers from choosing to work more than 10 hours per day. Even if that decision was wrong, it at worst left employers and employees in the status quo ante, while the legislature remained free to adopt other worker-protection laws that respected the workers' right to choose the terms of their employment. *Buck*, by contrast, allowed agents of the state to force a young Virginia woman named Carrie Buck to undergo a sterilization operation against her will, and to allow other states to permanently deprive countless others of their rights to bodily integrity and childbearing. And *Kelo* ended with the devastation of a neighborhood and a precedent that renders homeowners and businessowners across the United States vulnerable to condemnation essentially whenever local officials see fit.[144]

True, a court decision that mistakenly strikes down a constitutionally valid law may result in a precedent that stymies the legislature, but that risk is relatively remote since, as James Madison observed, the legislative branch is inherently stronger than the other branches. The powers of a legislature are "more extensive, and less susceptible of precise limits" than those of the judiciary or the executive, he wrote in *The Federalist*, and the legislature can "mask, under complicated and indirect measures, the encroachments which it makes on the co-ordinate departments." Legislatures represent the majority, and are motivated by timely political controversies, while courts often speak on behalf of unpopular minorities and operate much more slowly. Thus, he warned, legislatures are constantly "extending the sphere of [their] activity, and drawing all power into [their] impetuous vortex."[145] They are much more dangerous than courts.

It is still possible, of course, that a legislature can be effectively blocked from achieving important goals by an erroneous judicial precedent. But the reverse is also true: a decision wrongly upholding an unconstitutional law can result in a precedent that encourages further legislative abuse, and that decision can become part of the cultural background, making it vastly more difficult to overturn later. Consider *Plessy v. Ferguson*.[146] It took decades to erase this precedent, precisely because the Supreme Court's blessing on segregation encouraged further discriminatory laws and caused greater cultural entrenchment of racism. Society often comes to consider issues settled once the Court has spoken, often leading to copycat legislation in other states—and then another set of rules designed to prevent evasion of the previous law. The longer such laws remain on the books, the more reluctant courts become to overturn practices that have become widespread in the years since the prior decision.[147]

A judicial decision wrongly striking down a law can do serious damage. But legislatures and presidents are well equipped to defend their prerogatives against the judiciary, while individuals whose rights are violated by the government rarely have any realistic recourse if the courts fail to protect them. When the Supreme Court struck down popular New Deal legislation in the 1930s, Franklin Roosevelt's threat to pack the Court helped pressure the justices to reverse themselves. That, combined with his judicial appointments, meant that by the end of the decade, the Court had almost entirely accepted his preferred Progressive constitutional theory.[148] And in 2005 and 2006, Congress effectively barred courts from interfering with the operations of the Guantanamo Bay detention center, first by stripping courts of jurisdiction to hear cases brought by inmates and then, when the Supreme Court held that it could still hear some of these cases, by barring the president from releasing detainees.[149] The other branches thus have leverage against the courts. But people like Susette Kelo or Carrie Buck, whose rights are trampled upon by legislatures and ignored by courts, have no such checks or balances. Their only resort is the "amiable fiction" of asking politicians to change their minds.

The general judicial presumption in favor of upholding legislation clashes with our constitutional system's deeper commitments. In criminal law, we presume people innocent until proven guilty because it would be logically impossible to force them to prove a negative and because it is preferable to allow a guilty person to go free than to punish one who has committed no crime.[150] But a constitutional presumption in favor of upholding doubtful legislation risks infringing these principles. True, economic regulations are usually less severe than being convicted of a crime. But forcing someone to "to negative every conceivable basis" in order to prove such a regulation unconstitutional, and presuming that the government may limit a person's freedom until proven otherwise, still imposes the kind of unfairness our criminal law rejects.[151] It allows government to deprive people of liberty unjustly. As one court put it, "We cannot believe that construction a sound one, which indulges every reasonable presumption against the citizen, when the legislature deals with his rights, and gives him the benefit of every reasonable doubt, when his life and liberty are in jeopardy before the courts of the country."[152]

Legislative "Competency" Exists Only Within Constitutional Limits

Roosevelt argues that a judge should defer to the legislature whenever the legislature is better suited to balance the competing interests involved in a work of legislation. This "institutional competence factor" generally requires courts to presume laws to be constitutional, even though this will mean "strik[ing] down a good deal less than the Constitution actually prohibits,"[153] because courts are typically less able "to determine the right answer" than are legislatures.[154] Lawmakers can hold hearings, get advice from experts, ask for community input, and so forth, and are therefore in a better position than the courts to weigh the benefits and burdens of a proposed law. Thus "[i]f the legislature is acting in good faith—an important 'if'—then the possibility of obtaining right answers to that question will be increased if the Court does not attempt to decide the matter itself but simply accepts the legislative judgment."[155]

But this argument blurs the distinction between the right answer when it comes to policy and the right answer when it comes to constitutionality. When lawmakers debate what the tax rate should be, or whether the drinking age should be 21 or 18, it is proper for them to weigh the interests involved and draw a line that might not satisfy everybody. The matter is different when the legislature steps beyond its constitutional limits or violates individual rights. When that

149

happens, its competence is irrelevant; the question is whether it has acted within its legitimate authority. Roosevelt seems to acknowledge this when he counsels courts to strike down laws where "things seem to have gone drastically wrong" in the legislative process.[156] But without defining "wrong" or giving criteria for courts to detect it, this argument skips the most important question. Segregationists doubtless considered themselves to be acting in good faith when they violated the Fourteenth Amendment by separating the races. And nobody doubts that legislatures were *competent* at imposing segregation; indeed, they were disturbingly effective at it. The question at issue in *Brown v. Board of Education* and similar cases was instead whether such policies were within the legislature's constitutional authority.

According to Roosevelt, the institutional competence factor should lead courts to uphold even laws that the Constitution's language rules out of bounds, except when "defects in democracy" or historical abuses suggest that the legislature's good faith has been compromised. But as we have seen, courts cannot determine whether democracy has been defective without considering the rent seeking problems to which Roosevelt gives short shrift. Nor can history alone help a judge decide whether a law that discriminates against an emerging minority (*e.g.*, gays) should be treated like a bad-faith law that discriminates against a traditionally oppressed minority (*e.g.*, blacks) and should therefore be treated skeptically—or like a restriction of a minority that deserves minimal judicial protection (*e.g.*, alcohol drinkers), and thus left to the legislature's discretion.[157] That is a question about constitutionality, not policy. Matters of legislative competence play little role.

Nor can bad faith or oppression of minorities be the only reasons for courts to enforce the Constitution instead of deferring to legislative competence. Since elected officials enjoy only delegated, limited powers, they have no authority to go beyond constitutional limits even if they do so in good faith, and even if they carefully compare the costs and benefits of their actions. Nobody imagines that Congress had bad motives when it passed legislation to give the president a line-item veto, for example, or when it criminalized handgun possession within a certain radius of a school; nor was it incompetent to compare the costs and benefits of those proposals. Yet the Supreme Court rightly struck down those laws because

Congress has no power to alter the constitutional method for passing or vetoing legislation or to regulate activity that falls outside its commerce power.[158] Roosevelt's approach, by contrast, would invite judges to underenforce the Constitution and to assume that legislative competency entitles lawmakers to transgress constitutional limits so long as they act in good faith. This risks allowing judges to use subjective criteria when detecting good faith and to unjustifiably expand legislative power.

Legislatures play an important role in our constitutional structure, and it would be wrong for courts to take over the policymaking role that elected lawmakers enjoy. But just as judges are poorly equipped to weigh the costs and benefits of proposed legislation, they are also not prepared to determine whether the legislature's institutional competence is so great that it deserves the kind of underenforcing deference that Roosevelt recommends. The boundaries of legislative power should be set by the language of the Constitution, not by vague determinations of legislative competence, and courts are better equipped to decide where those constitutional boundaries lie than to decide whether those limits can be safely ignored or whether "leaving the legislature's judgment undisturbed will lead to fewer errors" than enforcing the Constitution as written.[159] Judges should focus on objective matters such as the text of a challenged law, its effects on the litigants, its impact on individual rights, the consequences of a precedent, and the explicit and implicit limits imposed by the Constitution. These matters will often be complicated, and judges will have to make hard choices. But assessing legislative competence does not help. Roosevelt's prescription—that courts should usually accept a legislative decision "if the legislature could rationally have thought that it produces net benefits to society"— ignores the very purpose of the Constitution.[160] That purpose is to put impervious boundaries around the legislature's ordinary cost-benefit analysis.

The murky institutional-competence factor adds little to the question of the judiciary's proper role except to perpetuate the Footnote Four dichotomy of individual rights: to encourage courts to underenforce the Constitution and to abandon some rights to the mercies of lawmakers while more scrupulously safeguarding others. But when courts uphold an unconstitutional law on the ground that legislators are competent to legislate with regard to the general subject

151

matter of that law, they shirk their responsibility in the name of vague appeals to democratic decisionmaking.

Progressivism's Elevation of Procedure over Substance Must Be Abandoned

Finally, and most important, we cannot avoid the substantive values underlying our constitutional order. Ever since the Progressive Era, legal thinkers have searched in vain for some way to avoid normative issues, either because they suppose that such matters are just subjective personal preferences or because they hope that the bitter conflicts that erupt over these subjects can be avoided by transferring our allegiance to the democratic process itself. In the end, these efforts are futile, because promoting majoritarian democracy is itself a normative value. We cannot determine whether the legislature's decision to discriminate against some minority is "reprehensible"[161] or a "defect[] in democracy"[162] without first having a preexisting idea of what a democracy *ought* to look like. We cannot say whether a legislature is competent to settle an issue, or whether it has fallen prey to unfair biases, without first having a substantive value (such as equality) to which we can compare it. No matter how we frame the question, we must know our normative goals before we can fashion appropriate means to achieve them. But if we have such goals, then democracy is not an end in itself, but a means toward advancing those goals. And such commitments give the judiciary a proper role—and a far better lodestar—in policing the boundaries of legislative discretion without deferring too much to the majority. Any theory of judicial deference based on moral agnosticism or on promoting process over substance must therefore be abandoned.

The argument that courts should avoid interfering because they are not as well equipped as legislatures to address complicated issues has some superficial plausibility. But a closer look reveals that it is more often an excuse for abdicating judicial duty. Litigants who argue over a law's constitutionality, after all, are usually not asking a judge to impose some solution to a complicated social problem, or to weigh the benefits and costs of alternative policies. They are asking the judge to decide whether what the legislature did choose meets constitutional standards. If a judge answers no and strikes down the law, he is not forcing legislators to do any particular thing but only declaring that they must not exceed the constitutional standard.[163]

This preserves legislative discretion within proper boundaries. Today's deferential approach, by contrast, gives lawmakers power to choose their own boundaries—often, as *Buck, Kelo,* and *Plessy* prove, with disastrous results.

Toward a Theory of Pro-Constitutional "Activism"

We have seen that many flaws in the prevailing understanding of the courts' role flow from assuming that the majority, or the legislature, has a basic right to govern others. This wolfish notion elevates the procedural means (democracy) over the substantive good (liberty), a fallacious approach with results that are often embarrassing, and sometimes horrifying. Judicial deference cannot be justified by the "amiable fiction" that voters can discipline officials who disregard the Constitution. Nor can it be defended on the grounds that the Constitution commits us to whatever emerges from the legislative process. Democracy is an important part of the constitutional system that protects our freedom—but it is only a part.

Of course, there is no perfect solution to the controversy over judicial activism. If any solution exists, it will originate in cultural attitudes toward the Constitution, not from lawyers' debates. That controversy is, after all, symptomatic of a deeper conflict about political philosophy, one that finds expression not only in the "red-blue" electoral map but in differing attitudes about the basic purpose of government: whether it exists to protect freedom, or whether it exists to enforce the majority's will.

What might a solution look like? A more wholesome understanding of the judiciary's role—which would make room for both "activism" and deference when appropriate—would begin with the text and context of the Constitution itself. Proper judicial engagement would enforce the Constitution as written, with a healthy respect for its primary goal of securing individual rights, instead of making exceptions to its terms or viewing it as a living document that can be molded to serve political exigencies, as courts so often do today. This would require courts to declare laws invalid—even popular laws—if they violate the Constitution's terms. On the other hand, courts should respect the role of the legislature where that role is clearly laid out in the Constitution.

For example, rather than interpreting the Commerce Clause to allow Congress to regulate virtually anything it considers worth regulating,[164] the liberty-oriented approach would adhere to the "first principle[]" that Congress has only limited and enumerated powers.[165] Rather than interpreting the Fifth Amendment's public-use requirement as allowing seizures of property whenever the legislature claims that redistributing property would benefit society, this approach would counsel a strict reading of that clause to bar officials from seizing one person's property for another's private use. But on matters that are clearly delegated to legislatures, such as the power to lay and collect taxes, regulate the military, or issue patents, lawmakers would have broad discretion—within the boundaries of the Constitution.

There are three steps that we could take today toward restoring a proper balance to our constitutional system of judicial review. The first would be to eliminate the double standard by which some rights are given meaningful judicial protection while other, equally important rights are treated like "poor relation[s]"[166] and accorded practically meaningless rational-basis scrutiny. That approach has no constitutional foundation, and leads to perverse results.

Second, and more fundamentally, courts should reexamine the Progressive inversion of constitutional priorities. For too long, legal and political elites have defined freedom as the right of the collective to enforce its will on individuals. By returning instead to the conception of liberty articulated in the Declaration—as the right of each person to do as he pleases with himself and the fruits of his labors, so long as he respects that right in others—we can properly understand how the Constitution preserves individual freedom by delegating a limited authority to democratic legislatures: rights exist prior to government and are the source of its legitimacy.[167] While the rule of the majority is a valuable part of the constitutional structure, limits on freedom must be justified by some genuine public purpose and must be no greater than necessary to accomplish that goal.

Most important, a jurisprudence rooted in this nation's substantive commitment to liberty must have a healthy respect for the natural-rights philosophy on which the Constitution was based. Modern theorists have claimed, with John Hart Ely, that "our society does not, rightly does not, accept the notion of a discoverable and objectively valid set of moral principles" to guide our constitutional course.[168] But actually, the opposite is true. Americans in general share, and rightly share, a belief in the basic truth of the principles enunciated in the Declaration of Independence. Our Constitution was written on the premise that objectively valid political principles and human rights do exist and can be known by lawyers and laymen alike. Today's abandonment of those principles has proven itself untenable and often destructive. Of course, as Chancellor James Kent said, judges should not render their decisions on "principles of abstract justice" alone.[169] But fidelity to the Constitution requires their allegiance to the principles articulated in the Declaration and incorporated in the Constitution. Judges should interpret the Constitution in ways that prioritize liberty, not democracy, and they should not hesitate to strike down laws that trample on individual rights.

Americans differ over important political issues, and the controversy over judicial activism is one manifestation of these differences. But we cannot hope to resolve these disagreements by shrugging at them or by replacing our constitutional order of limited government with one in which the majority always wins. A constitution can survive only among people who agree on basic precepts regarding political authority, justice and injustice, right and wrong. Lawyers, judges, and law professors should resist the temptation to proclaim themselves above it all, and by a pretense of objectivity regard all moral and political values as mere matters of preference to be settled by majority vote. Some things cannot and should not be subjected to vote. Judges fail in their responsibility when they abandon individual rights to the mercies of the legislature. Upholding the Constitution requires judges—no less than legislators, governors, or presidents—to respect the primacy of liberty.

6. Conclusion

In calling the Declaration of Independence the "conscience" of the Constitution, I have used the word advisedly. Whether we imagine it as a still, small voice, or Jiminy Cricket from Disney's *Pinocchio*, conscience is a quality within us that seems to stand outside our more mundane thoughts to guide our actions. It lies at the boundary between is and ought: it understands reasons and it gives reasons. It is the hallmark of a responsible person—or nation. When it comes to the American constitutional order, the Declaration of Independence gives us the standard: it stands above our political arguments to explain the basis and limits of rightful government. Readers of the Constitution should choose their route thereby.

Nineteenth-century Americans were curious about the conscience; philosophers debated its nature; writers sold children's stories about it. Even Mark Twain's greatest character, Huckleberry Finn, wrestles with his conscience before deciding, contrary to his upbringing, that his enslaved friend Jim deserves freedom. But no man of that era was more eloquent in discussing the conscience and its enemies than Frederick Douglass, himself an escaped slave, who as orator, newspaperman, diplomat, and civil-rights leader, is among America's greatest intellectuals. In an 1860 lecture on the evils of slavery, Douglass keenly expressed that quality of indefeasible individual responsibility that entitles all humans to freedom, and that slavery's defenders strove to deconstruct. The masters' physical cruelty, Douglass told his audience, was actually a comparatively minor aspect of their barbarism:

> It is only when we contemplate the slave as a moral and intellectual being, that we can adequately comprehend the unparalleled enormity of slavery. . . . The first work of slavery is to mar and deface those characteristics of its victims which distinguish *men* from *things*, and *persons* from *property*. Its first aim is to destroy all sense of high moral and religious responsibility. It reduces man to a mere machine. It cuts him

> off from his Maker, it hides from him the laws of God, and leaves him to grope his way from time to eternity in the dark, under the arbitrary and despotic control of a frail, depraved, and sinful fellow-man. As the serpent-charmer of India is compelled to extract the deadly teeth of his venomous prey before he is able to handle him with impunity, so the slave-holder must strike down the conscience of the slave before he can obtain the entire mastery over his victim. It is, then, the first business of the enslaver of men to blunt, deaden, and destroy the central principle of human responsibility.[1]

By depriving the slave of the power to choose for himself, and of the right to enjoy the fruits of his labors, the slave owner attempted to transform a man into a tool, into a device for the master's use rather than an independent, thinking being entitled to liberty. Yet the enslaved person always retains the ability to think and choose for himself, to enjoy his wise choices, suffer for his bad ones, and yearn for his freedom. All mature adults have this inalienable quality of personal choice. To make him the tool of another is to deny the basic reality of human existence. People are fallible, with personal biases and imperfect knowledge, incapable of precisely weighing other people's priorities or making good decisions for them. Attempting to do so clashes with each person's moral responsibility and independent judgment. The evil of slavery was thus twofold: it denied self-responsibility, and it made the slave subservient to another fallible, possibly corrupt, human mind. No slave can ever truly have his self taken away and vested in another. And if all men are created equal, no master can boast a degree of moral perfection that might entitle him to try.

Because they rejected equality and self-responsibility, defenders of slavery were forced to reject the Declaration of Independence. Assuming a basic right to govern others, they saw individual liberty as merely a gift they could dole out as they saw fit. The result was the corruption of both the individual citizen and American civic institutions. "Conscience is, to the individual soul, and to society," said Douglass, "what the law of gravitation is to the universe. It holds society together; it is the basis of all trust and confidence; it is the pillar of all moral rectitude. Without it, suspicion would take the place of trust; vice would be more than a match for virtue; men would prey upon each other, like the wild beasts of the desert; and earth would become a *hell*." A society in which some people claim the right to control the lives of others experiences not harmony, cooperation, and freedom, but bitterness, hostility, and strife. The people waste their energies scheming for political advantages or revenge, or hopelessly searching for protection from a legislative process that could target them next. Like Soraya M. or the victims of the dystopian tales of Jerome Bixby or Shirley Jackson, they are exposed to the same predatory dangers that government was supposed to protect them against; they are as vulnerable as they were in the state of nature, before the institution of civil society.

The Constitution was written to put a stop to such pointless plundering by drawing a boundary around politics—a shield that would protect people's rights from the political process. That shield is the law, and the Founders created it because, for all their faults and compromises, they knew that the ultimate goal of government was to secure the most basic right of all people: the right to be free.

When the Founders' compromises with slavery could no longer be sustained, Douglass and his allies demanded a return to the Declaration's principles, both individually and in the nation's fundamental law. "Interpreted as it *ought* to be interpreted," said Douglass in an 1852 address, "the Constitution is a GLORIOUS LIBERTY DOCUMENT."[2] He and other anti-slavery constitutionalists formulated a constitutional theory that brushed away the reactionary doctrines of states' rights and limitless legislative power, and restored the classical liberal principles of equality, liberty, and government by consent. All Americans were Americans primarily, and citizens of states only secondarily. They were entitled to federal protections that would ensure that both federal and state governments honor the primary value of liberty. No government may justly claim power to override people's rights at will. At the end of the Civil War, Republican leaders grasped the opportunity to amend the Constitution to ensure that these principles would not again be denied.

Sadly, their efforts were only partly successful. Although nothing so barbaric as chattel slavery remained, modern legal doctrines, and precedents like the *Slaughter-House Cases* and decisions from the 1930s, have marred the Fourteenth Amendment and perverted our understanding of the Constitution by turning away from the Declaration's orienting principles. The result is a body of law that prioritizes democracy over liberty—that encourages courts to defer to lawmakers and regulators and to shrug when politically influential factions exploit government power for their own private benefit. Like a bank guard abusing his trust by robbing the bank for himself, political leaders, instead of enforcing laws to protect individual rights, routinely take private property through eminent domain for private profit, restrict the freedom of workers and entrepreneurs so as to benefit established businesses, and expand government's reach into areas of our lives that the Founders meant to protect from their prying fingers. Lawyers, judges, and law professors, adhering to the wolfish view that government has a basic right to rule, and that individual rights are only privileges given to people for society's benefit, refuse to defend constitutional guarantees that were written to give life to the principles of the Declaration of Independence. The Constitution's real promise thus remains imperfectly redeemed.

Like an unheeded conscience, those principles still speak, waiting only for us to listen. Today, more and more Americans are realizing the dangers of expanding the scope of government and are protesting the continued calls for bailouts, handouts, entitlement programs, and restrictions on freedom, privacy, property rights, and other aspects of liberty. The time has come for the legal community to pay heed. The time has come to reject the notion that people have the right to control each other's lives and to take the fruits of their labor. The time has come to secure the blessings of liberty for ourselves and our posterity.

Notes

Introduction

1. John Locke, *Second Treatise of Civil Government*, § 57, in *John Locke: Two Treatises of Government*, rev. ed., Peter Laslett, ed. (New York: Cambridge University Press, 1963), p. 348.

2. Address at Sanitary Fair (April 18, 1864), in *Lincoln: Speeches and Writings 1859–1865*, Don Fehrenbacher, ed. (New York: Library of America, 1989), p. 589.

3. John C. Calhoun, "Disquisition on Government," in *Union and Liberty: The Political Philosophy of John C. Calhoun*, Ross M. Lence, ed. (Indianapolis: Liberty Fund, 1992), p. 42.

4. *Palko v. Connecticut*, 302 U.S. 319, 324–25 (1937).

Chapter 1

1. "Active Liberty: A Conversation with United States Supreme Court Justice Stephen Breyer and Professor Robert P. George," http://web.princeton.edu/sites/jmadison/calendar/flash/breyer.html.

2. See, for example, Charles Beard, *An Economic Interpretation of the Constitution of the United States* (New York: MacMillan, 1921).

3. See, for example, Stephen Holmes and Cass R. Sunstein, *The Cost of Rights: Why Liberty Depends on Taxes* (New York: Norton, 1999).

4. Robert Bork, *The Tempting of America: The Political Seduction of the Law* (New York: Free Press, 1990), pp. 353–54.

5. Ibid., p. 124.

6. James Madison, "Sovereignty" (1835), in *Writings of James Madison*, Gaillard Hunt, ed. (New York: G. P. Putnam's Sons, 1910), vol. 9, pp. 570–71.

7. Philip Kurland and Ralph Lerner, eds., *The Founders' Constitution* (Indianapolis: Liberty Fund, 1987), vol. 1, p. 632. See Edward Corwin, *The "Higher Law" Background of American Constitutional Law* (Indianapolis: Liberty Fund, 2008), p. 75.

8. Virginia Declaration of Rights ¶¶ 1–2 (1776).

9. Letter from Thomas Jefferson to Roger C. Weightman, June 24, 1826, in *Jefferson: Writings*, Merrill Peterson, ed. (New York: Library of America, 1984), p. 1517.

10. As Jefferson put it in his first inaugural address, "Sometimes it is said that man can not be trusted with the government of himself. Can he, then, be trusted with the government of others? Or have we found angels in the forms of kings to govern him?" Ibid., p. 494.

11. See John Locke, *Second Treatise of Civil Government*, chap. 6, in *John Locke: Two Treatises of Government*, rev. ed., Peter Laslett, ed. (New York: Cambridge University Press, 1963).

12. Letter to Isaac Tiffany, April 4, 1819, in *Jefferson: Political Writings*, Joyce Appleby and Terence Ball, eds. (New York: Cambridge University Press, 1999), p. 224.

13. See, for example, Letter from Thomas Jefferson to James Madison (September 6, 1789) in *Jefferson: Writings*, pp. 959–64; Letter from James Madison to Thomas Jefferson, *Madison: Writings*, Jack Rakove, ed. (New York: Library of America, 1999), pp. 473–77. See also Randy E. Barnett, *Restoring The Lost Constitution: The Presumption of Liberty* (Princeton: Princeton University Press, 2004), pp. 11–88.

14. Letter to Judge Spencer Roane (September 6, 1819), in *Jefferson: Writings*, p. 1426 (emphasis added).

15. "[T]he people's right to give their consent is itself derived from the equality of all men and therefore limits and directs what it is to which they may rightfully consent." Harry V. Jaffa, "Equality as a Conservative Principle," in *How to Think About the American Revolution* (Durham: Carolina Academic Press, 1978), pp. 41–42. See also Roger Pilon, "The Purpose and Limits of Government," *Cato's Letter* No. 13 (Washington: Cato Institute, 1999).

16. Barnett, ch. 10.

17. James Wilson, Speech in the Pennsylvania Ratification Convention, in *The Founders Constitution*, vol. 1 (December 4, 1787), p. 454. See also *Annals of Congress*, vol. 1 (August 15, 1789), pp. 759–60, in which Congressman Theodore Sedgwick opposed a bill of rights because it "might have gone into a very lengthy enumeration of rights; [it] might have declared that a man should have a right to wear his hat if he pleased; that he might get up when he pleased, and go to bed when he thought proper; but he would ask the gentleman whether he thought it necessary to enter these trifles in a declaration of rights, in a Government where none of them were intended to be infringed."

18. William Blackstone, *Commentaries on the Laws of England* (London: A. Strahan, 1809), vol. 4, p. 51.

19. Thomas Paine, "The Rights of Man: Part One," in *Thomas Paine: Writings* (New York: Library of America, 1995), p. 482.

20. James Madison, "Autobiographical Notes" (1832), in *James Madison: A Biography in His Own Words*, Merrill Peterson, ed. (New York: Newsweek, 1974), vol. 1, p. 41.

21. Thomas Jefferson, "Notes on the State of Virginia," in *Jefferson: Writings*, p. 285.

22. Henry Mayer, *A Son of Thunder: Patrick Henry and the American Republic* (New York: Grove Press, 1991), p. 361.

23. *Jefferson: Writings*, p. 285.

24. Ibid.

25. Virginia Statute for Religious Freedom, in ibid., pp. 346–48.

26 See also letter from George Washington to the Hebrew Congregation in Newport, RI, August 18, 1790, in John Rhodehamel, ed., *George Washington: Writings* (New York: Library of America, 1997), p. 767 ("The Citizens of the United States of America have a right to applaud themselves . . . [That] [a]ll possess alike liberty of consciences and immunities of citizenship. This now no more that toleration is spoken of. . . .").

27. James Madison, "Charters" (1792), in *Madison: Writings*, p. 502.

28. *Regents of the Univ. of Cal. v. Bakke*, 438 U.S. 265, 388 (1978) (opn. of Marshall, J.) ("The Declaration's self-evident truths and . . . unalienable rights were intended, however, to apply only to white men").

29. 60 U.S. (19 How.) 393 (1857).

30. Howard Zinn, *A People's History of the United States* (New York: Harper Perennial, 1990), p. 73.

31. Ibid., p. 74.

32. The term "anti-ideology" was popularized by William F. Buckley Jr., following Russell Kirk, *The Conservative Mind*, 7th ed. (Chicago: Regnery, 1986), p. iii.

33. See Harry V. Jaffa, *Original Intent and the Framers of the Constitution: A Disputed Question* (Washington: Regnery, 1994).

34. See Gordon Wood, *The Radicalism of the American Revolution* (New York: Knopf, 1991); Gordon Wood, *Empire of Liberty: A History of the Early Republic, 1789–1815* (New York: Oxford University Press, 2011).

35. 1 Stat. 1 (1776). The Declaration, along with the Constitution, the Northwest Ordinance of 1787, and the Articles of Confederation, were added to the United States Code in a supplement to volume 1, entitled "Organic Laws of the United States of America." See 1 U.S.C. xlv (2006).

36. To name just one example, in *Boumediene v. Bush*, 553 U.S. 723, 748 (2008), the Court relied on a resolution of the Continental Congress to interpret the meaning of habeas corpus. See also *Chisholm v. Georgia*, 2 U.S. (2 Dall.) 419, 471 (1793) (opn. of Jay, C. J.) (relying on the Declaration as source of law).

37. Minutes of the Board of Visitors of the University of Virginia, March 4, 1825, in *Jefferson: Writings*, p. 479. The Board—which consisted of James Madison, James Monroe, and others—determined that the Declaration would be taught to law students along with *The Federalist*, the Virginia Resolutions, Washington's Farewell Address, and the works of John Locke and Algernon Sidney as being "the best guides" for "the distinctive principles of the government of our State, and of that of the United States."

38. John C. Eastman, "The Declaration of Independence as Seen from the States," in *Declaration of Independence: Origins and Impact*, Scott Douglas Gerber, ed. (Washington: CQ Press, 2002), pp. 97–117.

39. Quoted in Douglas Kmeic and Stephen B. Presser, *The American Constitutional Order: History, Cases, and Philosophy* (Cincinnati: Anderson Publishing Co., 1998), p. 165.

40. *Troxel v. Granville*, 530 U.S. 57, 91–92 (2000) (Scalia, J., dissenting).

41. *Barnes v. Glen Theatre*, 501 U.S. 560, 574–75 (1991) (Scalia, J., dissenting).

42. The Founders were well aware that—in the words of Justice James Wilson, signer of the Constitution and of the Declaration—some people will use their natural liberty in ways that "may be justly censured as vicious and dishonourable," but "while they are not injurious to others," the Founders thought that generally "more unhappiness would result from depriving them of their liberty on account of their imprudence, than could be reasonably apprehended from the imprudent use of their liberty." James Wilson, "Lectures on Law," pt. 1, ch. VII, in *Collected Works of James Wilson*, Kermit L. Hall and Mark David Hall, eds. (Indianapolis: Liberty Fund, 2007), vol. 1, p. 639.

43. 539 U.S. 306, 378 (2003) (Thomas, J., dissenting). Justice Scalia joined Parts I through VII of this dissent rather than simply joining the whole of it. The dissent is only seven parts long—but at the end, separated by three asterisks, is Justice Thomas's reference to the Declaration. It is this part that Justice Scalia refused to join.

44. See Akhil Reed Amar, *The Bill of Rights: Creation and Reconstruction* (New Haven: Yale University Press, 1998), pp. 147–56.

45. *McCulloch v. Maryland*, 17 U.S. (4 Wheat.) 316, 421 (1819).

46. *Nat'l Fed'n of Indep. Bus. v. Sebelius*, 132 S. Ct. 2566, 2592 (2012).

47. *Congressional Globe*, 36th Cong., 1st sess. p. 2602 (1860).

48. *Congressional Globe*, 42nd Cong., 2nd sess. p. 844 (1872).

49. *Congressional Globe*, 39th Cong., 1st sess. p. 2961 (1866).

50. *Federalist* No. 1 (Alexander Hamilton), Jacob E. Cooke, ed. (Middletown, CT: Wesleyan University Press, 1961), p. 3.

51. *Lochner v. New York*, 198 U.S. 45, 75–76 (1905) (Holmes, J., dissenting).

52. *W. Va. Bd. of Ed. v. Barnette*, 319 U.S. 624, 638 (1943).

53. *Federalist* No. 51 (Madison), in Cooke, p. 349.

54. Ibid.

55. Ibid.; see also James Wilson, *Lectures on Law*, pt. 1, ch. X, in Hall, vol. 1, p. 690 ("In a state of nature, it is true, any one individual may act uncontrolled by others; but it is equally true, that, in such a state, every other individual may act uncontrolled by him. Amidst this universal independence, the dissensions and animosities between the interfering members of the society, would be numerous and ungovernable. The consequence would be, that each member, in such a natural state, would enjoy less liberty, and suffer more interruption and inconvenience, than he would under a civil government.").

56. See Garrett Hardin, "The Tragedy of the Commons," *Science* 162 (1968): 1243–48.

57. See, for example, R. Quentin Grafton et al., "Private Property and Economic Efficiency: A Study of a Common-Pool Resource," *Journal of Law and Economics* 43 (2000): 679–713 (using a real-life fishing example).

58. See, for example, Eric A. Posner and Alan O. Sykes, "Economic Foundations of the Law of the Sea," *American Journal of International Law* 104 (2010): 569–96, p. 571 ("[T]he sea contains a wealth of valuable resources, including food, minerals, energy, and materials for bioresearch. When such resources are unowned or found in a 'common pool,' they may be exploited inefficiently because of some familiar externality problems associated with the creation of property rights.").

59. See Robert Nozick, *Anarchy, State, and Utopia* (Cambridge: Harvard University Press, 1974), pp. 11–12 (describing rationality of state as rules for protecting resources). But see Anthony de Jasay, *Social Compact, Free Ride* (Indianapolis: Liberty Fund, 2008) (arguing that the social compact is not actually efficient).

60. *Federalist* No. 62 (James Madison), in Cooke, p. 421.

61. See James M. Buchanan, "Rent Seeking and Profit Seeking," in *The Logical Foundations of Constitutional Liberty*, (Indianapolis: Liberty Fund, 1999), vol. 1, p. 108 ("Rent seeking on the part of potential entrants in a setting where entry is either blocked or can at best reflect one-for-one substitution must generate social waste.").

62. *Federalist* No. 51 (James Madison), in Cooke, p. 352.

63. *Congressional Globe*, 33rd Cong., 1st sess., app. p. 137 (1854) (Sen. Petit). See also John C. Calhoun, "Speech on The Oregon Bill," in *Union and Liberty: The Political Philosophy of John C. Calhoun*, Ross M. Lence, ed. (Indianapolis: Liberty Fund, 1992), pp. 565–66; Alexander Stephens, "Cornerstone Speech, March 21, 1861, http://teachingamericanhistory.org/library/index.asp?documentprint=76.

64. Randy E. Barnett, "Was Slavery Unconstitutional before the Thirteenth Amendment: Lysander Spooner's Theory of Interpretation," *Pacific Law Journal* 28 (1997): 977–1014.

65. Charles Edward Merriam, *A History of American Political Theories* (New York: MacMillan, 1903), pp. 248–50.

66. Ibid., p. 311.

67. See Louis Menand, *The Metaphysical Club* (New York: Farrar, Strauss and Giroux, 2000).

68. Oliver Wendell Holmes, "Natural Law," *Harvard Law Review* 32 (1918): 41 ("Deep-seated preferences can not be argued about—you can not argue a man into liking a glass of beer—and therefore, when differences are sufficiently far reaching, we try to kill the other man rather than let him have his way.").

69. Ibid., p. 42.

70. See Philippa Foot, *Natural Goodness* (Oxford: Clarendon Press, 2001), pp. 15–16; John Herman Randall Jr., *Aristotle* (New York: Columbia University Press, 1960), pp. 250–53.

71. A thorough defense of natural-rights theory would require a full treatise and be beyond the scope of this book. I recommend the works of such classical liberal natural-rights thinkers as Douglas Den Uyl and Douglas Rasmussen, *Norms of Liberty: A Perfectionist Basis for Non-Perfectionist Politics* (University Park, PA: Pennsylvania State University Press, 2005); Tom G. Palmer, "Saving Rights Theory from Its Friends," in *Individual Rights Reconsidered: Are the Truths of the U.S. Declaration of Independence Lasting?* Tibor Machan, ed. (Stanford: Hoover Institution, 2001), pp. 35–85; Randy E. Barnett, *The Structure of Liberty* (Oxford: Oxford University Press, 1998); Larry Arnhart, *Darwinian Natural Right* (Albany: State University of New York Press, 1998); Tara Smith, *Moral Rights and Political Freedom* (Lanham, MD; Rowman & Littlefield, 1995); and Ayn Rand, *Capitalism: The Unknown Ideal* (New York: Signet, 1968). One common objection to these arguments is the charge that deriving rules of individual or group behavior from human nature is to commit the "naturalistic fallacy." This is answered most convincingly in Foot, *Natural Goodness*; Jan Tullberg and Brigitta S. Tullberg, "A Critique of the Naturalistic Fallacy Thesis," *Politics and the Life Sciences* 20, no. 2 (2001): 165–74; Philippa Foot, ed., *Theories of Ethics* (Oxford: Oxford University Press, 1976); Arnhart; Harry Binswanger, *The Biological Basis of Teleological Concepts* (Marina Del Rey, CA: Ayn Rand Institute Press, 1990); Roger D. Maters, *The Nature of Politics* (New Haven: Yale University Press, 1989); and W. D. Falk, *Ought, Reasons, and Morality* (New York: Cornell University Press, 1986). As Daniel Dennett writes, "[f]rom what can 'ought' be derived? The most compelling answer is this: ethics must *somehow* be based on an appreciation of human nature—on a sense of what a human being is or might be, and on what a human being might want to have or want to be. If *that* is naturalism, then naturalism is no fallacy." Daniel Dennett, *Darwin's Dangerous Idea: Evolution and the Meanings of Life* (New York: Simon & Schuster, 1995), p. 468. But I recognize that this is complicated and hotly contested philosophical ground.

72. Oliver Wendell Holmes, *The Common Law* (New York: Dover, 1991), p. 3.

73. See Adam Smith, *An Inquiry into the Nature and Causes of the Wealth of Nations* (Oxford: Oxford University Press, 1976) (1776), vol. 1, p. 26 ("Nobody ever saw a dog make a fair and deliberate exchange of one bone for another with another dog.").

74. *Black & White Taxicab & Transfer Co. v. Brown & Yellow Taxicab & Transfer Co.*, 276 U.S. 518, 533 (1928) (Holmes, J., dissenting).

75. Letter from Oliver Wendell Holmes to Alice Stopford Green (August 20, 1909), in *The Essential Holmes*, Richard Posner, ed. (Chicago: University of Chicago Press, 1992), p. 116.

76. Letter from Oliver Wendell Holmes to Harold Laski (September 15, 1916), in *The Holmes-Laski Letters*, Mark DeWolfe Howe, ed. (New York: Atheneum, 1953), vol. 1, pp. 18–19.

77. *Buck v. Bell*, 274 U.S. 200, 207 (1927).

78. 205 U.S. 349, 353 (1907). In a letter to Harold Laski dated January 29, 1926, Holmes elaborated: the idea of rights valid against government "seems to me like shaking one's fist at the sky, when the sky furnishes the energy that enables one to raise the fist." One might observe that it is entirely possible to shake one's fist at the sky—and to fly a rocket to the moon—notwithstanding. *Essential Holmes*, p. 235.

79. 250 U.S. 616, 624 (1919) (Holmes, J., dissenting).

80. See, for example, Harry Kalven Jr., *A Worthy Tradition: Freedom of Speech in America* (New York: Harper & Row, 1988), p. 144.

81. *Abrams*, 250 U.S. at 630 (Holmes, J., dissenting).

82. Ibid.

83. 249 U.S. 47, 52 (1919).

84. *Lochner*, 198 U.S. at 75–76 (Holmes, J., dissenting).

85. In Book 1 of Plato's *Republic*, Thrasymachus argues that justice is whatever serves "the interest of the stronger party."

86. Laurence H. Tribe, "The Curvature of Constitutional Space: What Lawyers Can Learn from Modern Physics," *Harvard Law Review* 103 (1989): 8.

87. Ibid., p. 7.

88. Laurence H. Tribe, *American Constitutional Law*, 2d ed. (Mineoala, NY: Foundation Press, 1988), p. 578.

89. Cass Sunstein, *Democracy and the Problem of Free Speech* (New York: Free Press, 1995), p. 30.

90. Ibid., pp. 34–35.

91. Ibid., p. 247.

92. Anthony de Jasay, *Justice and Its Surroundings* (Indianapolis: Liberty Fund, 2000), pp. 150–51.

93. William Lee Miller, *Arguing About Slavery* (New York: Vintage, 1995).

94. Palmer, "Rights Theory," p. 45.

95. Paraphrasing Sunstein, p. 30.

96. Bork, *Tempting of America*, p. 124.

97. Ibid., p. 249.

98. Ibid., p. 124.

99. Robert H. Bork, "Neutral Principles and Some First Amendment Problems," *Indiana Law Journal* 47 (1971): 10.

100. See Bork, *Tempting of America*, p. 121 ("It is doubtful that there are any moral 'facts,' as opposed to moral convictions. . . .").

101. Ibid., pp. 258–59.

102. Ibid., pp. 124–25 (emphasis added).

103. *First Treatise of Civil Government* § 27, in Laslett, ed., p. 195.

104. Ibid., § 2, p. 176.

Chapter 2

1. Kimberly Shankman and Roger Pilon, "Reviving the Privileges or Immunities Clause to Redress the Balance among States, Individuals, and the Federal Government," *Texas Review of Law & Politics* 3 (1998): 11.

2. Jacobus tenBroek, *Equal Under Law: The Antislavery Origins of the Fourteenth Amendment*, 2nd ed. (New York: Collier, 1965), ch. 4.

3. Akhil Reed Amar, *America's Constitution: A Biography* (New York: Random House, 2005), pp. 5–53; Daniel Farber, *Lincoln's Constitution* (Chicago: University of Chicago Press, 2003), pp. 26–91.

4. *Federalist* No. 15 (Alexander Hamilton), in *The Federalist*, Jacob E. Cooke, ed. (Middletown, CT: Wesleyan University Press, 1961), p. 93.

5. *Federalist* No. 33 (Alexander Hamilton), in ibid., p. 207.

6. Jonathan Elliot, ed., *Debates in the Several State Conventions on the Adoption of the Federal Constitution* (Washington: J. Elliot, 1836), vol. 3, p. 22.

7. Ibid., p. 94.

8. Ibid.

9. Elliot, vol. 5, p. 213.

10. Luther Martin, "The Genuine Information XII," in *Debate on the Constitution*, Bernard Bailyn, ed., (New York: Library of America, 1993), vol. 1, p. 658 (emphasis in original).

11. Elliot, vol. 5, p. 213.

12. Ibid.

13. Elliot, vol. 2, p. 444.

14. Ibid.

15. "Brutus XII," (February 7–14, 1788), in Elliot, vol. 2, pp. 173–74.

16. Federal Farmer, "Letter IV" (Oct. 12, 1787), in Elliot, vol. 1, p. 275.

17. See Akhil Reed Amar, "Of Sovereignty and Federalism," *Yale Law Journal* 96 (1987): 1462, n. 162.

18 22 U.S. (9 Wheat.) 1, 187 (1824); see also *Chisolm v. Georgia*, 2 U.S. (2 Dall.) 419, 470 (1793) (opn. of Jay, C. J.) ("the people, in their collective and national capacity, established the present Constitution").

19. 17 U.S. (4 Wheat.) 316, 403–04 (1819). Justice Kennedy's words almost two centuries later are apt: "The Framers split the atom of sovereignty. It was the genius of their idea that our citizens would have two political capacities, one state and one federal, each with its own direct relationship, its own privity, its own set of mutual rights and obligations to the people who sustain it and are governed by it." *U.S. Term Limits, Inc. v. Thornton*, 514 U.S. 779, 838 (1995) (Kennedy, J., concurring).

20. See William W. Freehling, *Prelude to Civil War: The Nullification Controversy in South Carolina, 1816–1836* (Oxford: Oxford University Press, 1992); Manisha Sinha, *The Counter-Revolution of Slavery: Politics and Ideology in Antebellum South Carolina* (Chapel Hill: University of North Carolina Press, 2000); and Timothy Sandefur, "How Libertarians Ought to Think About the U.S. Civil War," *Reason Papers* 28 (2006): 61–83.

21. Thomas Jefferson, Kentucky Resolutions (1798), in *Jefferson: Writings*, Merrill Peterson, ed. (New York: Library of America, 1984), p. 449.

22. John C. Calhoun, *A Discourse on the Constitution and Government of the United States*, in *Union and Liberty: The Political Philosophy of John C. Calhoun*, Ross M. Lence, ed. (Indianapolis: Liberty Fund, 1992), p. 86.

23. Farber, p. 34.

24. Herman Belz, ed., *The Webster-Hayne Debate on the Nature of the Union* (Indianapolis: Liberty Fund, 2000), p. 136.

25. Ibid., p. 126.

26. Ibid., p. 136.

27. Ibid., p. 174.

28. "Address to the People of South Carolina, by Their Delegates in Convention" (1832), in *State Papers on Nullification* (Boston: Dutton & Wentworth, 1834), pp. 40–43.

29. William Blackstone, *Commentaries on the Common Law* (London: A. Strahan, 1809), vol. 1, p. 156.

30. Ibid., p. 49.

31. Ibid., p. 156.

32. Ibid., p. 157.

33. Julian S. Waterman, "Thomas Jefferson and Blackstone's Commentaries," *Illinois Law Review* 27 (1933): 649–52.

34. St. George Tucker, *Blackstone's Commentaries* (Clark, N.: Lawbook Exchange, 2008), vol. 1, Appx. A, p. 3; vol. 2, Appx. G, pp. 19–20 (quoting James Madison).

35. Ibid., vol. 1, p. 49, n. 5.

36. Robert M. Cover, Book Review, *Blackstone's Commentaries*, St. George Tucker, ed., *Columbia Law Review* 70 (1970): 1475–94.

37. Abel Upshur, *Enquiry into the True Nature and Character of Our Federal Government* (Petersburg, VA: Edmund & Jullian C. Ruffin, 1840), p. 78.

38. Henry St. George Tucker, *Lectures on Constitutional Law* (Richmond: Shepherd and Colin, 1843), pp. 33–36 (Quoting Joseph Story).

39. N. Beverley Tucker, *A Series of Lectures on the Science of Government* (Philadelphia: Carey and Hart, 1845), pp. 73–74.

40. 21 Pa. 147 (1853). *Sharpless* is among the most fascinating of antebellum constitutional decisions. It illustrates the debate over the limits of sovereignty that echoed through American legal history up until the outbreak of the war. See Timothy Sandefur, *Cornerstone of Liberty: Property Rights in 21st Century America* (Washington: Cato Institute, 2006), pp. 64–67. The dissents, sadly, were not printed in the official state reports, but can be found in volume 2 of the *American Law Register* for 1854. Justice Lewis' dissenting opinion appears at page 80, and Justice Lowrie's at page 27. See also Ellis L. Waldron, "*Sharpless v. Philadelphia*: Jeremiah Black and the Parent Case on the Public Purpose of Taxation," *Wisconsin Law Review* (1953): 48–75.

41. *Sharpless*, 21 Pa. at 160.

42. Ibid.

43. Ibid. at 161. In fact, Black contradicted himself on this point. Contrary to his assertion that states possessed "full and uncontrolled power" except where specifically denied by the state constitution, Black accepted the existence of unwritten limits on state power: "The whole of a public burden cannot be thrown on a single individual, under the pretence of taxing him," for example, even though no written provision of the Constitution forbids this; such a prohibition "was not necessary," because such a legislative act "would not be a law, but an attempt to pronounce a judicial sentence, order or decree." Ibid. at 168. This, as Waldron observes, is the theory later called "substantive due process." Waldron, p. 75. Black did not seem to recognize his self-contradiction. Ibid., p. 64.

44. *Sharpless*, 21 Pa. at 160.

45. *Sharpless*, *American Law Register* 2, pp. 87, 97 (Lewis, J., dissenting).

46. Henry Hughes, *Treatise on Sociology, Theoretical and Practical* (Philadelphia: Lippincott, Grambo and Co., 1854), pp. 185–86. By "use," Hughes meant the common-law concept of "use," which entitles a person to the profits of a piece of land, but not to actual ownership.

NOTES FOR PAGES 40–43

47. William Harper, *Memoir on Slavery* (Charleston: James S. Burges, 1838), p. 7.

48. John C. Calhoun, *A Disquisition on Government*, in *Union and Liberty*, Lence, ed., p. 42.

49. Ibid.

50. Calhoun, speech on the Oregon Bill, in ibid., p. 566.

51. See John C. Calhoun, Speech on the Force Bill (Feb. 15–16, 1833), in ibid., pp. 443–44.

52. Amar, *America's Constitution*, pp. 38–53; Freehling, pp. 165–66.

53. Madison's clash with Calhoun and his allies is described in Drew McCoy's superb book, *The Last of the Fathers: James Madison and the Republican Legacy* (Cambridge: Cambridge University Press, 1989).

54. James Madison, "Sovereignty" (1835), in *Writings of James Madison*, Gaillard Hunt, ed., (New York: G. P. Putnam's Sons, 1910), vol. 9, pp. 570–71.

55. George A. Lipsky, *John Quincy Adams: His Theory and Ideas* (New York: Thomas Y. Crowell Co., 1965). See especially ch. 12.

56. *The Jubilee of the Constitution* was one of the most popular publications of the era, selling more than 8,000 copies in a matter of weeks. See Paul C. Nagel, *John Quincy Adams: A Public Life, A Private Life* (Harvard: Harvard University Press, 1997), p. 372.

57. John Quincy Adams, *The Jubilee of the Constitution* (New York: Samuel Colman, 1848), p. 20.

58. Ibid., p. 9.

59. Ibid., p. 30.

60. John Quincy Adams, *An Oration Addressed to the Citizens of the Town of Quincy on the Fourth of July, 1831, the Fifty-Fifth Anniversary of the Independence of the United States of America* (Boston: Richardson, Lord and Holbrook, 1831), p. 22.

61. Ibid., p. 35.

62. Ibid., p. 37.

63. Belz, *Webster-Hayne Debate*, p. 144.

64. Adams was hardly alone in these beliefs. Joseph Story made the same arguments in his *Commentaries on the Constitution* (Boston: Hilliard, Gray and Co., 1833), vol. 1, bk. 2, §§ 205-08, as did several other Northern leaders. Nor did all Southerners agree with the entire states' rights theory. For example, John Taylor of Caroline's 1820 book *Construction Construed and Constitutions Vindicated* rejected absolute Blackstonian sovereignty, and objected to the very word. But in 1823, in his *New Views of the Constitution of the United States*, he argued that the Constitution was a league of sovereign states, and appeared to back away from his arguments against absolute sovereignty.

65. See Anne-Marie Taylor, *Young Charles Sumner and the Legacy of the American Enlightenment, 1811–1851* (Amherst: University of Massachusetts Press, 2001), pp. 275–78.

66. See John M. Taylor, *William Henry Seward: Lincoln's Right Hand Man* (Washington: Potomac Books, 1991), pp. 69–70.

67. See William Lee Miller, *Arguing About Slavery* (New York: Knopf, 1996), pp. 448–49.

68. 46 U.S. (5 How.) 215 (1847).

69. S. P. Chase, *An Argument for the Defendant Submitted to the Supreme Court of the United States in the Case of Wharton Jones vs. John Van Zandt* (Cincinnati: R. P. Donogh and Co., 1847), pp. 93–94. Chase is paraphrasing from the opinion of his great-grandfather, Justice Samuel Chase, in *Calder v. Bull*, 3 U.S. (3 Dall.) 386, 388 (1798).

70. *Kohl v. United States*, 91 U.S. (1 Otto) 367, 373 (1876). *Kohl* upheld an 1872 condemnation of land to construct a post office in Ohio.

71. Article II section 1 requires that the President be a "natural born Citizen." Article I section 2 requires that Congressmen and Senators be "citizen[s] of the United States."

72. Josiah Quincy, *Memoir of the Life of John Quincy Adams* (Boston: Phillips, Samson, and Co., 1858), p. 114.

73. Charles Francis Adams, ed., *Memoirs of John Quincy Adams* (Philadelphia: J. B. Lippincott, 1875), vol. 5, p. 308.

74. *State v. Claiborne*, 19 Tenn. 331, 340 (1838). See also *Amy v. Smith*, 11 Ky. 326, 334 (1822) ("Free negroes and mulattoes are, almost everywhere, considered and treated as a degraded race of people; insomuch so, that, under the constitution and laws of the United States, they cannot become citizens of the United States.")

75. *Elkison v. Deliesseline*, 8 F. Cas. at 493 (C.C.D.S.C. 1823).

76. Ibid. Johnson wrote the decision sitting as a Circuit Judge.

77. 1 Op. Atty. Gen. 659 (1824).

78. Freehling, p. 115.

79. 2 Op. Atty. Gen. 426 (1831).

80. H. Jefferson Powell, "Attorney General Taney & the South Carolina Police Bill," *Green Bag (Second Series)* 5 (2001): 84–85.

81. Quoted in Herman von Holst, *The Constitutional and Political History of the United States* (Chicago: Callaghan and Co., 1881), vol. 3, p. 137.

82. *Deliesseline*, 8 F. Cas. at 494.

83. *Congressional Globe*, 31st Cong. 1st sess., App., p. 284 (1850).

84. Ibid., p. 288.

85. Ibid.

86. Ibid., p. 290.

87. Howard Jay Graham, "The Early Antislavery Backgrounds of the Fourteenth Amendment," *Wisconsin Law Review* (1950): 498.

88. *Crandall v. State*, 10 Conn. 339, 370 (1834). Crandall operated a school to teach black children, which outraged citizens of Canterbury, Connecticut. Unable to drive Crandall out through threats and violence, locals persuaded the state legislature to enact a law closing the school. Crandall continued to teach, and was arrested and tried for "harbouring and boarding coloured persons." Crandall's conviction was eventually reversed on a technicality, but continued harassment forced her to close her school. See Henry Mayer, *All on Fire: William Lloyd Garrison and the Abolition of Slavery* (New York: Norton, 1998), pp. 145–89.

89. William Jay, *An Inquiry into the Character and Tendency of the American Colonization and American Anti-Slavery Societies*, 3rd ed. (New York: Leavitt, Lord, and Co., 1835), pp. 39–46.

90. Lysander Spooner, *The Unconstitutionality of Slavery* (Boston: Burt Franklin, facsimile ed. n.d. (1860)); William Goodell, *Slavery and Antislavery* (New York: William Harnet, 1852); Beriah Green, *The Chattel Principle* (New York: American Anti-Slavery Society, 1839); Gerrit Smith, *Letter of Gerrit Smith to Hon. Henry Clay* (New York: American Anti-Slavery Society, 1839); Joel Tiffany, *A Treatise on the Unconstitutionality of American Slavery* (Cleveland: J. Calyer, 1849); Frederick Douglass, "The Constitution of the United States: Is It Pro-Slavery or Antislavery?" (1860), in *Frederick Douglass: Selected Speeches and Writings*, Philip S. Foner and Yuval Taylor, eds. (Chicago: Lawrence Hill Books, 1999), pp. 380–90.

91. Frederick Douglass, "The *Dred Scott* Decision" (1857), in ibid., p. 357; see also Spooner, p. 188 ("[T]here is no legal ground for denying that the terms 'the people of the United States,' included the whole of the then people of the United States. And if the whole of the people are the parties to it, it must, if possible, be so construed as to make it such a contract as each and every individual might reasonably agree to.").

92. See also Spooner, p. 101 (arguing that slaves were citizens).

93. See also Charles Sumner, *Freedom National, Slavery Sectional* (Boston: Ticknor, Reed and Fields, 1852), pp. 52–53.

94. Douglass, "The *Dred Scott* Decision," p. 357. Although Douglass began his abolitionist career under Garrison's tutelage, they split over the latter's belief that the Constitution was a pro-slavery document and therefore corrupt. See Henry Mayer, *All on Fire: William Lloyd Garrison and the Abolition of Slavery* (New York: Norton, 1998), p. 428; and William McFeely, *Frederick Douglass* (New York: Norton, 1991), pp. 168–69. Most writers who have addressed this schism have regarded Douglass's arguments as weak or even disingenuous—unfairly, in my view. See, for example, Mayer, p. 429 (describing Douglass's embrace of antislavery constitutionalism as "pragmatic" and "chimerical"). So far as I know, only three books—Peter C. Myers, *Frederick Douglass: Race and the Rebirth of American Liberalism* (Lawrence: University of Kansas Press, 2008), pp. 83–109; James A. Colaiaco, *Frederick Douglass and the Fourth of July* (New York: Palgrave MacMillan, 2006), pp. 163–87; and Nicholas Buccola, *The Political Thought of Frederick Douglass* (New York: NYU Press, 2012)—have even attempted a fair and thorough discussion of Douglass' constitutional views.

95. Joel Tiffany, *A Treatise on Government, and Constitutional Law, Being an Inquiry into the Source and Limitation of Governmental Authority, According to the American Theory* (Albany: Weare C. Little, 1867), pp. 50–51.

96. Ibid., p. 26.

97. Ibid., p. 372.

98. Tiffany, *A Treatise on the Unconstitutionality of American Slavery*, pp. 88–89.

99. Spooner, *The Unconstitutionality of Slavery*, p. 90.

100. Ibid., p. 92.

101. Ibid., p. 57.

102. John C. Calhoun, *A Discourse on the Constitution and Government of the United States*, in *Union and Liberty: The Political Philosophy of John C. Calhoun*, Ross M. Lence, ed. (Indianapolis: Liberty Fund, 1992), p. 116.

103. Speech on the Force Bill, Lence, p. 443.

104. *A Constitutional View of the Late War Between the States* (Philadelphia: National Publishing Co., 1868), vol. 1, pp. 18–37.

105. Jefferson Davis, *The Rise and Fall of the Confederate Government* (New York: Appleton and Co., 1912), vol. 1, p. 120.

106. Tiffany, *A Treatise on Government*, p. 372.

107. 10 Op. Atty. Gen. 382, 383 (1862).

108. G. Edward White, *Law in American History Vol. 1: From The Colonial Years Through The Civil War* (New York: Oxford University Press, 2012), pp. 376–78.

109. *Dred Scott v. Sandford*, 60 U.S. (19 How.) 393, 404 (1857).

110. Ibid. at 404–05.

111. Ibid. at 406.

112. Ibid. at 407.

113. Abraham Lincoln, Address at Cooper Institute, February 27, 1860, in Don Fehrenbacher, ed., *Lincoln: Speeches and Writings 1859–1865* (New York: Library of America, 1989), pp. 111–30.

114. *Dred Scott*, 60 U.S. (19 How.) at 420.

115. Ibid. at 572–73 (Curtis, J., dissenting).

116. Ibid. at 582 (Curtis, J., dissenting).

117. Ibid. at 580.

118. *Opinion of the Justices*, 44 Me. 505 (1857).

119. 20 N.Y. 562 (N.Y. 1860).

120. *Congressional Globe*, 35th Cong., 2nd sess., p. 983 (1859).

120. Ibid., p. 984.

122. Ibid., p. 985.

123. Ibid., p. 984. Professor David R. Upham has noted that Curtis may have been alluding to an unreported decision by Ohio Supreme Court Justice Nathan Reed, described in William H. Williams, "The Arrest of Non-Residents for Debt: Constitutionality of the Law," *Western Law Journal* 11 (1845): 266. See David R. Upham, "The Meanings of the 'Privileges and Immunities of Citizens' on the Eve of the Civil War," (Rough Draft, March 6, 2013), http://ssrn.com/abstract=2107460.

124. Jacobus tenBroek, *Equal Under Law*, rev. ed. (London: Collier MacMillan, 1969), p. 123.

125. Lincoln may have believed that signing was necessary. Mike Rappaport, "More on Why Lincoln Signed the 13th Amendment," *Liberty Law Blog*, December 20, 2012, http://libertylawsite.org/2012/12/20/more-on-why-lincoln-signed-the-13th-amendment/.

126. Charles Sumner, "Equality Before the Law Protected by National Statute, Speeches in the Senate on his Supplementary Civil Rights Bill, as an Amendment to the Amnesty Bill" (January 15, 17, and 31; February 5; and May 21, 1872), in *Works*, vol. 14, pp. 355, 407.

127. Michael Kent Curtis, *No State Shall Abridge: The Fourteenth Amendment and the Bill of Rights* (Durham, NC: Duke University Press, 1986), remains the leading history.

128. Robert J. Reinstein, "Completing the Constitution: The Declaration of Independence, Bill of Rights, and Fourteenth Amendment," *Temple Law Review* 66 (1993): 361–418.

129. Charles Sumner, "Our Domestic Relations: Power of Congress over the Rebel States" (1863), in *Works*, vol. 7, p. 507.

130. Ibid., p. 508.

131. Ibid., p. 513.

132. Ibid., p. 514.

133. Rebecca E. Zietlow, "Congressional Enforcement of Civil Rights and John Bingham's Theory of Citizenship," *Akron Law Review* 36 (2003): 717–760.

134. *Congressional Globe*, 35th Cong., 2nd sess., pp. 984–85 (1859) (statement of Rep. John Bingham).

135. Ibid., p. 985.

136. Sumner, "Equality Before the Law," in *Works*, vol. 14, p. 401.

137. Ibid., p. 407.

138. *Corfield v. Coryell*, 6 F. Cas. 546, 551-52 (C.C.E.D. Pa. 1823).

139. Ibid.

140. *Congressional Globe* 39th Cong., 1st sess., p. 2765 (1866) (quoting Coryell).

141. *Congressional Globe*, 42d Cong., 2nd sess., p. 844 (1872).

142. *Congressional Globe*, 39th Cong., 1st sess., p. 2542 (1866) (statement of Rep. John Bingham).

143. Ibid.

144. Ibid.

145. "Doughface" was a 19th-century slang term for "northern men of southern principles"—that is, Yankee defenders of slavery and states' rights.

146. Jeremiah S. Black, *Observations on Senator Douglas's Views of Popular Sovereignty as Expressed in Harper's Magazine for September, 1859*, 2nd ed. (1859), p. 18.

147. Jeremiah S. Black, "Open Letter to General Garfield," in Chauncey F. Black, ed., *Essays and Speeches of Jeremiah S. Black* (New York: Appleton and Co., 1886), pp. 300–01.

148. Ibid., p. 301.

149. See Ibid., p. 299.

150. Jeremiah S. Black, "The Character of Mr. Seward: Reply to C. F. Adams, Sr.," in ibid., p. 147.

151. Waldron, p. 55.

152. Mary Black Clayton, *Reminiscences of Jeremiah Sullivan Black* (St. Louis: Christian Publishing Co., 1887), p. 128.

153. 74 U.S. (7 Wall.) 506 (1868) (challenging the use of military tribunals to try a newspaper publisher for printing "incendiary" articles against Reconstruction); see also William Norwood Brigance, *Jeremiah Sullivan Black: A Defender of the Constitution and the Ten Commandments* (Philadelphia: University of Pennsylvania Press, 1934), pp. 171–79.

154. 71 U.S. (4 Wall.) 2 (1866) (challenging the use of a military tribunal to try a civilian Confederate sympathizer who planned to raid a Union POW camp); see also Brigance, pp. 145–57.

155. 80 U.S. (13 Wall.) 581 (1871) (opposing the constitutionality of the criminal law sections of the 1866 Civil Rights Act); see also Brigance, pp. 198–200.

156. Brigance, pp. 180–96.

157. Ibid., pp. 200–01.

158. Ibid., p. 201.

159. See Timothy Sandefur, *The Right to Earn A Living* (Washington: Cato Institute, 2010), pp. 17–44.

160. 83 U.S. (16 Wall.) 36, 77 (1873).

161. See Ibid. at 78.

162. Ibid. at 78.

163. An intriguing parallel to what happened in *Slaughter-House* can be found in the California Supreme Court decision *People v. Brady*, 40 Cal. 198 (1870). In an earlier case, *Billings v. Hall*, 7 Cal. 1 (1857), the California Supreme Court had rejected the notion of absolute state sovereignty such as articulated in the *Sharpless* decision, concluding that "the spirit of free institutions is at war" with the notion of unlimited state sovereignty (ibid. at 13) because "this [would be] to put themselves in a worse condition than a state of nature, wherein they had the liberty to defend their rights against the injuries of others. . . . [B]y supposing that they have given up themselves to the absolute, arbitrary power of the legislator, they have disarmed themselves, and armed him to make a prey of them when he pleases." Ibid. at 11–12. But in 1870, shortly before *Slaughter-House* was decided, the court reversed itself. Echoing *Sharpless*, the court held that after declaring independence, "legislative power was . . . as complete in each American as in the British Parliament," 40 Cal. at 219. "The Federal Government was created by the compact of

sovereign States, and their continued existence in the uncontrolled exercise of their powers, is an essential element of the system," the court continued. States enjoyed "[t]he absolute right of uncontrolled local legislation upon all subjects most intimately connected with individual rights and most essential to the maintenance of personal liberty. . . ." Ibid. at 220. And, as *Slaughter-House* would do three years later, the *Brady* court concluded that the Fourteenth Amendment was not "intended to strike from the Constitution the fundamental idea upon which the Union was constructed—to rob the Government of its crowning glory and most beneficent principle." If the amendment had meant to provide federal protections against the power of state governments, "we should regard it as we would a law apparently legalizing murder or robbery." Ibid. Another parallel between *Slaughter-House* and *Brady* is the effect each had on racial minorities. While *Slaughter-House* signaled a retreat from Reconstruction efforts to protect former slaves, Brady rejected a constitutional challenge to a state law that prohibited Chinese immigrants or Chinese Americans from testifying against whites in court. Being denied the chance to testify against whites meant that the Chinese had virtually no protection against violence from white mobs. See Jean Pfaelzer, *Driven Out: The Forgotten War Against Chinese Americans* (Berkeley: University of California Press, 2007), p. 52.

164. *Slaughter-House*, 83 U.S. (16 Wall.) at 76.

165. Ibid.

166. Ibid. at 77.

167. Ibid. at 78.

168. William L. Royall, "The Fourteenth Amendment: the Slaughter-House Cases," *Southern Law Review* (New Series) 4 (1879): 579–80.

169. *Bartemeyer v. Iowa*, 85 U.S. (18 Wall.) 129, 140-41 (1873) (Field, J., concurring).

170. 92 U.S. (2 Otto) 542 (1875).

171. See Charles Lane, *The Day Freedom Died* (New York: Holt, 2008).

172. *Cruikshank*, 92 U.S. (2 Otto) at 552.

173. Ibid. at 553.

174. Ibid. at 553–55.

175. Ibid. at 552.

176. Senator Howard, for example, specifically identified "the right of the people peaceably to assemble and petition the Government for a redress of grievances" and "the right to keep and to bear arms" as rights protected under the Privileges or Immunities Clause. *Congressional Globe*, 39th Cong., 1st sess., p. 2765 (1866).

177. Clayton, p. 125. In their book, *The Slaughterhouse Cases*, Ronald Labbé and Jonathan Lurie argue that the butchers' attorney, John Campbell, exploited the case to advance an "agenda" attacking Reconstruction. In their view, Campbell—a former United States Supreme Court Justice who resigned his seat in 1861 to join the Confederate government—used the case to publicize the alleged corruption of the Louisiana legislature, and thereby attack integration. See Ronald Labbé and Jonathan Lurie, *The Slaughterhouse Cases* (Lawrence: University of Kansas Press, 2003), p. 192. This may indeed be part of the story. Compare Michael A. Ross, "Obstructing Reconstruction: John Archibald Campbell and the Legal Campaign against Louisiana's Republican Government, 1868–1873," *Civil War History* 49, no. 3 (2003): 235–53, with Robert Saunders Jr., *John Archibald Campbell: Southern Moderate, 1811–1889* (Tuscaloosa: University of Alabama Press, 1997). But we must not overlook Black's efforts on the other side. Portraying the legislature of Louisiana as corrupt doubtless served the interests of Reconstruction's opponents, but neutering the most crucial part of the Fourteenth Amendment, as the state's attorneys managed

to do, served that purpose even more. Whatever Campbell's motives in prosecuting the case against the Louisiana legislature, his interpretation of the amendment was at least consistent with that of its Framers. And Labbé and Lurie's interpretation may be unjust to Campbell. One of his biographers wrote that he "took a larger view of their purpose [*i.e.*, the authors of the Fourteenth Amendment] and caught a larger vision of the scope of its accomplishment. To his mind every person then within the jurisdiction of the United States and every child born, or person naturalized, was lifted, as it were, into the status of National citizenship, with the power of the National Government pledged to the protection of his rights, privileges, and immunities, and every State prohibited from making or enforcing any law abridging such rights and privileges. The singular spectacle is presented of the States Rights, Southern Democratic lawyer urging the broadest, largest National view and the Northern-Nationalist Republican Judge enforcing a much narrower application of the language, in ascertaining the intention of those who framed the amendment." Henry G. Connor, *John Archibald Campbell* (Boston: Houghton Mifflin, 1920), pp. 222–23.

178. Wilson R. Huhn, "The Legacy of *Slaughter-House, Bradwell,* and *Cruikshank* in Constitutional Interpretation," *Akron Law Review* 42 (2009): 1079; Douglas Blackmon, *Slavery by Another Name* (New York: Anchor, 2008), p. 172.

179. The exception was *Colgate v. Harvey*, 296 U.S. 404 (1935), but that was overruled in *Madden v. Kentucky*, 309 U.S. 83 (1940).

180. *Saenz v. Roe*, 526 U.S. 489, 503-04 (1999).

181. *District of Columbia v. Heller*, 554 U.S. 570 (2008).

182. *McDonald v. City of Chicago*, 130 S. Ct. 3020, 3030-31 (2010).

183. Transcript of Oral Argument, *McDonald v. Chicago*, No. 08-1521, p. 7.

184. McDonald, 130 S. Ct. at 3089 (Stevens, J., dissenting).

185. Ibid. (quoting J. Harvey Wilkinson, "The Fourteenth Amendment Privileges or Immunities Clause," *Harvard Journal of Law & Public Policy* 12 (1989): 52).

186. Gary Lawson, "The Rise and Rise of the Administrative State," *Harvard Law Review* 107 (1994): 1231–54.

187. Trisha Olson, "The Natural Law Foundation of the Privileges or Immunities Clause of the Fourteenth Amendment," *Arkansas Law Review* 48 (1995): 438.

188. *Federalist* No. 51 (James Madison), in Cooke, p. 349.

189. *Congressional Globe*, 39th Cong., 1st sess., p. 2542 (1866) (statement of Rep. John Bingham).

Chapter 3

1. G. Edward White, *The Constitution and the New Deal* (Cambridge, MA: Harvard University Press, 2000), pp. 241–68.

2. 87 U.S. (20 Wall.) 655 (1874).

3. 539 U.S. 558 (2003).

4. Magna Carta, ¶ 39.

5. For Coke, law was "a rational ordinance or directive judgment, commanding obedience to itself primarily because what it directs the citizens to do is reasonable and in that sense just," as opposed to "an act of will that derives its binding force from the threat of sanction." John Underwood Lewis, "Sir Edward Coke (1552–1634): His Theory of 'Artificial Reason' as a Context for Modern Basic Legal Theory," in *Law, Liberty, and Parliament: Selected Essays on the Writings of Sir Edward Coke*, Allen D. Boyer, ed. (Indianapolis: Liberty Fund, 2004), p. 110.

6. Prohibitions del Roy, 77 Eng. Rep. 1342, 1343, 12 Co. Rep. 63, 65 (K.B. 1607) (quoting Bracton).

7. Francis Bacon, "Aphorism 1," in *The Philosophical Works of Francis Bacon*, John M. Robertson, ed. (London: George Routledge & Sons, 1905), p. 613.

8. Plato, *Euthyphro* 10a–11b, in *The Collected Dialogues of Plato*, Edith Hamilton and Huntington Cairns, eds. (Princeton: Princeton University Press, 1973), pp. 178–79.

9. *Federalist* No. 51 (James Madison), in *The Federalist*, Jacob E. Cooke, ed. (Middletown, CT: Wesleyan University Press, 1961), p. 349.

10. Shirley Jackson, "The Lottery," (1948), in *The Lottery and Other Stories* (New York: Farrar, Strauss, & Giroux, 2005), pp. 219–302.

11. Jerome Bixby, "It's a Good Life" (1953), in *The Twilight Zone: The Original Stories*, Martin Harry Greenberg, et al., eds. (New York: Avon Books, 1985), pp. 125–45.

12. Although Jackson hints that the ritual has roots in some ancient harvest ceremony, we soon learn that, whatever its origin, the practice continues simply because it is old: "'There's always been a lottery,' he added petulantly." Jackson, p. 232.

13. Ibid., p. 235.

14. Lon L. Fuller, "Reason and Fiat in Case Law," *Harvard Law Review* 59 (1946): 388.

15. C. D. C. Reeve trans., *Aristotle: Politics* 1279a-b (Indianapolis: Hackett Publishing Company, 1998), pp. 77–78.

16. Of course, Aristotle did believe in natural slavery, though not on racial grounds, but he did not see slavery as a kind of *political* rule. See Jonathan Lear, *Aristotle: The Desire to Understand* (Cambridge: Cambridge University Press, 2007), pp. 197–200.

17. See Harry V. Jaffa, "Aristotle," in *History of Political Philosophy*, Leo Strauss and Joseph Cropsey, eds. (Chicago: Rand McNally, 1963), pp. 64–68, 74.

18. On the role of presumptions, see Richard Epstein, *Bargaining with the State* (Princeton: Princeton University Press, 1993), pp. 25–38.

19. John Locke, *Second Treatise of Civil Government*, § 137, in *John Locke: Two Treatises of Government*, rev. ed., Peter Laslett, ed. (New York: Cambridge University Press, 1963), p. 405.

20. Ibid. § 57, p. 348.

21. Freidoune Sahebham, *The Stoning of Soraya M.* (New York: Arcade Publishing, 2011), p. 53.

22. Ibid., p. 39.

23. Ibid., p. 51.

24. Ibid., p. 52.

25. Ibid., p. 86.

26. Ibid., p. 57.

27. Ibid., p. 59.

28. Ibid., p. 79.

29. Ibid., p. 91.

30. Antigone pours only a handful of dirt on the corpse of her brother, Polynices, in defiance of Creon's command. Robert Fagles, ed., *Sophocles: Three Theban Plays* (New York: Penguin, 1984), p. 71. Zahra buries only a few of Soraya's bones. Sahebham, p. 138. I discuss *Antigone* in depth in "Love and Solipsism: Law and Arbitrary Rule in Aeschylus, Shakespeare, Sophocles, and Anouilh," *Alabama Law Review* 64 (2013): 981-1011.

31. Francis Bacon, *Elements of the Common Lawes of England* (London: John Moore, 1630), p. 77.

32. Timothy Sandefur, "In Defense of Substantive Due Process, or, the Promise of Lawful Rule," *Harvard Journal of Law and Public Policy* 35 (2012): 340, n. 222.

33. *Federalist* No. 78 (Alexander Hamilton), in Cooke, p. 526.

34. Lon Fuller, *The Morality of Law*, 2nd ed. (New Haven: Yale University Press, 1969), p. 63.

35. Philippa Foot, *Virtues and Vices* (Berkeley: University of California Press, 1978), ch. 9.

36. Fuller, *The Morality of Law*, p. 122: "To speak of a legal system as an 'enterprise' implies that it may be carried on with varying degrees of success. This would mean that the existence of a legal system is a matter of degree."

37. See, for example, St. Thomas Aquinas, *Summa Theologiae*, Fathers of the English Dominican Province, trans. (Westminster, MD: Christian Classics, 1981), p. 995; William Blackstone, *Commentaries on the Common Law* (London: A. Strahan, 1809), vol. 1, p. 44; John Austin, *Lectures on Jurisprudence*, 3rd ed., Robert Campbell ed. (London: John Murray, 1869), vol. 1, p. 95; Roscoe Pound, *An Introduction to the Philosophy of Law*, rev. ed. (New Haven: Yale University Press, 1954), pp. 25–47; H. L. A. Hart, *The Concept of Law*, 2nd ed. (New Delhi: Oxford India Paperbacks, 2002), pp. 21–25; Fuller, *The Morality of Law*, ch. 2; Tara Smith, "Neutrality Isn't Neutral: On the Value of Value-Neutrality of the Rule of Law," *Washington University Jurisprudence Review* 4 (2011): 55–60.

38. 17 U.S. (4 Wheat.) 518, 580–82 (argument of Mr. Webster) (quoting Blackstone).

39. Ibid. at 582. Burke's actual wording was: "The properties of law are, first, that it should be known; secondly, that it should be fixed and not occasional. . . . No man in . . . any court upon earth, will say that is law, upon which, if a man going to his counsel should say to him, 'What is my tenure in law of this estate?' he would answer, 'Truly, sir, I know not; the court has no rule but its own discretion: they will determine.'" Edmund Burke, "Speech on Parliamentary Incapacitation," (January 31, 1770), in *Writings and Speeches of Edmund Burke*, Paul Langford, ed. (Oxford: Oxford University Press, 1981), vol. 2, p. 235.

40. Blackstone, vol. 1, p. 44.

41. Ibid.

42. See, for example, *Romer v. Evans*, 517 U.S. 620, 634 (1996); *City of Cleburne v. Cleburne Living Ctr.*, 473 U.S. 432, 443 (1985); *Merrifield v. Lockyer*, 547 F.3d 978, 991–92 (9th Cir. 2008).

43. Wallace Mendelson, "A Missing Link in the Evolution of Due Process," *Vanderbilt Law Review* 10 (1956): 125–37.

44. *Jones' Heirs v. Perry*, 18 Tenn. 59, 69–71 (1836). But see *Williamson v. Williamson*, 11 Miss. 715, 744–46 (1844), which although not differing from the *Perry* court on general principles, upheld the constitutionality of a law similar to that at issue in *Perry*.

45. Fuller, *The Morality of Law*, p. 39.

46. Mark David Agrast et al., *World Justice Project: Rule of Law Index 2010*, p. 8, http://worldjusticeproject.org/sites/default/files/WJP%20Rule%20of%20Law%20Index%202010_0.pdf.

47. "One would speak adequately if one were to attain the clarity that goes along with the underlying material, for precision ought not to be sought in the same way in all kinds of discourse. . . . [O]ne ought to be content, when speaking about such things and reasoning from such things, to point out the truth roughly and in outline, and when speaking about things that are so for the most part, and reasoning fro things of that sort, to reach conclusions that are also of that sort. . . . [I]t belongs to an educated person to look for just so much precision in each kind of discourse as the nature of the thing one is concerned with admits; for to demand demonstrations from a rhetorician seems about

like accepting probable conclusions from a mathematician." Joe Sachs, trans., *Aristotle: Nichomachean Ethics* 1094b (Newburyport, MA: Focus Publishing, 2002), p. 2.

48. *Anderson v. Bd. of Comm'rs of Cloud Cnty.*, 95 P. 583, 586 (Kan. 1908) (quoting Samuel P. Orth, "Special Legislation," *Atlantic Monthly*, Jan. 1906, p. 69).

49. Ibid.

50. 524 U.S. 417 (1998).

51. Ibid. at 439.

52. Ibid.

53. *Chi. Typographical Union v. Chi. Sun-Times*, 935 F.2d 1501, 1503 (7th Cir. 1991) (emphasis added) (citations omitted).

54. *Sunshine Security & Detective Agency v. Wells Fargo Armored Services Corp.*, 496 So. 2d 246 (Fla. Dist. Ct. App. 1986).

55. Ibid. at 246–47.

56. *Federalist* No. 78 (Alexander Hamilton), in Cooke, p. 525.

57. 3 U.S. (3 Dall.) 386 (1798).

58. Ibid. at 387.

59. Ibid. at 388.

60. Ibid.

61. Ibid. at 399 (Iredell, J., concurring).

62. Ibid.

63. *McDonald v. Chicago*, 130 S. Ct. 3020, 3058 (2010) (Scalia, J., concurring).

64. *Troxel v. Granville*, 530 U.S. 57, 91–92 (2000) (Scalia, J., dissenting).

65. *FCC v. Beach Communications, Inc.*, 508 U.S. 307, 314 (1993).

66. *Romer v. Evans*, 517 U.S. 620 (1996); *City of Cleburne v. Cleburne Living Center*, 473 U.S. 432 (1985); *Zobel v. Williams*, 457 U.S. 55 (1982); *Lawrence v. Texas*, 539 U.S. 558 (2003).

67. 517 U.S. at 632.

68. *Marbury v. Madison*, 5 U.S. (1 Cranch) 137 (1803).

69. *Hurdado*, 110 U.S. at 535–36. The Court quoted Webster's oral argument in *Dartmouth College*, 17 U.S. (4 Wheat.) at 581.

70. 41 Cal. 147 (1871).

71. Ibid. at 161.

72. Ibid. at 175.

73. Ibid. at 168.

74. Ibid. at 184.

75. Ibid. at 191.

76. Ibid. at 198.

77. Ibid. at 199.

78. 87 U.S. (20 Wall.) 655 (1874).

79. Ibid. at 663.

80. Ibid. at 664.

81. Ibid.

82. 539 U.S. 558 (2003).

83. Ibid. at 578.

84. Ron Paul, "Federal Courts and the Imaginary Constitution," August12, 2003, http://www.lewrockwell.com/paul/paul120.html.

85. Quoted in Barry Friedman, "The Importance of Being Positive: The Nature and Function of Judicial Review," *University of Cincinnati Law Review* 72 (2004): 1264, n. 44.

86. Lino A. Graglia, "*Lawrence v. Texas*: Our Philosopher-Kings Adopt Libertarianism as Our Official National Philosophy and Reject Traditional Morality as a Basis for Law," *Ohio State Law Journal* 65 (2004): 1139–50, pp. 1140–41. Indeed, Graglia argued that collective decisionmaking is the source of individual rights. Ibid., p. 1141. See also Lino A. Graglia, "Jaffa's Quarrel with Bork: Religious Belief Masquerading as Constitutional Argument," *Southern California Interdisciplinary Law Journal* 4 (1995): 711 ("by actually enacting and enforcing such laws [i.e., that violate rights], a society effectively demonstrates that there is no such right in that society.").

87. Graglia, "Philosopher Kings," p. 1140.

88. See Randy E. Barnett, "Justice Kennedy's Libertarian Revolution: *Lawrence v. Texas*," *2002–2003 Cato Supreme Court Review* (Washington: Cato Institute, 2003): 21–41.

89. *Lawrence*, 539 U.S. at 578.

Chapter 4

1. Robert Bork, *Coercing Virtue: The Worldwide Rule of Judges* (Washington: AEI Press, 2003), p. 55.

2. *Perry v. New Hampshire*, 132 S. Ct. 716, 730 (2012) (Thomas, J., concurring).

3. Daniel Dennett, *Darwin's Dangerous Idea* (New York: Touchstone, 1995), p. 74.

4. True, the Constitution commands that its rules be followed—but the legislature has also commanded that its rules be followed. It is not possible to choose between these two without some broader normative standard by which to rank the alternatives.

5. *Federalist* No. 33 (Alexander Hamilton), in *The Federalist*, Jacob E. Cooke, ed. (Middletown, CT: Wesleyan University Press, 1961), p. 207.

6. Ibid.

7. *Thomas v. Sorrell*, Vaughan, 330, 337, 124 Eng. Rep. 1098, 1102 (C.P. 1677).

8. William Blackstone, *Commentaries on the Common Law* (London: A. Strahan, 1809), vol. 1, p. 156.

9. *Taylor v. Porter & Ford*, 4 Hill 140, 145-46 (N.Y. Sup. Ct. 1843) (punctuation altered; italics added).

10. John Harrison, "Substantive Due Process and the Constitutional Text," *Virginia Law Review* 83 (1997): 493–558.

11. Ibid., p. 550.

12. Ibid., p. 547.

13. Ibid., p. 551.

14. 261 U.S. 86 (1923).

15. Ibid. at 91.

16. *Calder v. Bull*, 3 U.S. (3 Dall.) 386, 388 (1798).

17. *Day v. Savadge*, Hob. 85, 87, 80 Eng. Rep. 235, 237 (C.P. 1615). See John V. Orth, *Due Process of Law: A Brief History* (Lawrence, KS: University Press of Kansas, 2003), p. 24.

18. *Giddings v. Brown*, in *The Hutchinson Papers* (Albany: Joel Munsell, 1865), vol. 2 pp. 1–25. See also Paul Samuel Reinsch, *English Common Law in the Early American Colonies* (Clark, NJ: Lawbook Exchange, 2004), p. 16.

19. Frederick Mark Gedicks, "An Originalist Defense of Substantive Due Process: Magna Carta, Higher-Law Constitutionalism, and the Fifth Amendment," *Emory Law Journal* 58 (2009): 619–20.

20. *Bowman v. Middleton*, 1 S.C.L. (1 Bay) 252 (S.C. 1792).

21. *Trevett v. Weeden* (R.I. 1786), reprinted in Bernard Schwartz, ed., *The Bill of Rights: A Documentary History* (New York: Chelsea House, 1971), vol. 1, p. 417. See also Gedicks, pp. 627–28.

22. Gedicks, p. 644.

23. Robert E. Riggs, "Substantive Due Process in 1791," *Wisconsin Law Review* 1990: 1004.

24. *Federalist* No. 78 (Alexander Hamilton), in Cooke, p. 526.

25. Throughout *The Federalist*, Hamilton and Madison emphasized the importance of resisting popular sentiment in cases where "conduct of this kind has saved the people from very fatal consequences of their own mistakes." *Federalist* No. 71, ibid., p. 482–83 (Hamilton); see also *Federalist* No. 63, ibid., p. 425 (Madison).

26. 297 U.S. 1, 62-63 (1936).

27. Charles Howard McIlwain, *The High Court of Parliament and Its Supremacy* (New Haven: Yale University Press, 1910), p. 150.

28. James Madison, "Report on the Virginia Resolutions," in *Madison: Writings*, p. 645. I am indebted to Professor Nicholas Rosenkranz for this observation.

29. Quoted in Earl E. Pollock, *The Supreme Court and American Democracy: Case Studies on Judicial Review and Public Policy* (Westport, CT: Greenwood Publishing, 2009), p. 119; Gary McDowell, "The Perverse Paradox of Privacy," in *A Country I Do Not Recognize: The Legal Assault on American Values*, Robert Bork, ed. (Stanford: Hoover Institution, 2005), p. 64.

30. Raoul Berger, "'Law of the Land' Reconsidered," *Northwestern University Law Review* 74 (1979): 11–12.

31. Alexander Hamilton, Speech in the New York Assembly, Feb. 6, 1787, in *The Works of Alexander Hamilton*, Henry Cabot Lodge, ed. (New York: G. P. Putnam's Sons, 1885), vol. 8, p. 29.

32. *Anonymous*, 2 N.C. 28, 29–30 (1794).

33. 15 N.C. 1 (1833).

34. Ibid. at 9–10.

35. *Bradshaw v. Rodgers & Magee*, 20 Johns. 103, 106 (N.Y. Sup. Ct. 1822); *In re John & Cherry Streets*, 19 Wend. 659, 676–77 (N.Y. Sup. Ct. 1838); *In re Albany Street*, 11 Wend. 149, 151 (N.Y. Sup. Ct. 1834).

36. 13 U.S. (9 Cranch.) 43, 50–51 (1815).

37. 27 U.S. (2 Pet.) 627 (1829).

38. 17 U.S. (4 Wheat.) 518, 580–82 (1819) (argument of Mr. Webster).

39. 60 U.S. (19 How.) 393, 450 (1856).

40. Ryan C. Williams, "The One and Only Substantive Due Process Clause," *Yale Law Journal* 120 (2010): 408–512.

41. *Congressional Globe*, 39th Cong., 1st sess. p. 1089 (1866); see also ibid., p. 2459 (statement of Rep. Thaddeus Stevens) (Due Process Clause prevents states from "unlawfully depriving [persons] of life, liberty, or property"); p. 340 (statement of Sen. Edgar Cowan) (due process of law meant that "the rights of no free man, no man not a slave, can be infringed in so far as regards any of the great principles of English and American liberty"); p. 1294 (statement of Rep. James Wilson) (due process included the "great civil rights" referred to in the Civil Rights Act of 1866); p. 1833 (statement of Rep. William Lawrence) (due process means that "there [are] rights which are inherent, and of which a State cannot constitutionally deprive him," and citing cases).

42. Williams, p. 512.

43. Putting aside for present purposes the anti-slavery argument that a slave could not rightly come within the "property" protected by the Due Process Clause.

44. See Abraham Lincoln, "Address at Cooper Institute," February 27, 1860, in *Lincoln: Speeches and Writings 1859–1865*, Don Fehrenbacher, ed. (New York: Library of America, 1989), pp. 111–30.

45. 323 U.S. 214 (1944).

46. 163 U.S. 537 (1896).

47. Gedicks, p. 667.

48. Ibid., quoting Michael Kent Curtis, *No State Shall Abridge: The Fourteenth Amendment and the Bill of Rights* (Durham, NC: Duke University Press, 1986), p. 183.

49. Letter from James Madison to Thomas Jefferson (October 17, 1788), in *Madison: Writings*, p. 420.

50. See *Federalist* No. 84 (Alexander Hamilton), in Cooke, pp. 575–81.

51. James Wilson, Speech in Pennsylvania Ratification Convention, in *Debate on the Constitution*, Bernard Bailyn, ed. (New York: Library of America, 1993), vol. 1, pp. 807–10.

52. Letter from James Madison to Thomas Jefferson (October 17, 1788), *in Madison: Writings*, p. 420.

53. Gedicks, p. 667.

54. *Poe v. Ullman*, 367 U.S. 497, 542-43 (1961) (Harlan, J., dissenting).

55. Ibid., p. 543 (internal citations omitted).

56. See Eugene V. Rostow, "The Democratic Character of Judicial Review," *Harvard Law Review* 66 (1952): 193-224, p. 194 ("The attack on judicial review as undemocratic rests on the premise that the Constitution should be allowed to grow without a judicial check. . . . But the Constitution of the United States does not establish a parliamentary government, and attempts to interpret American government in a parliamentary perspective break down in confusion and absurdity.").

57. See letter from James Madison to James Monroe (October 5, 1786), in *Writings of James Madison*, Ralph Ketcham, ed. (Indianapolis: Hackett Publishing, 2006), pp. 28–29 ("There is no maxim in my opinion which is more liable to be misapplied, and which therefore more needs elucidation than the current one that the interest of the majority is the political standard of right and wrong. Taking the word 'interest' as synonymous with 'Ultimate happiness,' in which sense it is qualified with every necessary moral ingredient, the proposition is no doubt true. But taking it in the popular sense, as referring to immediate augmentation of property and wealth, nothing can be more false. In the latter sense it would be in the interest of the majority in every community to despoil & enslave the minority of individuals. . . . In fact, it is only reestablishing under another name, and a more specious form, force as the measure of right. . . .").

58. Letter from James Madison to Thomas Jefferson (October 17, 1788), in *Madison: Writings*, p. 421.

59. *Federalist* No. 10 (James Madison), in Cooke, p. 84.

60. Ibid., pp. 79–80.

61. Ibid., p. 79.

62. Andrew T. Hyman, "The Little Word 'Due,'" *Akron Law Review* 38 (2005): 34.

63. *Federalist* No. 78 (Alexander Hamilton), in Cooke, pp. 524–25.

64. Robert H. Bork, "Neutral Principles and Some First Amendment Problems," *Indiana Law Journal* 47 (1971): 10. Bork stuck to his argument on this point, as well. See Robert H. Bork, "The Judge's Role in Law and Culture," *Ave Maria Law Review* 1 (2003): 28

("The sole task of the [judge] . . . is to translate the . . . legislator's morality into a rule to govern unforeseen circumstances.") Note that Bork begged the question, because he assumes that impartiality is a value that a judge is bound to follow. Presumably, judges should be impartial if and only if the majority instructs the judge to be impartial. But then how does that account for Bork's recognition (p. 76) of the "obvious moral rightness" of *Brown v. Board of Education*, given that there was no majority preference for equal treatment in that case?

65. William H. Rehnquist, "The Notion of a Living Constitution," *Texas Law Review* 54 (1976): 704.

66. Thomas Jefferson, letter to Judge Spencer Roane (September 6, 1819), in *Jefferson: Writings*, p. 1426.

67. Nelson Lund and John McGinnis, "*Lawrence v. Texas* and Judicial Hubris," *Michigan Law Review* 102 (2004): 1556.

68. Nelson Lund, "Rousseau and Direct Democracy (With A Note on the Supreme Court's Term Limits Decision)," *Journal of Contemporary Legal Issues* 13 (2004): 459–510, p. 466. See also ibid., p. 472 ("Hobbes . . . does not seem to establish, by adequate argument or evidence, the claims about natural or inherent rights that we find in the Virginia Declaration of Rights and the Declaration of Independence."); p. 474 ("Locke appears not to have established what the Declaration of Independence says is self-evident. Like the Declaration, Locke just asserts it.").

69. Lund and McGinnis, p. 1591.

70. Lund, "Rousseau," p. 466.

71. Lund and McGinnis, p. 1560 (emphasis added).

72. Ibid., p. 1557.

73. Borrowing the term from Samuel Scheffler, "Potential Congruence," in *Morality and Self-Interest*, Paul Bloomfield, ed. (New York: Oxford University Press, 2008), p. 118.

74. To name just two recent examples, Justice Clarence Thomas dissented in *Lawrence v. Texas*, 539 U.S. 558, 605 (2003) (Thomas, J., dissenting), while admitting that he believed the statute challenged in that case was "uncommonly silly." Justice John Paul Stevens, author of *Kelo v. New London*, later acknowledged that he disagreed with the policy outcome but believed the decision was required as a matter of constitutional interpretation. See John Paul Stevens, "Judicial Predilections," *Nevada Law Journal* 6 (2005): 4 ("My own view is that the allocation of economic resources that result from the free play of market forces is more likely to produce acceptable results in the long run than the best-intentioned plans of public officials.").

75. See Philip Soper, "In Defense of Classical Natural Law in Legal Theory: Why Unjust Law is No Law at All," *Canadian Journal of Law & Jurisprudence* 20 (2007): 221 ("The assumption that natural law looses a judge to do whatever she wants, ignoring even clear texts, is wrong. Natural law . . . empowers her, at most, to reach decisions she believes are required by her own views of a sound, defensible moral and political theory.").

76. *Lochner v. New York*, 198 U.S. 45, 76 (1905) (Holmes, J., dissenting).

77. See, e.g., *Boumediene v. Bush*, 553 U.S. 723, 739–52 (2008) (reviewing common law contours of habeas corpus).

Chapter 5

1. Abraham Lincoln, "Address at Sanitary Fair" (April 18, 1864), in *Lincoln: Speeches and Writings 1859–1865*, Don Fehrenbacher, ed. (New York: Library of America, 1989), p. 589.

2. 5 U.S. (1 Cranch) 137 (1803). See Mary Sarah Bilder, "The Corporate Origins of Judicial Review," *Yale Law Journal* 116 (2006): 503–66; William Michael Treanor, "Judicial Review Before Marbury," *Stanford Law Review* 58 (2005): 455–562; and Robert J. Reinstein and Mark C. Rahdert, "Reconstructing *Marbury*," *Arkansas Law Review* 57 (2005): 729–834.

3. *Federalist* No. 78 (Alexander Hamilton) in *The Federalist*, Jacob E. Cooke, ed. (Middletown, CT: Wesleyan University Press, 1961), p. 521. See also James Wilson, *Lectures on Law*, pt. 1, chap. XI, in Kermit L. Hall and Mark David Hall, eds., *Collected Works of James Wilson* (Indianapolis: Liberty Fund, 2007), vol. 1, p. 743 (Judicial review "is far from throwing any disparagement upon the legislative authority of the United States. It does not confer upon the judicial department a power superiour [*sic*], in its general nature, to that of the legislature; but it confers upon it, in particular instances, and for particular purposes, the power of declaring and enforcing the superiour [*sic*] power of the constitution—the supreme law of the land.").

4. "Appendix: Correspondence between Mr. Justice Field and the Other Members of the Court with Regard to His Retiring from the Bench," 168 U.S. 713, 717 (1897).

5. All judicial officers, after all, are required to take an oath to support "not a person, a party, an office, or even a nation, but the Constitution itself." Kermit Roosevelt III, *The Myth of Judicial Activism* (New Haven: Yale University Press, 2006), p. 23.

6. *Federalist* No. 10 (James Madison), in Cooke, ed., p. 57 (emphasis added).

7. Ibid., p. 65.

8. *Federalist* No. 51 (James Madison), in Cooke, p. 352.

9. Letter from James Madison to James Monroe (October 5, 1786), in *Writings of James Madison*, Gaillard Hunt, ed., (New York: G. P. Putnam's Sons, 1901), vol. 2, p. 273.

10. James M. Buchanan and Gordon Tullock, *The Calculus of Consent* (Ann Arbor: University of Michigan Press, 1992).

11. Ibid., p. 287 ("[T]he profitability of investment in [political organization] is a direct function of the size of the total public sector and an inverse function of the 'generality' of the government budget.... The organized pressure group thus arises because differential advantages are expected to be secured through the political process....").

12. *Federalist* No. 10 (James Madison), in Cooke, p. 61.

13. *Federalist* No. 51 (James Madison), ibid., p. 349.

14. But see *Kelo v. New London*, 545 U.S. 469 (2005).

15. But see *Nat'l Fed'n of Indep. Bus. v. Sebelius*, 132 S. Ct. 2566 (2012).

16. See *Federalist* No. 84 (Alexander Hamilton), in Cooke, p. 579 ("Why . . . should it be said that the liberty of the press shall not be restrained, when no power is given by which restrictions may be imposed?").

17. *Federalist* No. 51 (James Madison), ibid., p. 351.

18. See *Federalist* No. 71 (Alexander Hamilton), ibid., p. 482 ("When occasions present themselves in which the interests of the people are at variance with their inclinations, it is the duty of the persons whom they have appointed to be the guardians of those interests to withstand the temporary delusion in order to give them time and opportunity for more cool and sedate reflection. Instances might be cited in which a conduct of this kind has saved the people from very fatal consequences of their own mistakes, and has procured lasting monuments of their gratitude to the men who had courage and magnanimity enough to serve them at the peril of their displeasure.").

19. *Federalist* No. 78 (Alexander Hamilton), ibid., p. 527.

20. Even Socrates, whose right to freedom of speech was spectacularly destroyed by the majority in Athens, still regarded himself as a creature of the *nomoi*, subservient even

to the point of death. Plato, *Crito*, 50b-52d, in *The Collected Dialogues of Plato*, Edith Hamilton and Huntington Cairns, eds. (Princeton: Princeton University Press, 1973), pp. 35–37.

21. Thomas Jefferson, "Notes on Virginia," in *Jefferson: Writings*, Merrill Peterson, ed. (New York: Library of America, 1984), p. 245.

22. Stephen Breyer, *Active Liberty: Interpreting Our Democratic Constitution* (New York: Knopf, 2005).

23. Ibid., p. 5 (quoting Benjamin Constant, *The Liberty of the Ancients Compared with That of the Moderns* (1819), *in The Political Writings of Benjamin Constant*, Biancamaria Fontana, ed. (New York: Cambridge University Press, 1988), p. 316. Constant himself did not elevate the liberty of the ancients over that of the moderns. In his famous article, Constant contended that "our happy revolution" had created "freedom and peace" in a way that was "totally unknown to the free nations of antiquity":

> You find among [the ancients] almost none of the enjoyments which
> we have just seen form part of the liberty of the moderns. All private
> actions were submitted to a severe surveillance. No importance was
> given to individual independence, neither in relation to opinions,
> nor to labor, nor, above all, to religion. The right to choose one's own
> religious affiliation, a right which we regard as one of the most pre-
> cious, would have seemed to the ancients a crime and a sacrilege. In
> the domains which seem to us the most useful, the authority of the
> social body interposed itself and obstructed the will of individuals. . . .
> Thus among the ancients the individual, almost always sovereign
> in public affairs, was a slave in all his private relations. As a citizen,
> he decided on peace and war; as a private individual, he was con-
> strained, watched and repressed in all his movements; as a member
> of the collective body, he interrogated, dismissed, condemned, beg-
> gared, exiled, or sentenced to death his magistrates and superiors; as
> a subject of the collective body he could himself be deprived of his
> status, stripped of his privileges, banished, put to death, by the discre-
> tionary will of the whole to which he belonged. Among the moderns,
> on the contrary, the individual, independent in his private life, is, even
> in the freest of states, sovereign only in appearance. His sovereignty
> is restricted and almost always suspended. If, at fixed and rare inter-
> vals, in which he is again surrounded by precautions and obstacles,
> he exercises this sovereignty, it is always only to renounce it.

Constant originally drew his distinction between ancient and modern liberty to emphasize the importance of individual freedom over and above social participation—precisely the opposite lesson that Justice Breyer draws.

24. Breyer, *Active Liberty*, p. 37.

25. Ibid., p. 49.

26. Stephen Breyer, *Making Our Democracy Work: A Judge's View* (New York: Knopf, 2010), p. 1.

27. Ibid., p. 5.

28. Ibid., p. 6.

29. Ibid., p. 162.

30. Ibid., p. 163.

31. Ibid., pp. 163–64.

32. See Eric Foner, *The Story of American Freedom* (New York: Norton, 1998), p. 140 ("[N]early all Progressives agreed that freedom must be infused with new meaning.").

33. John Locke, *Second Treatise of Civil Government* § 57 in *Two Treatises of Government*, rev. ed., Peter Laslett, ed. (Cambridge: Cambridge University Press, 1967), p. 324.

34. John Dewey, "The Future of Liberalism," *Journal of Politics* 32, no. 9 (1935): 225–30.

35. Foner, p. 144.

36. See Michael McGerr, *A Fierce Discontent: The Rise and Fall of the Progressive Movement in America* (New York: Oxford University Press, 2003), p. 81.

37. Samuel J. Konefsky, *The Legacy of Holmes and Brandeis* (New York: Collier Books, 1961), p. 105.

38. In his 1938 book, *The Administrative Process* (New Haven: Yale University Press, 1938), p. 155, James M. Landis, chairman of the Securities and Exchange Commission, argued that "[t]he rise of the administrative process represented the hope that policies to shape [economic] fields could most adequately be developed by men bred to the facts. That hope is still dominant, but its possession bears no threat to our ideal of the 'supremacy of the law.' Instead, it lifts it to new heights where the great judge, like a conductor of a many-tongued symphony, from what would otherwise be discord, makes known through the voice of many instruments the vision that has been given him of man's destiny upon this earth." As Bruce A. Williams and Albert R. Matheny observe, this romanticism "allow[ed] Landis to avoid the troubling issue of the degree to which democratic values are contradicted by regulatory policy-making within administrative agencies." *Democracy, Dialogue, and Environmental Disputes* (New Haven: Yale University Press, 1995), p. 15. I thank my colleague Damien M. Schiff for bringing this passage to my attention.

39. Konefsky, p. 112.

40. As Louis Menand has put it, the Progressives "shift[ed] the totem of legitimacy from premises to procedures. We know an outcome is right not because it was derived from immutable principles, but because it was reached by following the correct procedures." Louis Menand, *The Metaphysical Club* (New York: Farrar, Srauss and Giroux, 2001), p. 432. Cf. Ralph Ketcham, *James Madison: A Biography* (Charlottesville: University of Virginia Press, 1990), p. 43 ("[James] Madison had at the foundation of his political education a supreme emphasis on the ends, not the means, of government. . . . A great gulf, therefore, separates the thought of Madison (and other founding fathers) from that of believers in such later concepts of . . . simple majoritarian democracy, who denied that principles of justice and virtue can be identified and made the foundations of government, and therefore have a higher sanction than the will of the majority.").

41. Menand, p. 432.

42. See Grant Gilmore, *The Death of Contract* (Columbus: Ohio State University Press, 1974), pp. 16–21 (describing Holmes' attempt to fashion a value-free theory of contract); G. Edward White, *Tort Law in America: An Intellectual History* (New York: Oxford University Press, 1980), p. 74 ("[I]n proclaiming the incomprehensibility or the current irrelevance of traditional moral values, the Realists, like their counterparts in history or political science or philosophy, were identifying themselves with moral relativism."); and Albert W. Alschuler, "The Descending Trail: Holmes' Path of the Law One Hundred Years Later," *Florida Law Review* 49 (1997): 380–86 (detailing Holmes' attempt to separate law from morals).

43. *Federalist* No. 78 (Alexander Hamilton), in Cooke, p. 525.

44. Letter from Oliver Wendell Holmes to Harold Laski (March 4 1920), in Mark De Wolfe Howe, *The Holmes-Laski Letters 1916–1935* (New York: Atheneum Press, 1963), vol. 1, p. 249. See also Walter Berns, "The Supreme Court as Republican Schoolmaster: Constitutional Interpretation and the 'Genius of the People,'" in *The Supreme Court and American Constitutionalism*, Bradford Wilson and Ken Masugi, eds. (Lanham: Rowman and Littlefield, 1998), p. 11.

45. See Menand, p. 409 ("[R]ights are created not for the good of individuals, but for the good of society. Individual freedoms are manufactured to achieve group ends.").

46. Jefferson, "First Inaugural Address," in *Jefferson: Writings*, p. 494.

47. Bork, *Tempting of America*, p. 139.

48. Ibid., p. 124.

49. Ibid., p. 139.

40. Ibid., p. 183; cf. *Federalist* No. 84 (Alexander Hamilton), in Cooke, p. 579 ("They [*i.e.*, bills of rights] would contain various exceptions to powers which are not granted; and, on this very account, would afford a colorable pretext to claim more than were granted."); Letter from James Madison to Thomas Jefferson (October 17, 1788), in *Madison: Writings*, Jack Rakove, ed. (New York: Library of America, 1999), p. 420 (explaining that a bill of rights must be "so framed as not to imply powers not meant to be included in the enumeration" of powers in Article I, Section 8).

51. Bork, *Tempting of America*, p. 166.

52. See Randy E. Barnett, "The Ninth Amendment: It Means What It Says," *Texas Law Review* 85 (2006): 1–82.

53. Robert H. Bork, "Neutral Principles and Some First Amendment Problems," *Indiana Law Journal* 47 (1971): 10.

54. Bork does acknowledge that the Bill of Rights restricts the majority—but he also holds that the Bill of Rights is itself a set of privileges granted by, and thus revocable by, the majority.

55. See Harry V. Jaffa, *Storm Over the Constitution* (Lanham, MD: Lexington Books, 1999).

56. 478 U.S. 186, 204 (1986) (Blackmun, J., dissenting) (citation omitted); Bork, *Tempting of America*, p. 121.

57. Ibid., p. 122.

58. Letter from Thomas Jefferson to James Monroe (May 20, 1782), in *Jefferson: Writings*, p. 779.

59. Bork, *Tempting of America*, pp. 121–22.

60. Ibid., p. 54; see also Mark R. Levin, *Men in Black: How the Supreme Court Is Destroying America* (Washington, DC: Regnery Publishing, 2005), pp. 26–33 ("[T]he framers did not intend to grant general authority to the judiciary to rule on the constitutionality of legislative acts. . . . Marshall's ruling in *Marbury* was nothing short of a counter-revolution.").

61. Bork, *Tempting of America*, p. 54.

62. 198 U.S. 45 (1905).

63. 545 U.S. 469 (2005).

64. David E. Bernstein, *Rehabilitating Lochner* (Chicago: University of Chicago Press, 2011).

65. 198 U.S. at 53.

66. Ibid. at 57.

67. Ibid. at 61.

68. Ibid. at 53.
69. Ibid. at 56.
70. Roscoe Pound, "Mechanical Jurisprudence," *Columbia Law Review* 8 (1908): 605–23.
71. Theodore Roosevelt, "A Confession of Faith" (1912), in *The Works of Theodore Roosevelt: Social Justice and Popular Rule*, Herman Hagedorn, ed. (New York: Scribner's Sons, 1926), vol. 17, pp. 254, 264.
72. Ibid., p. 262.
73. Bernstein, *Rehabilitating Lochner*, p. 32.
74. David N. Mayer, "The Myth of 'Laissez-Faire Constitutionalism': Liberty of Contract During the *Lochner* Era," *Hastings Constitutional Law Quarterly* 36 (2009): 227.
75. 291 U.S. 502 (1934).
76. See, for example, *FCC v. Beach Communications, Inc.*, 508 U.S. 307, 313–15 (1993) (detailing the "paradigm of judicial restraint" that is rational basis).
77. *United States v. Carolene Prods. Co.*, 304 U.S. 144, 152 n.4 (1938).
78. Ibid. at 152, n.4.
79. Bernstein, *Rehabilitating Lochner*, p. 122.
80. David Bernstein, "The Role of *Lochner* in the Health Care Litigation," *Jurist Forum*, March 21, 2012, http://jurist.org/forum/2012/03/david-bernstein-lochner.php.
81. Timothy Sandefur, *The Right to Earn A Living* (Washington: Cato Institute, 2010), ch. 6.
82. See, for example, David N. Mayer, *Liberty of Contract: Rediscovering a Lost Constitutional Right* (Washington: Cato Institute, 2011), p. 123, n. 37.
83. An exception is the heightened protection for "privacy rights," a legacy of the realignment within Progressive liberalism during the years following World War II. Some liberals came to reject morally-neutral Progressivism and returned to a natural-rights theory regarding certain privacy rights. Others resisted this innovation. Witness Justice Hugo Black's dispute with Justice William O. Douglas in *Griswold* and similar cases. The same change can be seen in the efforts of civil rights advocates like Martin Luther King, who, though an ordinary Progressive on economic matters, invoked the Declaration of Independence to attack the segregation laws that Progressives had implemented a generation earlier.
84. See, for example, *Dolan v. City of Tigard*, 512 U.S. 374, 392 (1994); *United States v. Carlton*, 512 U.S. 26, 41–42 (U.S. 1994) (Scalia and Thomas, JJ., concurring in judgment); *Hettinga v. United States*, 677 F.3d 471, 480–83 (D.C. Cir. 2012) (Brown and Sentelle, JJ., concurring).
85. *Kelo*, 545 U.S. at 483.
86. Ibid. at 484.
87. Ibid. at 518 (Thomas, J., dissenting).
88. *Lochner*, 198 U.S. at 56.
89. *Beach Communications*, 508 U.S. at 323 n. 3 (Stevens, J., concurring in the judgment). See also *City of Cleburne v. Cleburne Living Ctr.*, 473 U.S. 432, 451 (1985) (Stevens, J., concurring) (arguing for more realistic rational basis review).
90. *Adkins v. Children's Hosp.*, 261 U.S. 525, 546 (1923).
91. Thomas Reed Powell, "The Judiciality of Minimum Wage Legislation," *Harvard Law Review* 37 (1924): 555–56.
92. Roosevelt, *Myth*, p. 3.
93. Ibid., pp. 24–36.
94. Ibid., p. 29.
95. Ibid., p. 33.

96. *Guinn v. Legislature of Nevada*, 71 P.3d 1269 (Nev. 2003), *reh'g denied*, 76 P.3d 22 (Nev. 2003) (per curiam), *cert. denied sub nom. Angle v. Guinn*, 541 U.S. 957 (2004), *overruled by Nevadans for Nevada v. Beers*, 142 P.3d 339, 348 (Nev. 2006) (per curiam). I tell the story of this astonishing case in "A Private Little *Bush v. Gore*, or, How Nevada Violated the Republican Guarantee and Got Away with It," *Texas Review of Law & Politics* 9 (2004): 105–45.

97. *Guinn*, 71 P.3d at 1272.

98. Ibid. at 1275.

99. "Recent Case, Constitutional Interpretation: Nevada Supreme Court Sets Aside a Constitutional Amendment Requiring a Two-Thirds Majority for Passing a Tax Increase Because It Conflicts with a Substantive Constitutional Right," *Harvard Law Review* 117 (2004): 977–78.

100. *Guinn*, 76 P.3d at 22 ("Against . . . the democratic process . . . we balanced the interests fostered by the supermajority requirement.").

101. Breyer, *Active Liberty*, p. 48.

102. Redistribution does not necessarily take the form of actual transfer payments. Any legislative action that has the potential of benefiting a particular group and burdening others will be subject to such pressures. Occupational licensing, for example, is routinely subject to rent-seeking pressures, as economic groups seek to protect themselves against competition from newcomers. See Sandefur, *Right to Earn a Living*, chapter 7. Because occupational licensing serves as a barrier to entry, established businesses often lobby the government to establish licensing regimes that will close the market to at least some degree, enabling the insiders to raise their prices securely. See, for example, Walter Gellhorn, "The Abuse of Occupational Licensing," *University of Chicago Law Review* 44 (1976): 6–27.

103. Roosevelt, *Myth*, p. 25.

104. 427 U.S. 297 (1976) (per curiam).

105. *Dukes v. City of New Orleans*, 501 F.2d 706, 712, 712 n. 7 (5th Cir. 1974).

106. Ibid. at 712 n.6.

107. Ibid. at 711.

108. Ibid. at 712.

109. 427 U.S. at 303; see also ibid. at 306 (describing the ordinance as "exclusively [an] economic regulation").

110. Ibid. at 305.

111. Ibid. at 304.

112. Christopher J. Duerksen and Mary C. Bean, "Land and the Law 1986: The Perils of Prognostication," *Urban Lawyer* 18 (1986): 954.

113. Clifford L. Weaver and Christopher J. Duerksen, "Central Business District Planning and the Control of Outlying Shopping Centers," *Urban Law Annual* 14 (1977): 68.

114. See, for example, Allen D. Boyer, "Samuel Williston's Struggle with Depression," *Buffalo Law Review* 42 (1994): 20 ("Existing [formalist] rules were elevated into the category of self-evident verities. . . . [T]he law turned a blind eye to social and economic concerns—thereby setting itself, deliberately or unwittingly, against social change.").

115. Roosevelt, *Myth*, pp. 136–37.

116. McCloskey, p. 50.

117. See *Kelo*, 545 U.S. at 521–22 (Thomas, J., dissenting) ("If ever there were justification for intrusive judicial review of constitutional provisions that protect

'discrete and insular minorities,' surely that principle would apply with great force to the powerless groups and individuals the Public Use Clause protects.") (citation omitted).

118. 467 U.S. 837, 844 (1984).

119. Roosevelt, *Myth*, p. 26.

120. Ibid., pp. 33–34.

121. See *San Remo Hotel L.P. v. City and County of San Francisco*, 27 Cal.4th 643, 697 (2002) (Brown, J., dissenting) ("[T]he majority's exception for legislatively created permit fees is mere sophism, particularly where the legislation affects a relatively powerless group and therefore the restraints inherent in the political process can hardly be said to have worked.").

122. Robert G. McCloskey, "Economic Due Process and the Supreme Court: An Exhumation and Reburial," *Supreme Court Review* 1962: 50 (citation omitted).

123. Roosevelt, *Myth*, pp. 213–14.

124. Ibid, p. 216.

125. Ibid.

126. Cf., e.g.,"Brutus VI," in *Debate on the Constitution*, Bernard Bailyn, ed. (New York: Library of America, 1993), vol. 1, pp. 618–19 ("It is as absurd to say, that the power of Congress is limited by these general expressions, 'to provide for the common safety, and general welfare,' as it would be to say, that it would be limited, had the constitution said they should have power to lay taxes, &c. at will and pleasure. Were this authority given, it might be said, that under it the legislature could not do injustice, or pursue any measures, but such as were calculated to promote the public good, and happiness. For every man, rulers as well as others, are bound by the immutable laws of God and reason, always to will what is right. It is certainly right and fit, that the governors of every people should provide for the common defence and general welfare; every government, therefore, in the world, even the greatest despot, is limited in the exercise of his power. But however just this reasoning may be, it would be found, in practice, a most pitiful restriction. The government would always say, their measures were designed and calculated to promote the public good; and there being no judge between them and the people, the rulers themselves must, and would always, judge for themselves.").

127. See Timothy Sandefur, "Mine and Thine Distinct: What *Kelo* Says About Our Path," *Chapman Law Review* 10 (2005): 1–48.

128. Roosevelt, *Myth*, p. 136.

129. Ibid., p. 98.

130. The public choice dynamics of eminent domain abuse have been discussed at length. See, for example, Sandefur, "Mine And Thine Distinct," pp. 34–37; Stephen J. Jones, "Trumping Eminent Domain Law: An Argument for Strict Scrutiny Analysis under the Public Use Requirement of the Fifth Amendment," *Syracuse Law Review* 50 (2000): 306; and Donald J. Kochan, "'Public Use' and the Independent Judiciary: Condemnation in an Interest-Group Perspective," *Texas Review of Law & Politics* 3 (1998): 49–116. For more on the rent-seeking problem in *Lochner*, see Alan J. Meese, "Will, Judgment, and Economic Liberty: Mr. Justice Souter and the Mistranslation of the Due Process Clause," *William & Mary Law Review* 41 (1999): 3–64; and Michael J. Phillips, "Entry Restrictions in the *Lochner* Court," *George Mason Law Review* 4 (1996): 405–54.

131. Roosevelt, *Myth*, pp. 124–25.

132. I have contended that, at least early in development, they have none. Timothy Sandefur, "Liberal Originalism: A Past for the Future," *Harvard Journal of Law & Public Policy* 27 (2004): 522–25.

133. See *Kelo*, 545 U.S. at 521–22 (Thomas, J., dissenting).

134. The judiciary itself is also subject to public choice pressures. What else are amicus briefs but so much judicial lobbying? As philosopher Anthony de Jasay notes, private-interest groups not only seek to maximize their gains from legislation but also to devise a constitutional order that will give them the best opportunities for such legislation. See Anthony de Jasay, *Justice and Its Surroundings* (Indianapolis: Liberty Fund, 1998), p. 83. The constitutional revolution of the New Deal is best seen as a major shift in the direction of increasing such opportunities. See John O. McGinnis, "The Original Constitution and Its Decline: A Public Choice Perspective," *Harvard Journal of Law & Public Policy* 21 (1997): 204–08. In addition, the current fights over judicial nominations are a function of the benefits—economic or otherwise—that interest groups expect to obtain or fear losing, depending on the makeup of the judiciary.

135. See Steven M. Simpson, "Judicial Abdication and the Rise of Special Interests," *Chapman Law Review* 6 (2003): 201–05; and Timothy Sandefur, "Is Economic Exclusion A Legitimate State Interest? Four Recent Cases Test the Boundaries," *William & Mary Bill of Rights Journal* 14 (2006): 1036–48.

136. *Washington v. Seattle Sch. Dist. No. 1*, 458 U.S. 457, 486 (1982) (quoting *San Antonio Indep. Sch. Dist. v. Rodriguez*, 411 U.S. 1, 28 (1973)).

137. See, for example, *Communications Workers of Am. v. Beck*, 487 U.S. 735 (1988); *Worcester v. Georgia*, 31 U.S. (6 Pet.) 515 (1832).

138. 47 C.F.R. § 64.1200 (2002).

139. *U.S. Security v. F.T.C.*, 282 F. Supp. 2d 1285, 1292 (W.D. Okla. 2003), *rev'd sub nom. Mainstream Marketing Services, Inc. v. F.T.C.*, 358 F.3d 1228 (10th Cir. 2004), *cert. denied*, 543 U.S. 812 (2004).

140. 798 N.E.2d 941 (2003).

141. See John C. Eastman, "Philosopher King Courts: Is the Exercise of Higher Law Authority Without a Higher Law Foundation Legitimate?" *Drake Law Review* 54 (2006): 834.

142. Roosevelt, *Myth*, p. 108.

143. 274 U.S. 200 (1927).

144. Timothy Sandefur, *Cornerstone of Liberty: Property Rights in 21st Century America* (Washington: Cato Institute, 2006), pp. 97–106.

145. *Federalist* No. 48 (James Madison), in Cooke, p. 333.

146. 163 U.S. 537 (1896).

147. See, for example, *Dickerson v. United States*, 530 U.S. 428, 443 (2000) ("We do not think there is such justification for overruling *Miranda*. *Miranda* has become embedded in routine police practice to the point where the warnings have become part of our national culture.").

148. Jeff Shesol, *Supreme Power: Franklin Roosevelt vs. the Supreme Court* (New York: Norton, 2010); G. Edward White, *The Constitution and the New Deal* (Cambridge: Harvard University Press, 2000). By 1949, all of the justices were nominees of Franklin Roosevelt and Harry Truman.

149. Aziz Z. Huq, "The Political Path of Detention Policy," *American Criminal Law Review* 48 (2011): 1542–43.

150. Cf. *Schlup v. Delo*, 513 U.S. 298, 324–25 (1995) ("The quintessential miscarriage of justice is the execution of a person who is entirely innocent. Indeed, concern about the injustice that results from the conviction of an innocent person has long been at the core of our criminal justice system. That concern is reflected, for example, in the 'fundamental value determination of our society that it is far worse to convict an innocent man than to let a guilty man go free.'" (quoting *In re Winship*, 397 U.S. 358, 372 (1970) (Harlan, J., concurring))).

151. *Beach Communications*, 508 U.S. at 315.

152. *Sadler v. Langham*, 34 Ala. 311, 321 (1859).

153. Roosevelt, *Myth*, p. 25

154. Ibid., p. 24.

155. Ibid., pp. 24–25.

156. Ibid., p. 25.

157. This analogy is adopted from Roosevelt, *Myth*, pp. 96–99.

158. *Clinton v. New York*, 524 U.S. 417 (1998); *United States v. Lopez*, 514 U.S. 549 (1995).

159. Roosevelt, *Myth*, p. 25.

160. Ibid., p. 25.

161. Ibid., p. 98.

162. Ibid., p. 27.

163. "An American judge, armed with the right to declare laws unconstitutional . . . cannot compel the people to make laws, but at least he can constrain them to be faithful to their own laws and remain in harmony with themselves." Alexis de Tocqueville, *Democracy in America*, ed., J. P. Mayer, trans. George Lawrence (New York: Harper Perennial, 1969), p. 269.

164. See, for example, *Gonzalez v. Raich*, 545 U.S. 1 (2005).

165. *United States v. Lopez*, 514 U.S. 549, 552 (1995).

166. *Dolan v. City of Tigard*, 512 U.S. 374, 392 (1994).

167. See Thomas Jefferson, letter to Isaac Tiffany (April 4, 1819), in *Jefferson: Political Writings*, Joyce Appleby and Terence Ball, eds. (Cambridge: Cambridge University Press, 1999), p. 224 ("Liberty . . . is unobstructed action according to our will, within the limits drawn around us by the equal rights of others.").

168. John Hart Ely, *Democracy and Distrust: A Theory of Judicial Review* (Cambridge: Harvard University Press, 1980), p. 54.

169. *Yates v. People*, 6 Johns. 337, 494 (N.Y. 1810).

Conclusion

1. Frederick Douglass, "The Nature of Slavery," in *Frederick Douglass: Autobiographies*, Henry Louis Gates Jr., ed. (New York: Library of America, 1994), pp. 420–21.

2. Frederick Douglass, *Oration Delivered in Corinthian Hall, Rochester* (Rochester, NY: Lee, Mann and Co., 1852), p. 36.

Index

Note to index: an n following a page number indicates a note on that page.

195

About the Author

Timothy Sandefur is an adjunct scholar at the Cato Institute and a Principal Attorney at the Pacific Legal Foundation, a non-profit legal foundation headquartered in Sacramento, California, dedicated to defending economic liberty and private property rights. Sandefur is the author of *Cornerstone of Liberty: Property Rights in 21st Century America* (2006) and *The Right to Earn A Living: Economic Freedom and The Law* (2010).

Cato Institute

Founded in 1977, the Cato Institute is a public policy research foundation dedicated to broadening the parameters of policy debate to allow consideration of more options that are consistent with the principles of limited government, individual liberty, and peace. To that end, the Institute strives to achieve greater involvement of the intelligent, concerned lay public in questions of policy and the proper role of government.

The Institute is named for Cato's Letters, libertarian pamphlets that were widely read in the American Colonies in the early 18th century and played a major role in laying the philosophical foundation for the American Revolution.

Despite the achievement of the nation's Founders, today virtually no aspect of life is free from government encroachment. A pervasive intolerance for individual rights is shown by government's arbitrary intrusions into private economic transactions and its disregard for civil liberties. And while freedom around the globe has notably increased in the past several decades, many countries have moved in the opposite direction, and most governments still do not respect or safeguard the wide range of civil and economic liberties.

To address those issues, the Cato Institute undertakes an extensive publications program on the complete spectrum of policy issues. Books, monographs, and shorter studies are commissioned to examine the federal budget, Social Security, regulation, military spending, international trade, and myriad other issues. Major policy conferences are held throughout the year, from which papers are published thrice yearly in the Cato Journal. The Institute also publishes the quarterly magazine Regulation.

In order to maintain its independence, the Cato Institute accepts no government funding. Contributions are received from foundations, corporations, and individuals, and other revenue is generated from the sale of publications. The Institute is a nonprofit, tax-exempt, educational foundation under Section 501(c)3 of the Internal Revenue Code.

CATO INSTITUTE
1000 Massachusetts Ave., N.W.
Washington, D.C. 20001
www.cato.org